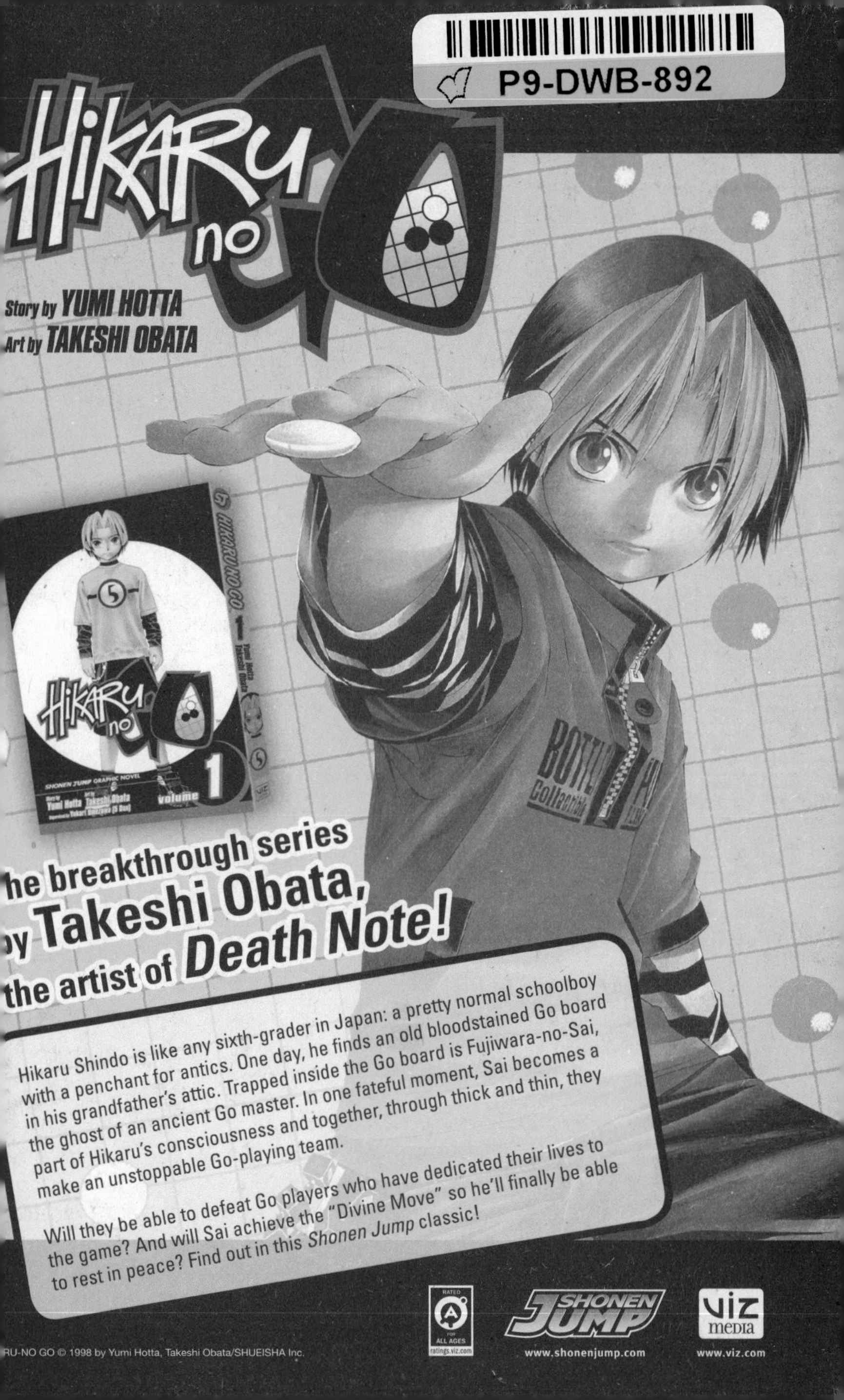
P9-DWB-892
HIKARU no GO
Story by YUMI HOTTA
Art by TAKESHI OBATA
HIKARU NO GO 1
SHONEN JUMP GRAPHIC NOVEL
volume 1
he breakthrough series
y Takeshi Obata,
the artist of Death Note!
Hikaru Shindo is like any sixth-grader in Japan: a pretty normal schoolboy with a penchant for antics. One day, he finds an old bloodstained Go board in his grandfather's attic. Trapped inside the Go board is Fujiwara-no-Sai, the ghost of an ancient Go master. In one fateful moment, Sai becomes a part of Hikaru's consciousness and together, through thick and thin, they make an unstoppable Go-playing team.
Will they be able to defeat Go players who have dedicated their lives to the game? And will Sai achieve the "Divine Move" so he'll finally be able to rest in peace? Find out in this Shonen Jump classic!
RATED A FOR ALL AGES ratings.viz.com
SHONEN JUMP
www.shonenjump.com
viz media
www.viz.com
RU-NO GO © 1998 by Yumi Hotta, Takeshi Obata/SHUEISHA Inc.

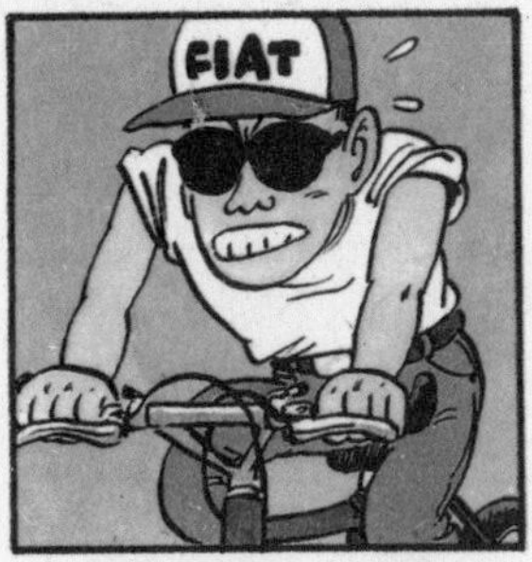
FIAT

鳥山明

I've recently slacked off on my exercise routine, getting lazy and using the motorcycle or the car to run short errands. As a result, I now have a sizeable gut. I thought to myself, "This'll be bad if it goes on any longer!", so I made the decision that I'd at least *try* to get in shape by riding a bicycle. That was the theory, anyway. In practice, I always end up looking at women along the way and riding slower than dirt. You couldn't really call it "exercise"...

–Akira Toriyama, 1986

Artist/writer Akira Toriyama burst onto the manga scene in 1980 with the wildly popular **Dr. Slump**, a science fiction comedy about the adventures of a mad scientist and his android "daughter." In 1984 he created his hit series **Dragon Ball**, which ran until 1995 in Shueisha's best-selling magazine **Weekly Shonen Jump**, and was translated into foreign languages around the world. Since **Dragon Ball**, he has worked on a variety of short series, including **Cowa!**, **Kajika**, **SandLand**, and **Neko Majin**, as well as a children's book, **Toccio the Angel**. He is also known for his design work on video games, particularly the **Dragon Warrior** RPG series. He lives with his family in Japan.

DRAGON BALL VOL.4
SHONEN JUMP Manga Edition

STORY AND ART BY
AKIRA TORIYAMA

English Adaptation/Gerard Jones
Translation/Lillian Olsen
Touch-up Art & Lettering/Wayne Truman
Design/Sean Lee
Editor/Jason Thompson

In the original Japanese edition, DRAGON BALL and DRAGON BALL Z
are known collectively as the 42-volume series DRAGON BALL.
The English DRAGON BALL Z was originally volumes 17–42 of the Japanese
DRAGON BALL.

Printed in Canada

Published by VIZ Media, LLC
P.O. Box 77010
San Francisco, CA 94107

10
First printing, March 2003
Tenth printing, February 2018

SHONEN JUMP MANGA

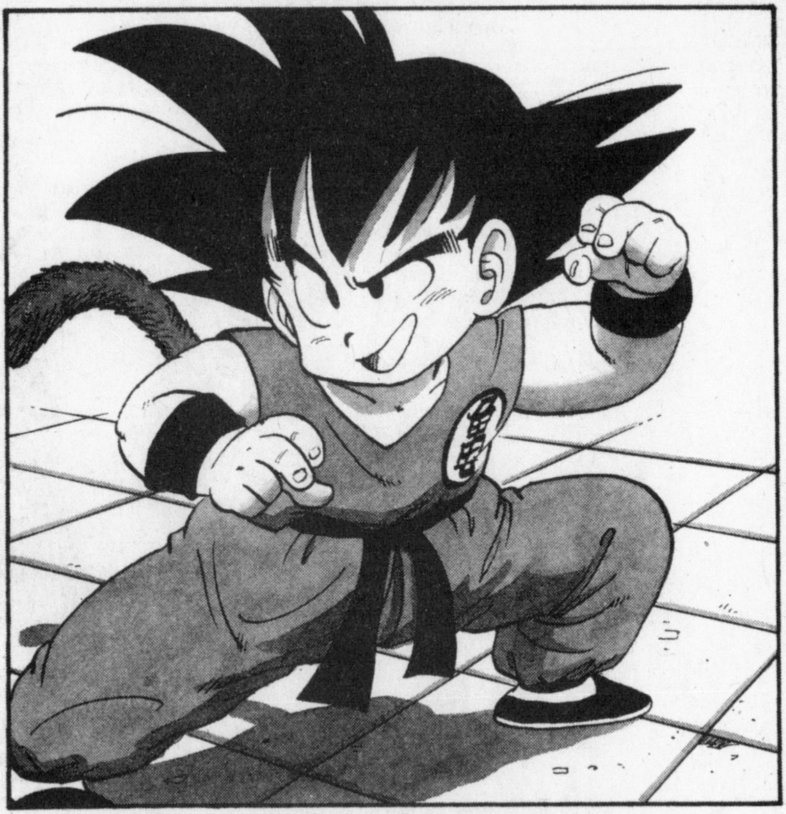

DRAGON BALL

Vol. 4

DB: 4 of 42

STORY AND ART BY
AKIRA TORIYAMA

THE MAIN CHARACTERS

Son Goku
Young Goku has always been stronger than normal. His grandfather Gohan gave him the *nyoibô*, a magic staff, and Kame-Sen'nin gave him the *kinto'un*, a magic flying cloud. He once had a monkey's tail, but he lost it under strange circumstances in Vol. 2.

Oolong
Immature, shapeshifting Oolong was originally a villain that Goku and Bulma defeated.

Bulma
A genius inventor, Bulma met Goku on her quest for the seven magical Dragon Balls.

Pu'ar
Yamcha's shapeshifting friend.

Yamcha
Yamcha used to be a desert bandit, but he went to the city to be Bulma's boyfriend. He uses "Fist of the Wolf-Fang" kung-fu.

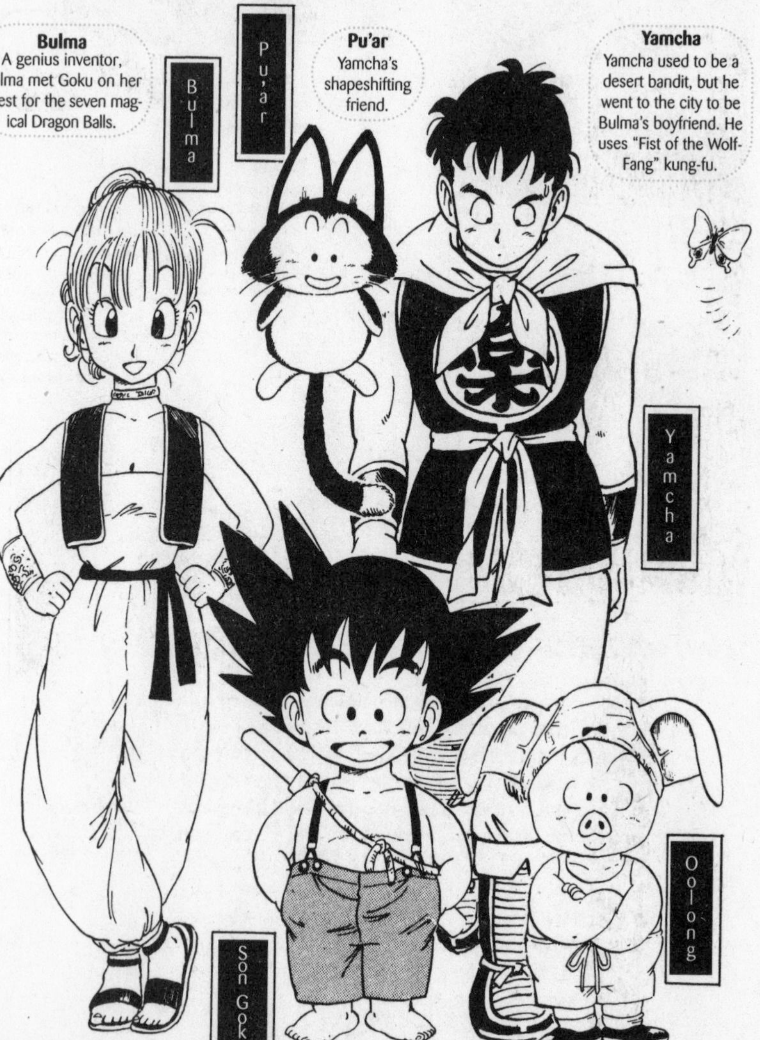

Pu'ar
Bulma
Yamcha
Oolong
Son Goku

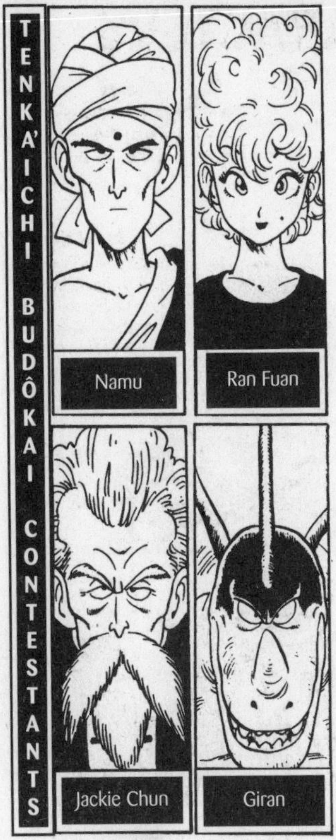
TENKA'ICHI BUDÔKAI CONTESTANTS
Namu
Ran Fuan
Jackie Chun
Giran

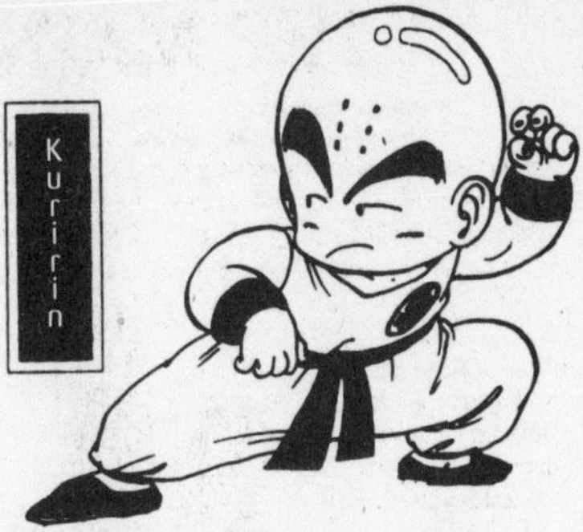
Kuririn

Kuririn

A sometimes trustworthy young fighter. Like Goku, he has become super-strong from Kame-Sen'nin's difficult training.

Kame-Sen'nin (The "Turtle Hermit")

A tricky old martial artist (also known as the *muten-rôshi*, or "Invincible Old Master") who trained Goku's grandfather, Son Gohan, and has now trained Goku and Kuririn. Is there any martial arts move he doesn't know?

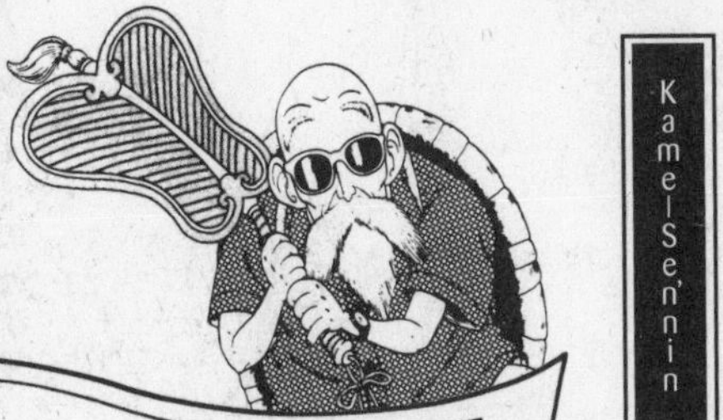
Kame-Sen'nin

Long, long ago, in the mountains, there lived a young boy named Son Goku. His simple life was interrupted by Bulma, a girl from the city who took Goku with her on her quest for the seven magical "Dragon Balls." After many dangerous adventures with Bulma, Goku decided that what he really wanted was to be stronger, so he went to the great martial artist Kame-Sen'nin to be trained. Now, after 8 months of tough training, Goku and his fellow student Kuririn have entered the "Strongest Under the Heavens" fighting tournament...but what a tournament! And what fighters!

DRAGON BALL 4

CONTENTS

ドラゴンボール

DRAGON BALL

Tale 37 • Match No. 2

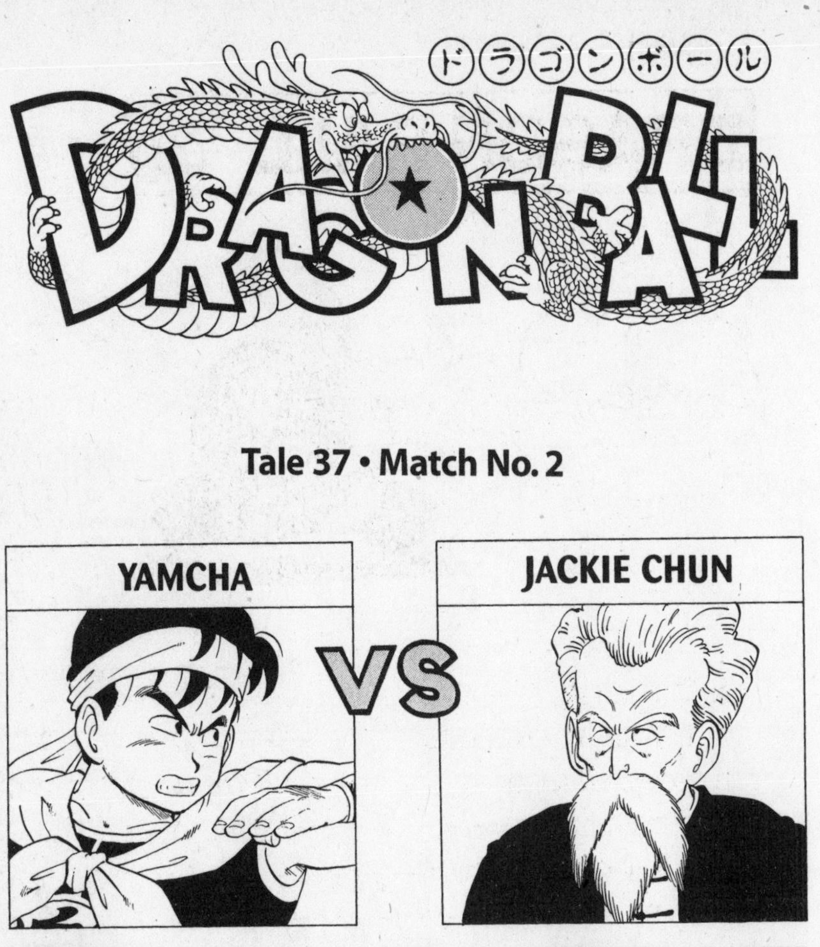
JACKIE CHUN
VS
YAMCHA

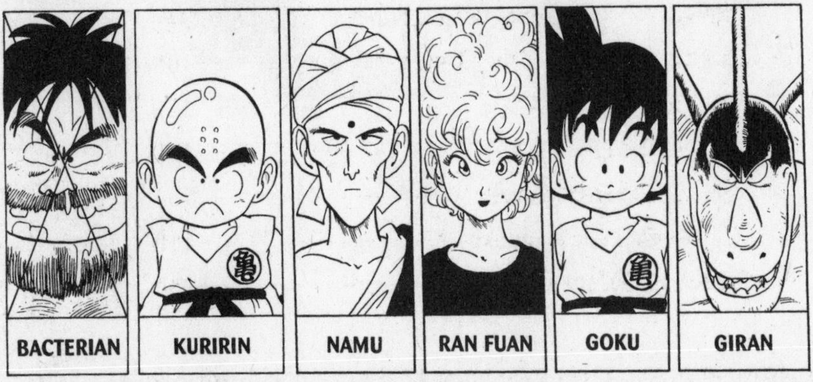
GIRAN
GOKU
RAN FUAN
NAMU
KURIRIN
BACTERIAN

Tale 37
Match No. 2

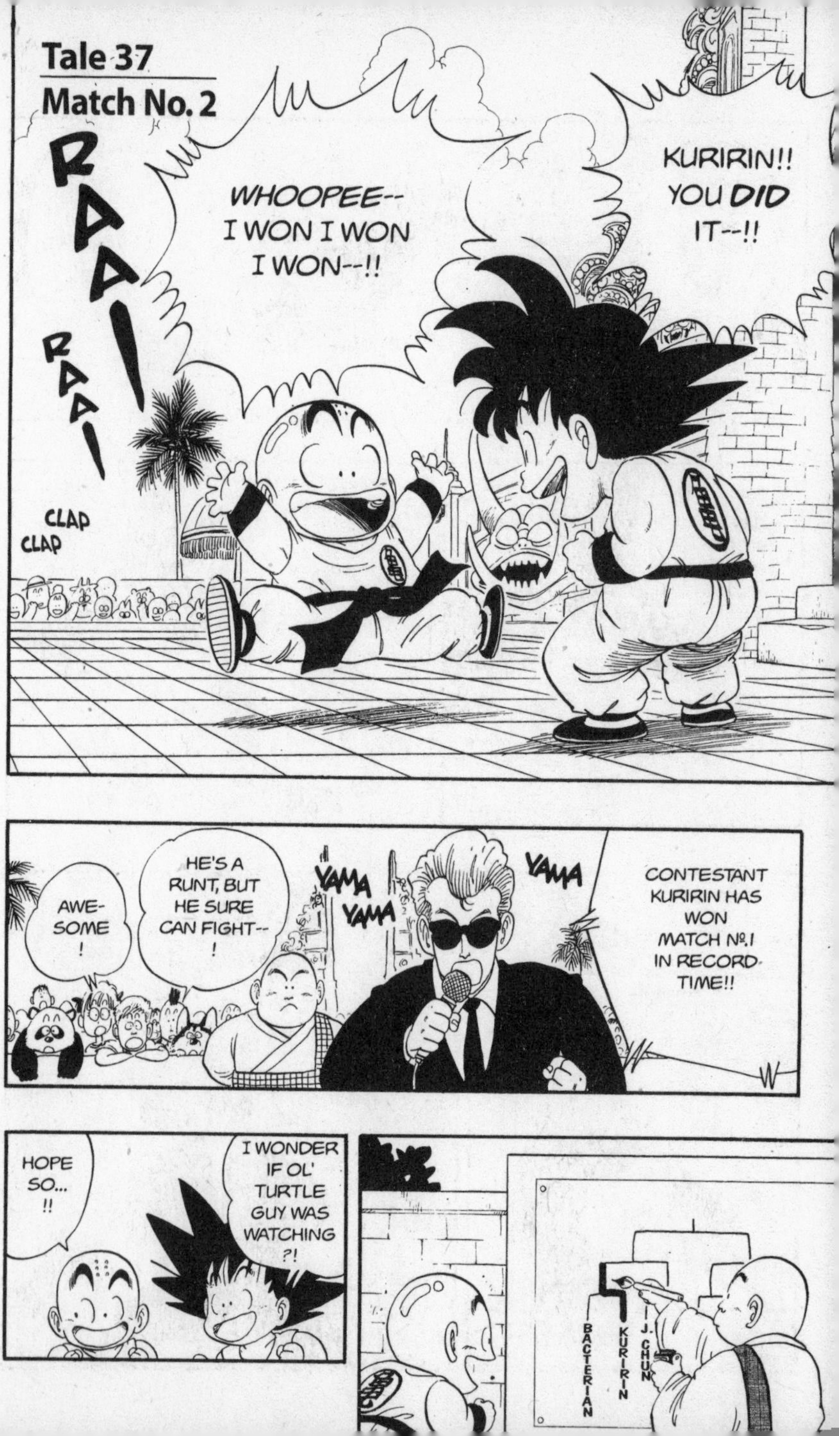
KURIRIN!! YOU DID IT--!!
WHOOPEE-- I WON I WON I WON--!!
RAAAI
RAAI
CLAP CLAP
CONTESTANT KURIRIN HAS WON MATCH №.1 IN RECORD TIME!!
YAMA
YAMA YAMA
HE'S A RUNT, BUT HE SURE CAN FIGHT--!
AWE-SOME!
J. CHUN
KURIRIN
BACTERIAN
I WONDER IF OL' TURTLE GUY WAS WATCHING?!
HOPE SO...!!

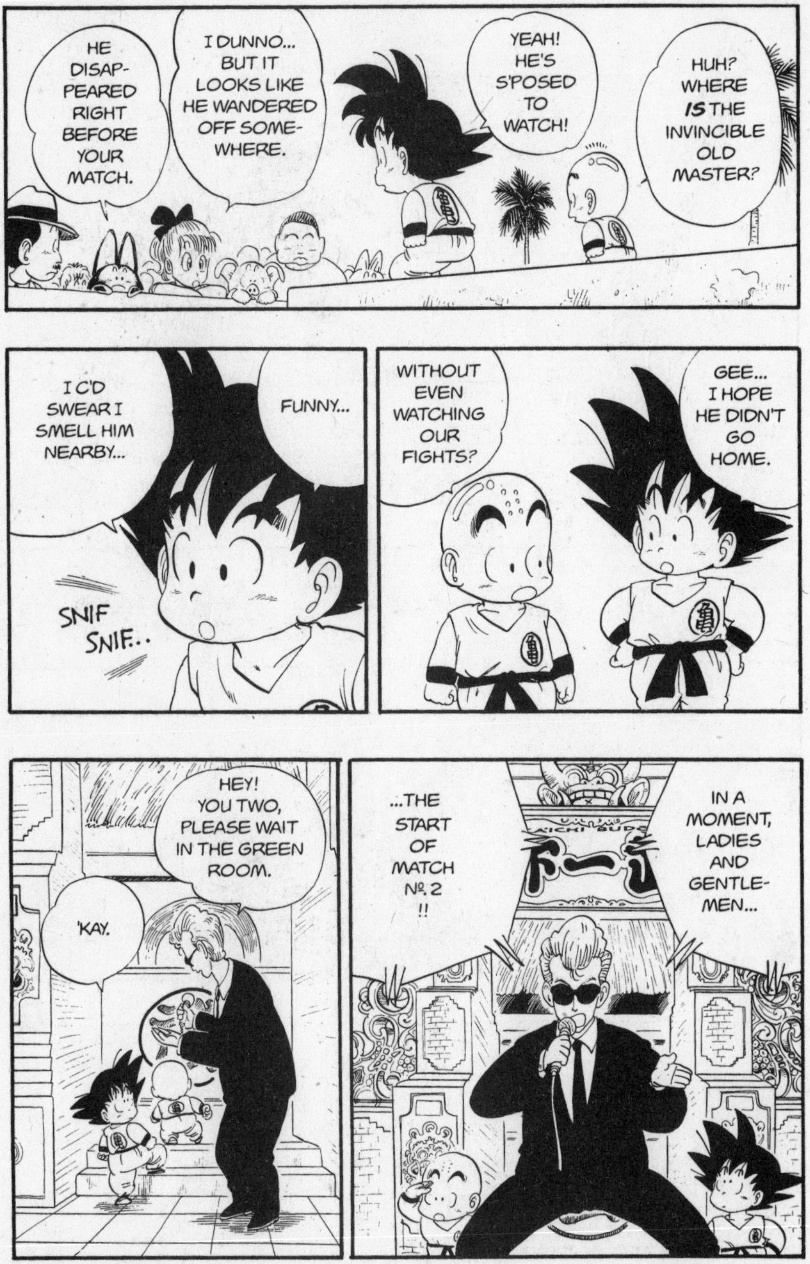
HUH? WHERE IS THE INVINCIBLE OLD MASTER?
YEAH! HE'S S'POSED TO WATCH!
I DUNNO... BUT IT LOOKS LIKE HE WANDERED OFF SOME-WHERE.
HE DISAP-PEARED RIGHT BEFORE YOUR MATCH.
GEE... I HOPE HE DIDN'T GO HOME.
WITHOUT EVEN WATCHING OUR FIGHTS?
FUNNY...
I C'D SWEAR I SMELL HIM NEARBY...
SNIF SNIF...
IN A MOMENT, LADIES AND GENTLE-MEN...
...THE START OF MATCH №. 2 !!
HEY! YOU TWO, PLEASE WAIT IN THE GREEN ROOM.
'KAY.

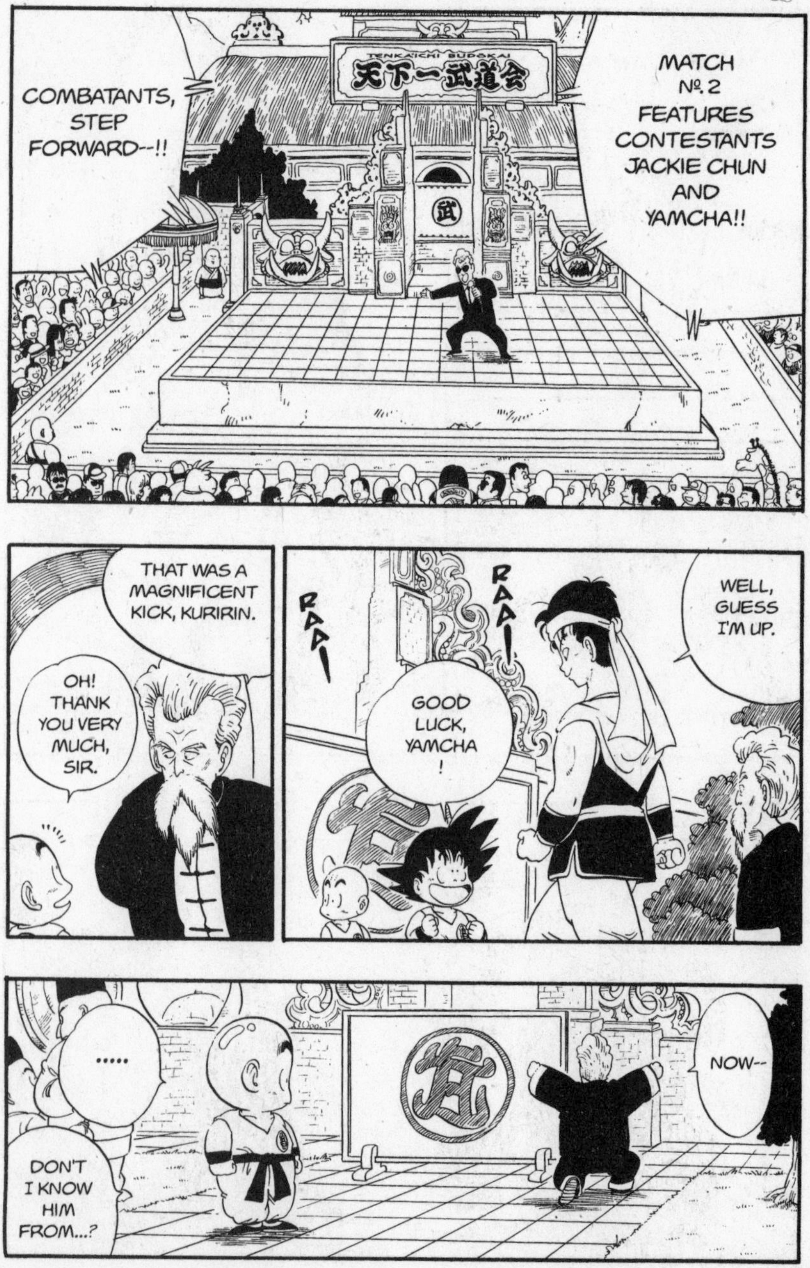
MATCH №.2 FEATURES CONTESTANTS JACKIE CHUN AND YAMCHA!!
TENKAICHI BUDOKAI
天下一武道会
COMBATANTS, STEP FORWARD--!!
WELL, GUESS I'M UP.
RAAI
RAAI
GOOD LUCK, YAMCHA!
THAT WAS A MAGNIFICENT KICK, KURIRIN.
OH! THANK YOU VERY MUCH, SIR.
NOW--
.....
DON'T I KNOW HIM FROM...?

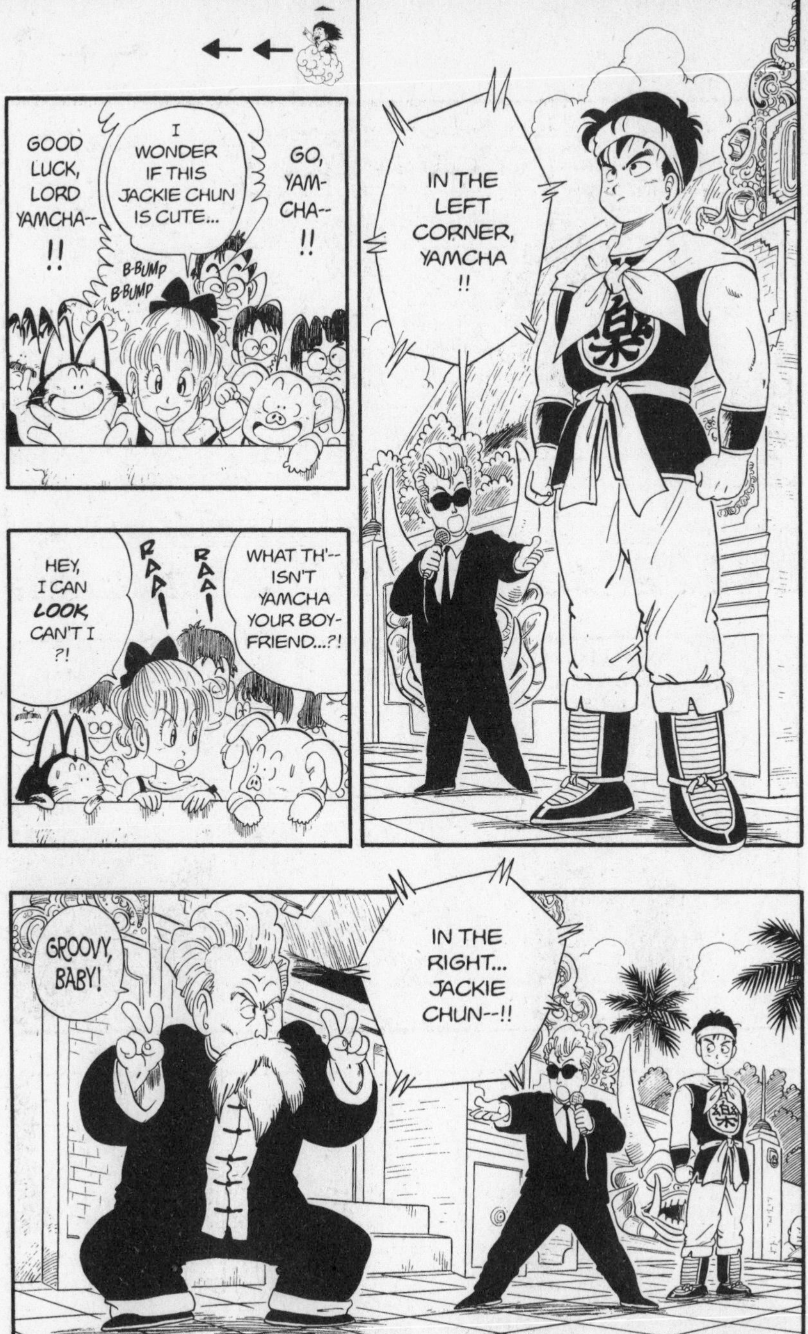
IN THE LEFT CORNER, YAMCHA!!
GO, YAMCHA--!!
I WONDER IF THIS JACKIE CHUN IS CUTE...
B-BUMP B-BUMP
GOOD LUCK, LORD YAMCHA--!!
WHAT TH'-- ISN'T YAMCHA YOUR BOYFRIEND...?!
RAA
RAA
HEY, I CAN *LOOK*, CAN'T I?!
IN THE RIGHT... JACKIE CHUN--!!
GROOVY, BABY!

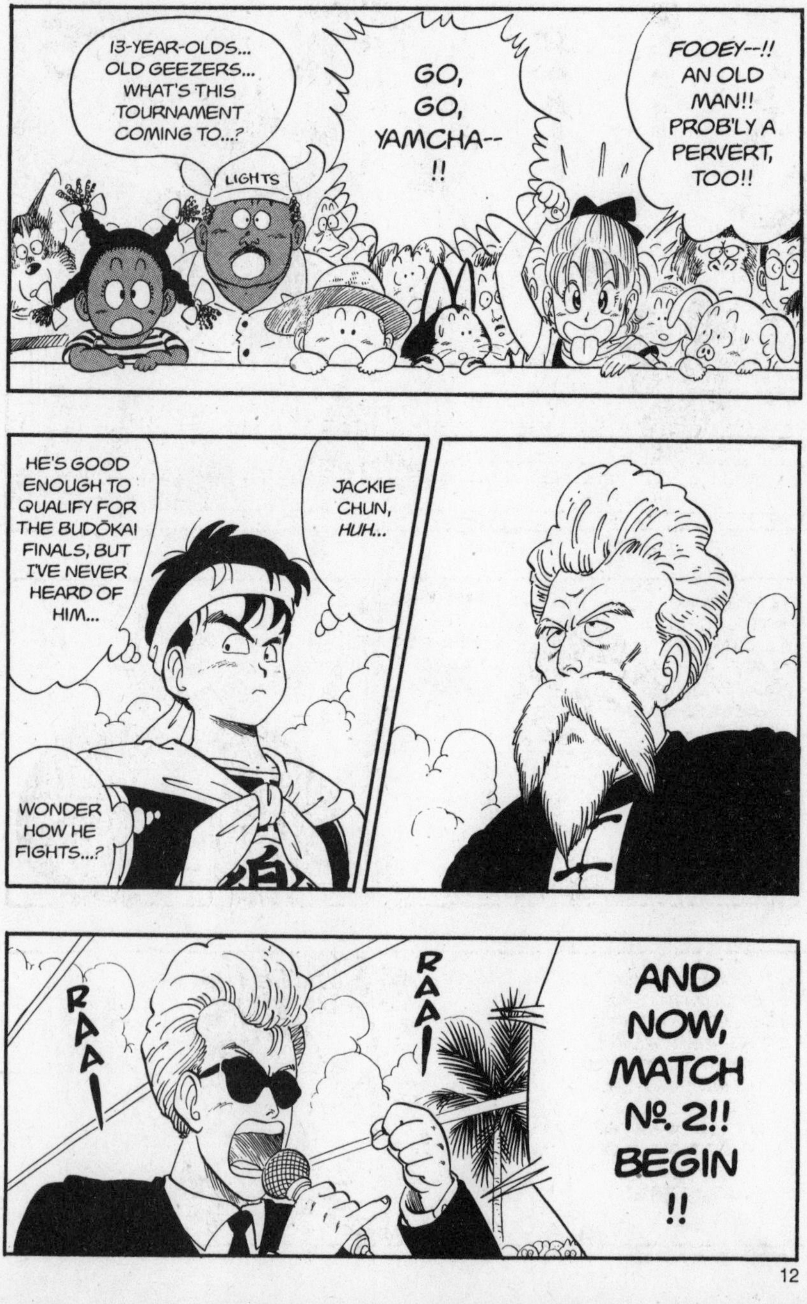
FOOEY--!! AN OLD MAN!! PROB'LY A PERVERT, TOO!!
GO, GO, YAMCHA--!!
13-YEAR-OLDS... OLD GEEZERS... WHAT'S THIS TOURNAMENT COMING TO...?
LIGHTS
JACKIE CHUN, HUH...
HE'S GOOD ENOUGH TO QUALIFY FOR THE BUDŌKAI FINALS, BUT I'VE NEVER HEARD OF HIM...
WONDER HOW HE FIGHTS...?
AND NOW, MATCH №. 2!! BEGIN!!
RAAI
RAAI

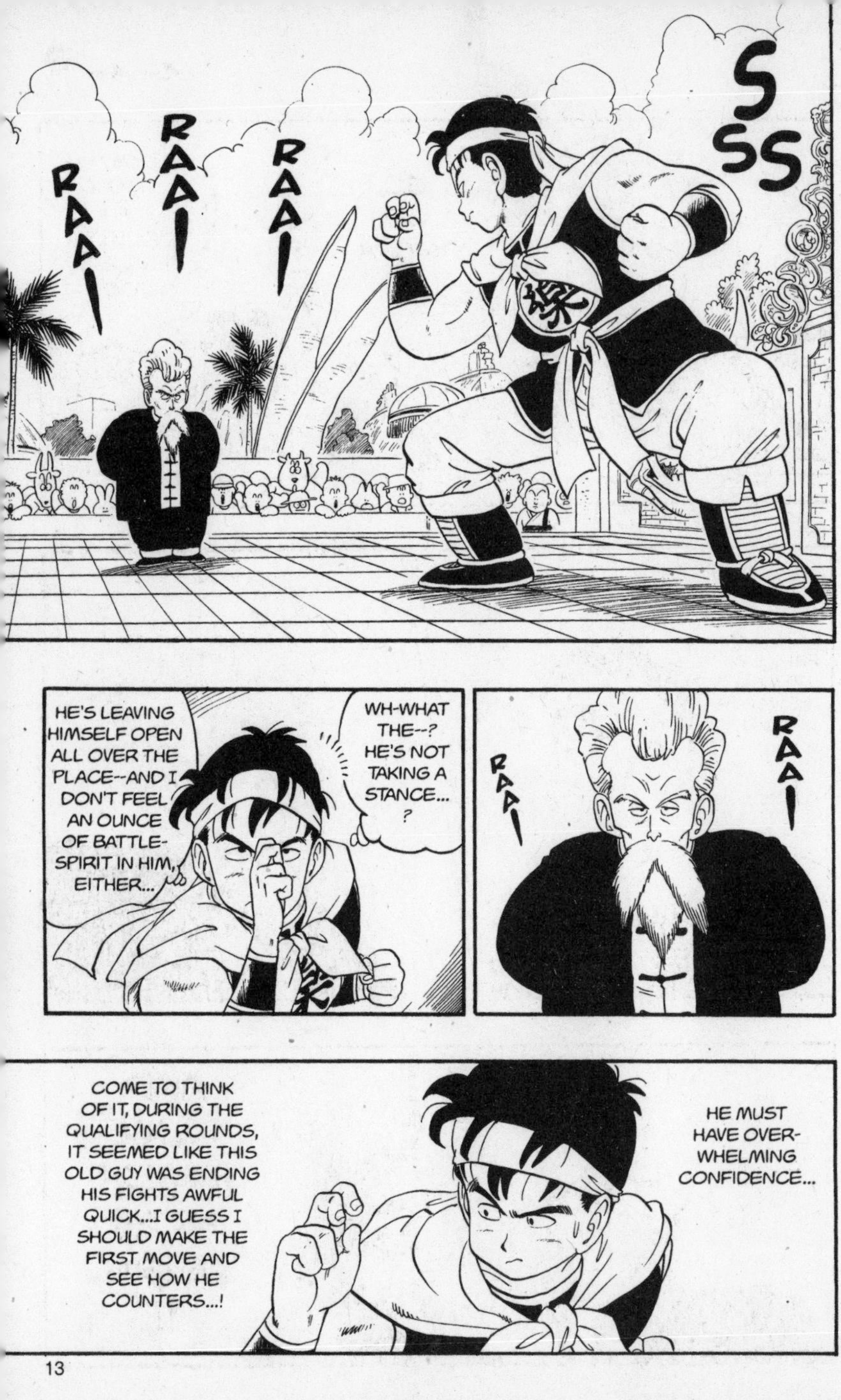
SSS
RAAI
RAAI
RAAI
RAAI
RAAI
WH-WHAT THE--? HE'S NOT TAKING A STANCE...?
HE'S LEAVING HIMSELF OPEN ALL OVER THE PLACE--AND I DON'T FEEL AN OUNCE OF BATTLE-SPIRIT IN HIM, EITHER...
HE MUST HAVE OVER-WHELMING CONFIDENCE...
COME TO THINK OF IT, DURING THE QUALIFYING ROUNDS, IT SEEMED LIKE THIS OLD GUY WAS ENDING HIS FIGHTS AWFUL QUICK...I GUESS I SHOULD MAKE THE FIRST MOVE AND SEE HOW HE COUNTERS...!

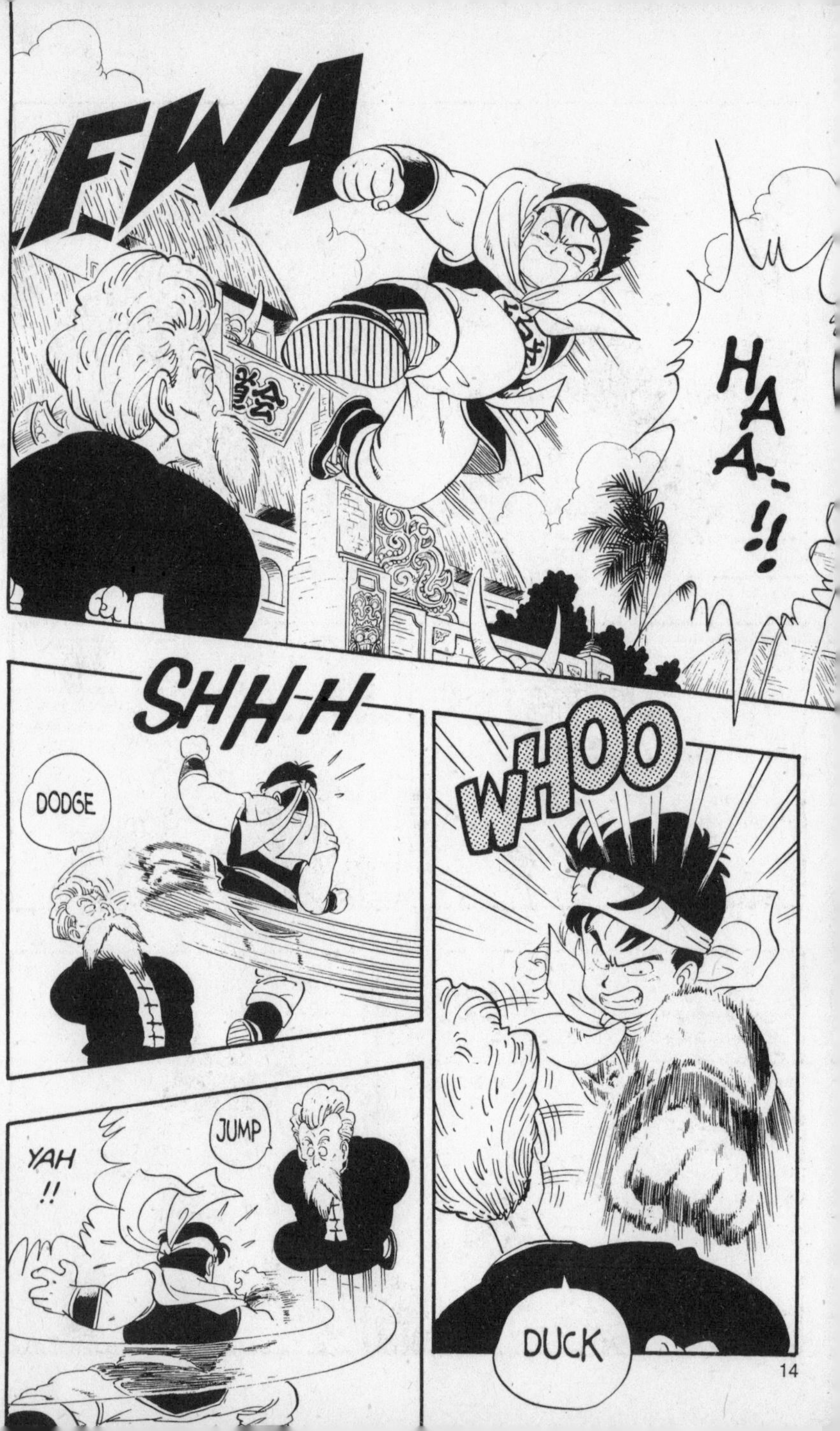
HAA-!!
FWA
WHOO
DUCK
SHH-H
DODGE
JUMP
YAH !!

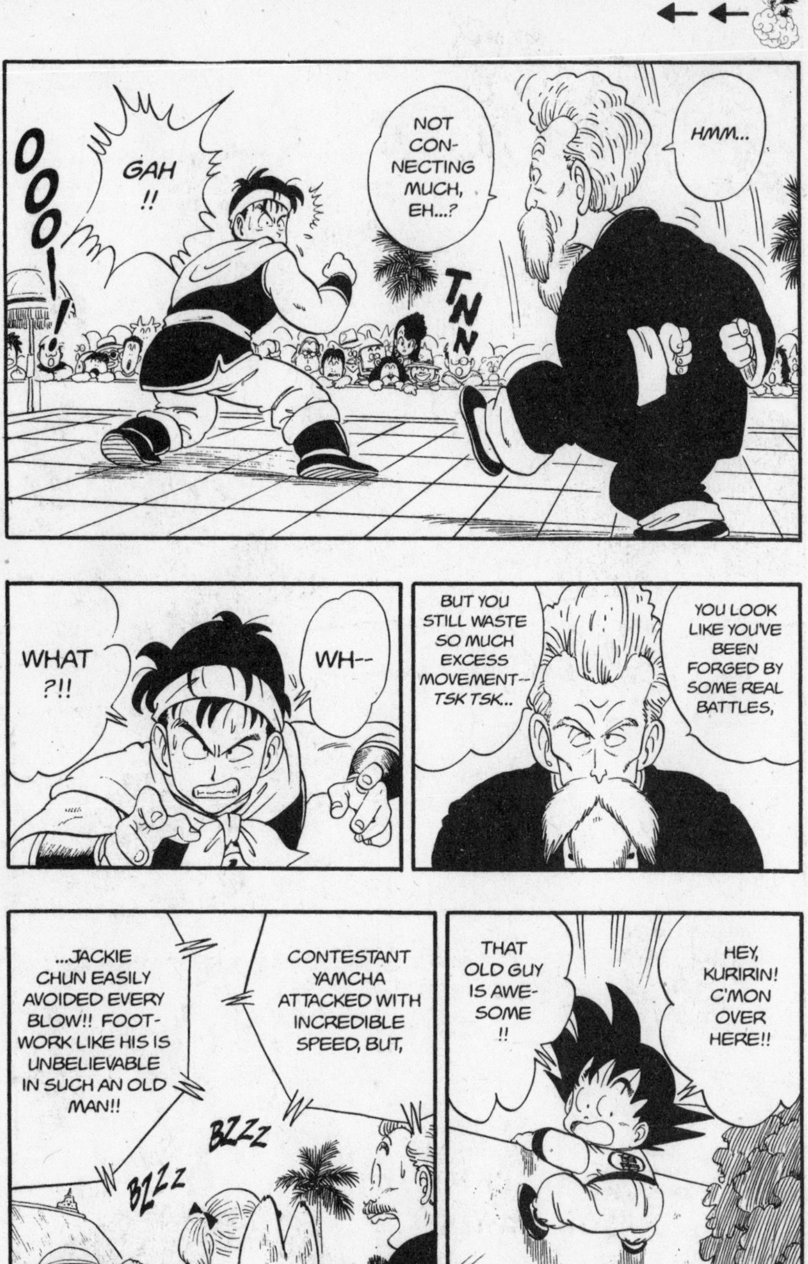
HMM...
NOT CON-NECTING MUCH, EH...?
TNN
GAH !!
OOO-!
YOU LOOK LIKE YOU'VE BEEN FORGED BY SOME REAL BATTLES,
BUT YOU STILL WASTE SO MUCH EXCESS MOVEMENT-- TSK TSK...
WH--
WHAT ?!!
HEY, KURIRIN! C'MON OVER HERE!!
THAT OLD GUY IS AWE-SOME !!
CONTESTANT YAMCHA ATTACKED WITH INCREDIBLE SPEED, BUT,
...JACKIE CHUN EASILY AVOIDED EVERY BLOW!! FOOT-WORK LIKE HIS IS UNBELIEVABLE IN SUCH AN OLD MAN!!
BZZZ
BZZZ

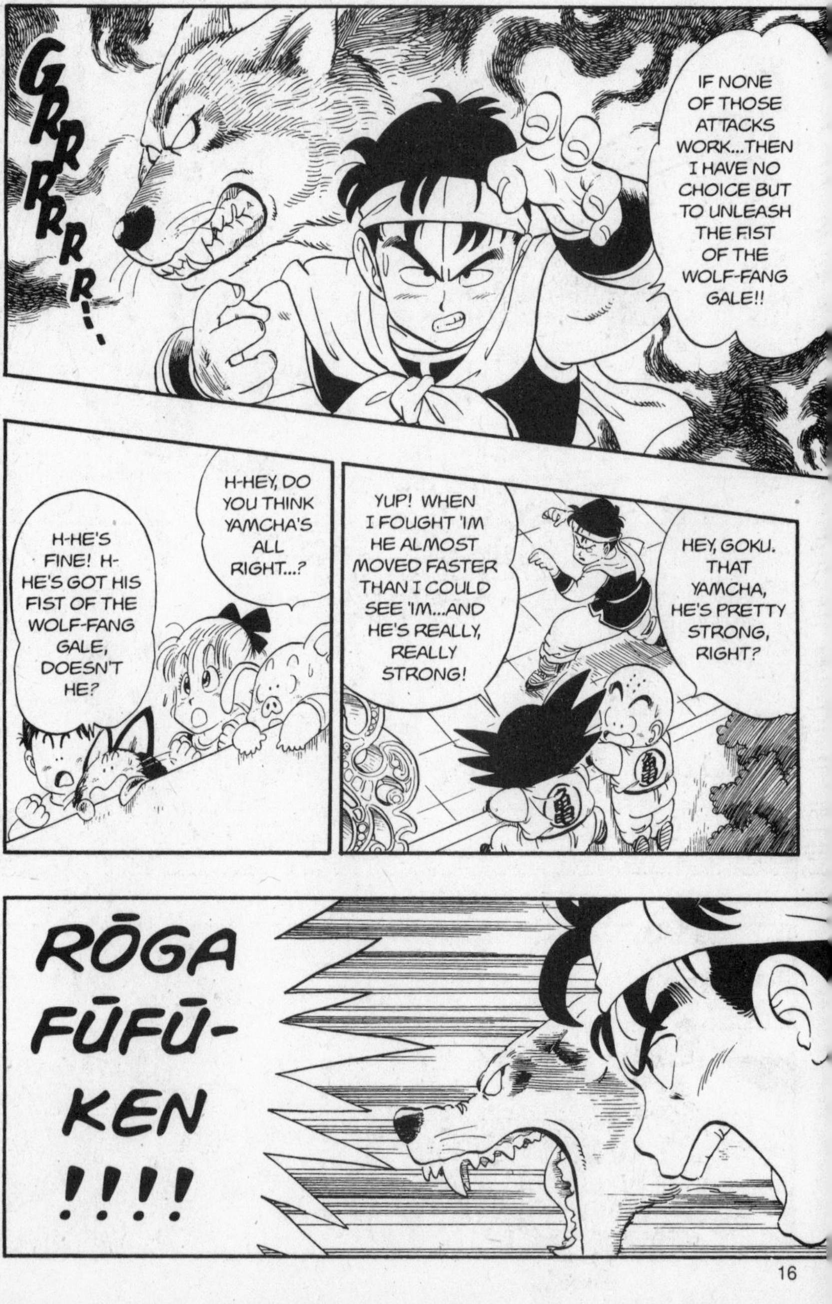
IF NONE OF THOSE ATTACKS WORK...THEN I HAVE NO CHOICE BUT TO UNLEASH THE FIST OF THE WOLF-FANG GALE!!
GRRRRRR...
HEY, GOKU. THAT YAMCHA, HE'S PRETTY STRONG, RIGHT?
YUP! WHEN I FOUGHT 'IM HE ALMOST MOVED FASTER THAN I COULD SEE 'IM...AND HE'S REALLY, REALLY STRONG!
H-HEY, DO YOU THINK YAMCHA'S ALL RIGHT...?
H-HE'S FINE! H-HE'S GOT HIS FIST OF THE WOLF-FANG GALE, DOESN'T HE?
RŌGA FŪFŪ-KEN!!!!

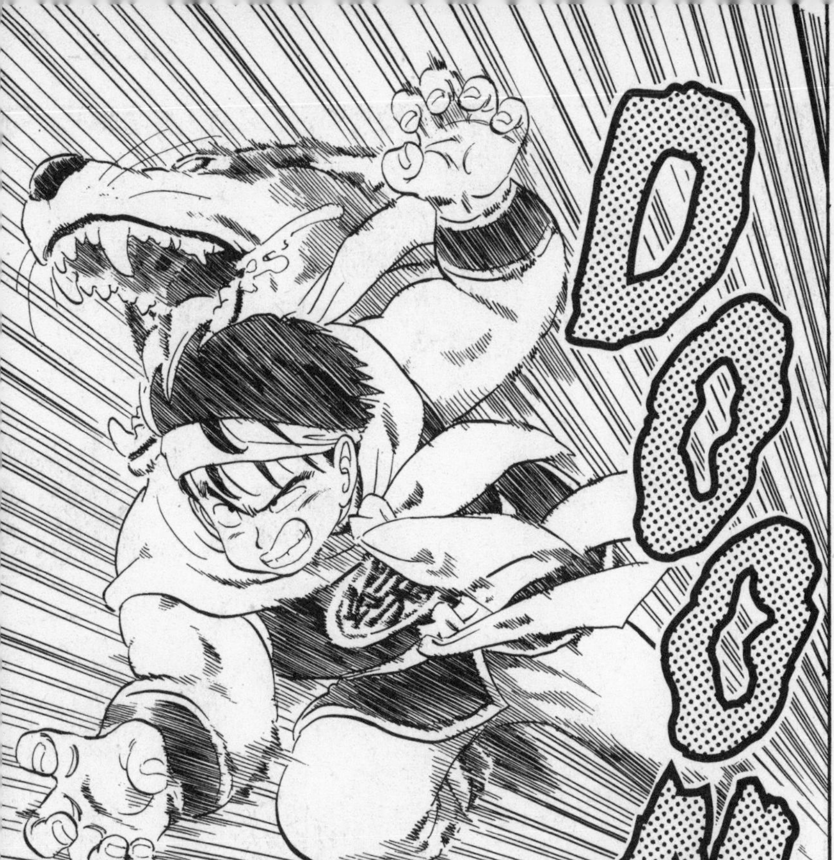
DOOOM!
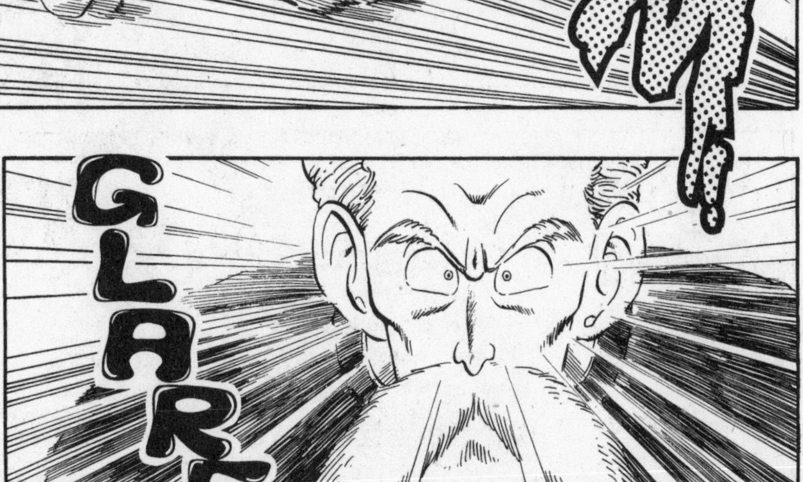
GLARE

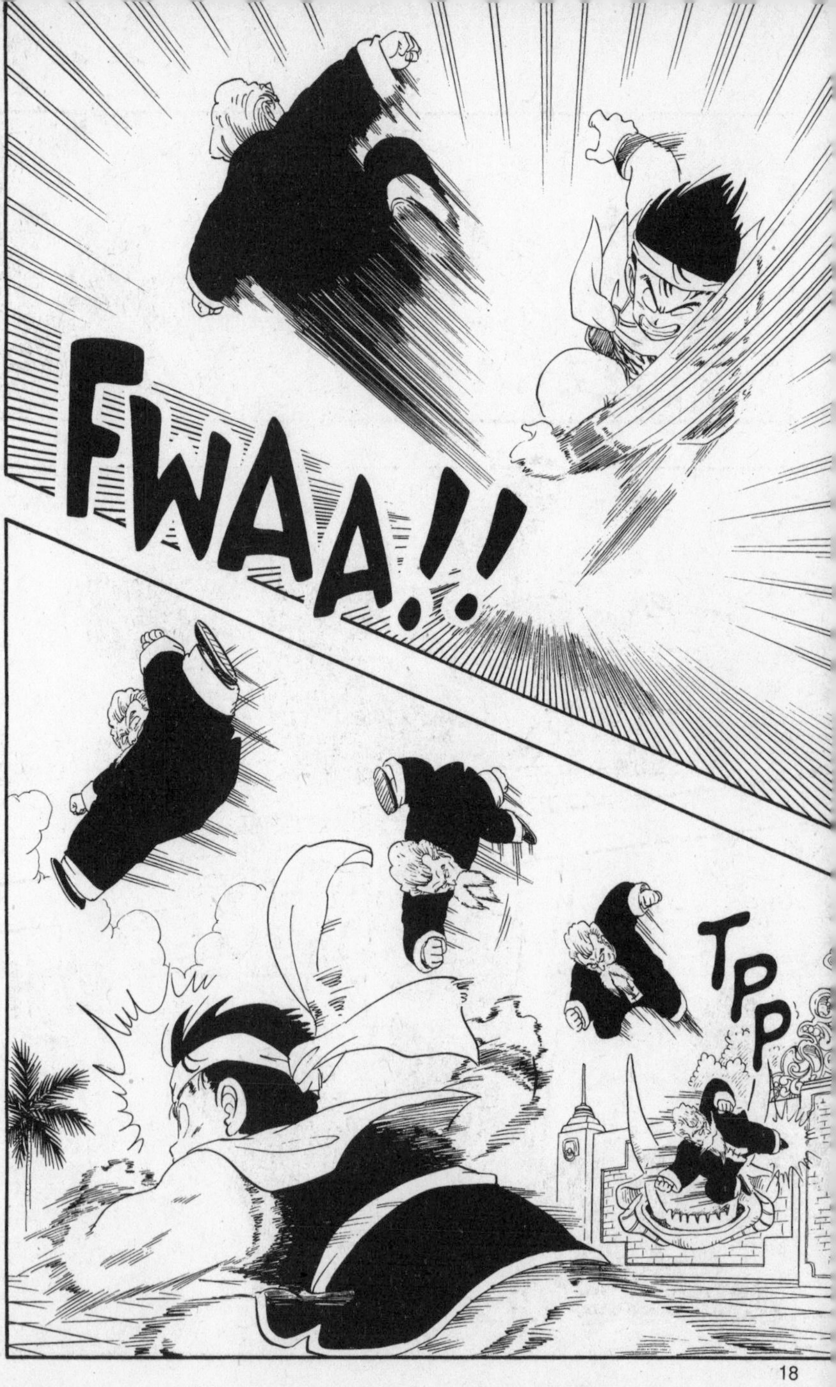
FWAA!!
TPP

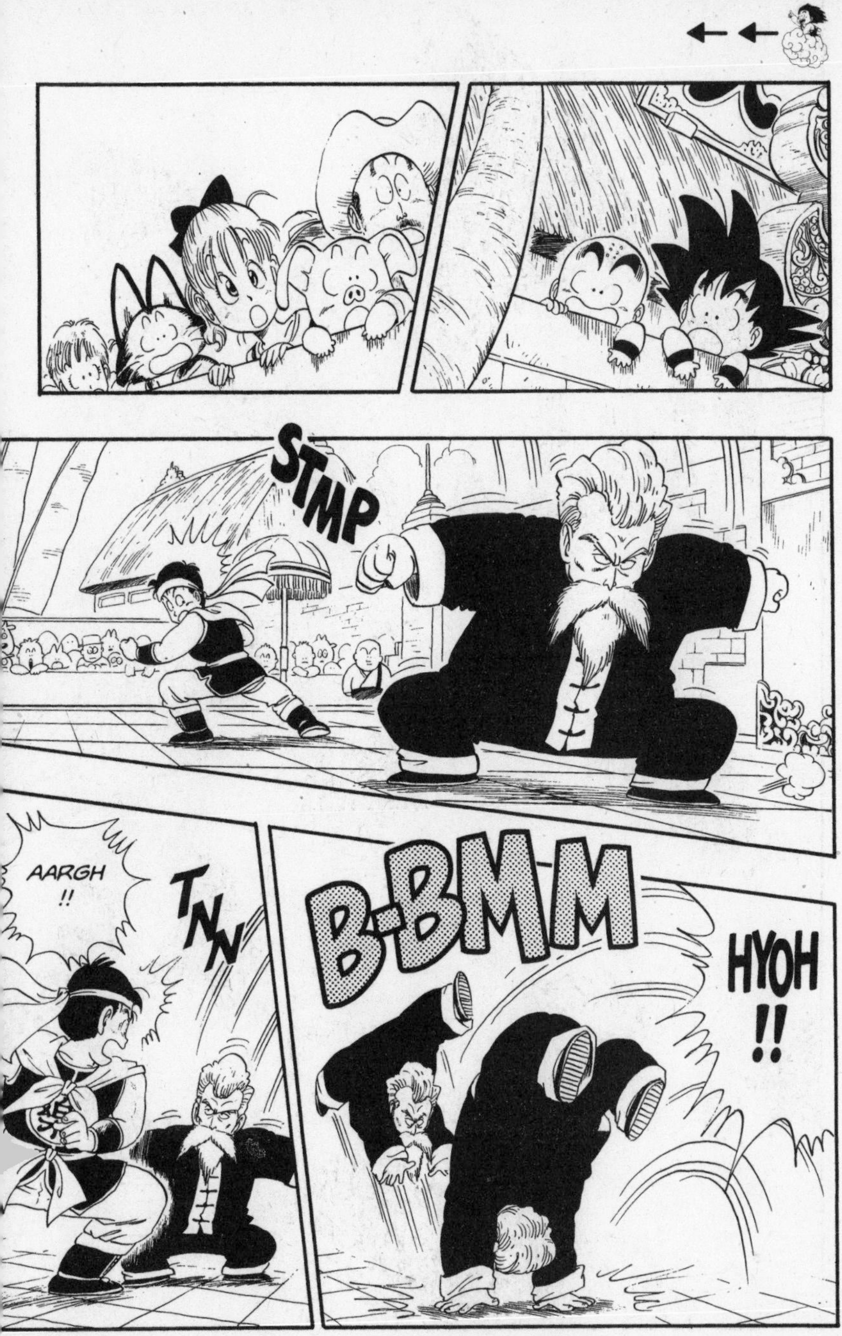
STMP
B-BMMM
HYOH !!
TNN
AARGH !!

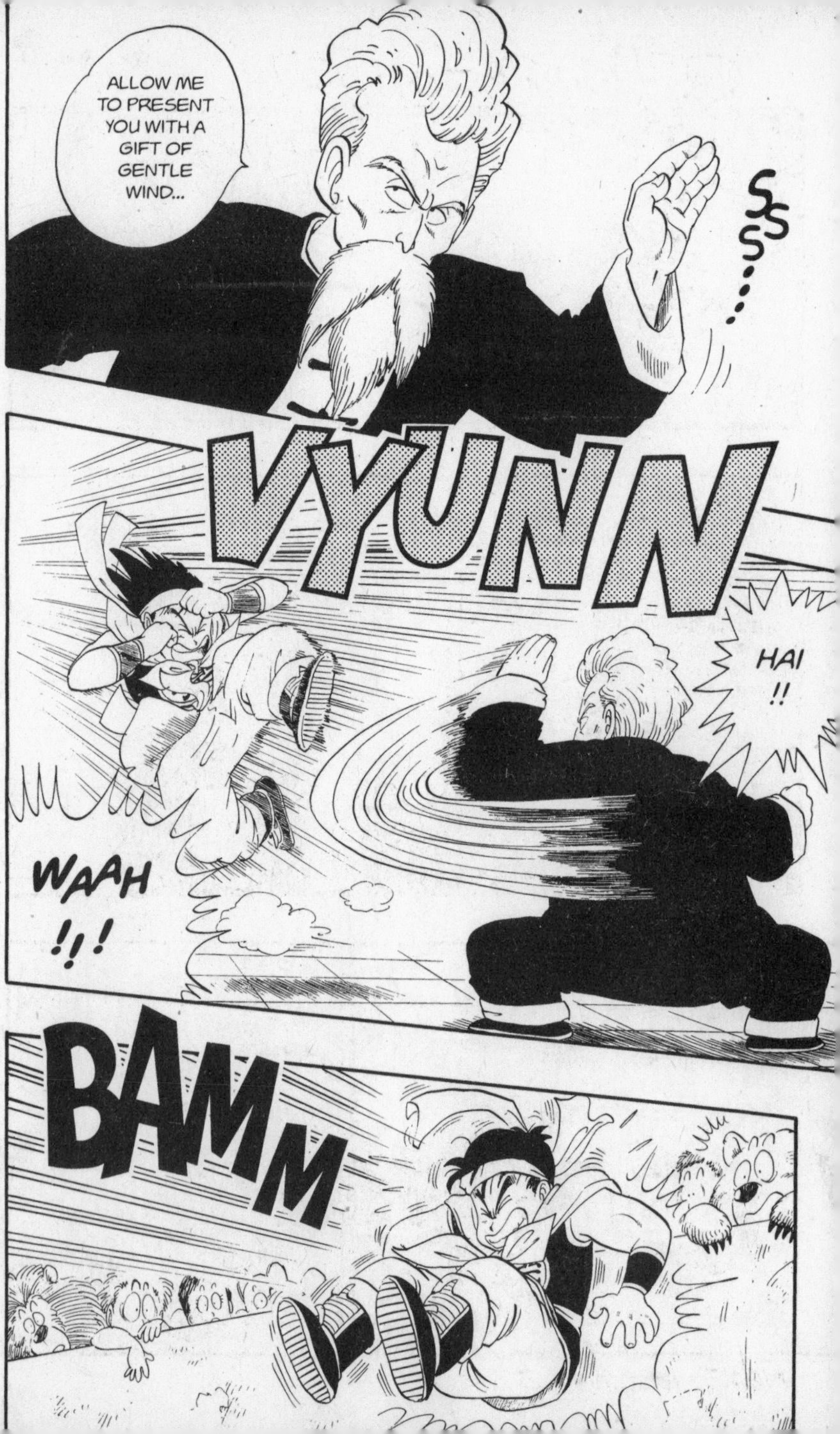

ALLOW ME TO PRESENT YOU WITH A GIFT OF GENTLE WIND...
SSS...
VYUNN
HAI !!
WAAH !!!
BAMM

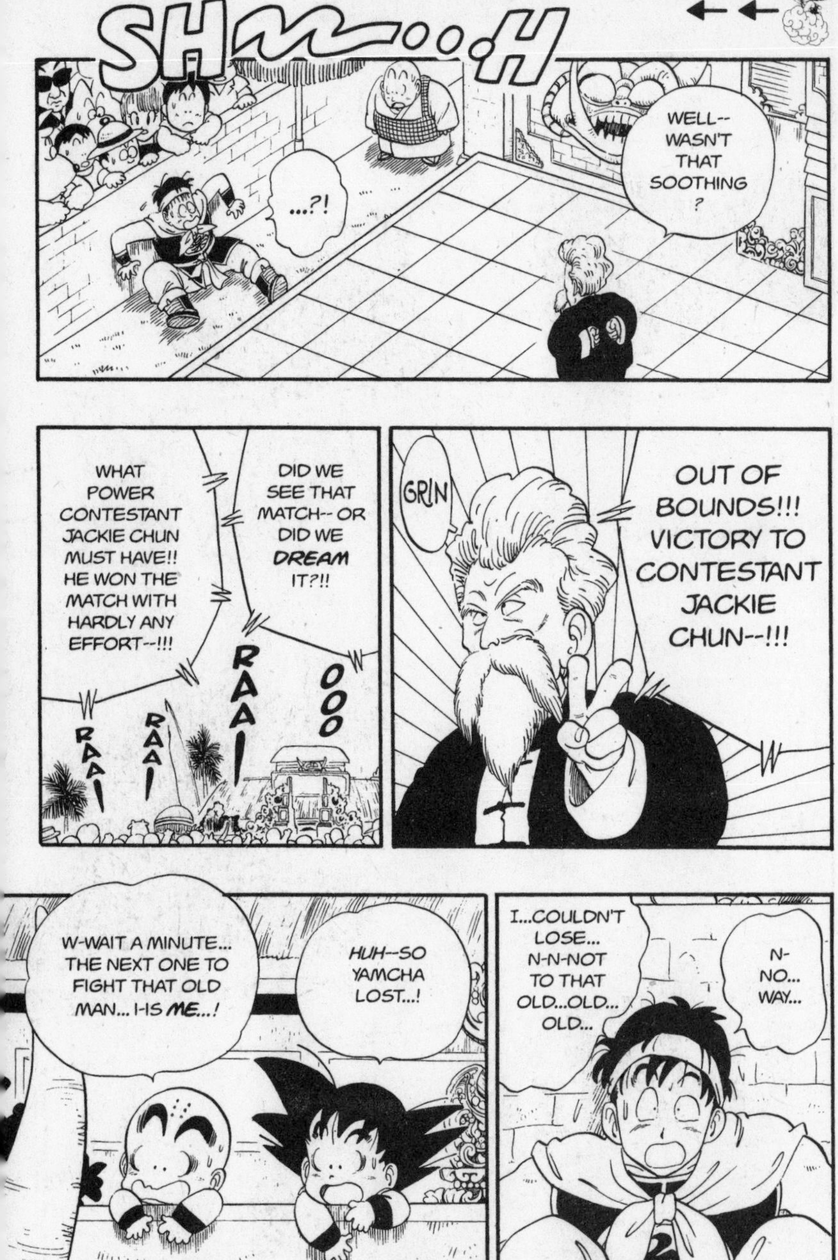
SHMOOOH
WELL-- WASN'T THAT SOOTHING?
...?!
OUT OF BOUNDS!!! VICTORY TO CONTESTANT JACKIE CHUN--!!!
GRIN
DID WE SEE THAT MATCH-- OR DID WE *DREAM* IT?!!
WHAT POWER CONTESTANT JACKIE CHUN MUST HAVE!! HE WON THE MATCH WITH HARDLY ANY EFFORT--!!!
RAAA!
OOO
RAAA!
RAAA!
N- NO... WAY...
I...COULDN'T LOSE... N-N-NOT TO THAT OLD...OLD... OLD...
HUH--SO YAMCHA LOST...!
W-WAIT A MINUTE... THE NEXT ONE TO FIGHT THAT OLD MAN... I-IS *ME*...!

NEXT: Match №. 3

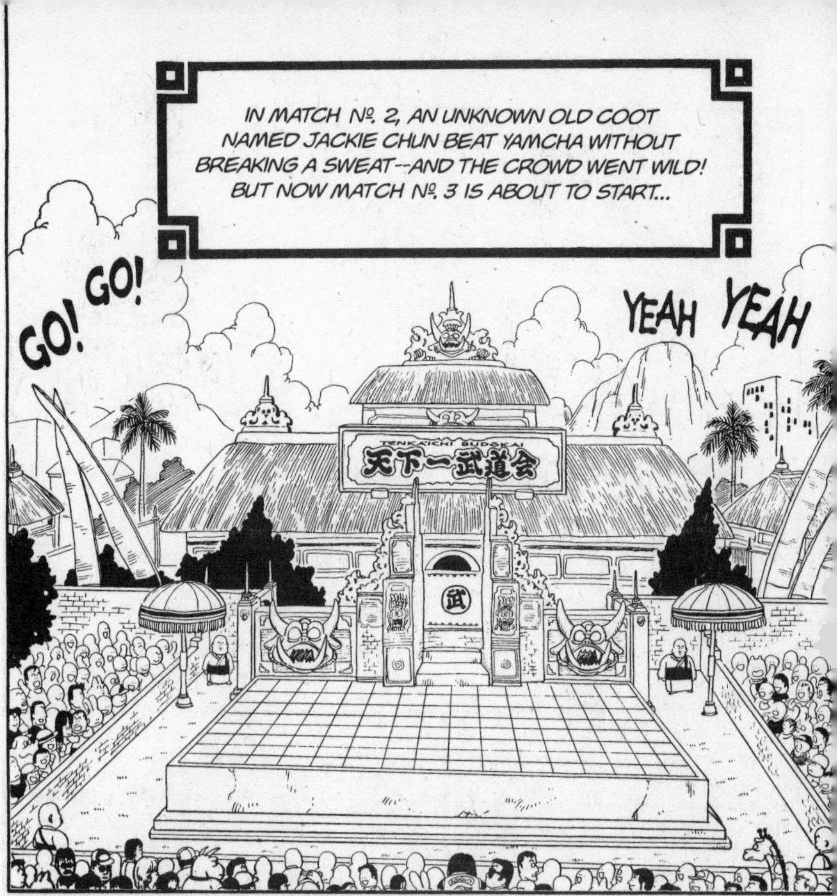
IN MATCH №. 2, AN UNKNOWN OLD COOT NAMED JACKIE CHUN BEAT YAMCHA WITHOUT BREAKING A SWEAT--AND THE CROWD WENT WILD! BUT NOW MATCH №. 3 IS ABOUT TO START...
YEAH YEAH
GO! GO!
TENKAICHI BUDOKAI
天下一武道会
武

Tale 38 • Water and Cheesecake

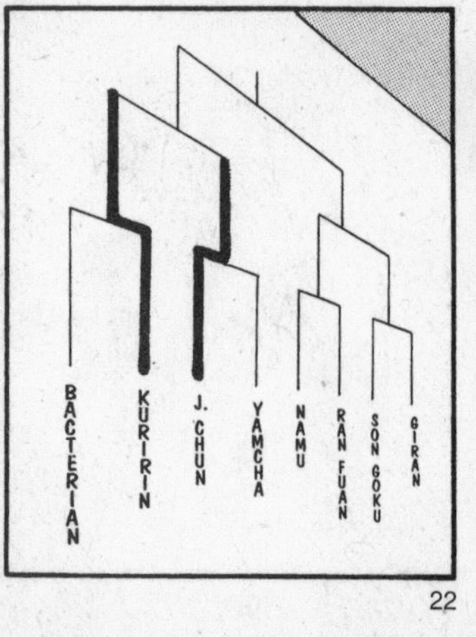
BACTERIAN
KURIRIN
J. CHUN
YAMCHA
NAMU
RAN FUAN
SON GOKU
GIRAN

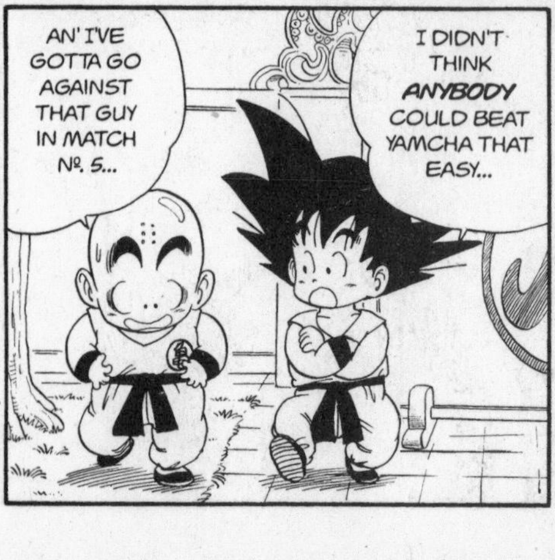
I DIDN'T THINK *ANYBODY* COULD BEAT YAMCHA THAT EASY...
AN' I'VE GOTTA GO AGAINST THAT GUY IN MATCH №. 5...

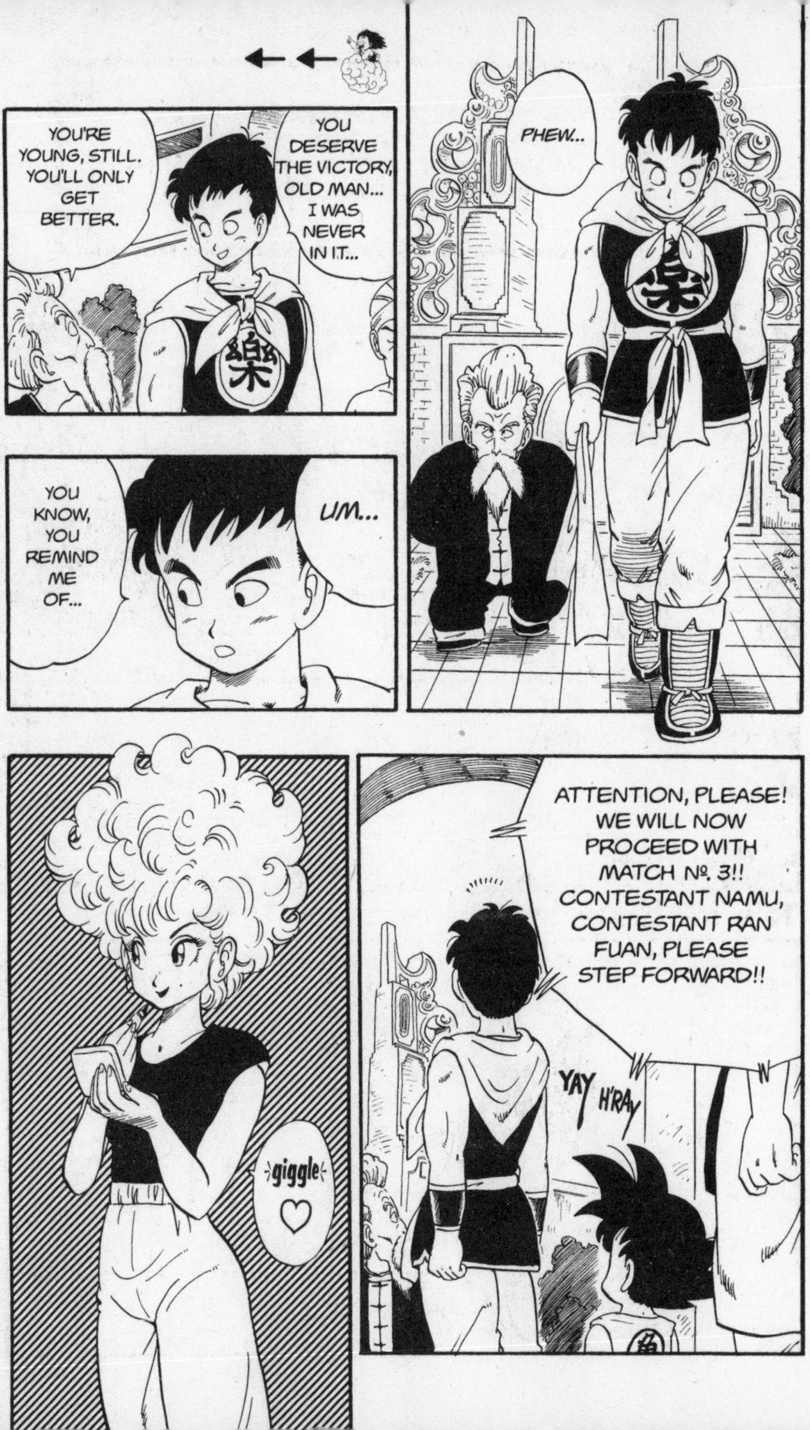
PHEW...
YOU DESERVE THE VICTORY, OLD MAN... I WAS NEVER IN IT...
YOU'RE YOUNG, STILL. YOU'LL ONLY GET BETTER.
UM...
YOU KNOW, YOU REMIND ME OF...
ATTENTION, PLEASE! WE WILL NOW PROCEED WITH MATCH №. 3!! CONTESTANT NAMU, CONTESTANT RAN FUAN, PLEASE STEP FORWARD!!
YAY
H'RAY
giggle
♥

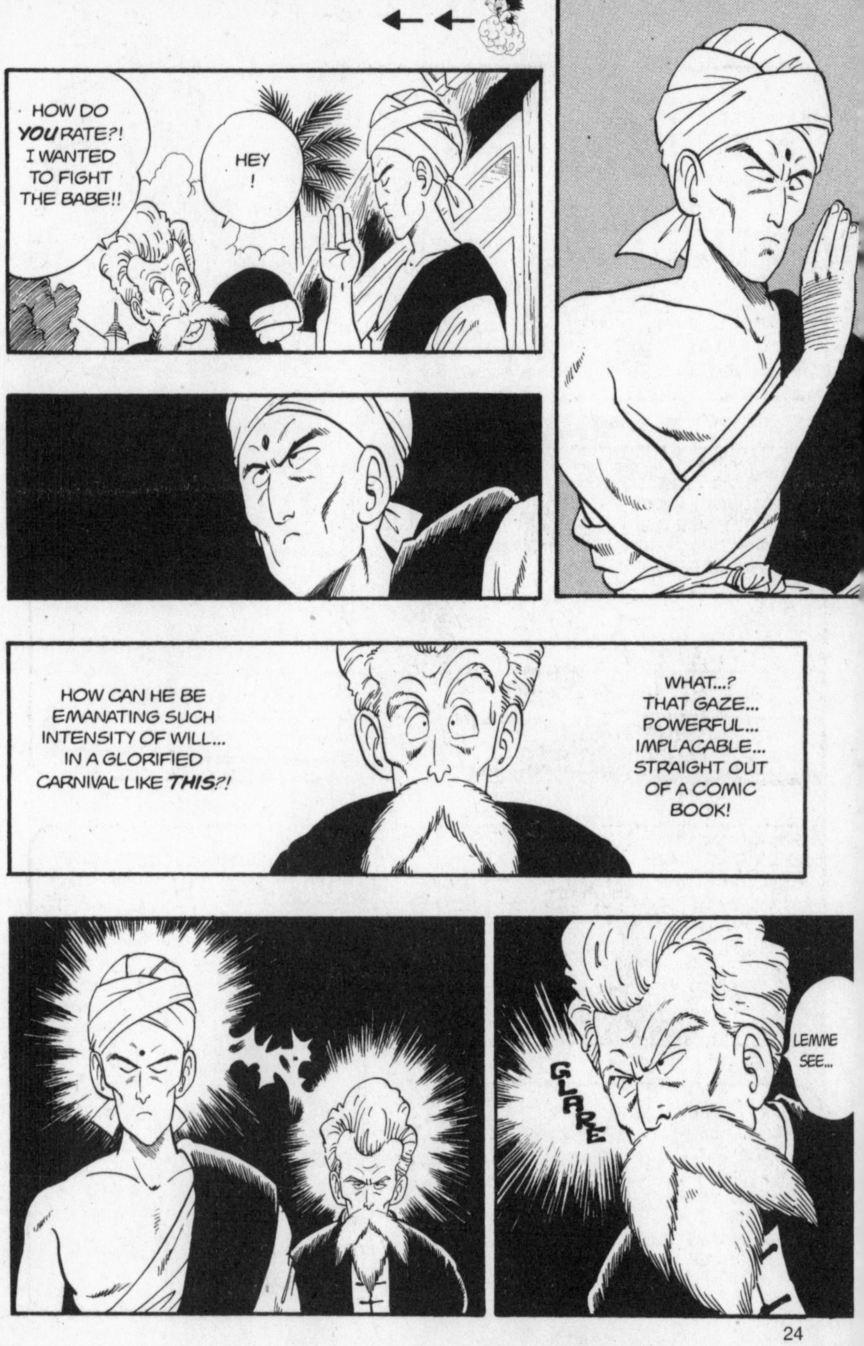
HEY !
HOW DO *YOU* RATE?! I WANTED TO FIGHT THE BABE!!
WHAT...? THAT GAZE... POWERFUL... IMPLACABLE... STRAIGHT OUT OF A COMIC BOOK!
HOW CAN HE BE EMANATING SUCH INTENSITY OF WILL... IN A GLORIFIED CARNIVAL LIKE *THIS*?!
LEMME SEE...
GLARE

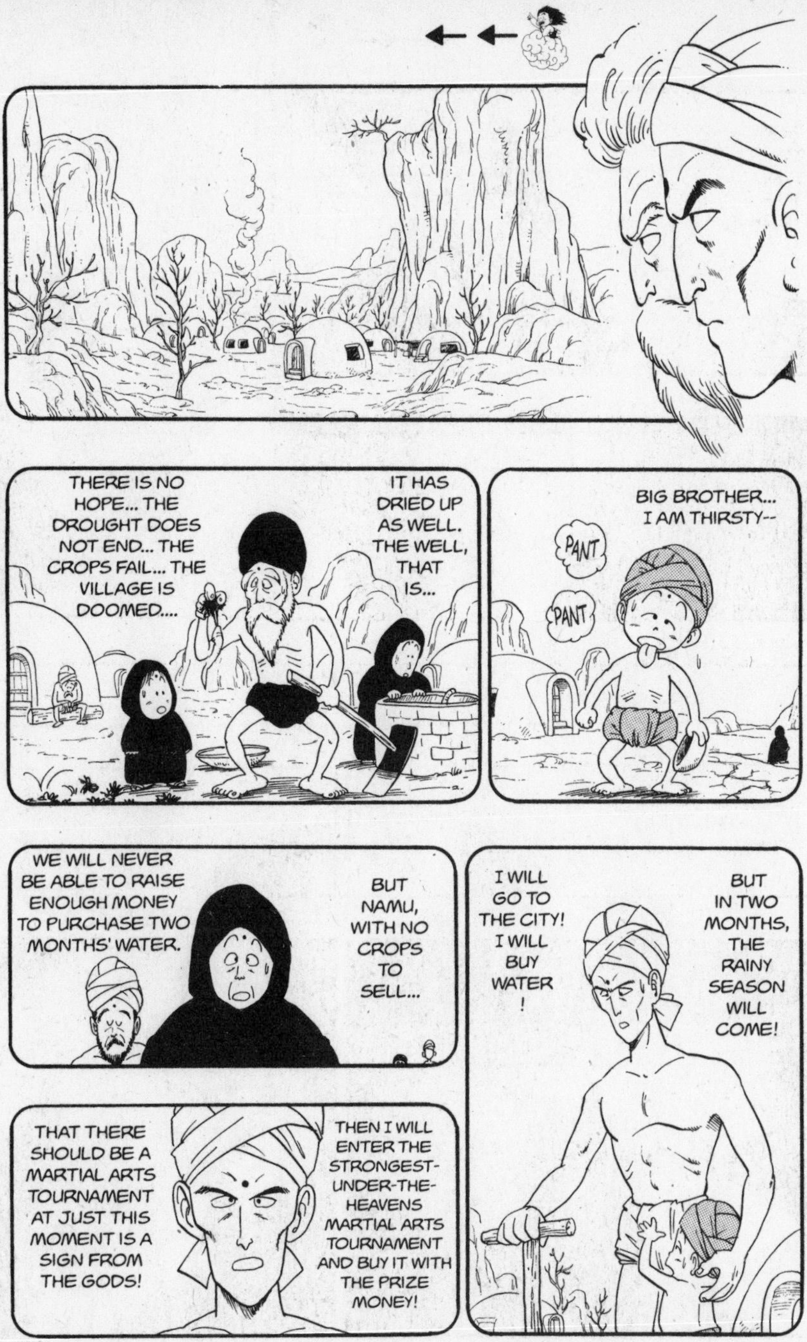
BIG BROTHER... I AM THIRSTY--
PANT
PANT
IT HAS DRIED UP AS WELL. THE WELL, THAT IS...
THERE IS NO HOPE... THE DROUGHT DOES NOT END... THE CROPS FAIL... THE VILLAGE IS DOOMED....
BUT IN TWO MONTHS, THE RAINY SEASON WILL COME!
I WILL GO TO THE CITY! I WILL BUY WATER!
BUT NAMU, WITH NO CROPS TO SELL...
WE WILL NEVER BE ABLE TO RAISE ENOUGH MONEY TO PURCHASE TWO MONTHS' WATER.
THEN I WILL ENTER THE STRONGEST-UNDER-THE-HEAVENS MARTIAL ARTS TOURNAMENT AND BUY IT WITH THE PRIZE MONEY!
THAT THERE SHOULD BE A MARTIAL ARTS TOURNAMENT AT JUST THIS MOMENT IS A SIGN FROM THE GODS!

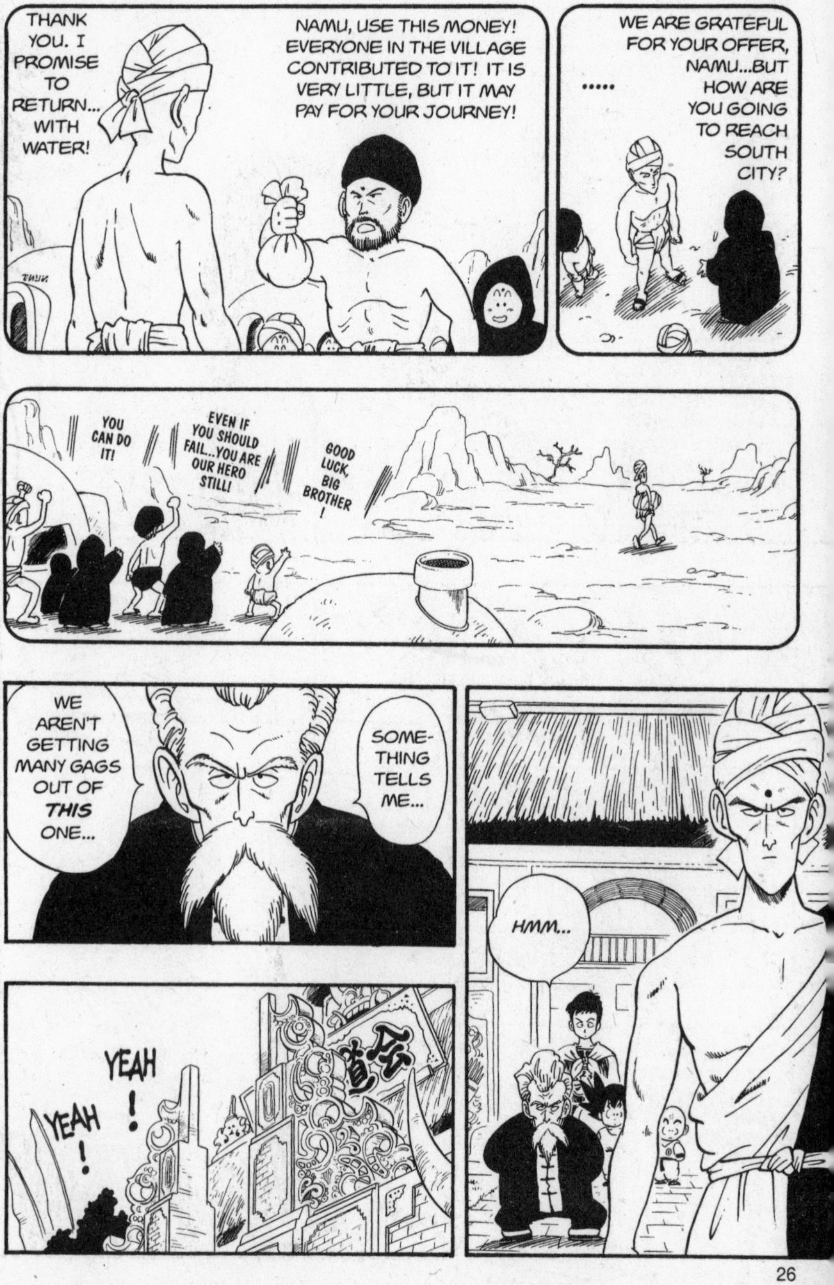
WE ARE GRATEFUL FOR YOUR OFFER, NAMU...BUT HOW ARE YOU GOING TO REACH SOUTH CITY?
.....
NAMU, USE THIS MONEY! EVERYONE IN THE VILLAGE CONTRIBUTED TO IT! IT IS VERY LITTLE, BUT IT MAY PAY FOR YOUR JOURNEY!
THANK YOU. I PROMISE TO RETURN... WITH WATER!
GOOD LUCK, BIG BROTHER!
EVEN IF YOU SHOULD FAIL...YOU ARE OUR HERO STILL!
YOU CAN DO IT!
HMM...
SOME-THING TELLS ME...
WE AREN'T GETTING MANY GAGS OUT OF *THIS* ONE...
YEAH!
YEAH!

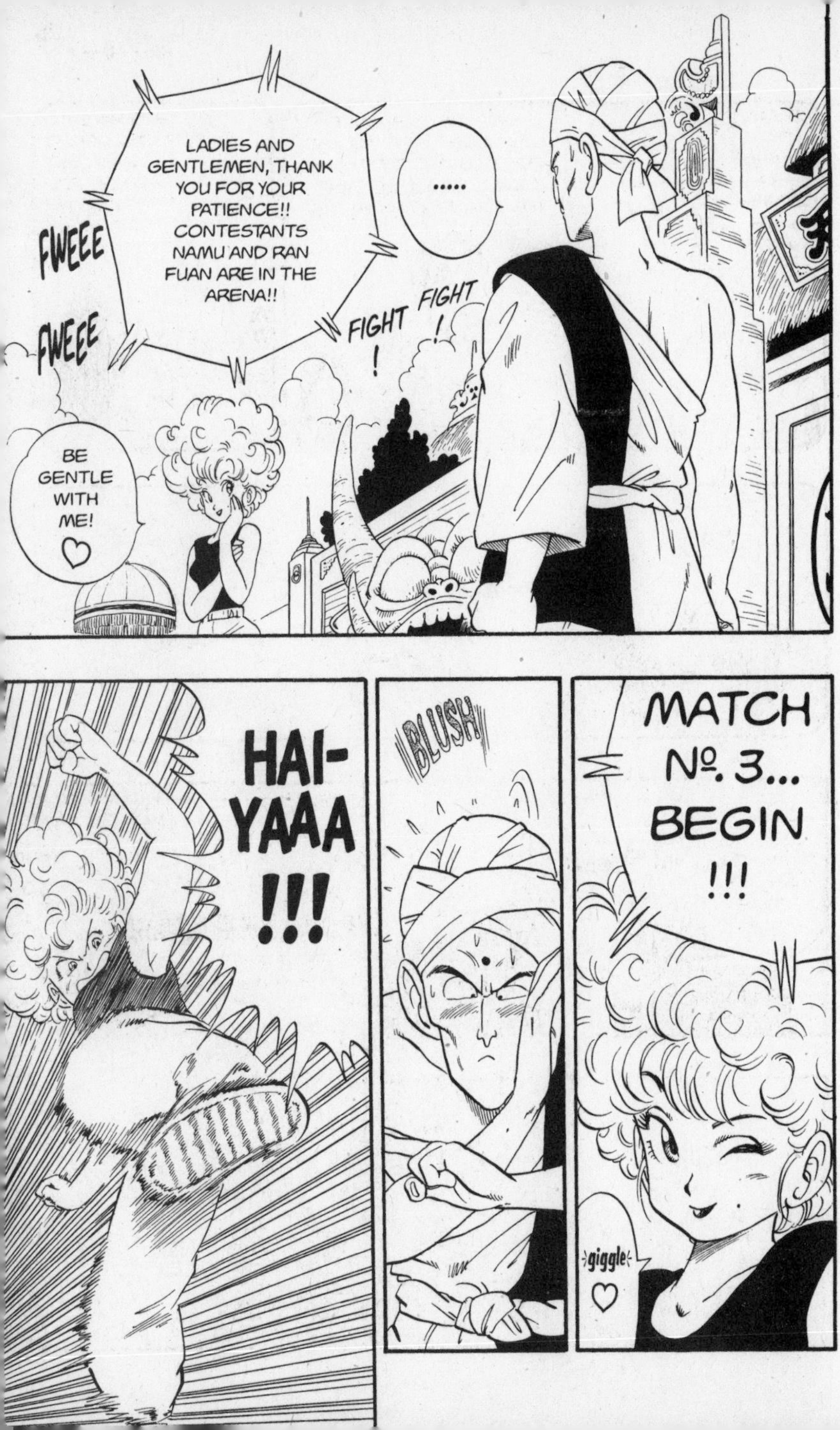
.....
LADIES AND GENTLEMEN, THANK YOU FOR YOUR PATIENCE!! CONTESTANTS NAMU AND RAN FUAN ARE IN THE ARENA!!
FWEEE
FWEEE
FIGHT! FIGHT!
BE GENTLE WITH ME! ♡
MATCH №. 3... BEGIN!!!
giggle ♡
BLUSH
HAI-YAAA!!!

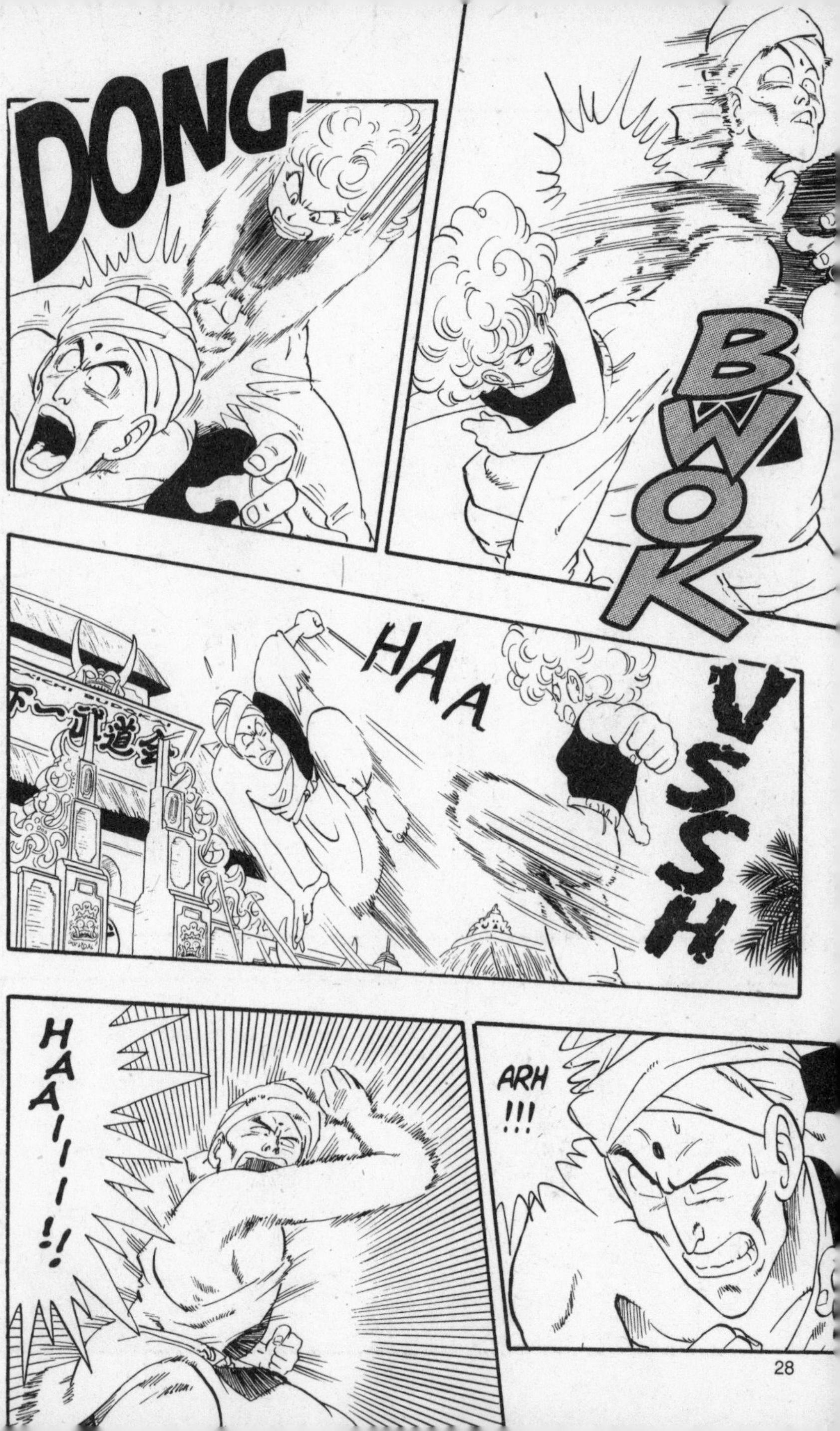
BWOK
DONG
VSSH
HAA
ARH!!!
HAAIIII!!

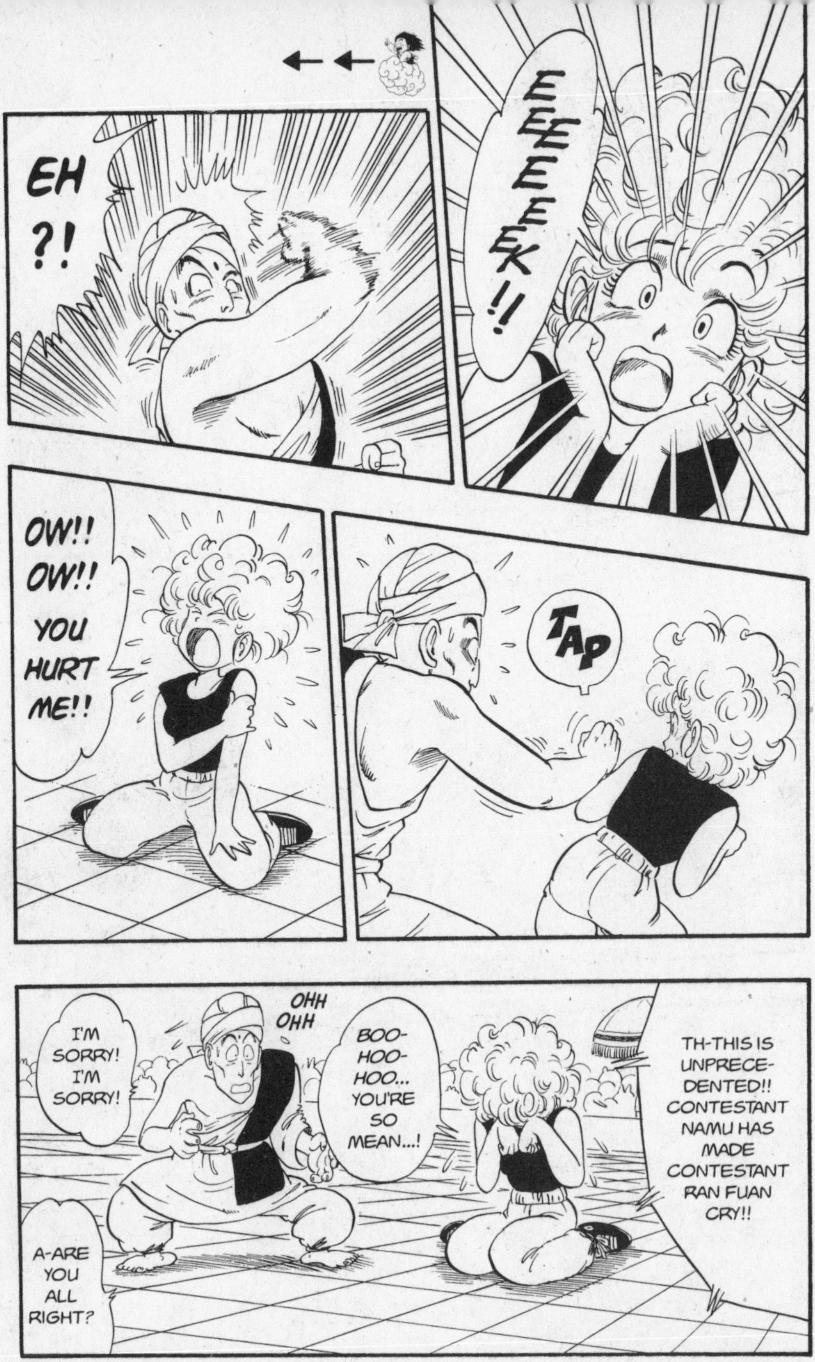
EEEEEEK!!
EH ?!
TAP
OW!! OW!! YOU HURT ME!!
TH-THIS IS UNPRECEDENTED!! CONTESTANT NAMU HAS MADE CONTESTANT RAN FUAN CRY!!
BOO-HOO-HOO... YOU'RE SO MEAN...!
OHH OHH
I'M SORRY! I'M SORRY!
A-ARE YOU ALL RIGHT?

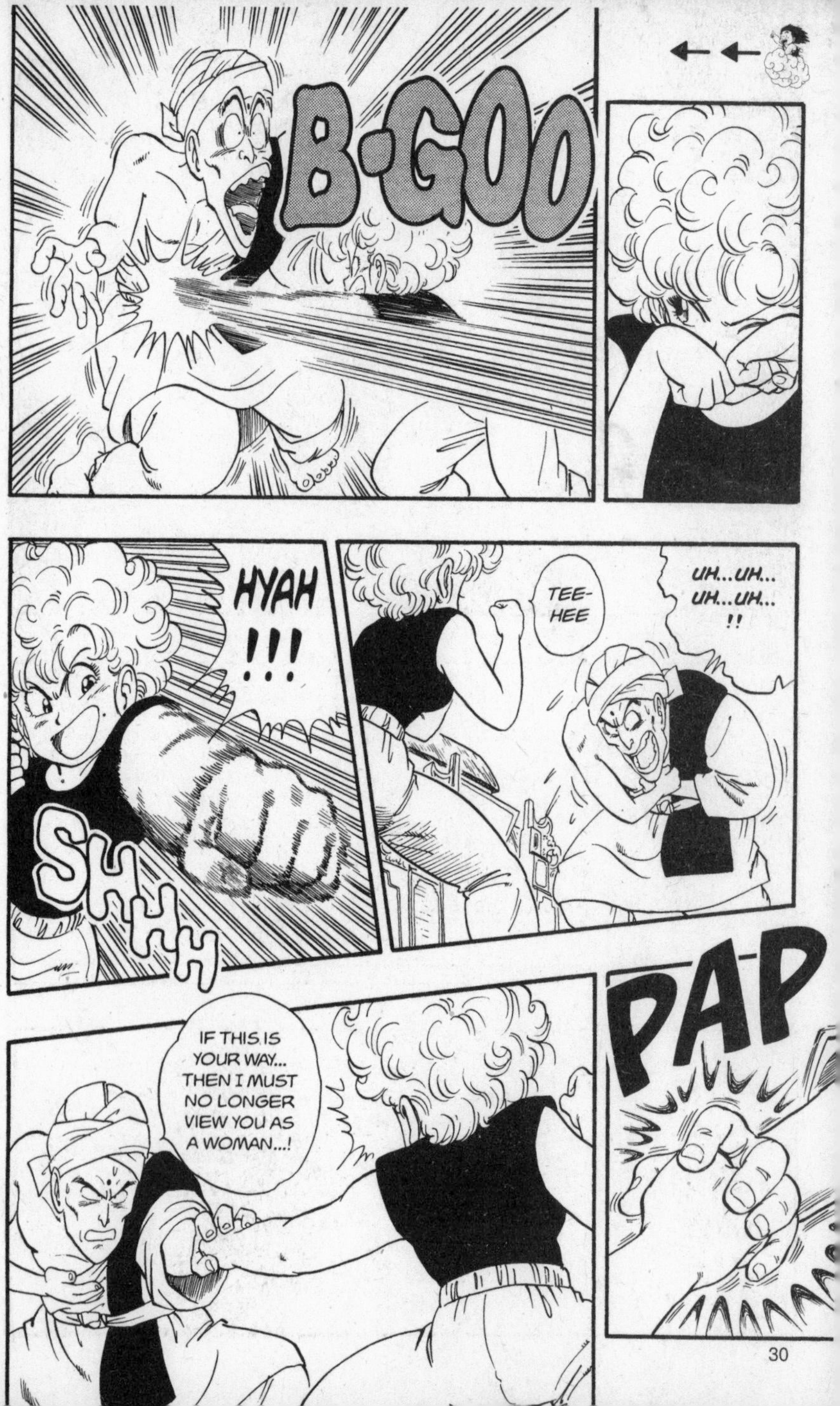
B-GOO
UH...UH... UH...UH... !!
TEE-HEE
HYAH !!!
SHHHH
PAP
IF THIS IS YOUR WAY... THEN I MUST NO LONGER VIEW YOU AS A WOMAN...!

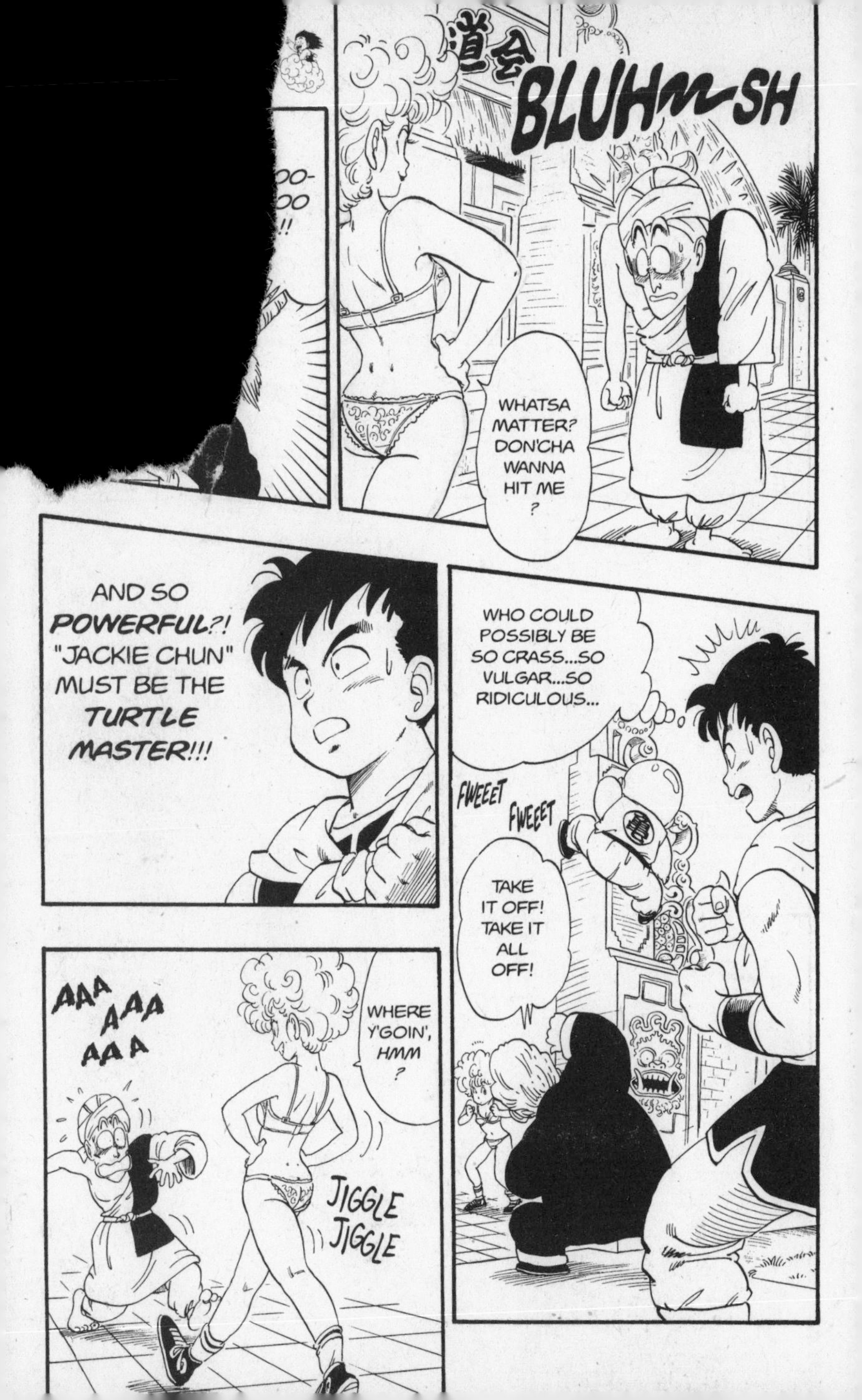

BLUHMSH
WHATSA MATTER? DON'CHA WANNA HIT ME?
WHO COULD POSSIBLY BE SO CRASS...SO VULGAR...SO RIDICULOUS...
FWEEET FWEEET
TAKE IT OFF! TAKE IT ALL OFF!
AND SO POWERFUL?! "JACKIE CHUN" MUST BE THE TURTLE MASTER!!!
WHERE Y'GOIN', HMM?
AAA AAA AAA
JIGGLE JIGGLE

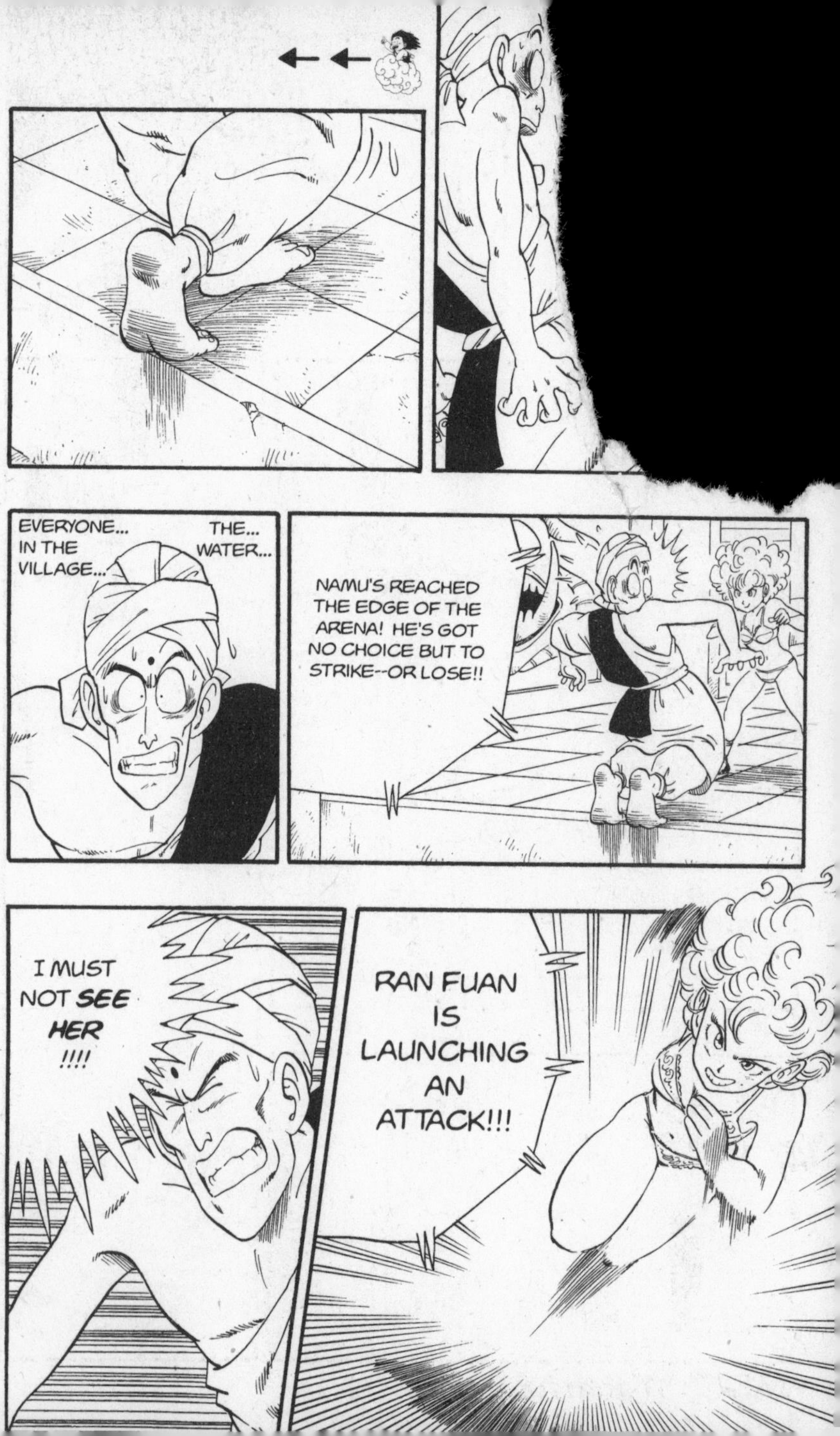
NAMU'S REACHED THE EDGE OF THE ARENA! HE'S GOT NO CHOICE BUT TO STRIKE--OR LOSE!!
EVERYONE... IN THE VILLAGE...
THE... WATER...
RAN FUAN IS LAUNCHING AN ATTACK!!!
I MUST NOT SEE HER !!!!

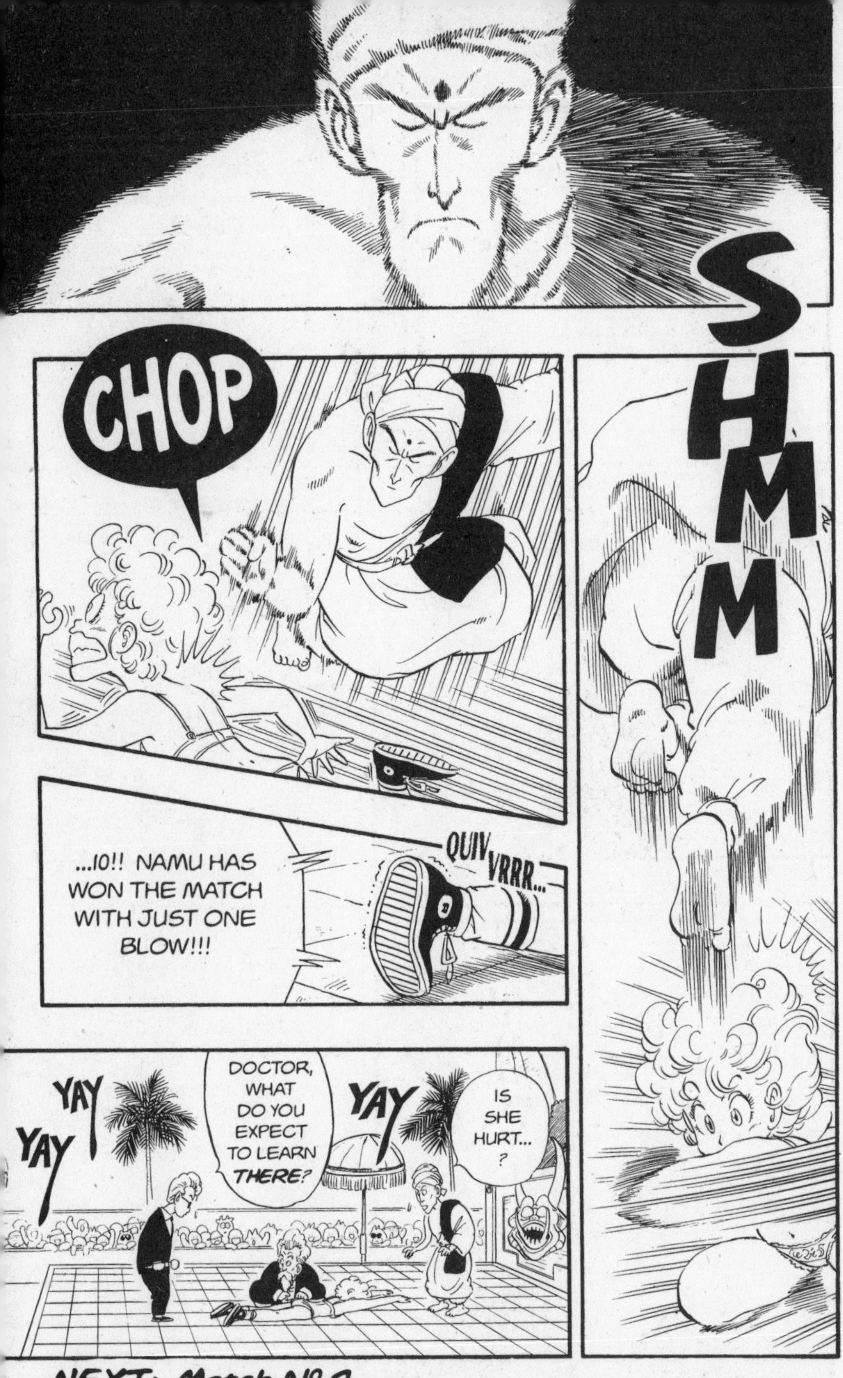
SHMM
CHOP
QUIV VRRR...
...10!! NAMU HAS WON THE MATCH WITH JUST ONE BLOW!!!
IS SHE HURT...?
YAY
DOCTOR, WHAT DO YOU EXPECT TO LEARN *THERE?*
YAY
YAY

NEXT: Match №. 4

Tale 39

Monster Smash!

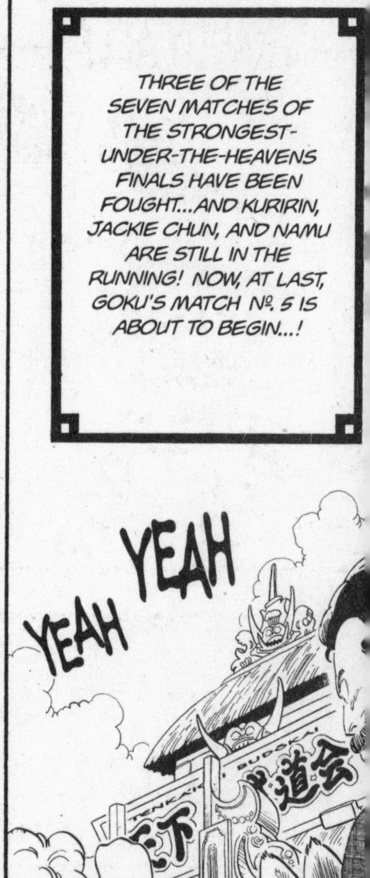

THREE OF THE SEVEN MATCHES OF THE STRONGEST-UNDER-THE-HEAVENS FINALS HAVE BEEN FOUGHT...AND KURIRIN, JACKIE CHUN, AND NAMU ARE STILL IN THE RUNNING! NOW, AT LAST, GOKU'S MATCH №. 5 IS ABOUT TO BEGIN...!
YEAH
YEAH
TENKAICHI BUDOKAI

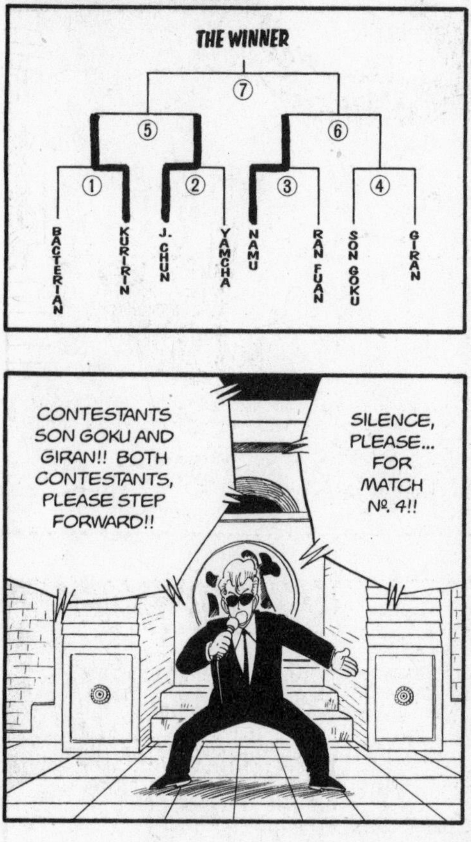

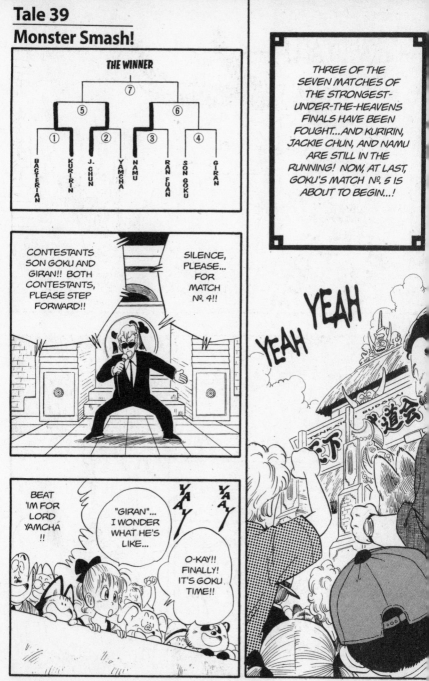

THE WINNER
⑦
⑤
⑥
①
②
③
④
BACTERIAN
KURIRIN
J. CHUN
YAMCHA
NAMU
RAN FUAN
SON GOKU
GIRAN
SILENCE, PLEASE... FOR MATCH №. 4!!
CONTESTANTS SON GOKU AND GIRAN!! BOTH CONTESTANTS, PLEASE STEP FORWARD!!
YAAAY
YAAAY
"GIRAN"... I WONDER WHAT HE'S LIKE...
O-KAY!! FINALLY! IT'S GOKU TIME!!
BEAT 'IM FOR LORD YAMCHA !!

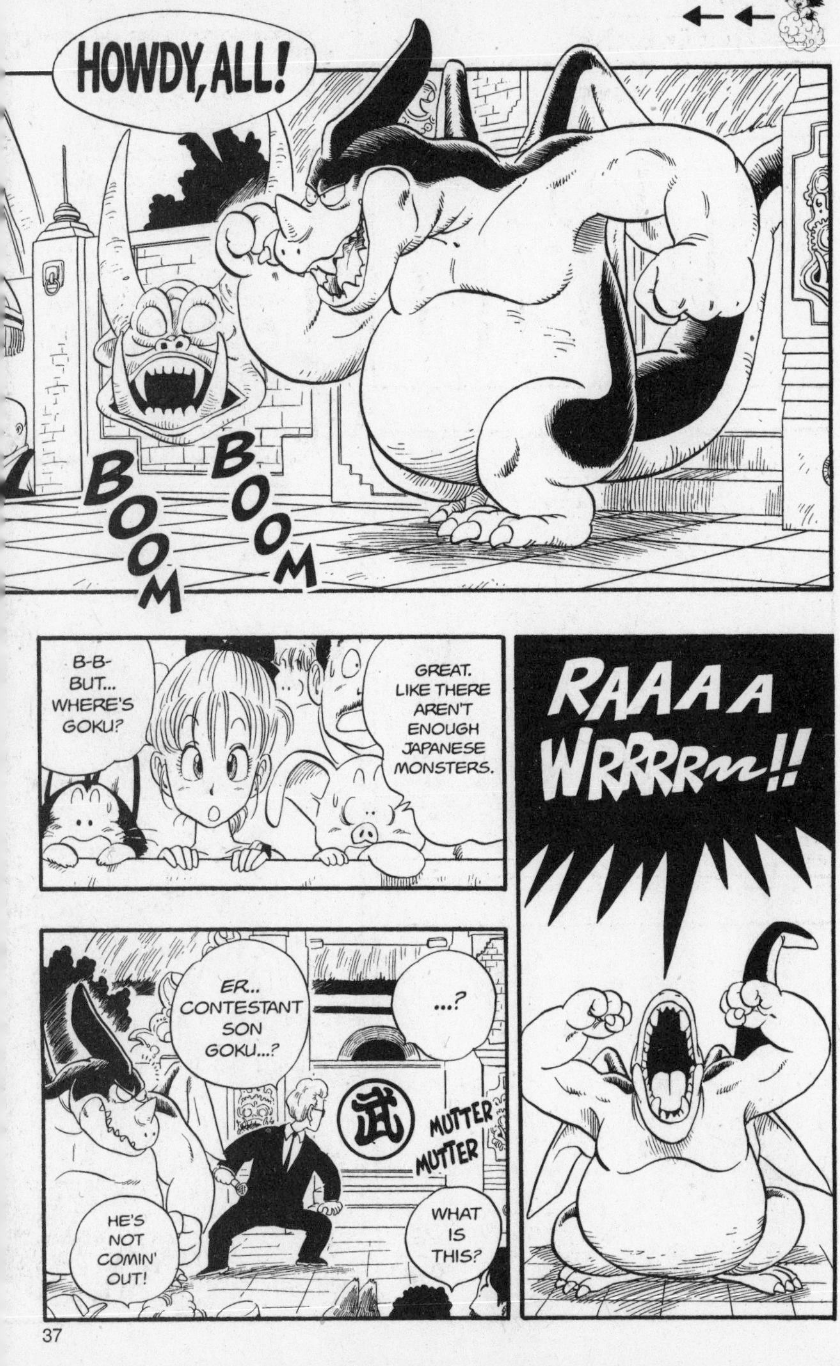

HOWDY, ALL!
BOOM
BOOM
RAAAA WRRRRn!!
GREAT. LIKE THERE AREN'T ENOUGH JAPANESE MONSTERS.
B-B-BUT... WHERE'S GOKU?
...?
ER... CONTESTANT SON GOKU...?
MUTTER MUTTER
WHAT IS THIS?
HE'S NOT COMIN' OUT!

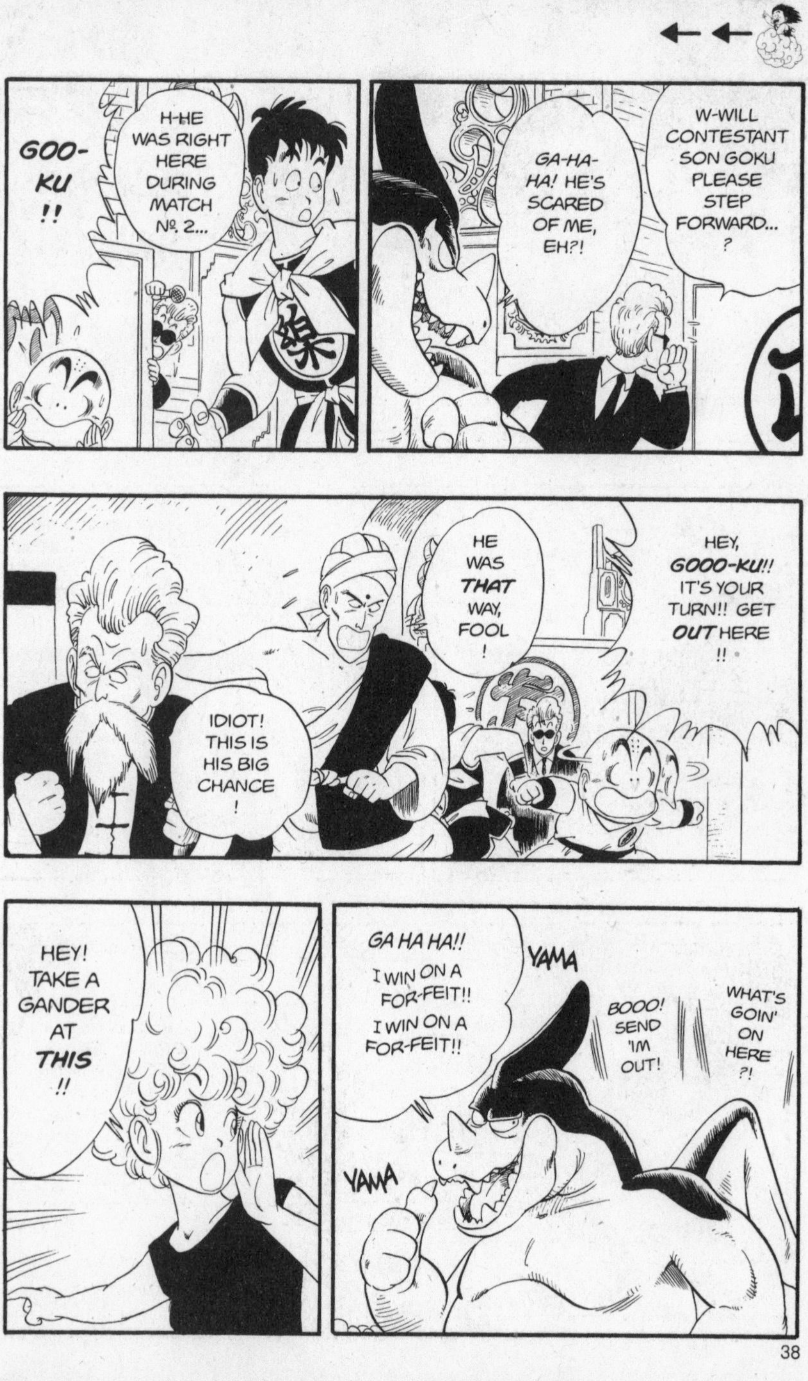
W-WILL CONTESTANT SON GOKU PLEASE STEP FORWARD...?
GA-HA-HA! HE'S SCARED OF ME, EH?!
H-HE WAS RIGHT HERE DURING MATCH №. 2...
GOO-KU!!
HEY, GOOO-KU!! IT'S YOUR TURN!! GET OUT HERE!!
HE WAS THAT WAY, FOOL!
IDIOT! THIS IS HIS BIG CHANCE!
WHAT'S GOIN' ON HERE?!
BOOO! SEND 'IM OUT!
YAMA
GA HA HA!! I WIN ON A FOR-FEIT!! I WIN ON A FOR-FEIT!!
YAMA
HEY! TAKE A GANDER AT THIS!!

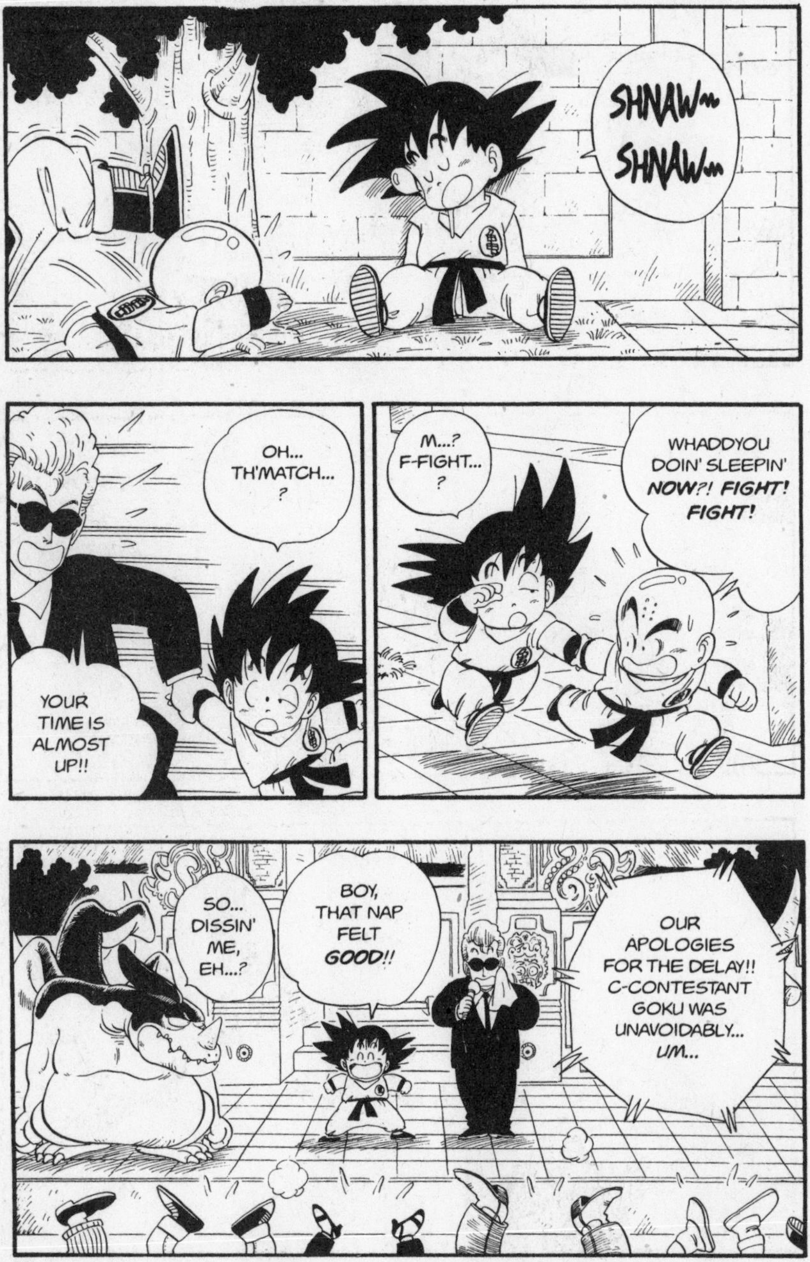
SHNAW... SHNAW...
WHADDYOU DOIN' SLEEPIN' NOW?! FIGHT! FIGHT!
M...? F-FIGHT... ?
OH... TH'MATCH... ?
YOUR TIME IS ALMOST UP!!
OUR APOLOGIES FOR THE DELAY!! C-CONTESTANT GOKU WAS UNAVOIDABLY... UM...
BOY, THAT NAP FELT GOOD!!
SO... DISSIN' ME, EH...?

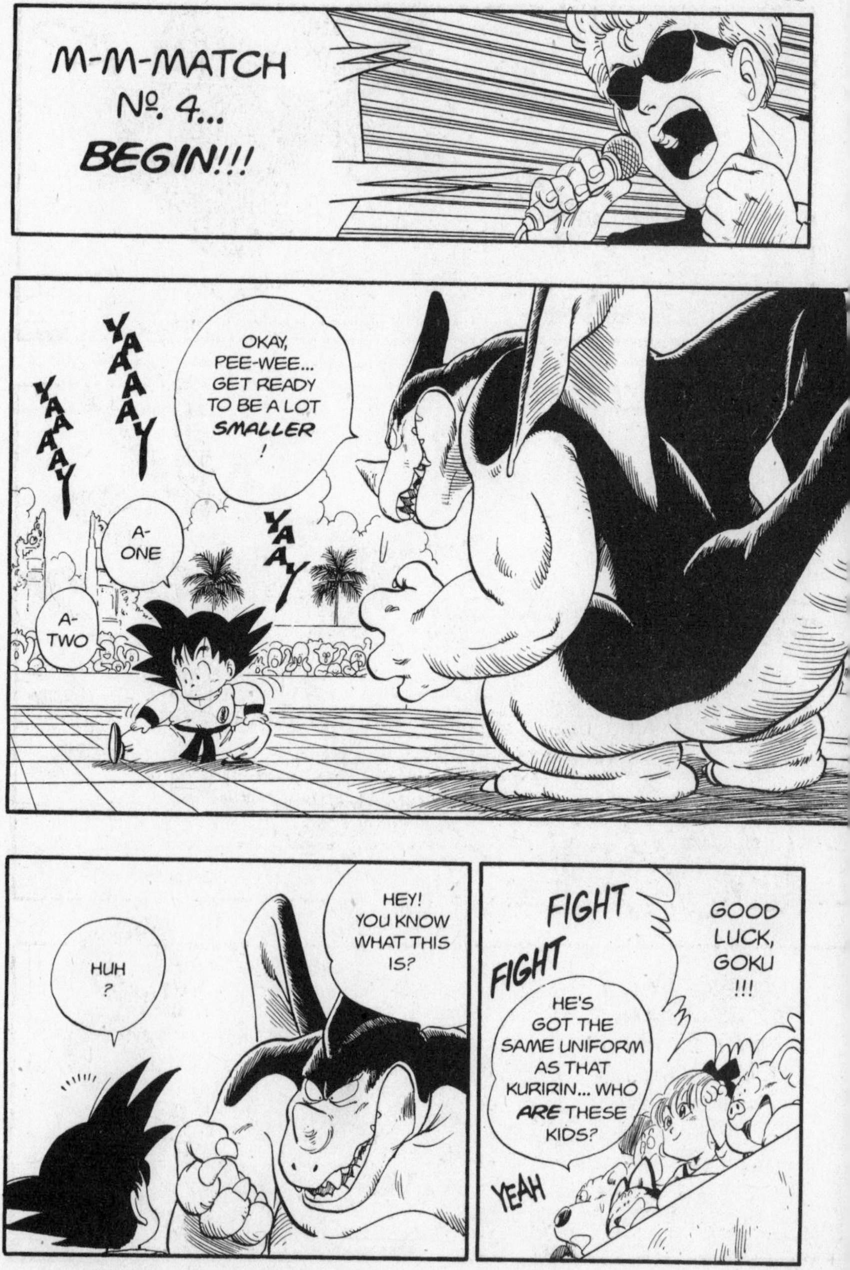

M-M-MATCH
Nº. 4...
BEGIN!!!
OKAY, PEE-WEE... GET READY TO BE A LOT SMALLER !
YAAAAY
YAAAAY
YAAY
A- ONE
A- TWO
GOOD LUCK, GOKU !!!
FIGHT
FIGHT
HE'S GOT THE SAME UNIFORM AS THAT KURIRIN... WHO ARE THESE KIDS?
YEAH
HEY! YOU KNOW WHAT THIS IS?
HUH ?

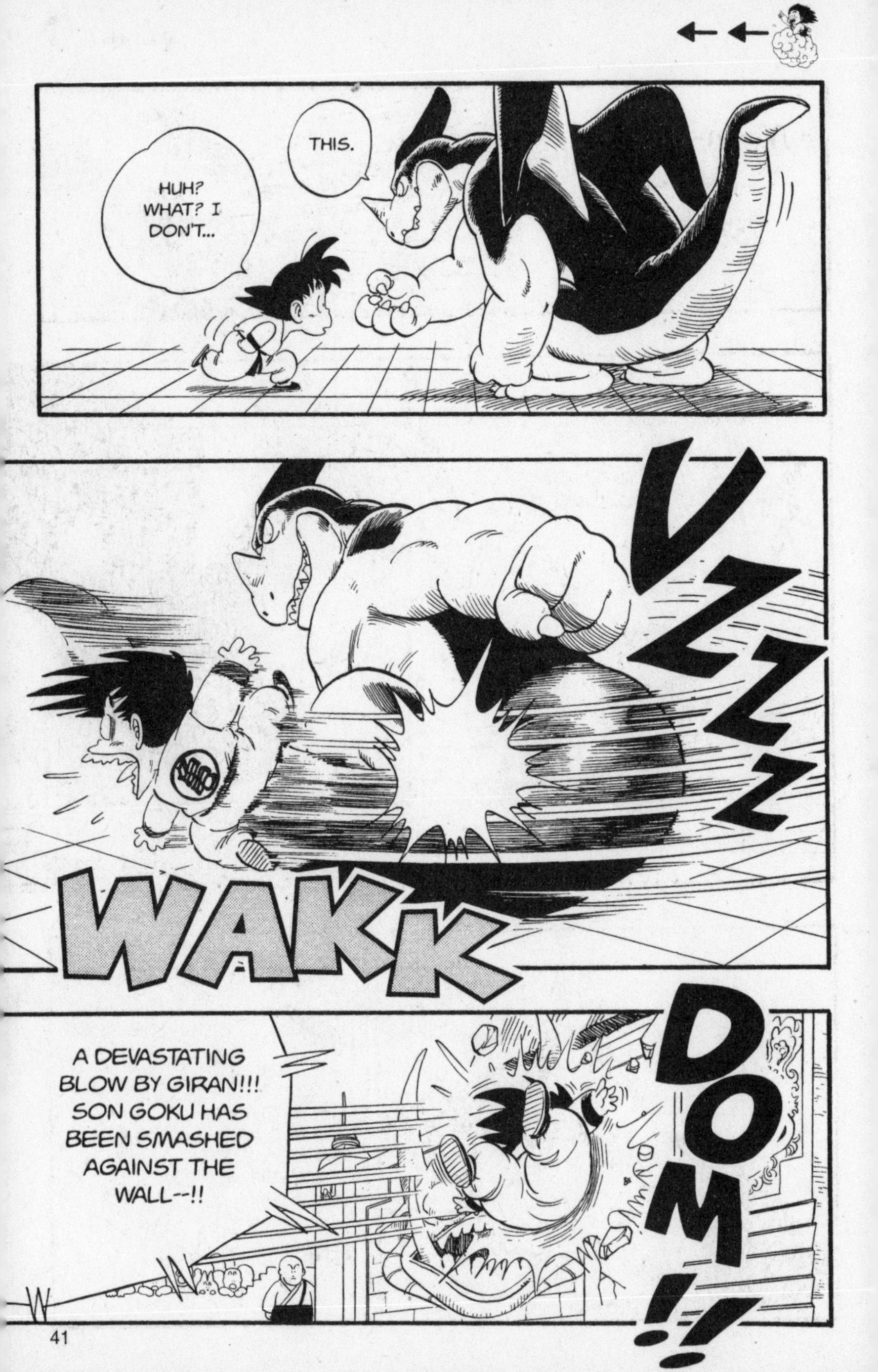

THIS.
HUH? WHAT? I DON'T...
VZZZZ
WAKK
DOM!!
A DEVASTATING BLOW BY GIRAN!!! SON GOKU HAS BEEN SMASHED AGAINST THE WALL--!!

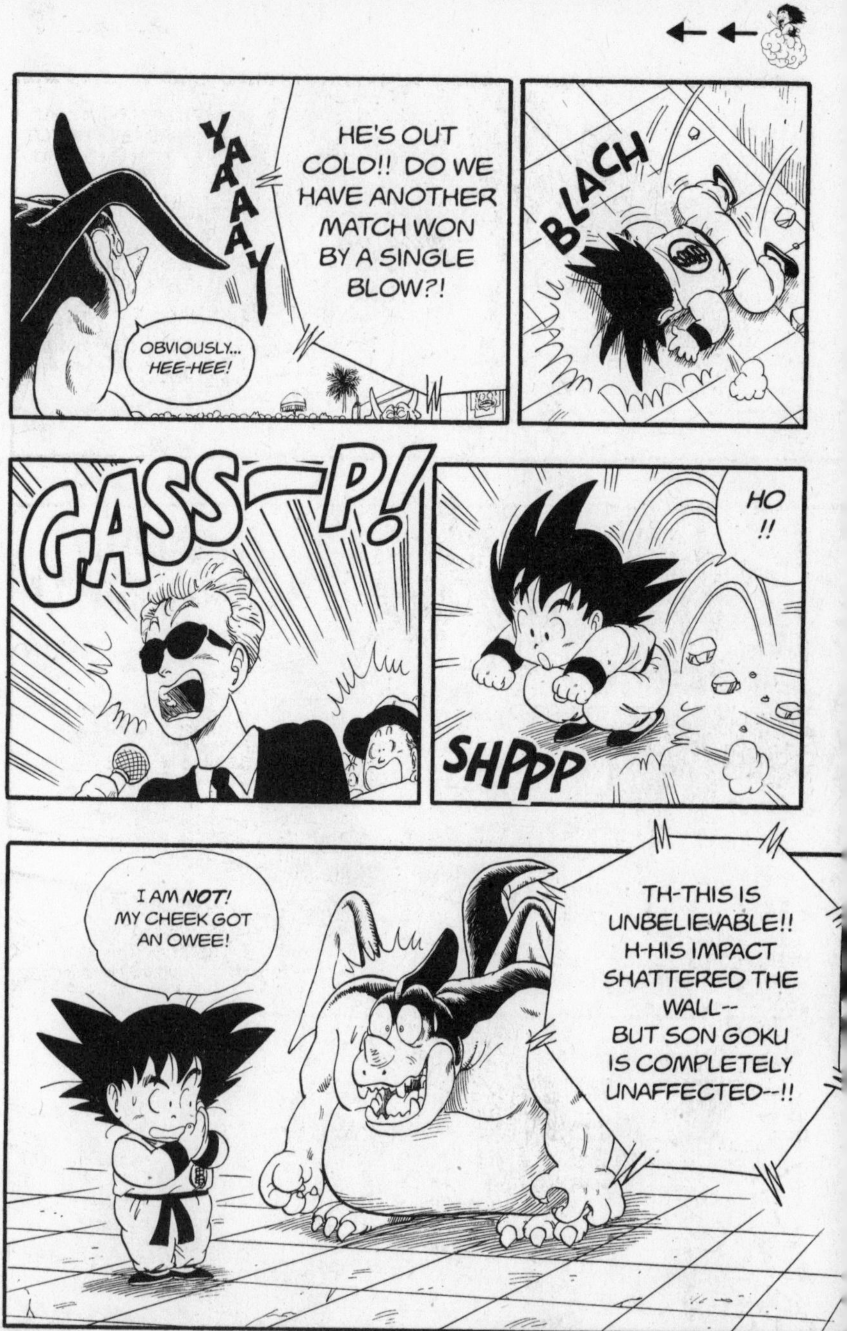
BLACH
YAAAAY
HE'S OUT COLD!! DO WE HAVE ANOTHER MATCH WON BY A SINGLE BLOW?!
OBVIOUSLY... HEE-HEE!
HO !!
SHPPP
GASS—P!
TH-THIS IS UNBELIEVABLE!! H-HIS IMPACT SHATTERED THE WALL-- BUT SON GOKU IS COMPLETELY UNAFFECTED--!!
I AM NOT! MY CHEEK GOT AN OWEE!

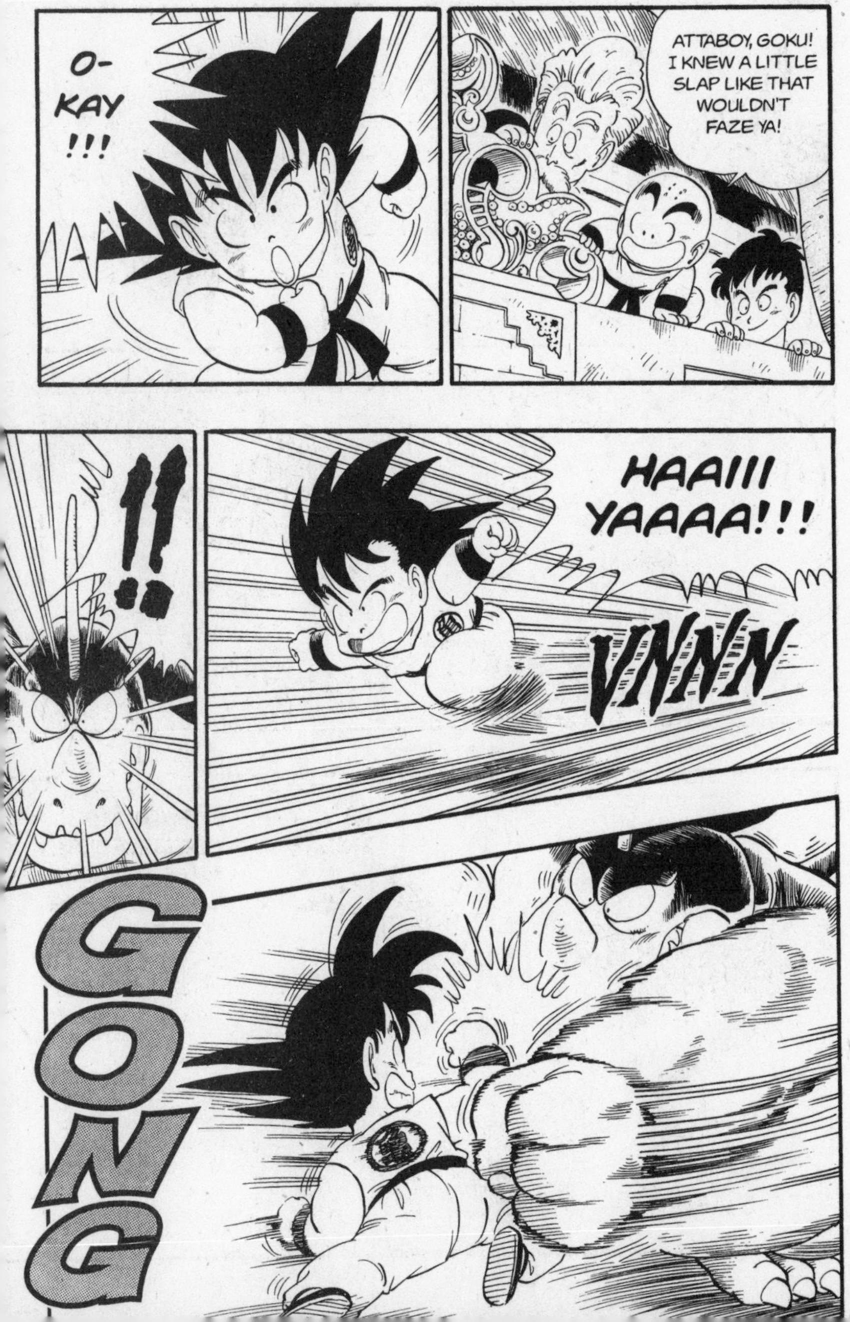
ATTABOY, GOKU! I KNEW A LITTLE SLAP LIKE THAT WOULDN'T FAZE YA!
O-KAY!!!
HAAIII YAAAA!!!
VNNN
!!
GONG

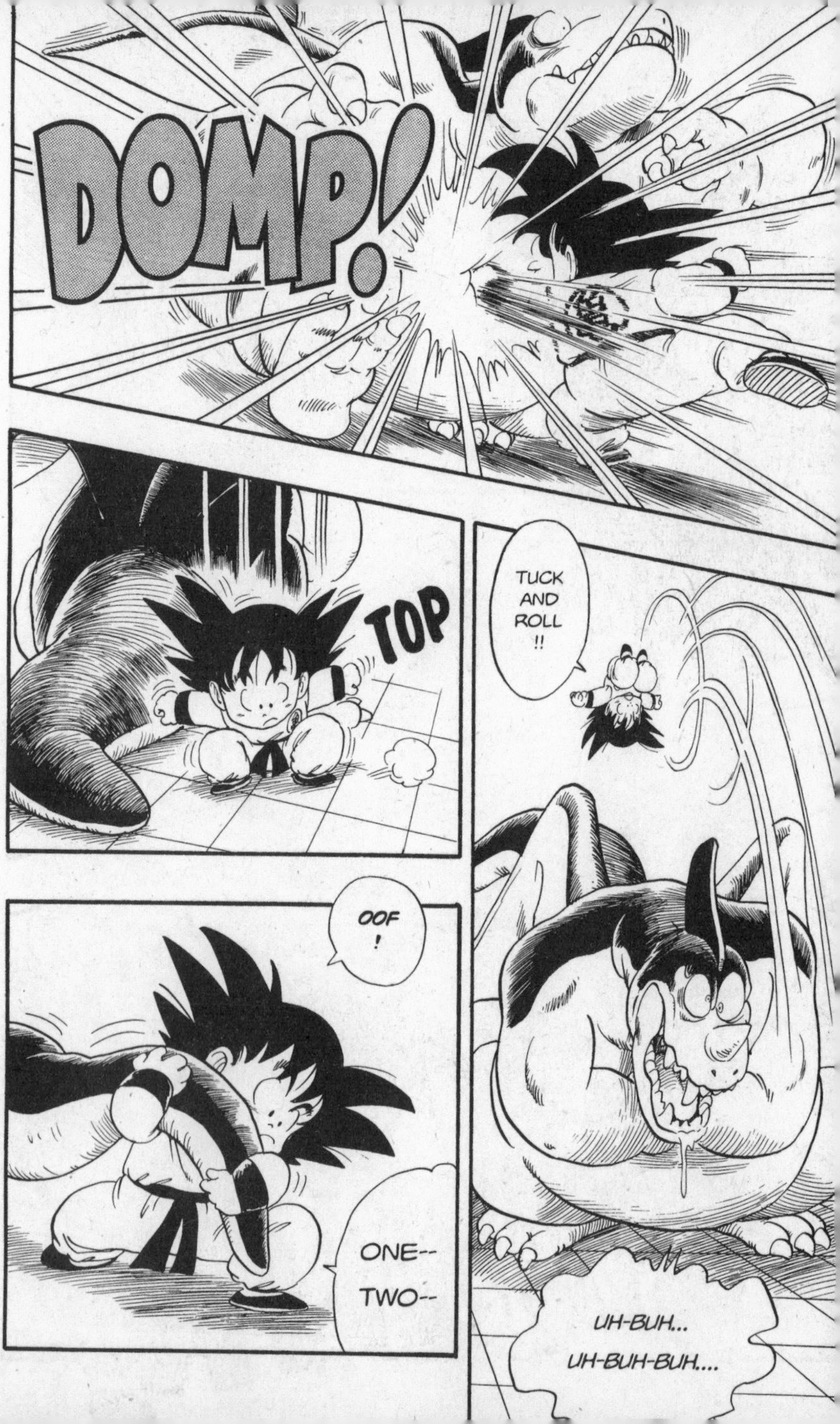
DOMP!
TUCK AND ROLL !!
UH-BUH... UH-BUH-BUH....
TOP
OOF !
ONE-- TWO--

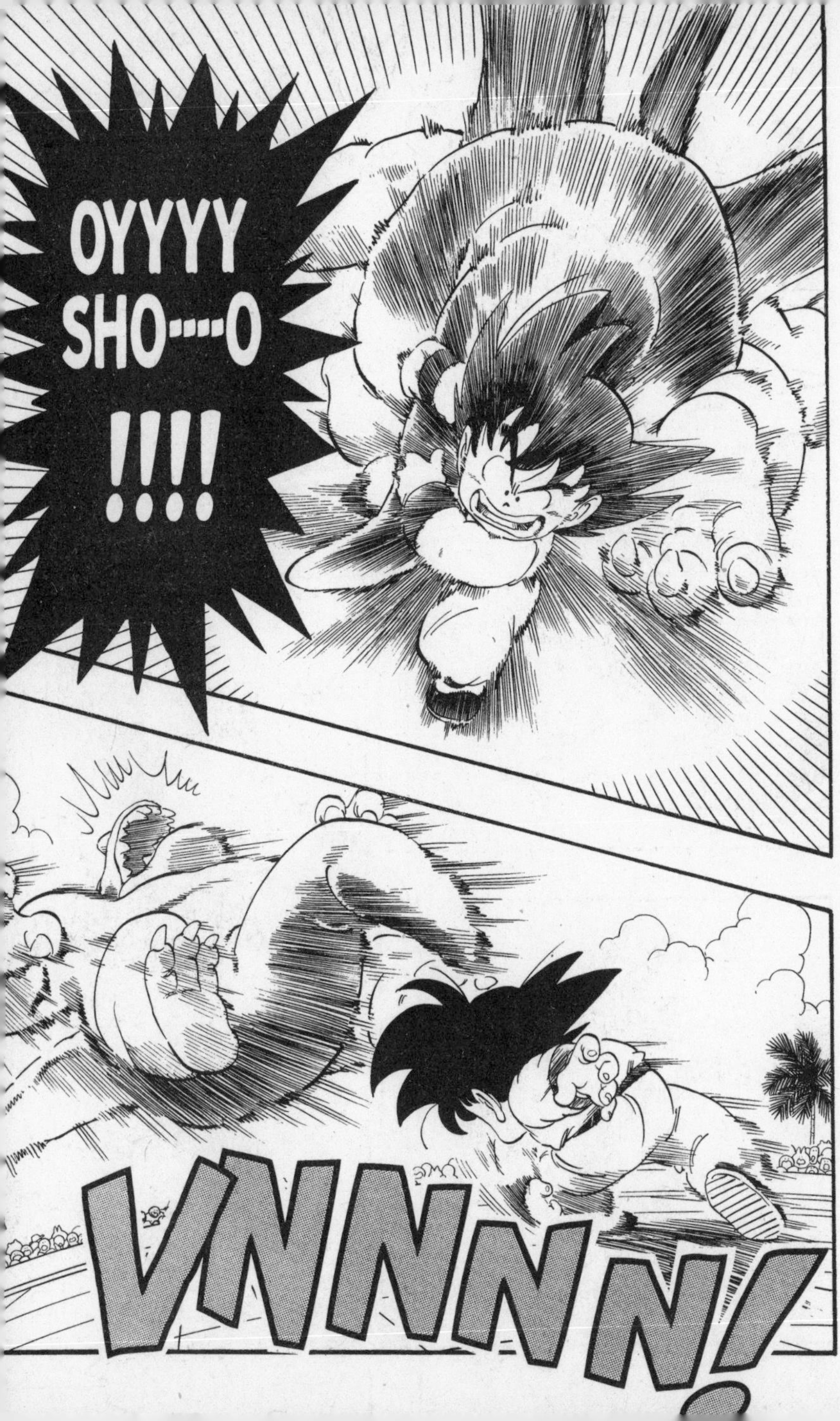
OYYYY SHO----O !!!!
VNNNN!

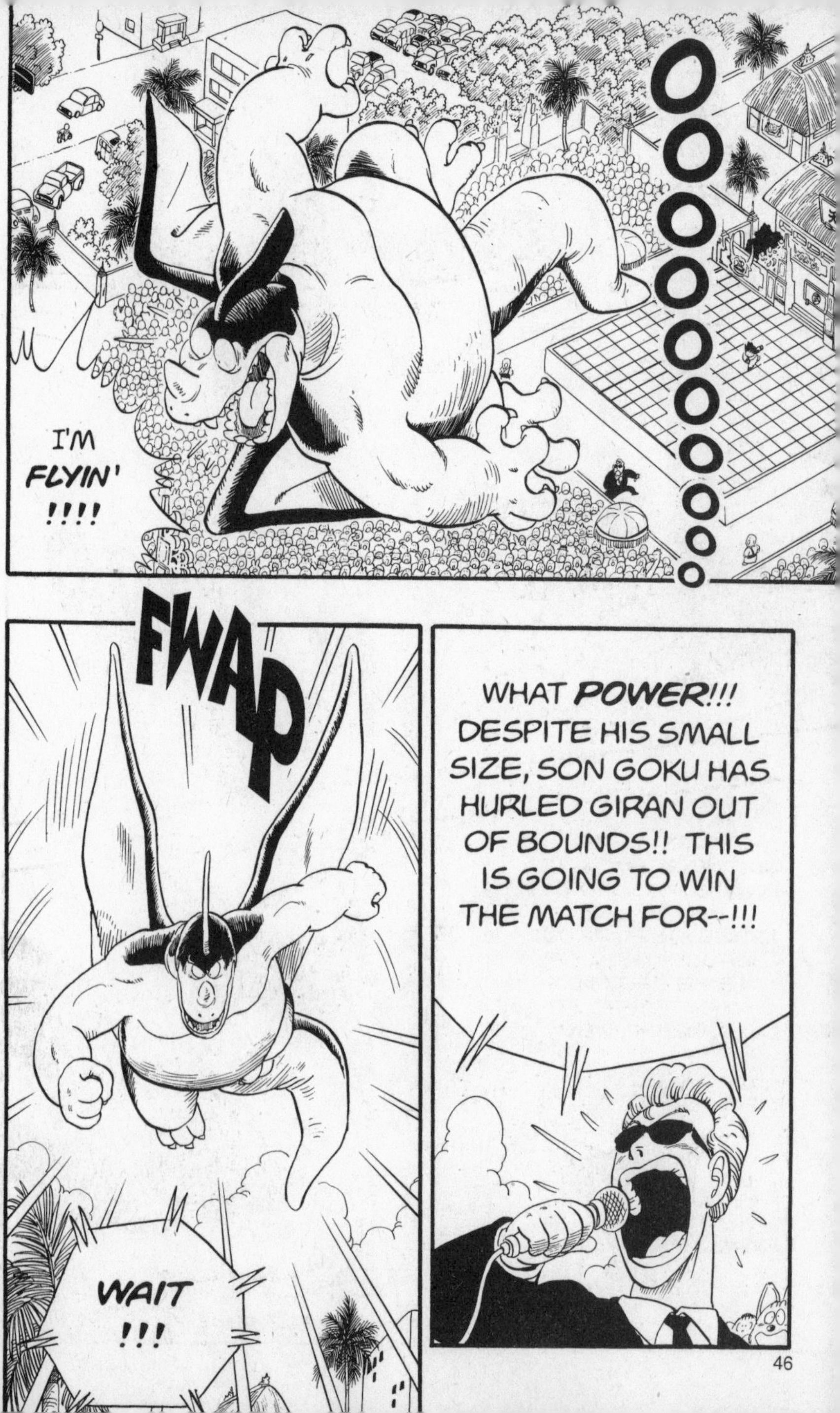
OOOOOOOOOOOOO
I'M FLYIN' !!!!
WHAT POWER!!! DESPITE HIS SMALL SIZE, SON GOKU HAS HURLED GIRAN OUT OF BOUNDS!! THIS IS GOING TO WIN THE MATCH FOR--!!!
FWAP
WAIT !!!

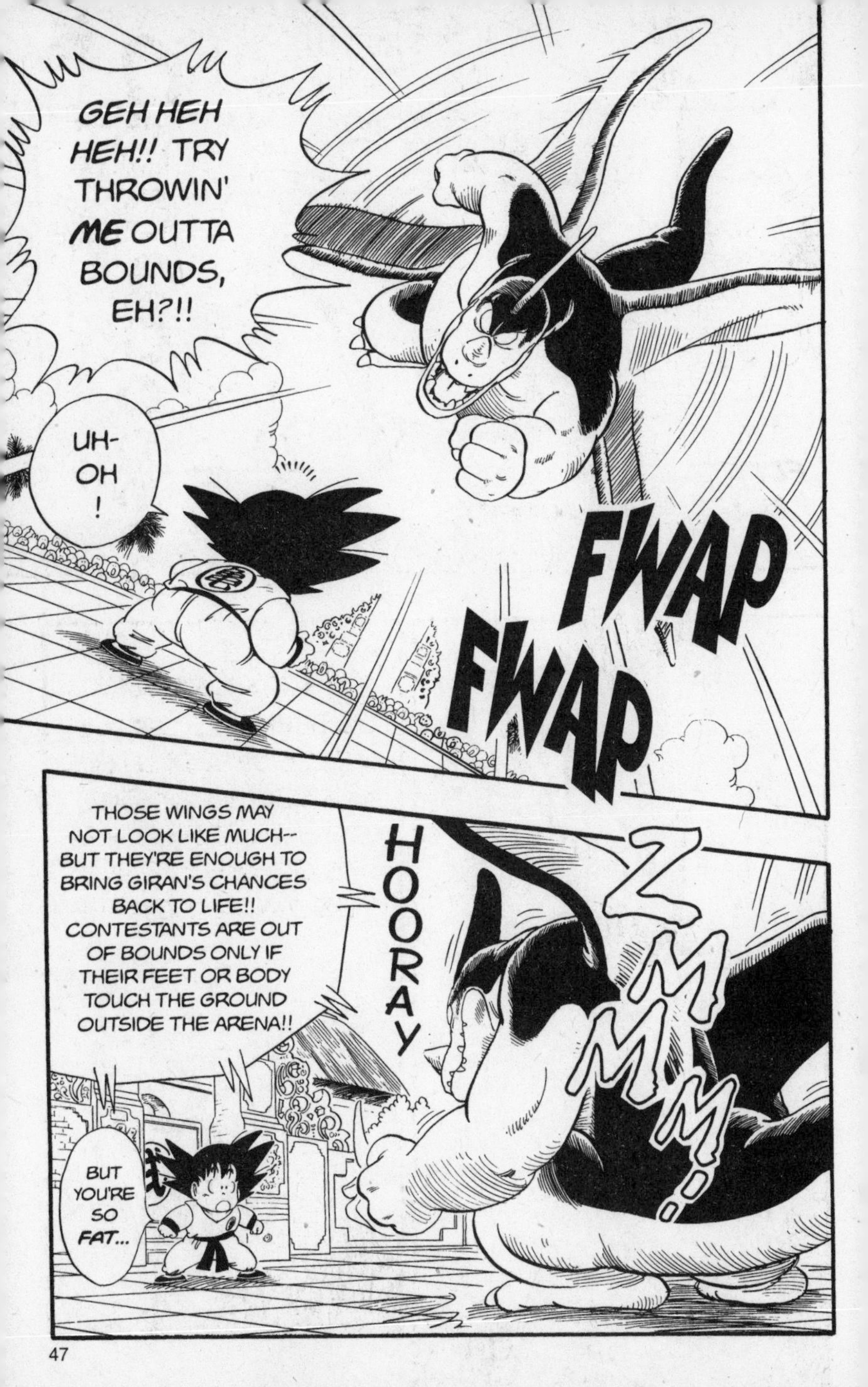
GEH HEH HEH!! TRY THROWIN' ME OUTTA BOUNDS, EH?!!
UH-OH!
FWAP FWAP
THOSE WINGS MAY NOT LOOK LIKE MUCH-- BUT THEY'RE ENOUGH TO BRING GIRAN'S CHANCES BACK TO LIFE!! CONTESTANTS ARE OUT OF BOUNDS ONLY IF THEIR FEET OR BODY TOUCH THE GROUND OUTSIDE THE ARENA!!
HOORAY
ZMMMM...
BUT YOU'RE SO FAT...

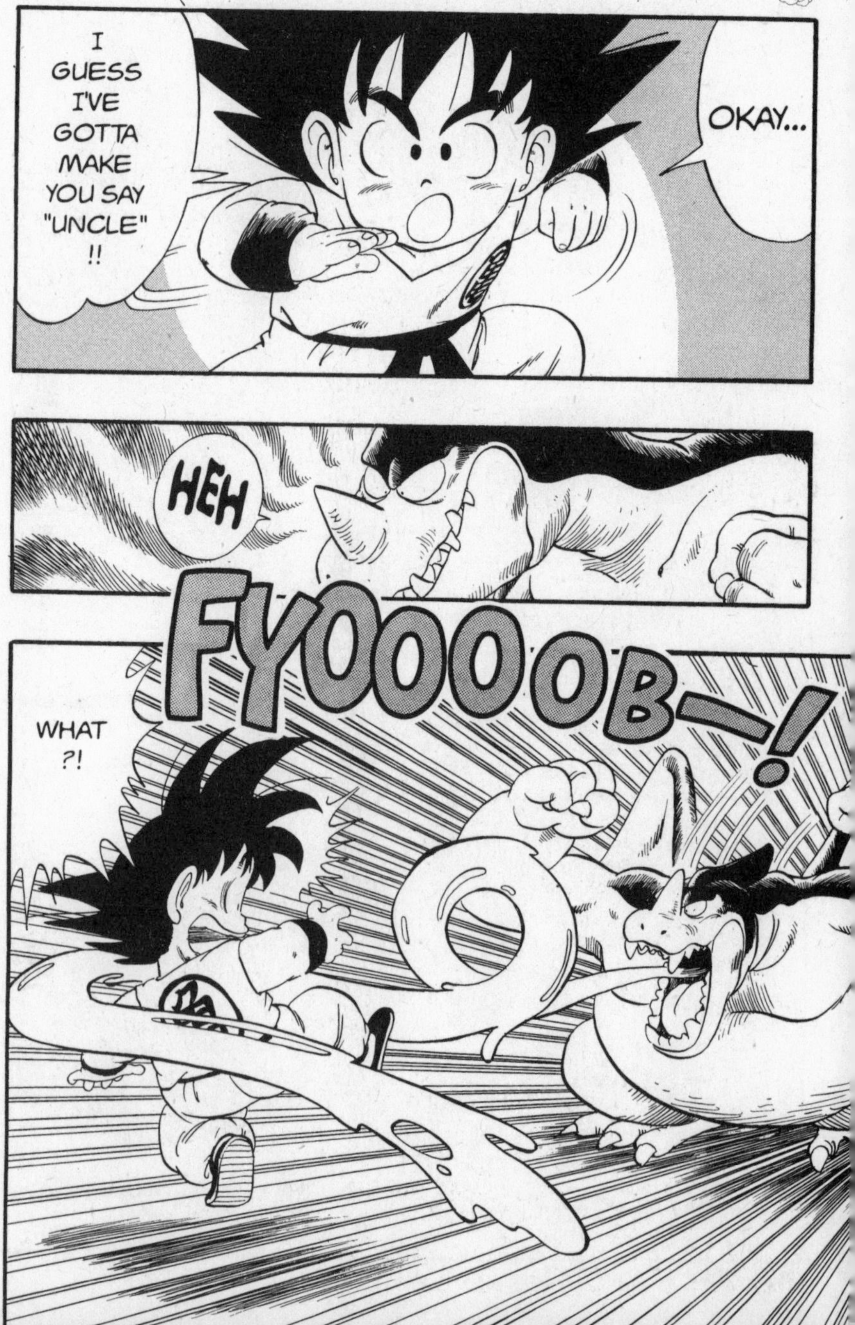
OKAY...
I GUESS I'VE GOTTA MAKE YOU SAY "UNCLE" !!
HEH
FYOOOOB—!
WHAT ?!

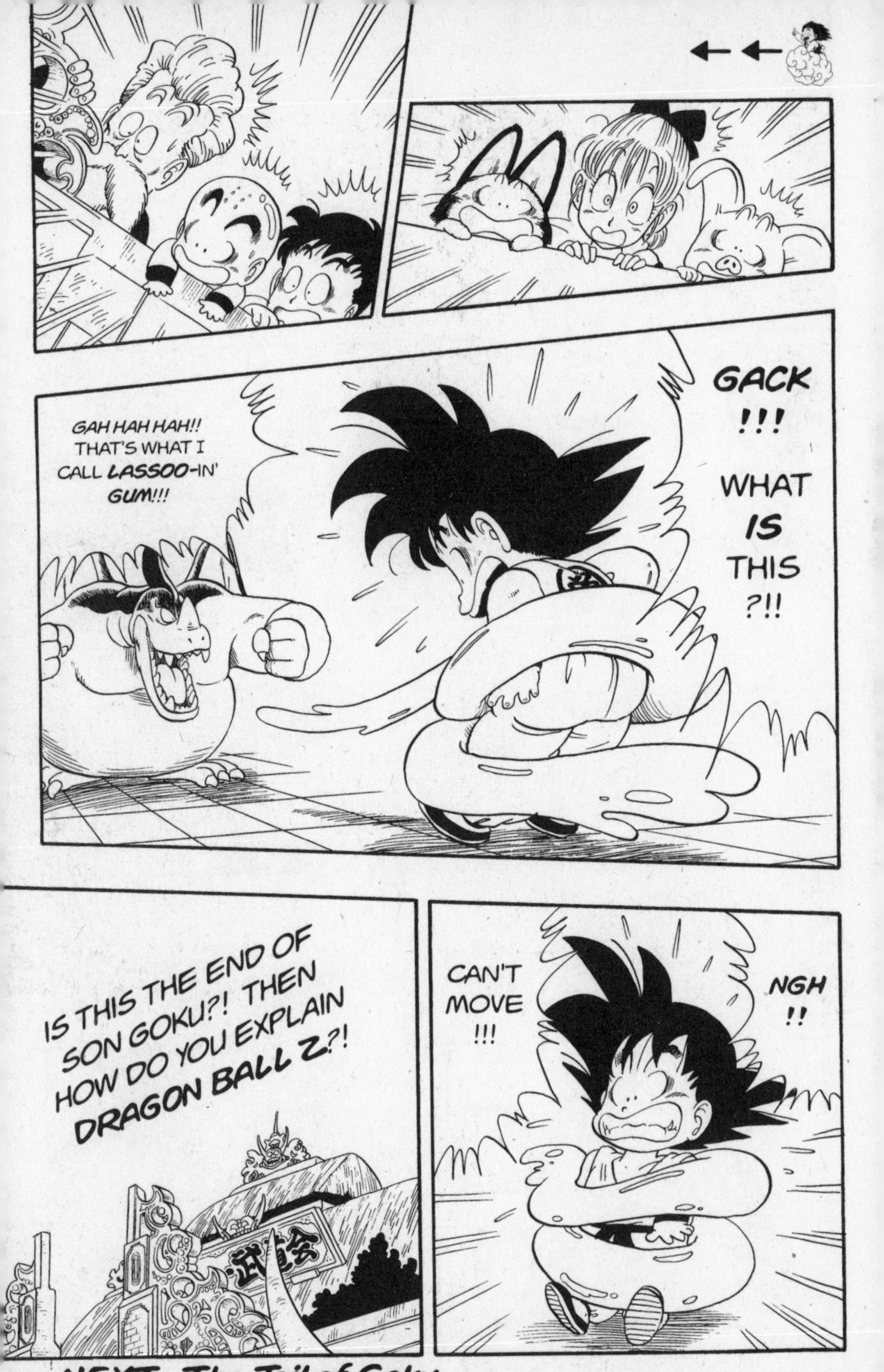
GACK!!!
WHAT IS THIS?!!
GAH HAH HAH!! THAT'S WHAT I CALL LASSOO-IN' GUM!!!
NGH!!
CAN'T MOVE!!!
IS THIS THE END OF SON GOKU?! THEN HOW DO YOU EXPLAIN DRAGON BALL Z?!

NEXT: The Tail of Goku

Tale 40 • The Tail of Goku

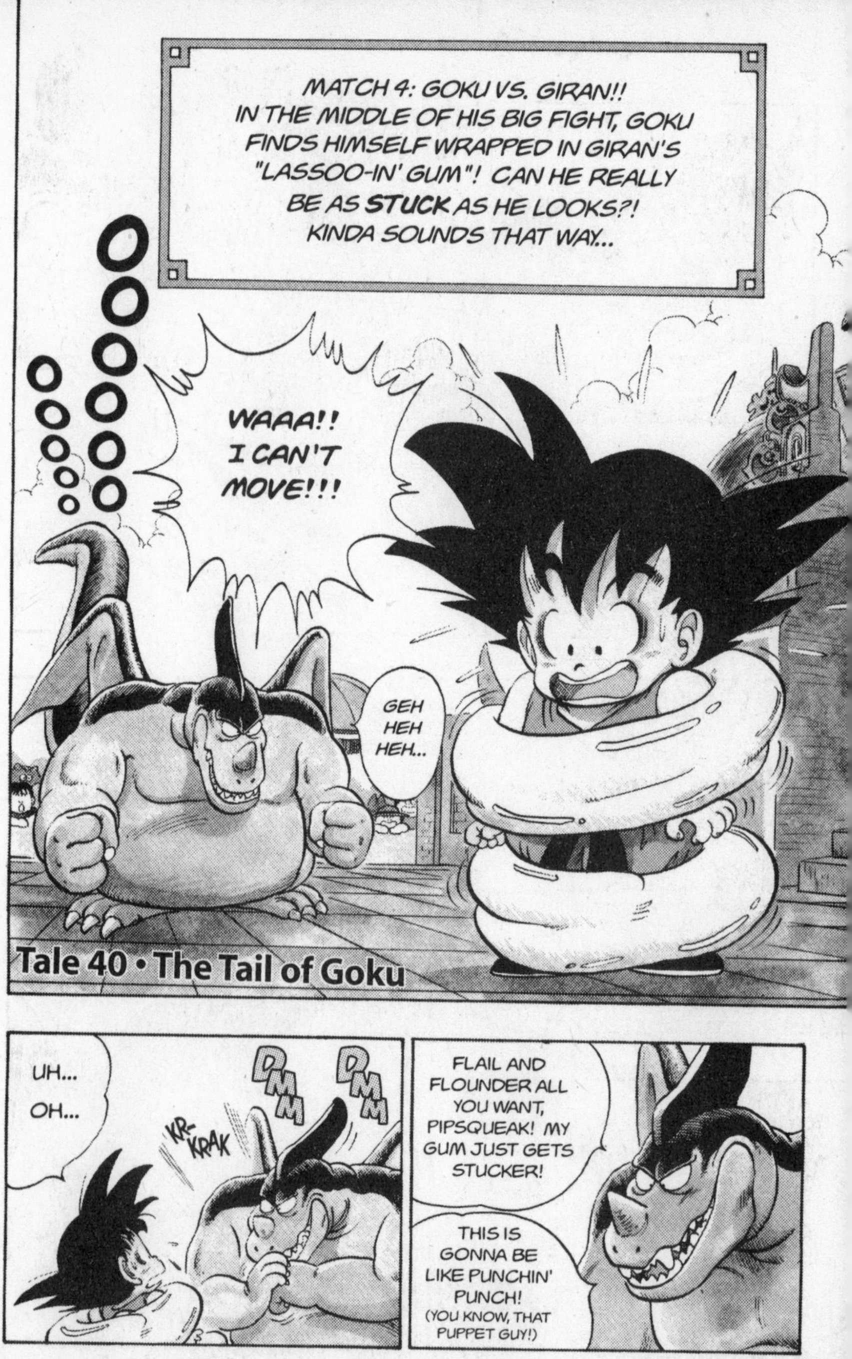
MATCH 4: GOKU VS. GIRAN!! IN THE MIDDLE OF HIS BIG FIGHT, GOKU FINDS HIMSELF WRAPPED IN GIRAN'S "LASSOO-IN' GUM"! CAN HE REALLY BE AS **STUCK** AS HE LOOKS?! KINDA SOUNDS THAT WAY...
OOOOOOO
OOOOOO
WAAA!! I CAN'T MOVE!!!
GEH HEH HEH...
FLAIL AND FLOUNDER ALL YOU WANT, PIPSQUEAK! MY GUM JUST GETS STUCKER!
THIS IS GONNA BE LIKE PUNCHIN' PUNCH! (YOU KNOW, THAT PUPPET GUY!)
DMM
DMM
UH... OH...
KR-KRAK

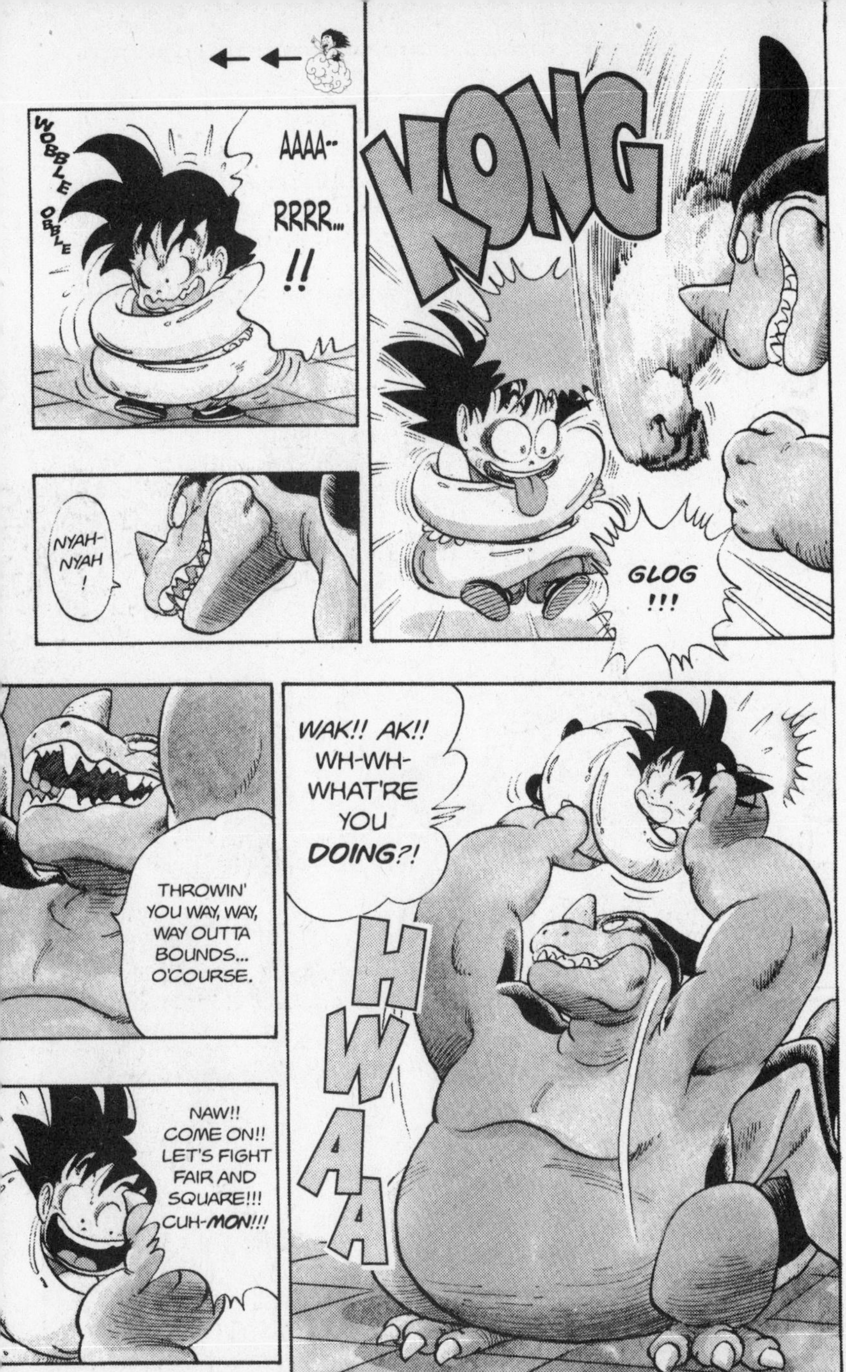

KONG
GLOG !!!
WOBBLE OBBLE
AAAA-- RRRR... !!
NYAH-NYAH !
WAK!! AK!! WH-WH-WHAT'RE YOU **DOING**?!
HWAAA
THROWIN' YOU WAY, WAY, WAY OUTTA BOUNDS... O'COURSE.
NAW!! COME ON!! LET'S FIGHT FAIR AND SQUARE!!! CUH-**MON**!!!

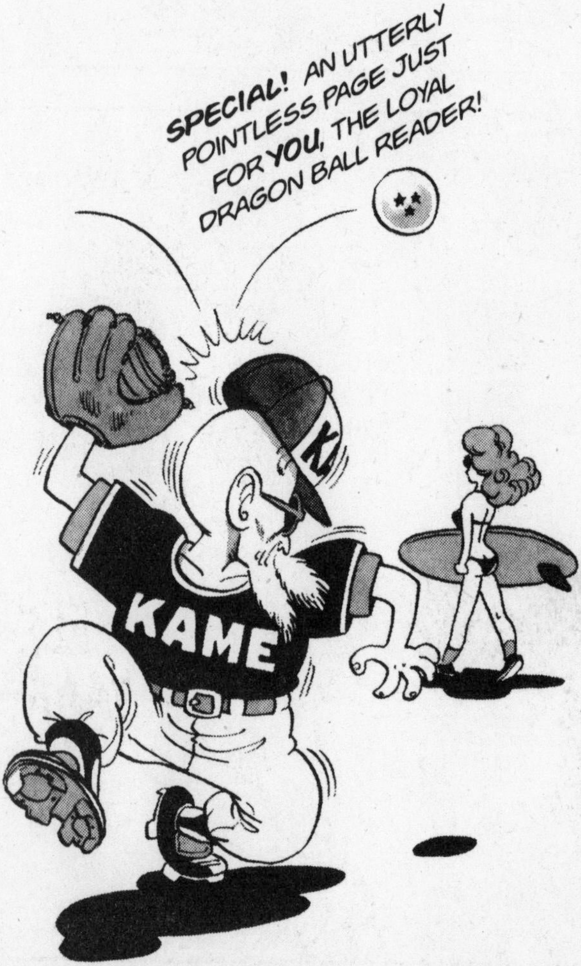
SPECIAL! AN UTTERLY POINTLESS PAGE JUST FOR YOU, THE LOYAL DRAGON BALL READER!
KAME

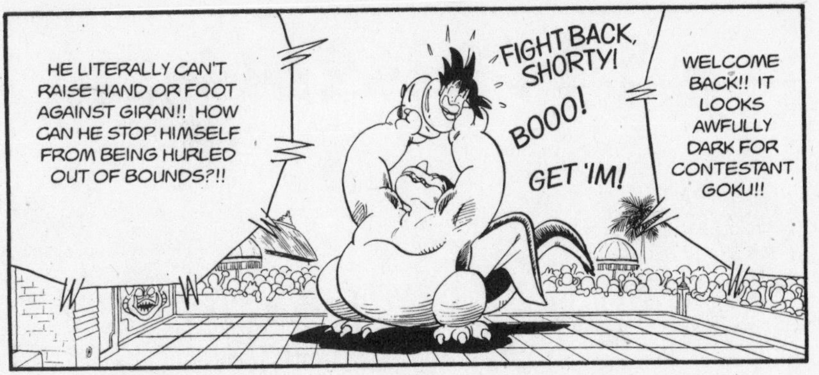
WELCOME BACK!! IT LOOKS AWFULLY DARK FOR CONTESTANT GOKU!!
FIGHT BACK, SHORTY!
BOOO!
GET 'IM!
HE LITERALLY CAN'T RAISE HAND OR FOOT AGAINST GIRAN!! HOW CAN HE STOP HIMSELF FROM BEING HURLED OUT OF BOUNDS?!!

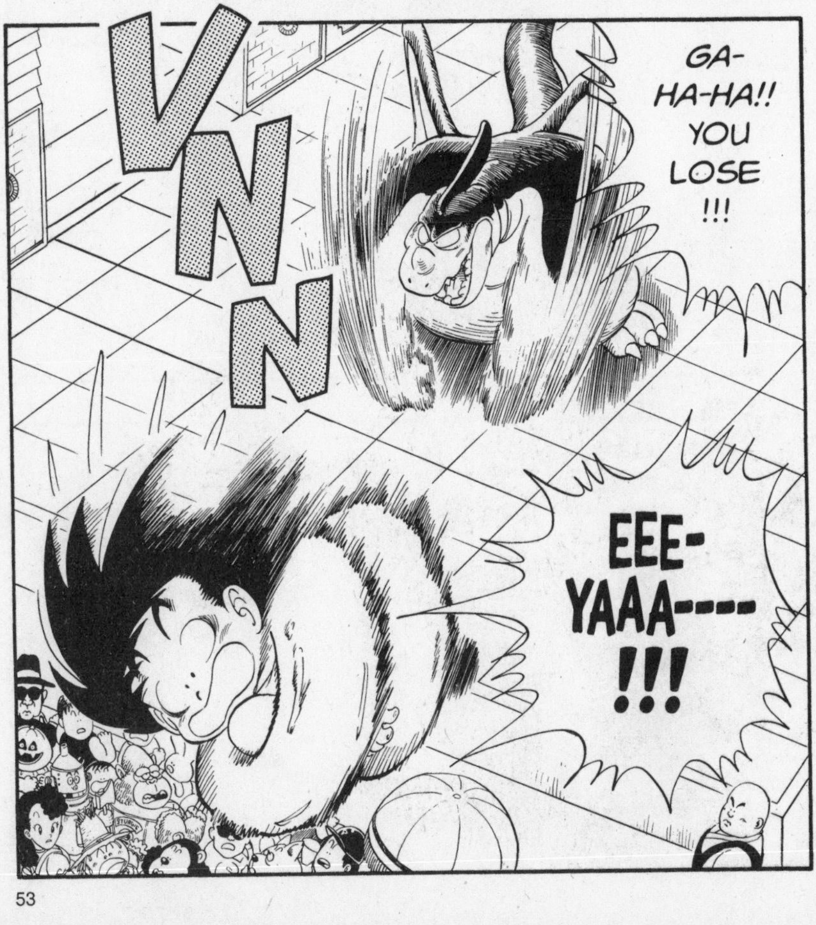
GA-HA-HA!! YOU LOSE!!!
VNN
EEE-YAAA----!!!

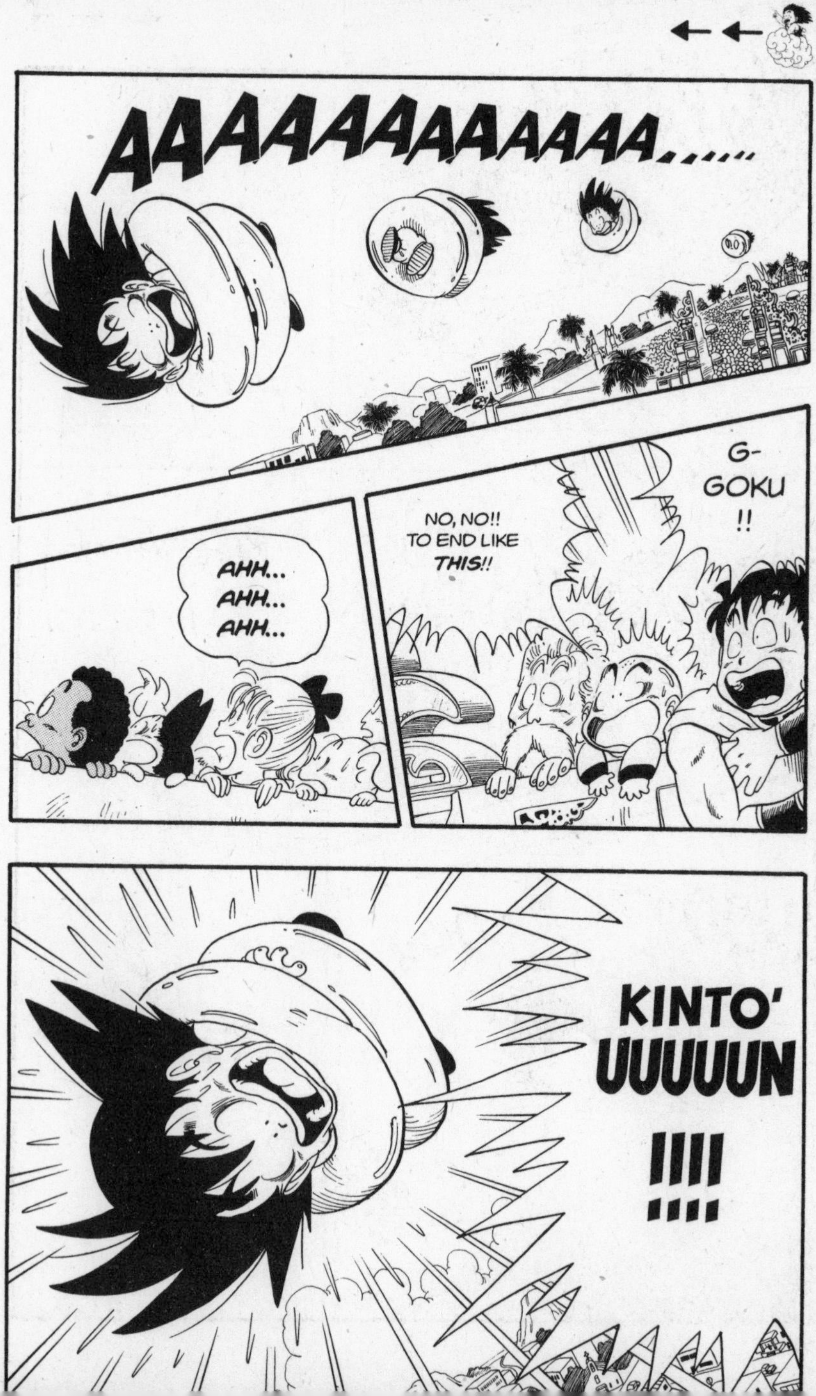
AAAAAAAAAAAA......
G-GOKU!!
NO, NO!! TO END LIKE THIS!!
AHH... AHH... AHH...
KINTO' UUUUUN!!!!

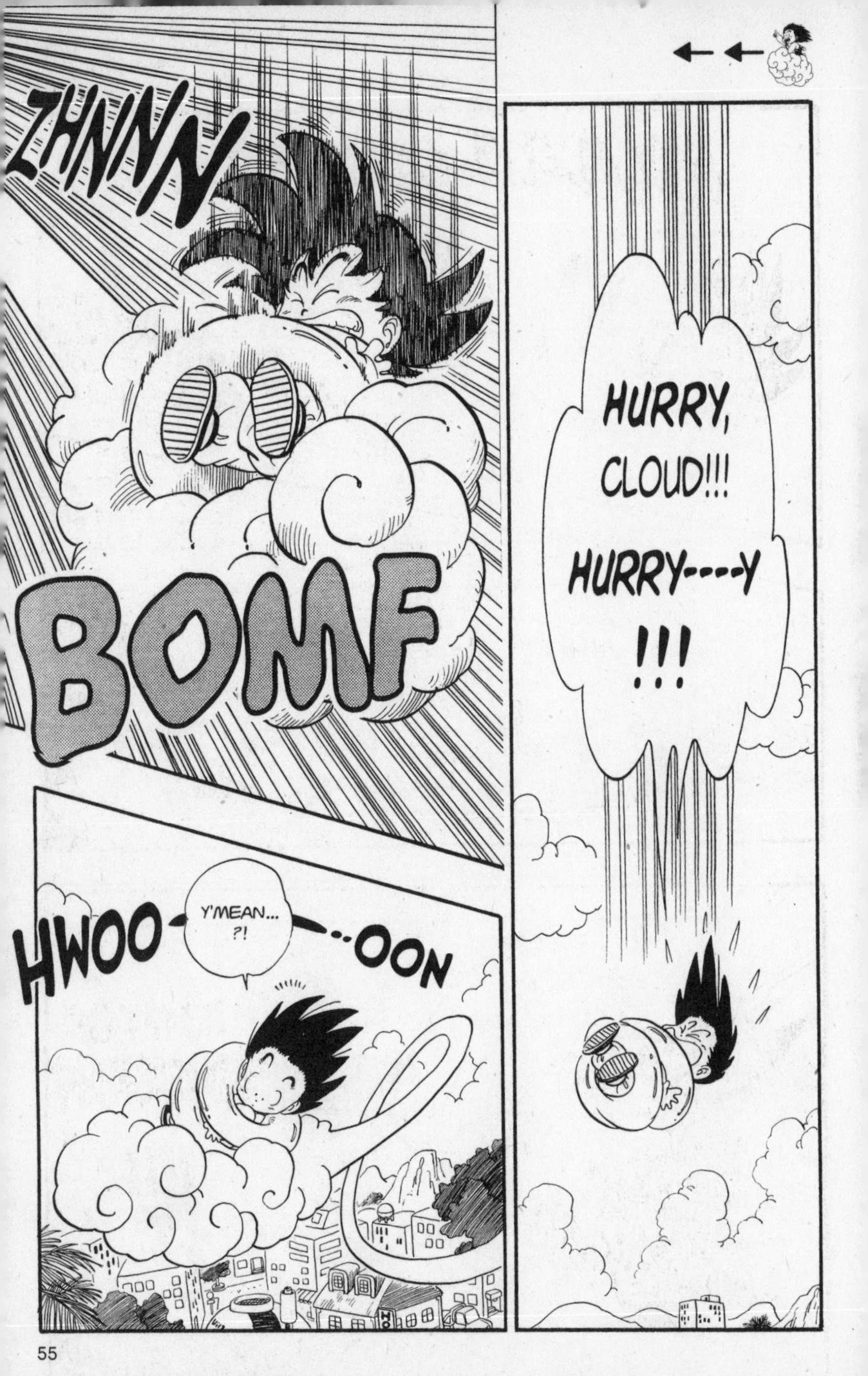
HURRY, CLOUD!!!
HURRY----Y !!!
ZHNNN
BOMF
HWOO---OON
Y'MEAN... ?!

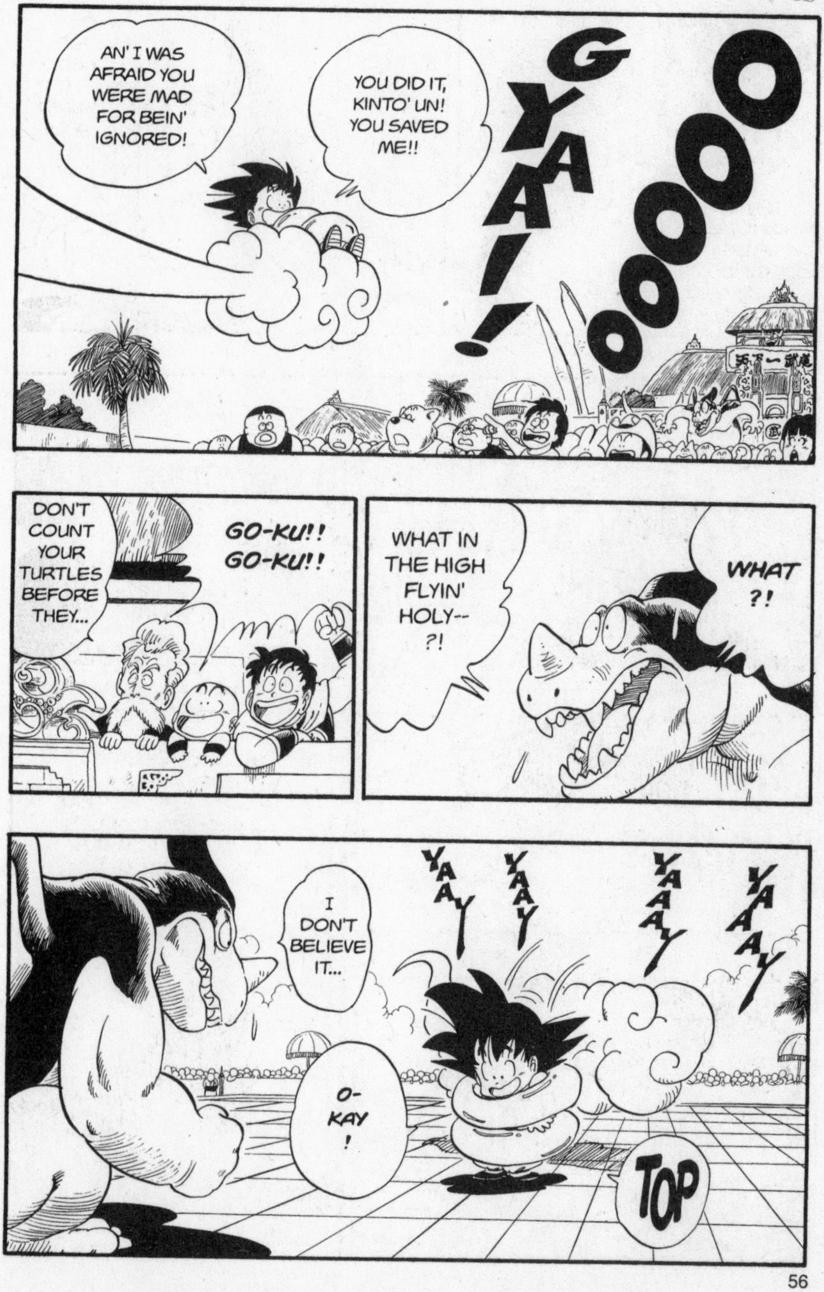
GYAA!!
OOOOOOO
YOU DID IT, KINTO' UN! YOU SAVED ME!!
AN' I WAS AFRAID YOU WERE MAD FOR BEIN' IGNORED!
WHAT ?!
WHAT IN THE HIGH FLYIN' HOLY-- ?!
GO-KU!! GO-KU!!
DON'T COUNT YOUR TURTLES BEFORE THEY...
YAAAAY
YAAAAY
YAAAY
YAAY
I DON'T BELIEVE IT...
TOP
O-KAY!

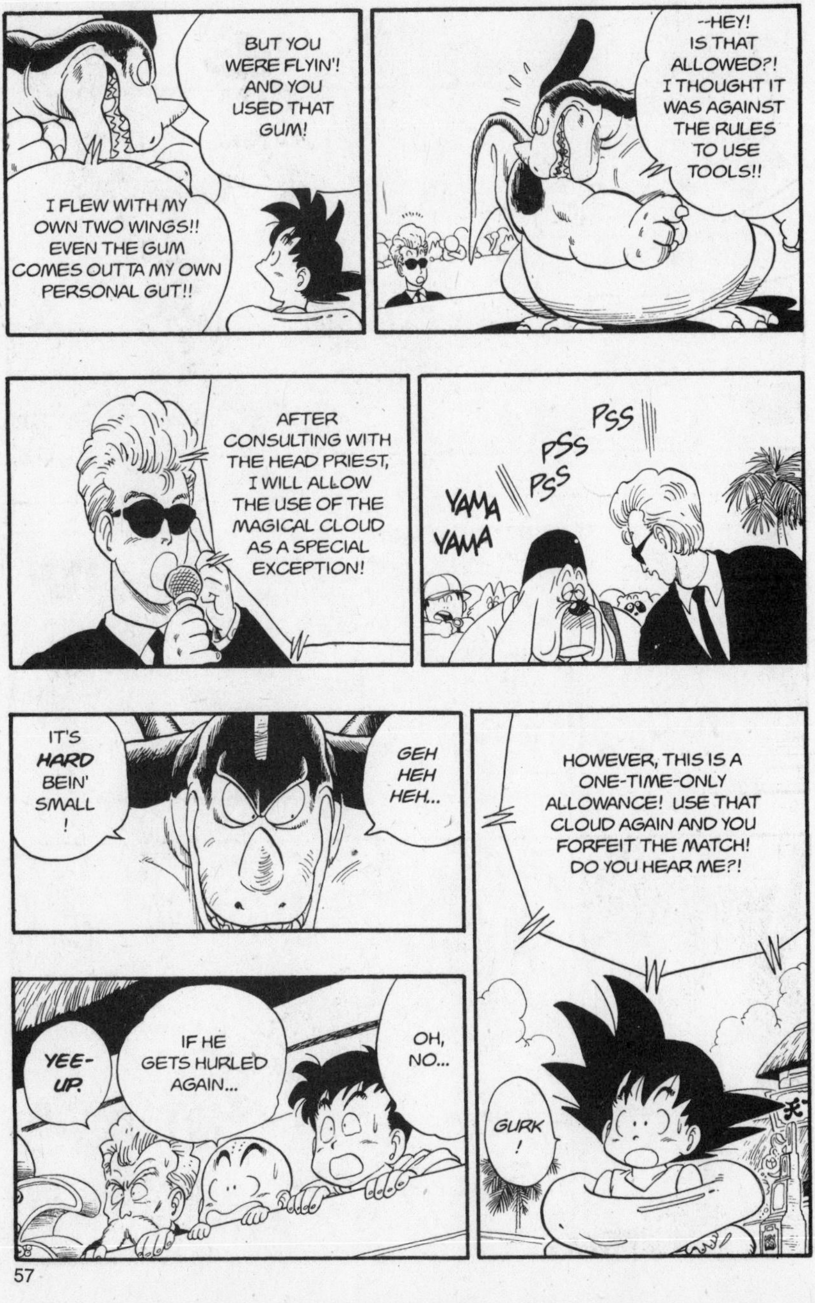
--HEY! IS THAT ALLOWED?! I THOUGHT IT WAS AGAINST THE RULES TO USE TOOLS!!
BUT YOU WERE FLYIN'! AND YOU USED THAT GUM!
I FLEW WITH MY OWN TWO WINGS!! EVEN THE GUM COMES OUTTA MY OWN PERSONAL GUT!!
PSS
PSS
PSS
YAMA YAMA
AFTER CONSULTING WITH THE HEAD PRIEST, I WILL ALLOW THE USE OF THE MAGICAL CLOUD AS A SPECIAL EXCEPTION!
HOWEVER, THIS IS A ONE-TIME-ONLY ALLOWANCE! USE THAT CLOUD AGAIN AND YOU FORFEIT THE MATCH! DO YOU HEAR ME?!
GURK!
GEH HEH HEH...
IT'S **HARD** BEIN' SMALL!
OH, NO...
IF HE GETS HURLED AGAIN...
YEE-UP.

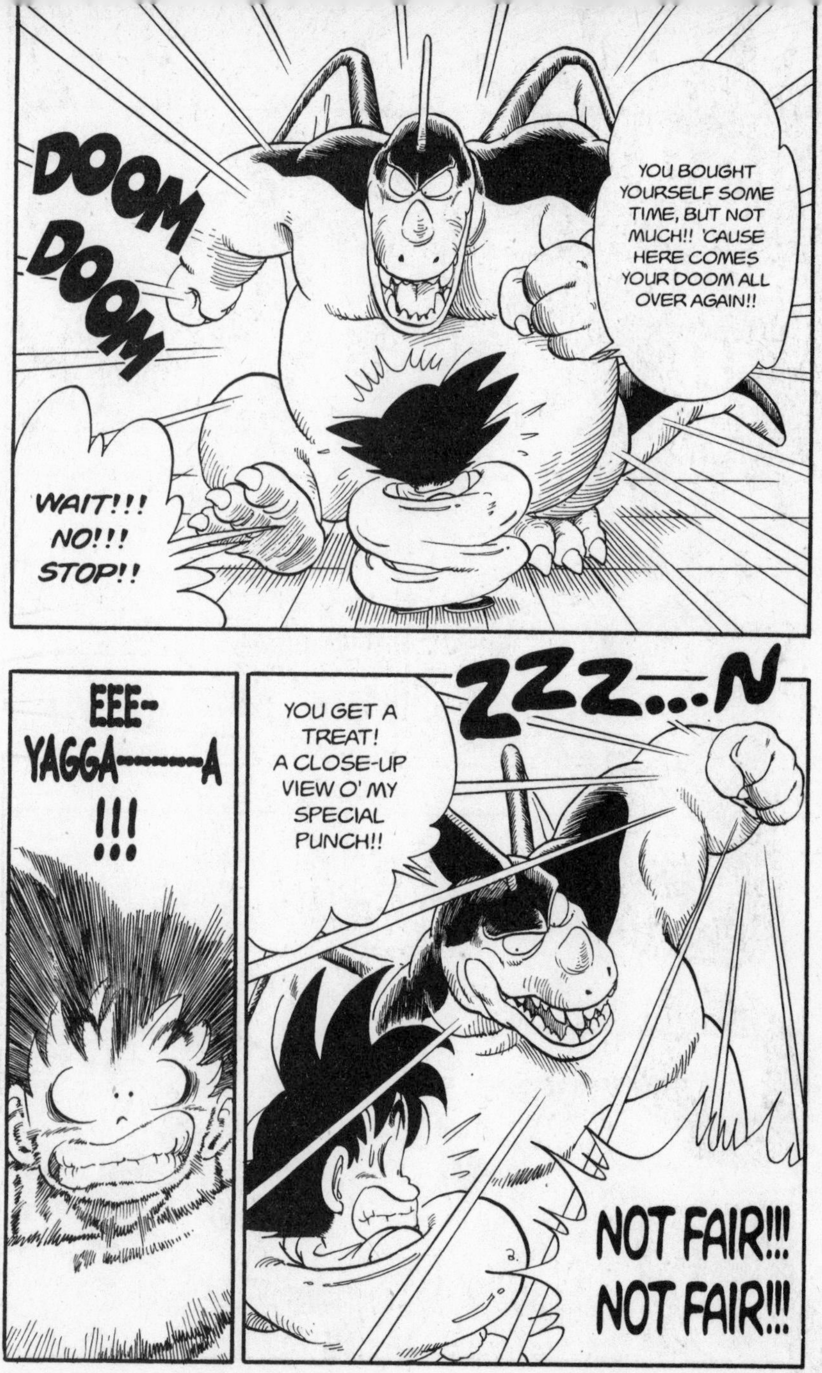
YOU BOUGHT YOURSELF SOME TIME, BUT NOT MUCH!! 'CAUSE HERE COMES YOUR DOOM ALL OVER AGAIN!!
DOOM DOOM
WAIT!!! NO!!! STOP!!
ZZZ...N
YOU GET A TREAT! A CLOSE-UP VIEW O' MY SPECIAL PUNCH!!
NOT FAIR!!! NOT FAIR!!!
EEE-YAGGA--------A !!!

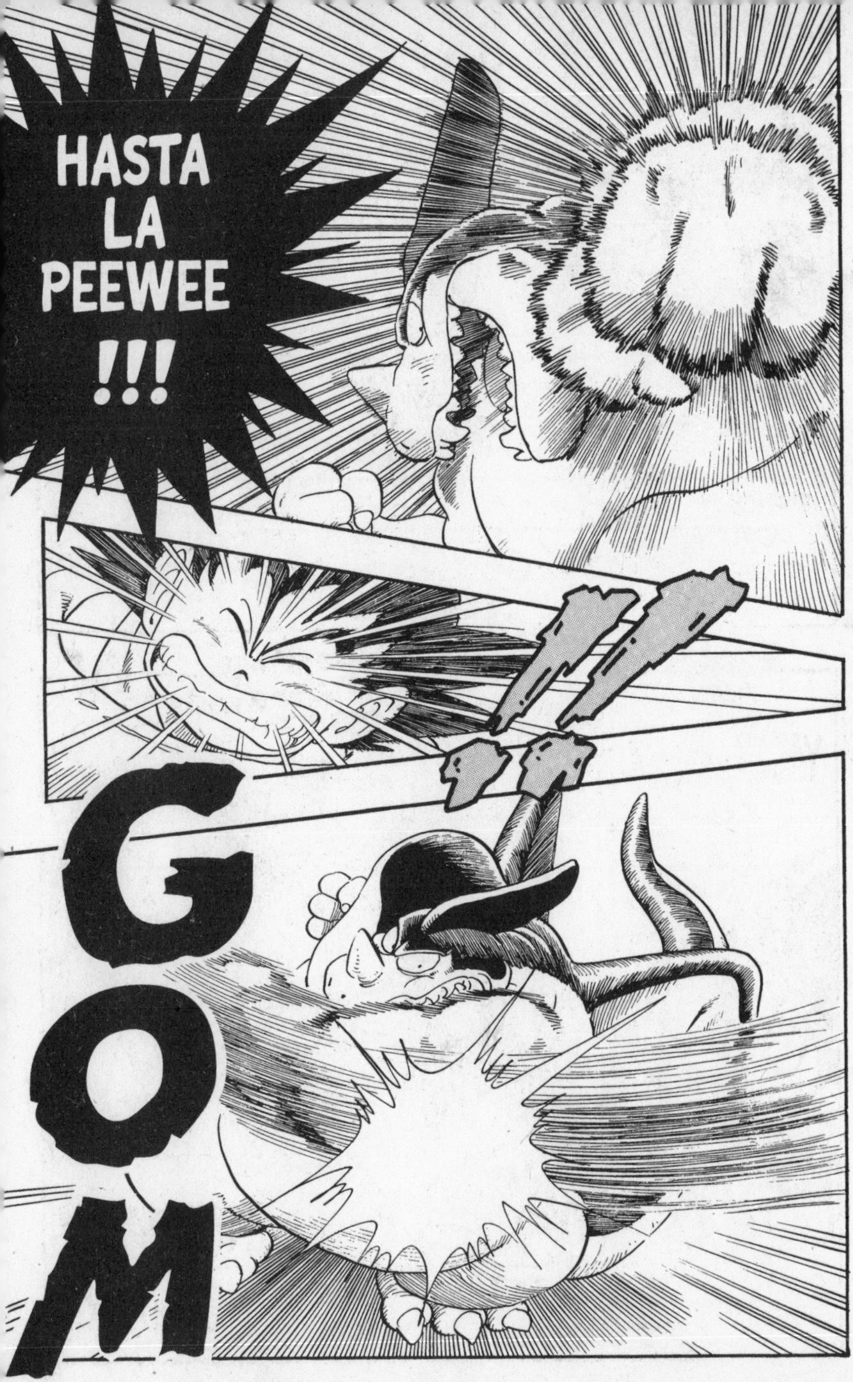
HASTA LA PEEWEE !!!
GOM

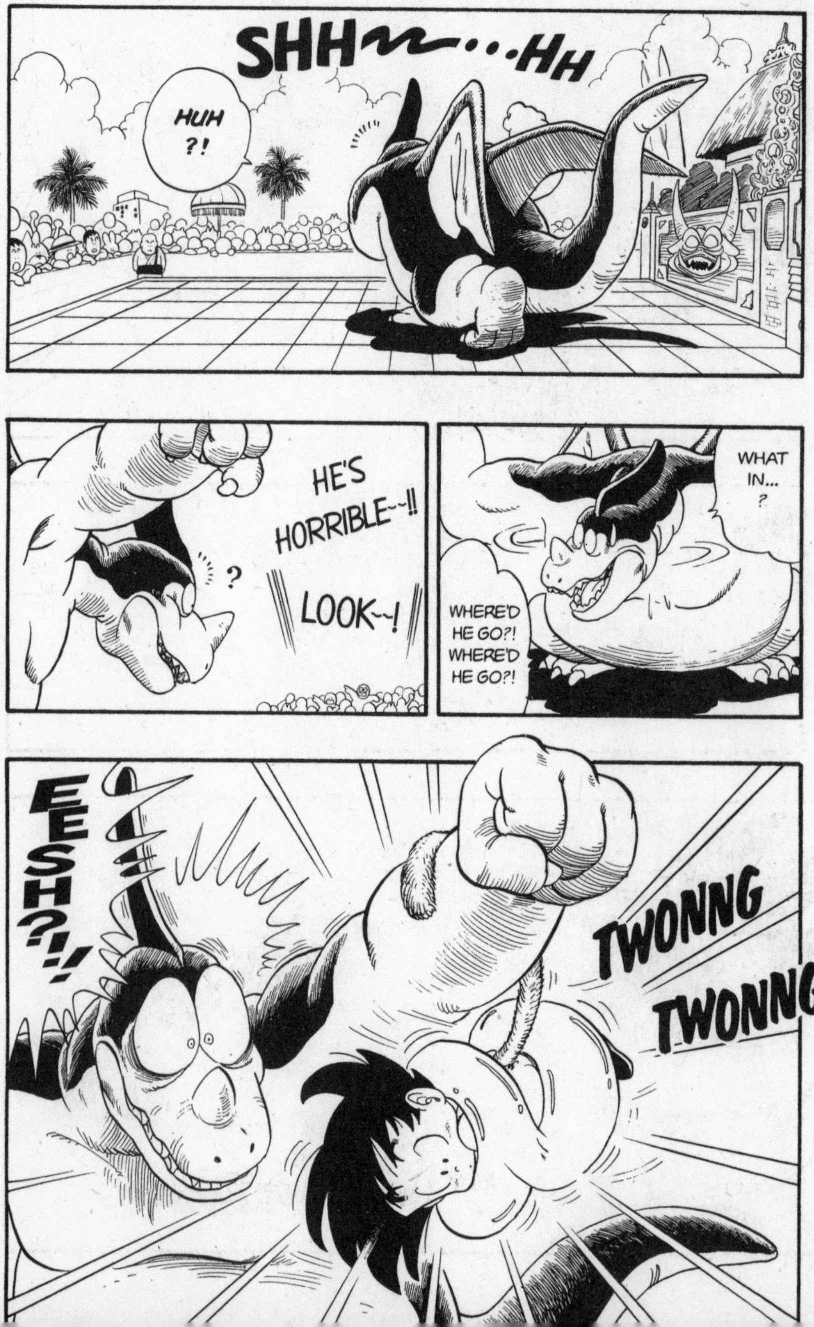
SHH~...HH
HUH ?!
WHAT IN... ?
WHERE'D HE GO?! WHERE'D HE GO?!
HE'S HORRIBLE~~!!
LOOK~~!
?
EESH?!!
TWONNG
TWONNG

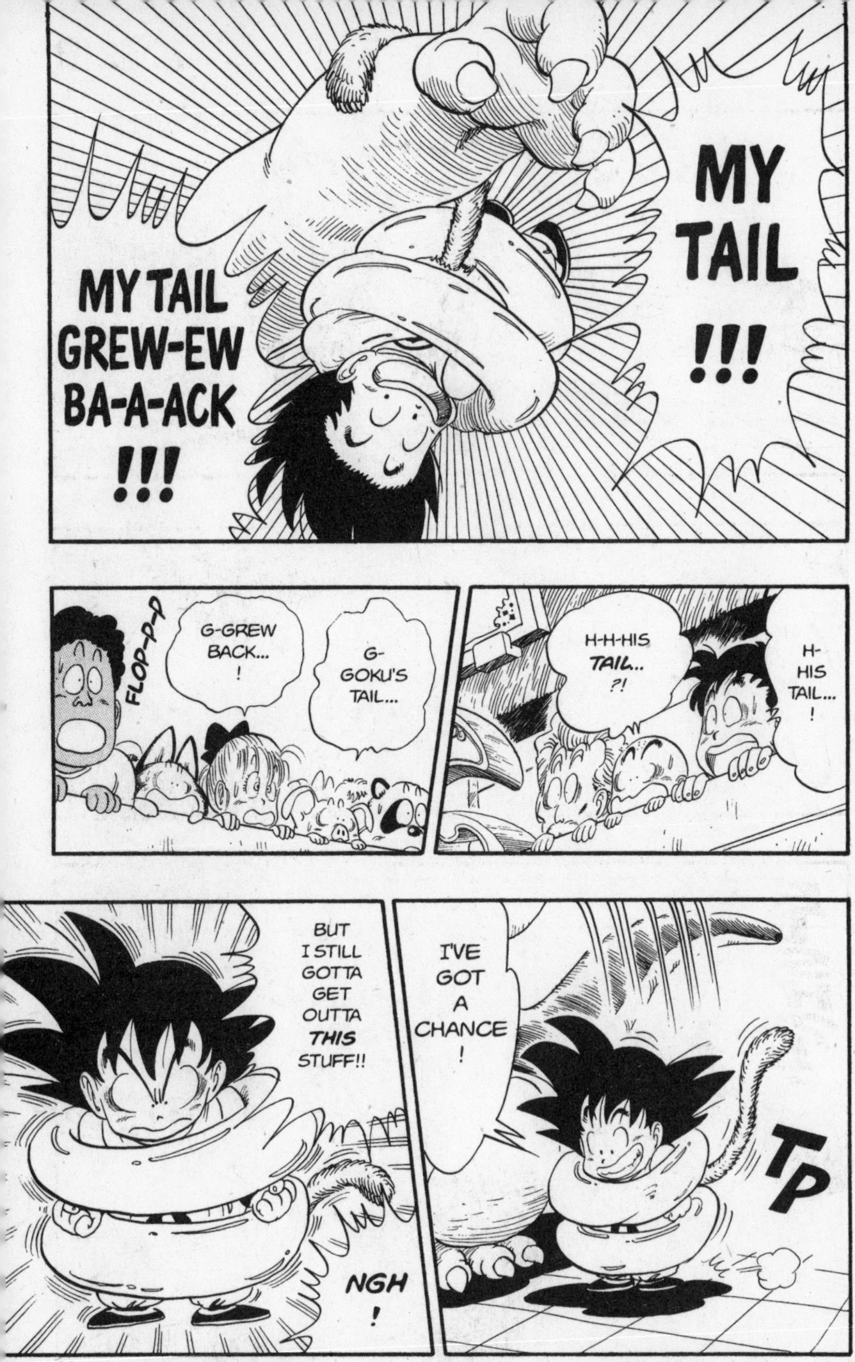
MY TAIL !!!
MY TAIL GREW-EW BA-A-ACK !!!
H- HIS TAIL... !
H-H-HIS TAIL... ?!
G- GOKU'S TAIL...
G-GREW BACK... !
FLOP-P-P
I'VE GOT A CHANCE !
TP
BUT I STILL GOTTA GET OUTTA THIS STUFF!!
NGH !

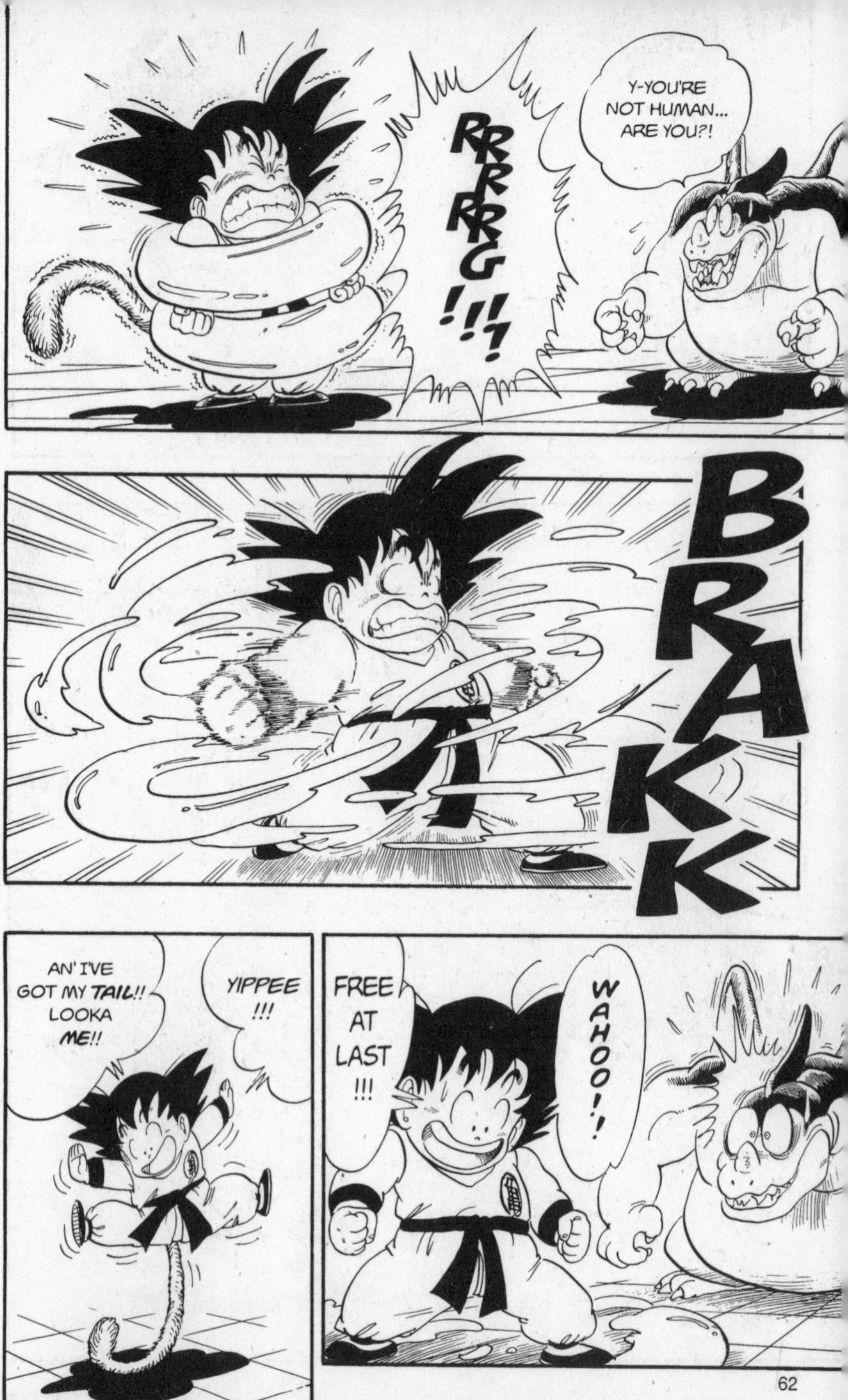
Y-YOU'RE NOT HUMAN... ARE YOU?!
RRRRG!!!?
BRAKK
WAHOO!!
FREE AT LAST!!!
YIPPEE!!!
AN' I'VE GOT MY TAIL!! LOOKA ME!!

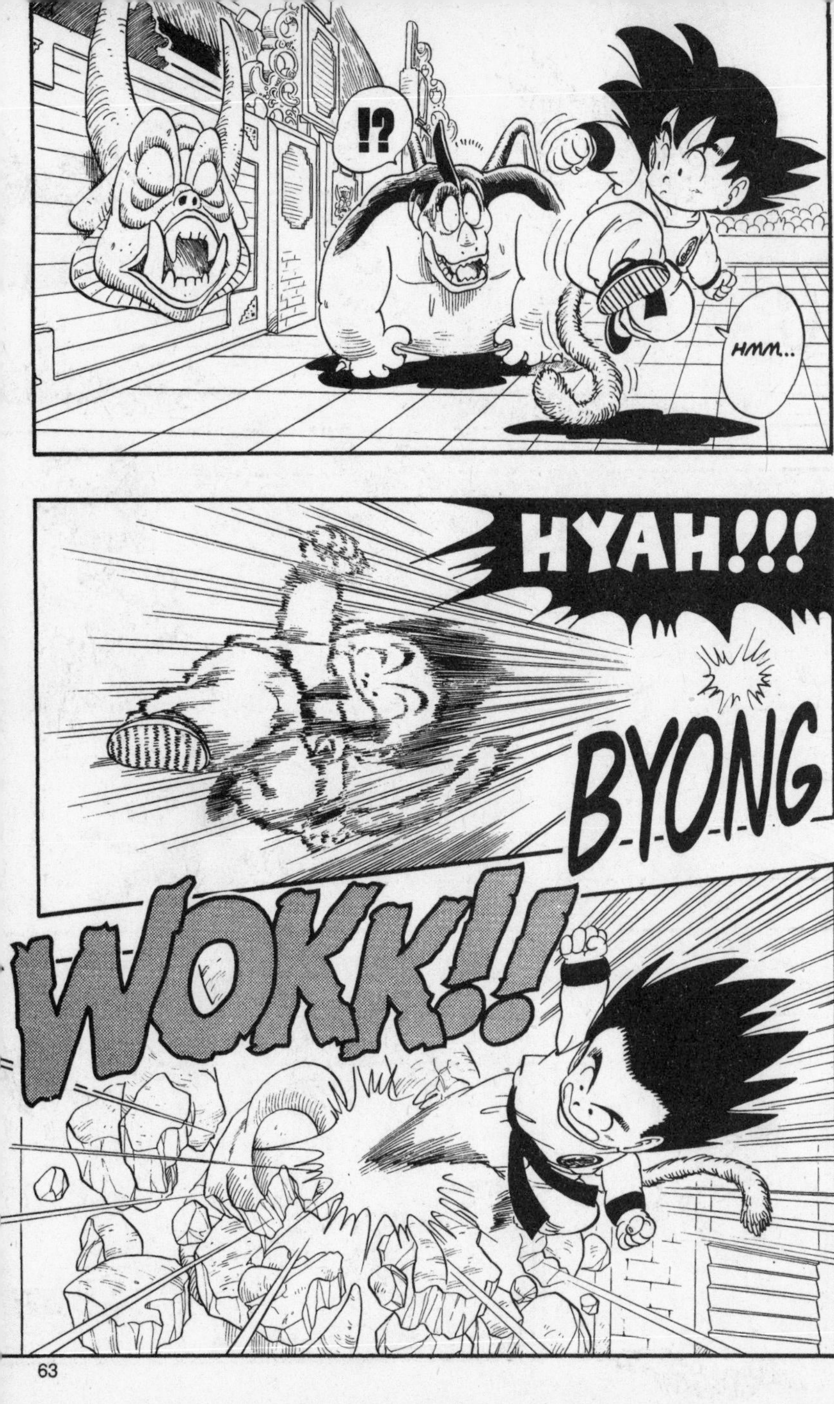
HMM..
!?
HYAH!!!
BYONG
WOKK!!

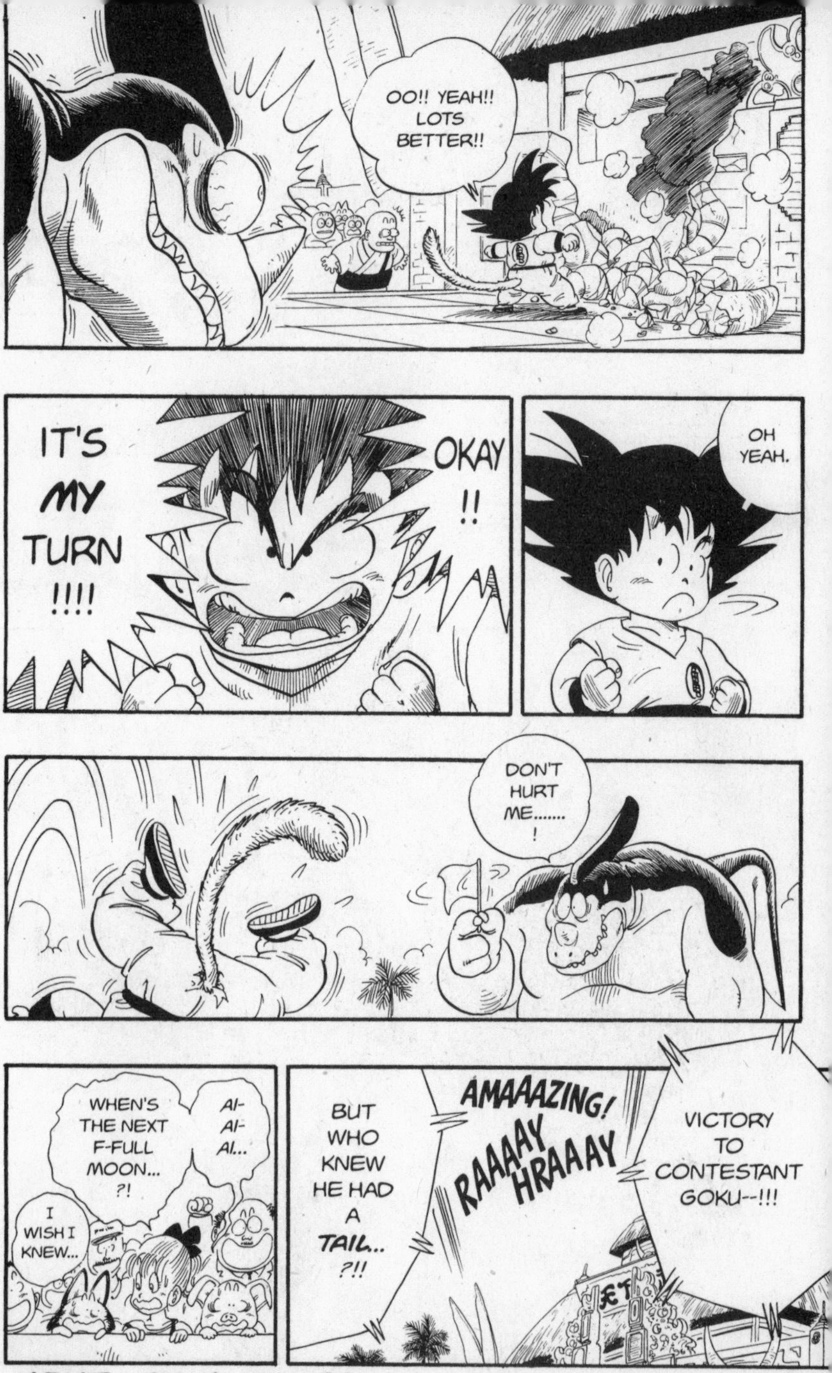
OO!! YEAH!! LOTS BETTER!!
OH YEAH.
OKAY!!
IT'S MY TURN!!!!
DON'T HURT ME.......!
VICTORY TO CONTESTANT GOKU--!!!
AMAAAZING!
RAAAAY HRAAAY
BUT WHO KNEW HE HAD A TAIL...?!!
AI-AI-AI...
WHEN'S THE NEXT F-FULL MOON...?!
I WISH I KNEW...

NEXT: Who's Next?!

ドラゴンボール

DRAGON BALL

Tale 41

Kuririn vs. Jackie Chun

DRAGON BALL
41

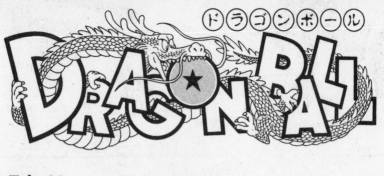

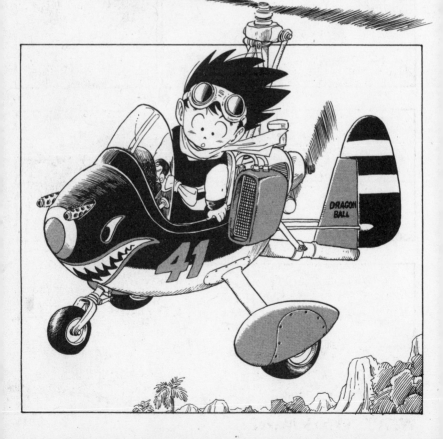

Tale 41
Kuririn VS. "Jackie Chun"

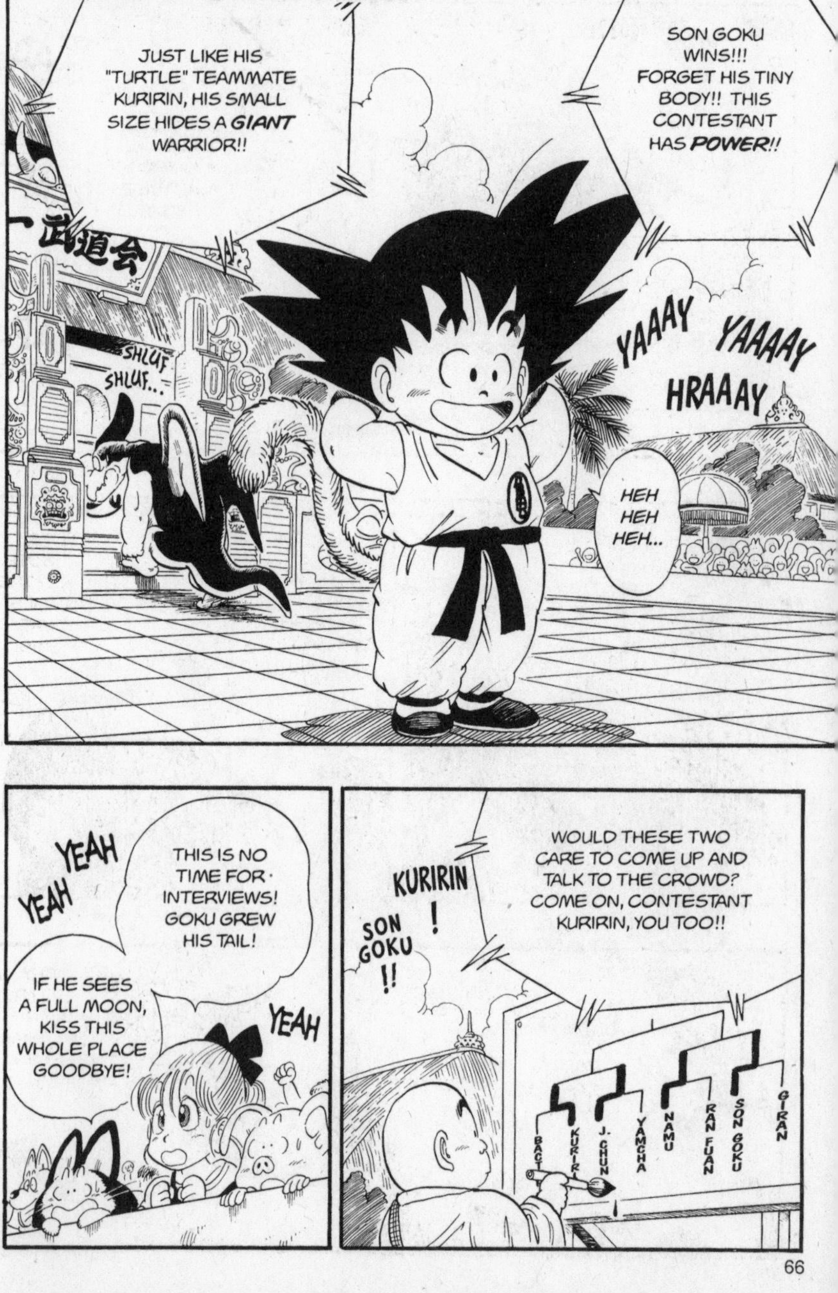
SON GOKU WINS!!! FORGET HIS TINY BODY!! THIS CONTESTANT HAS **POWER**!!
JUST LIKE HIS "TURTLE" TEAMMATE KURIRIN, HIS SMALL SIZE HIDES A ***GIANT*** WARRIOR!!
YAAAAY
YAAAY
HRAAAY
HEH HEH HEH...
SHLUF SHLUF...
WOULD THESE TWO CARE TO COME UP AND TALK TO THE CROWD? COME ON, CONTESTANT KURIRIN, YOU TOO!!
KURIRIN!
SON GOKU!!
GIRAN
SON GOKU
RAN FUAN
NAMU
YAMCHA
J. CHUN
KURIRI
BACT
THIS IS NO TIME FOR INTERVIEWS! GOKU GREW HIS TAIL!
IF HE SEES A FULL MOON, KISS THIS WHOLE PLACE GOODBYE!
YEAH
YEAH
YEAH

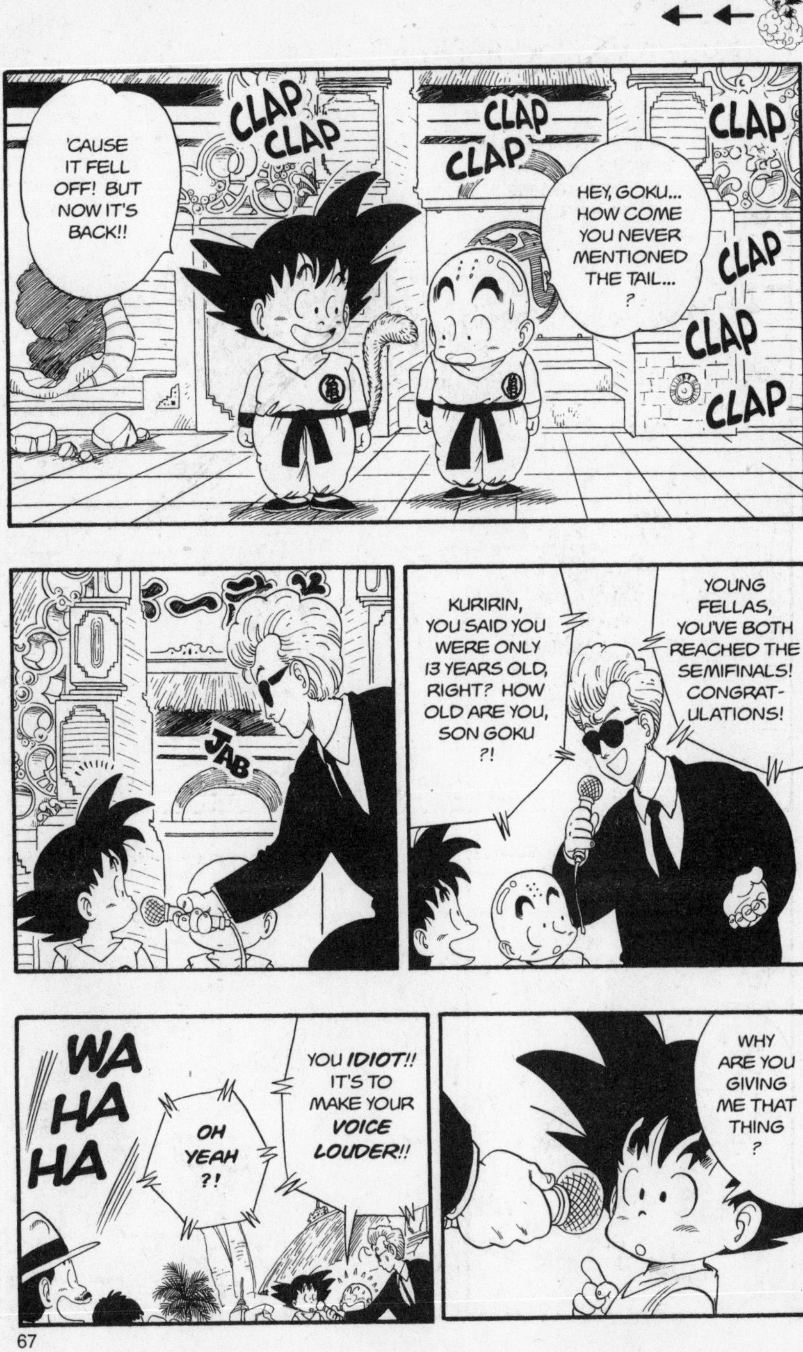
CLAP
CLAP
CLAP
HEY, GOKU... HOW COME YOU NEVER MENTIONED THE TAIL... ?
CLAP
CLAP
CLAP
CLAP CLAP
'CAUSE IT FELL OFF! BUT NOW IT'S BACK!!
YOUNG FELLAS, YOU'VE BOTH REACHED THE SEMIFINALS! CONGRATULATIONS!
KURIRIN, YOU SAID YOU WERE ONLY 13 YEARS OLD, RIGHT? HOW OLD ARE YOU, SON GOKU ?!
JAB
WHY ARE YOU GIVING ME THAT THING ?
YOU IDIOT!! IT'S TO MAKE YOUR VOICE LOUDER!!
OH YEAH ?!
WA HA HA

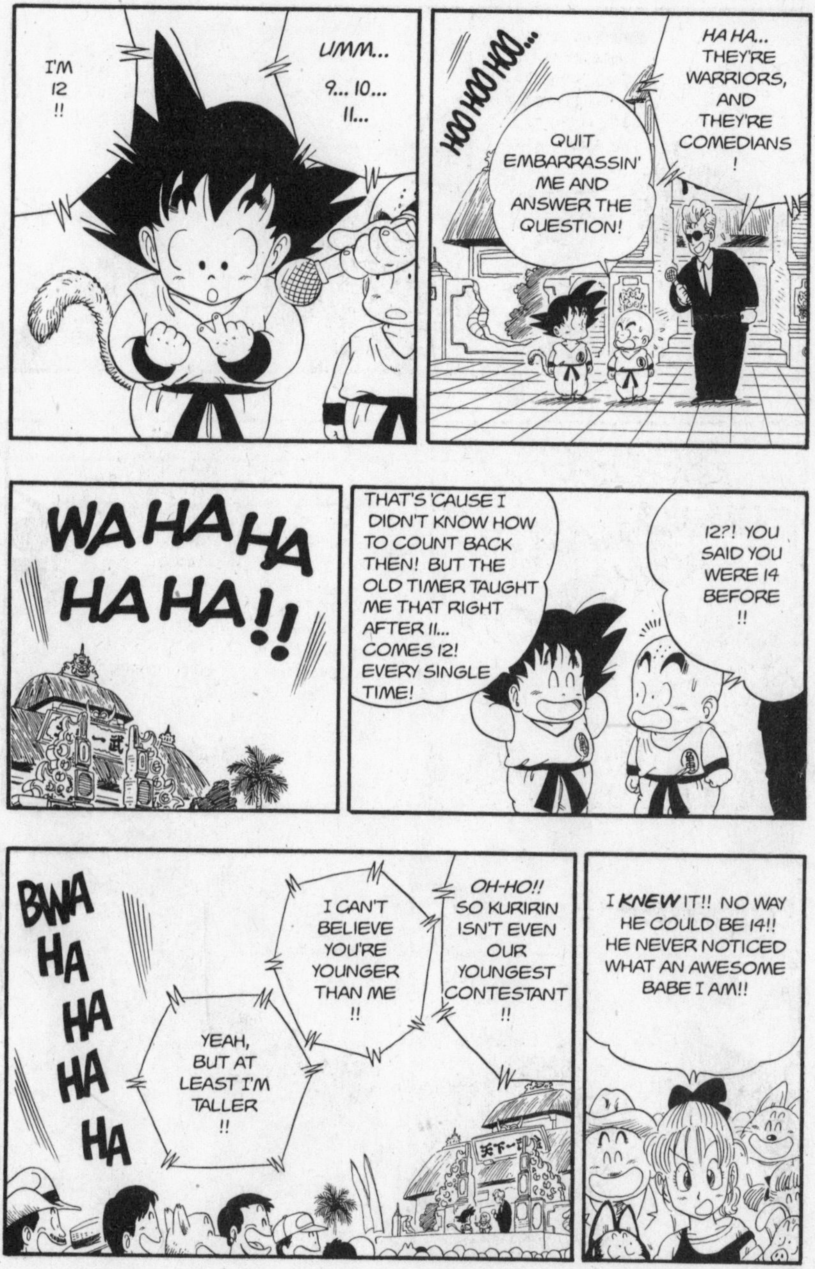
HA HA... THEY'RE WARRIORS, AND THEY'RE COMEDIANS !
HOO HOO HOO...
QUIT EMBARRASSIN' ME AND ANSWER THE QUESTION!
UMM... 9... 10... 11...
I'M 12 !!
12?! YOU SAID YOU WERE 14 BEFORE !!
THAT'S 'CAUSE I DIDN'T KNOW HOW TO COUNT BACK THEN! BUT THE OLD TIMER TAUGHT ME THAT RIGHT AFTER 11... COMES 12! EVERY SINGLE TIME!
WA HA HA HA HA!!
I KNEW IT!! NO WAY HE COULD BE 14!! HE NEVER NOTICED WHAT AN AWESOME BABE I AM!!
OH-HO!! SO KURIRIN ISN'T EVEN OUR YOUNGEST CONTESTANT !!
I CAN'T BELIEVE YOU'RE YOUNGER THAN ME !!
BWA HA HA HA HA HA
YEAH, BUT AT LEAST I'M TALLER !!

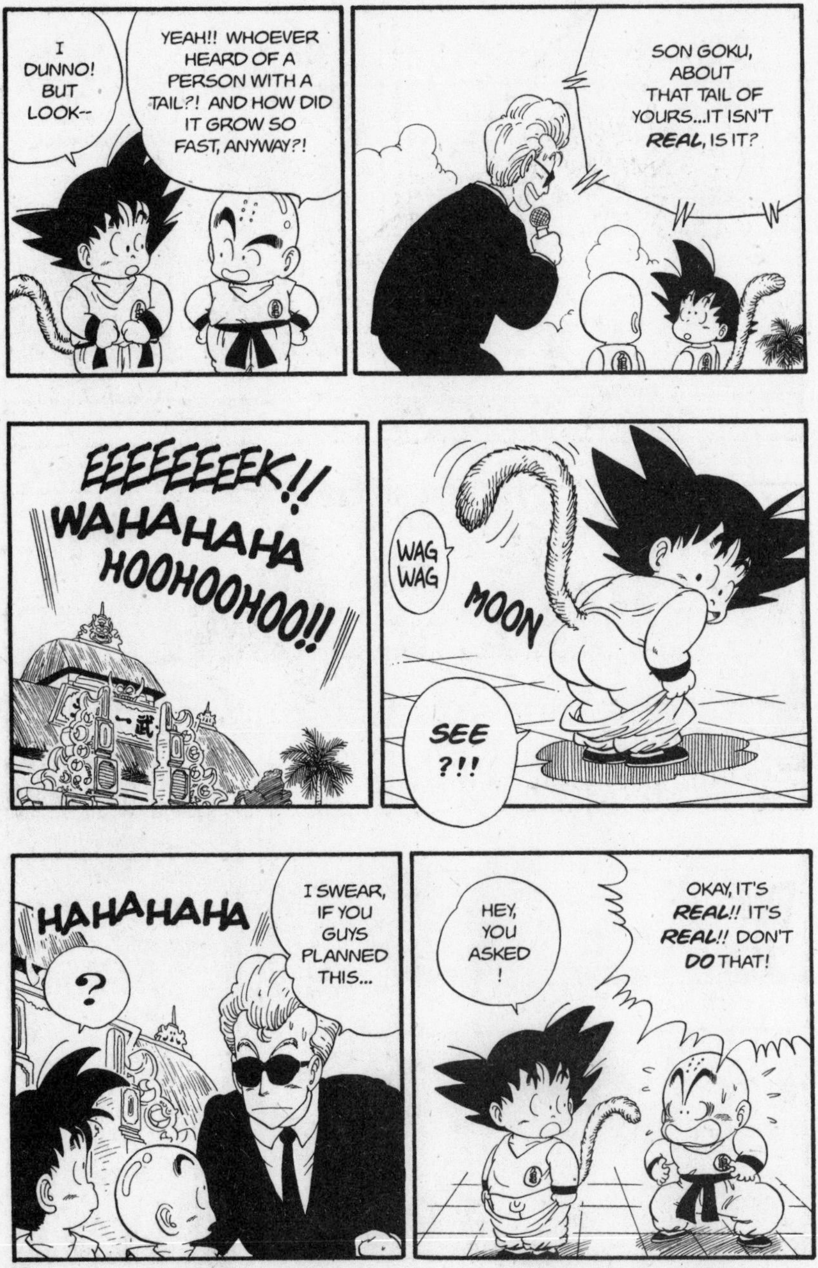
SON GOKU, ABOUT THAT TAIL OF YOURS...IT ISN'T REAL, IS IT?
YEAH!! WHOEVER HEARD OF A PERSON WITH A TAIL?! AND HOW DID IT GROW SO FAST, ANYWAY?!
I DUNNO! BUT LOOK--
WAG WAG
MOON
SEE ?!!
EEEEEEEEK!!
WAHAHAHA
HOOHOOHOO!!
OKAY, IT'S REAL!! IT'S REAL!! DON'T DO THAT!
HEY, YOU ASKED!
I SWEAR, IF YOU GUYS PLANNED THIS...
HAHAHAHA
?

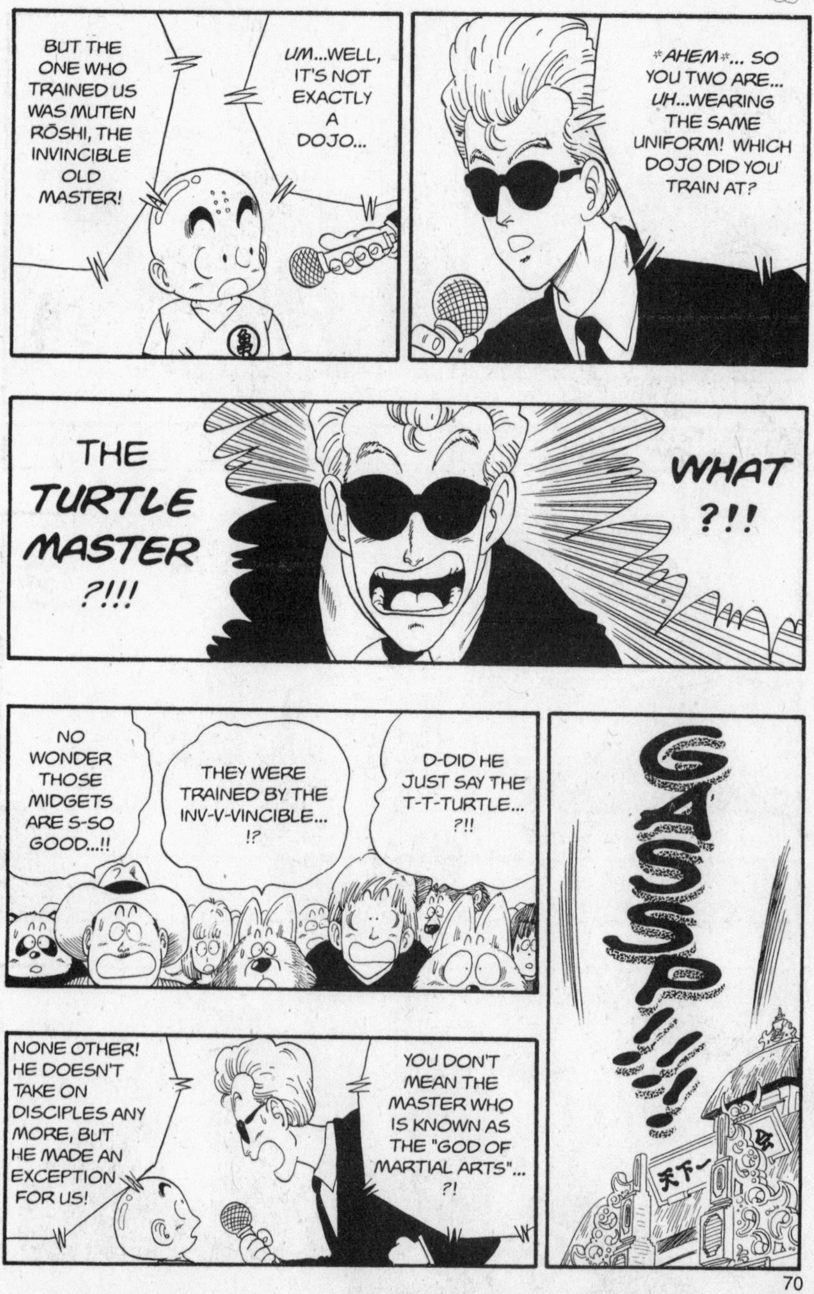
AHEM... SO YOU TWO ARE... UH...WEARING THE SAME UNIFORM! WHICH DOJO DID YOU TRAIN AT?
UM...WELL, IT'S NOT EXACTLY A DOJO...
BUT THE ONE WHO TRAINED US WAS MUTEN RŌSHI, THE INVINCIBLE OLD MASTER!
WHAT ?!!
THE TURTLE MASTER ?!!!
GASSP!!!!
天下一
D-DID HE JUST SAY THE T-T-TURTLE... ?!!
THEY WERE TRAINED BY THE INV-V-VINCIBLE... !?
NO WONDER THOSE MIDGETS ARE S-SO GOOD...!!
YOU DON'T MEAN THE MASTER WHO IS KNOWN AS THE "GOD OF MARTIAL ARTS"... ?!
NONE OTHER! HE DOESN'T TAKE ON DISCIPLES ANY MORE, BUT HE MADE AN EXCEPTION FOR US!

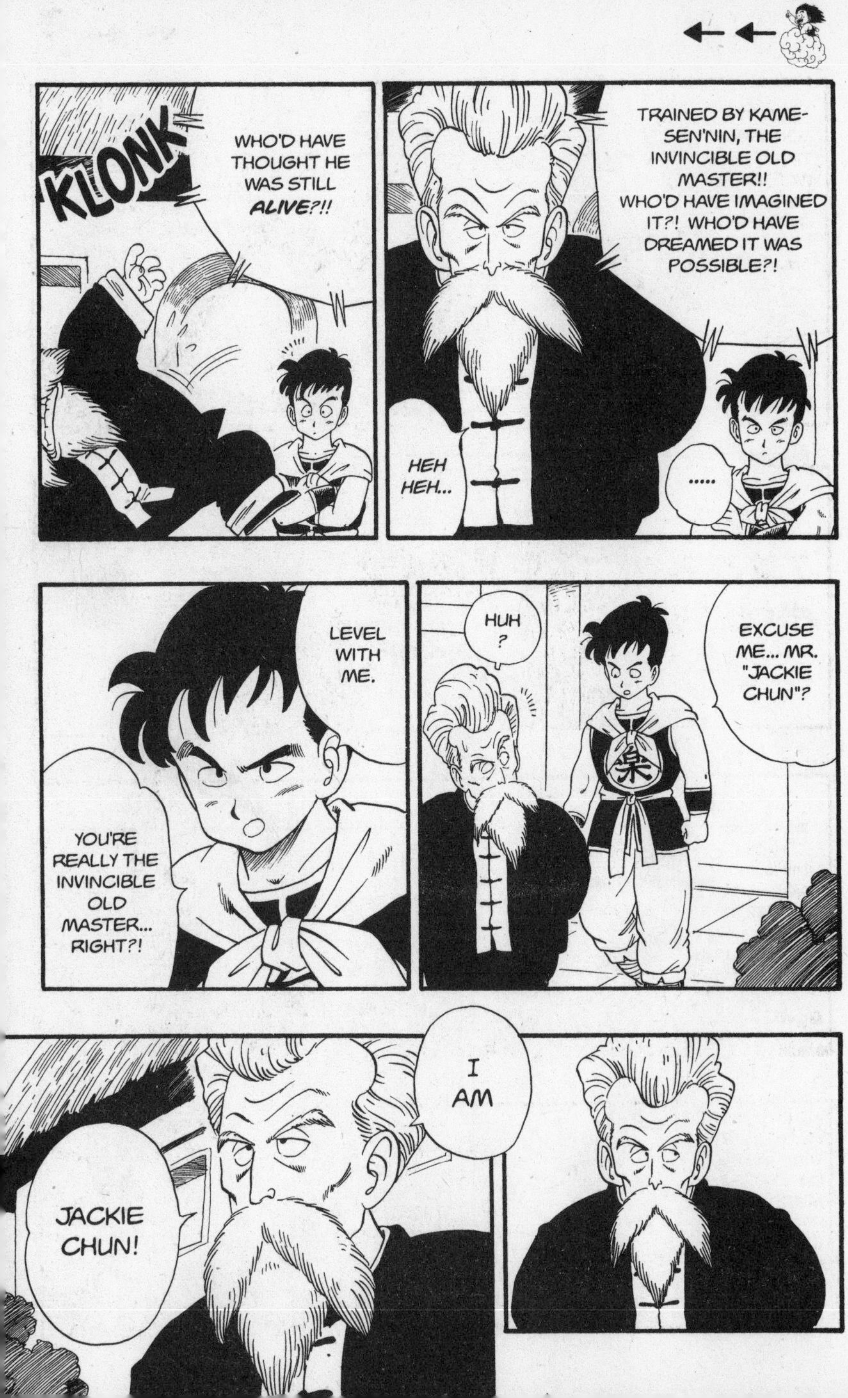

TRAINED BY KAME-SEN'NIN, THE INVINCIBLE OLD MASTER!! WHO'D HAVE IMAGINED IT?! WHO'D HAVE DREAMED IT WAS POSSIBLE?!
HEH HEH...
......
KLONK
WHO'D HAVE THOUGHT HE WAS STILL ALIVE?!!
EXCUSE ME... MR. "JACKIE CHUN"?
HUH?
LEVEL WITH ME.
YOU'RE REALLY THE INVINCIBLE OLD MASTER... RIGHT?!
I AM
JACKIE CHUN!

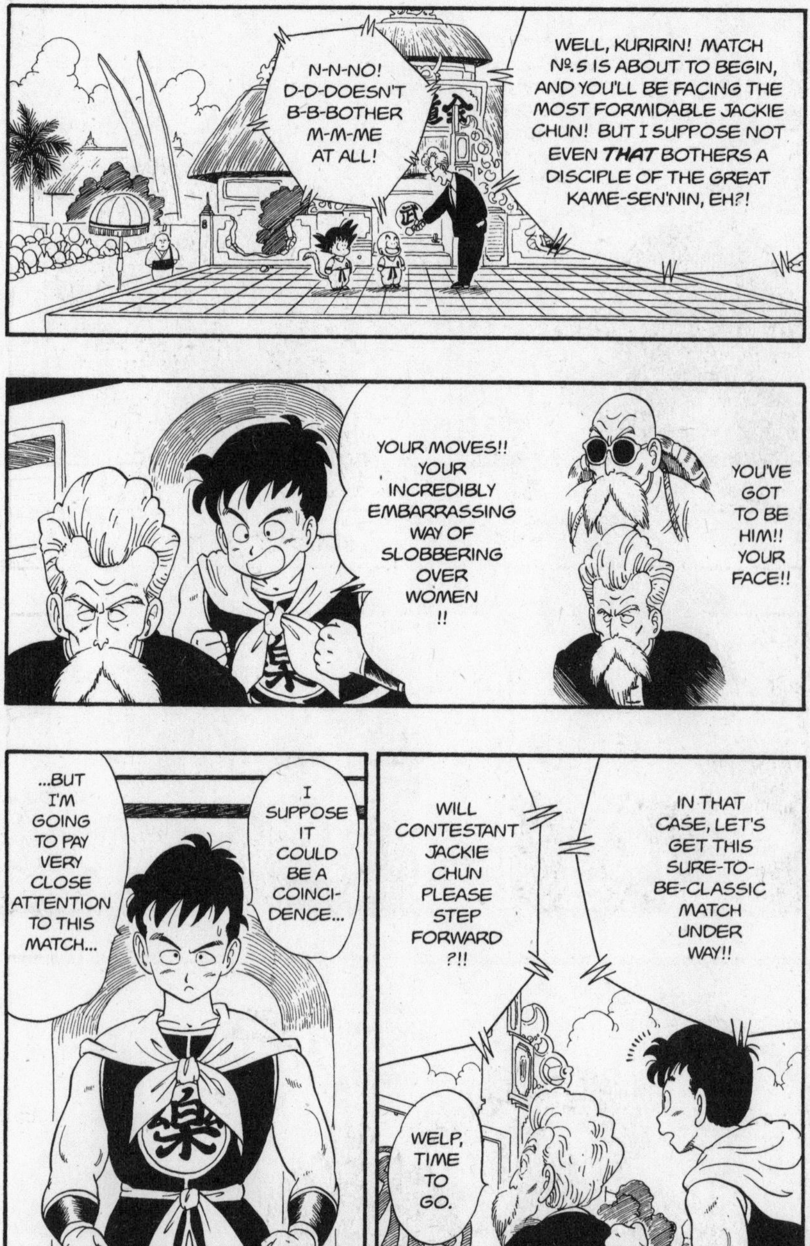
WELL, KURIRIN! MATCH №.5 IS ABOUT TO BEGIN, AND YOU'LL BE FACING THE MOST FORMIDABLE JACKIE CHUN! BUT I SUPPOSE NOT EVEN *THAT* BOTHERS A DISCIPLE OF THE GREAT KAME-SEN'NIN, EH?!
N-N-NO! D-D-DOESN'T B-B-BOTHER M-M-ME AT ALL!
YOU'VE GOT TO BE HIM!! YOUR FACE!!
YOUR MOVES!! YOUR INCREDIBLY EMBARRASSING WAY OF SLOBBERING OVER WOMEN !!
IN THAT CASE, LET'S GET THIS SURE-TO-BE-CLASSIC MATCH UNDER WAY!!
WILL CONTESTANT JACKIE CHUN PLEASE STEP FORWARD ?!!
WELP, TIME TO GO.
I SUPPOSE IT COULD BE A COINCI-DENCE...
...BUT I'M GOING TO PAY VERY CLOSE ATTENTION TO THIS MATCH...

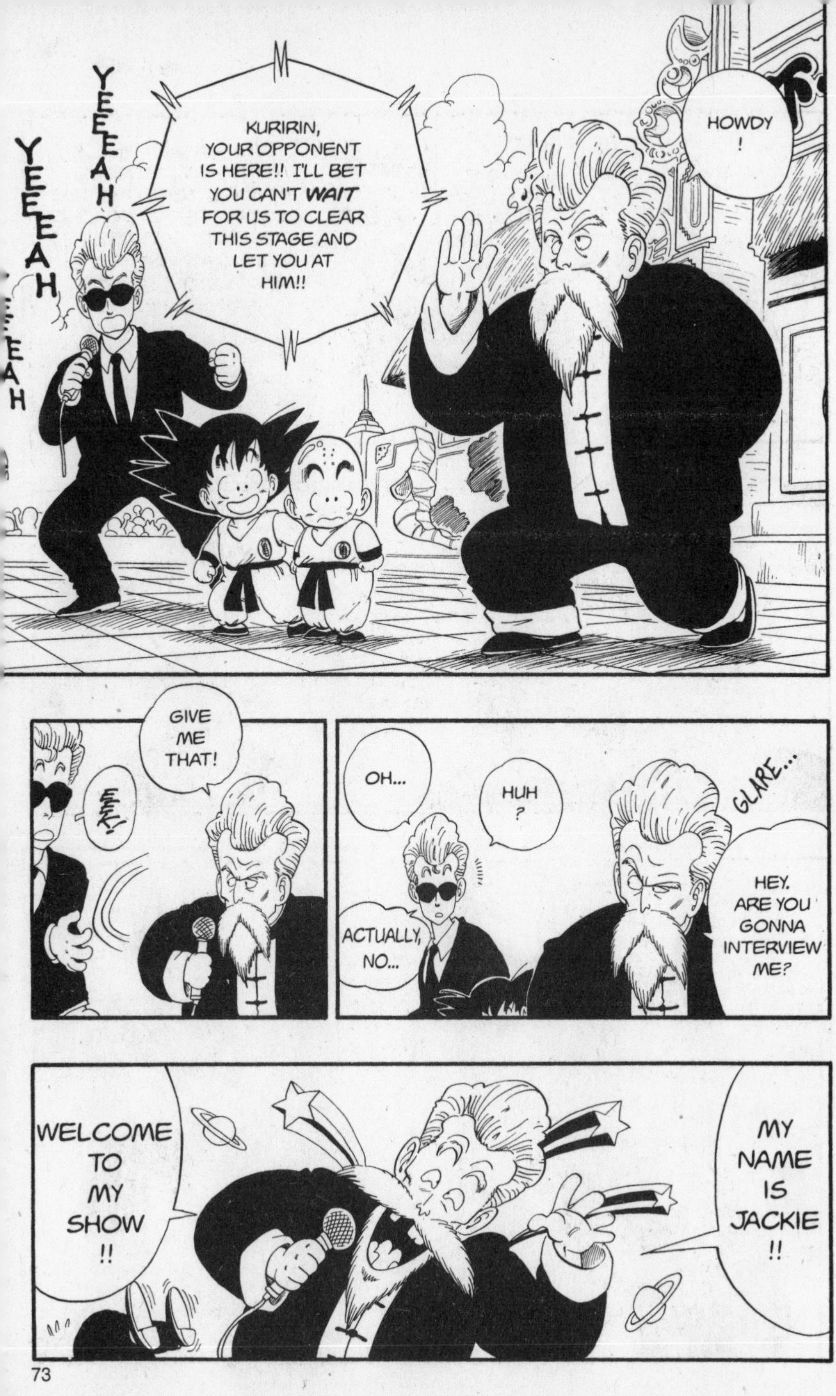
HOWDY!
KURIRIN, YOUR OPPONENT IS HERE!! I'LL BET YOU CAN'T WAIT FOR US TO CLEAR THIS STAGE AND LET YOU AT HIM!!
YEEEAH
YEEEAH
GLARE...
HEY. ARE YOU GONNA INTERVIEW ME?
HUH?
OH...
ACTUALLY, NO...
GIVE ME THAT!
EEK!
MY NAME IS JACKIE!!
WELCOME TO MY SHOW!!

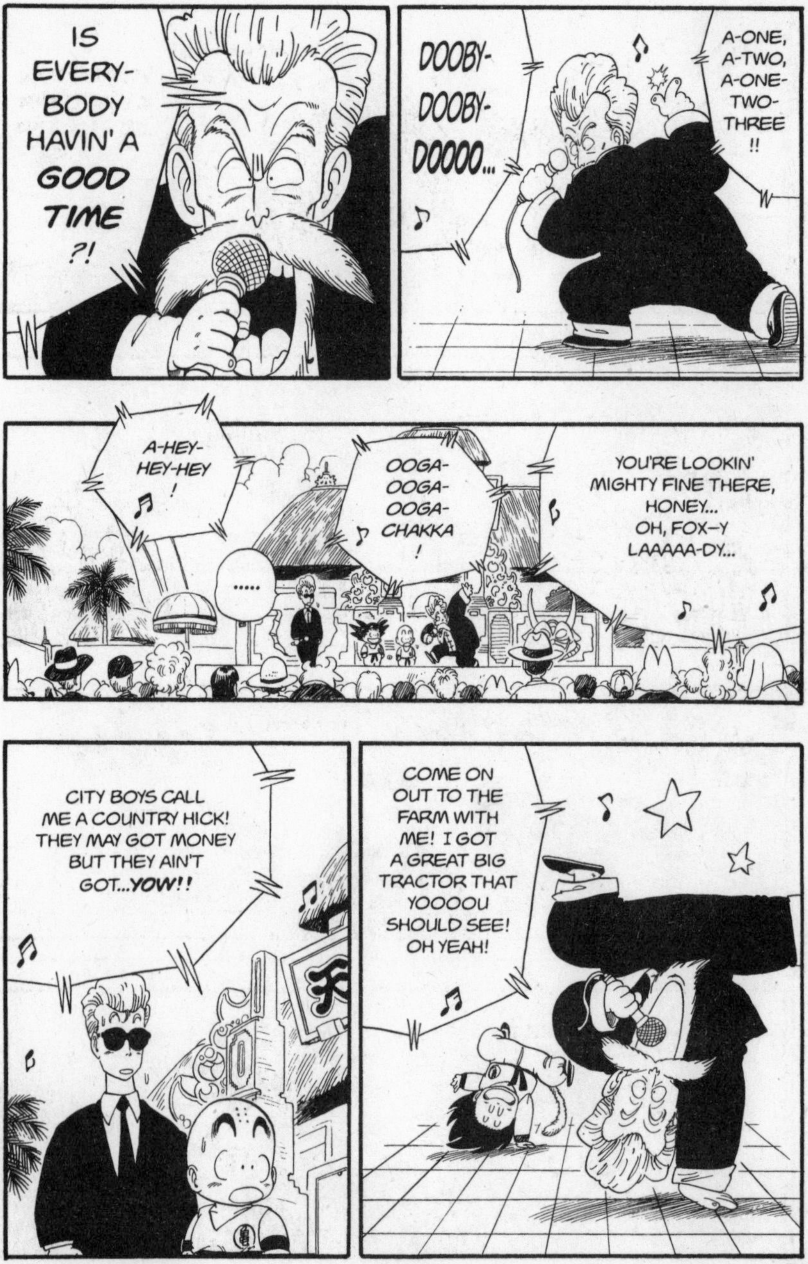
A-ONE, A-TWO, A-ONE-TWO-THREE!!
DOOBY-DOOBY-DOOOO...
IS EVERYBODY HAVIN' A GOOD TIME?!
YOU'RE LOOKIN' MIGHTY FINE THERE, HONEY... OH, FOX-Y LAAAAA-DY...
OOGA-OOGA-OOGA-CHAKKA!
A-HEY-HEY-HEY!
......
COME ON OUT TO THE FARM WITH ME! I GOT A GREAT BIG TRACTOR THAT YOOOOU SHOULD SEE! OH YEAH!
CITY BOYS CALL ME A COUNTRY HICK! THEY MAY GOT MONEY BUT THEY AIN'T GOT...YOW!!

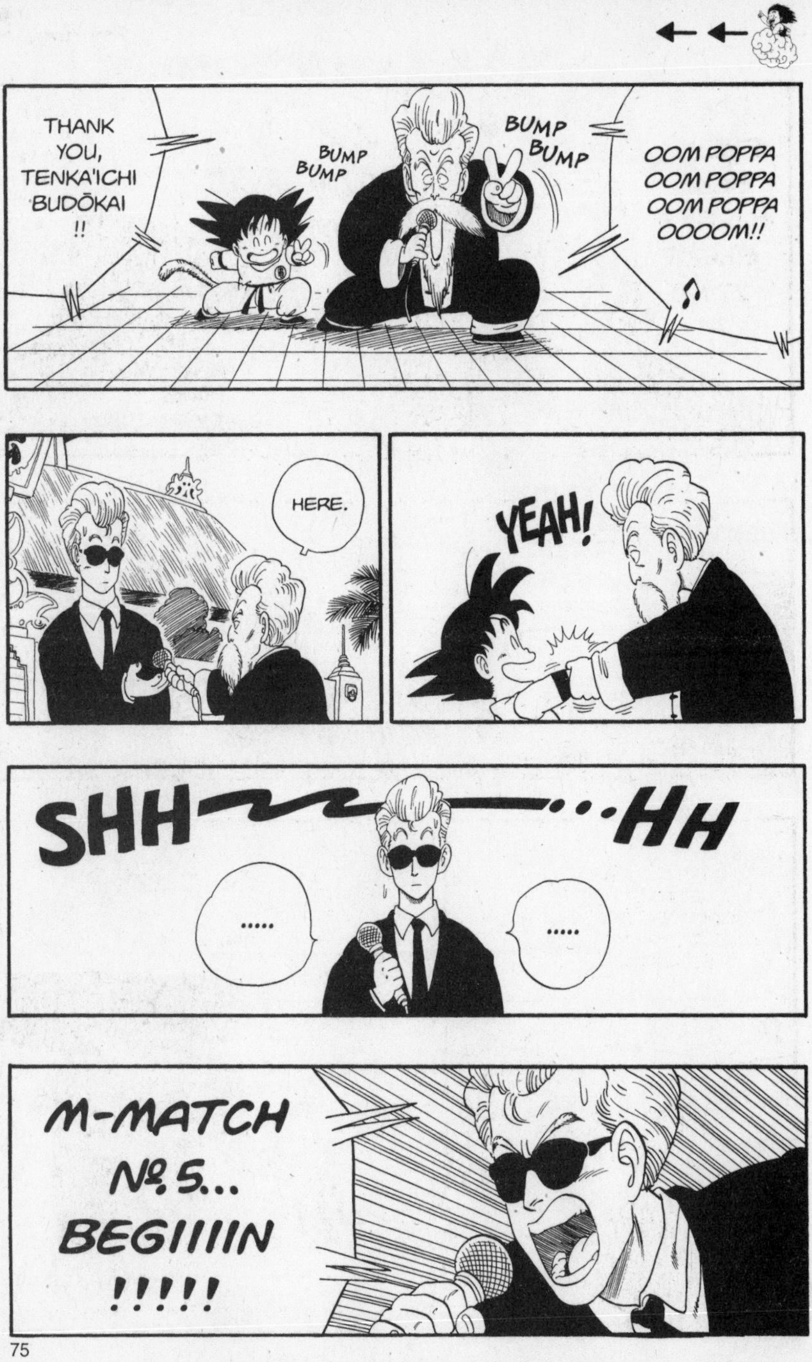
OOM POPPA OOM POPPA OOM POPPA OOOOM!!
BUMP BUMP
BUMP BUMP
THANK YOU, TENKA'ICHI BUDŌKAI !!
YEAH!
HERE.
.....
.....
SHH—…HH
M-MATCH №. 5... BEGIIIIN !!!!!

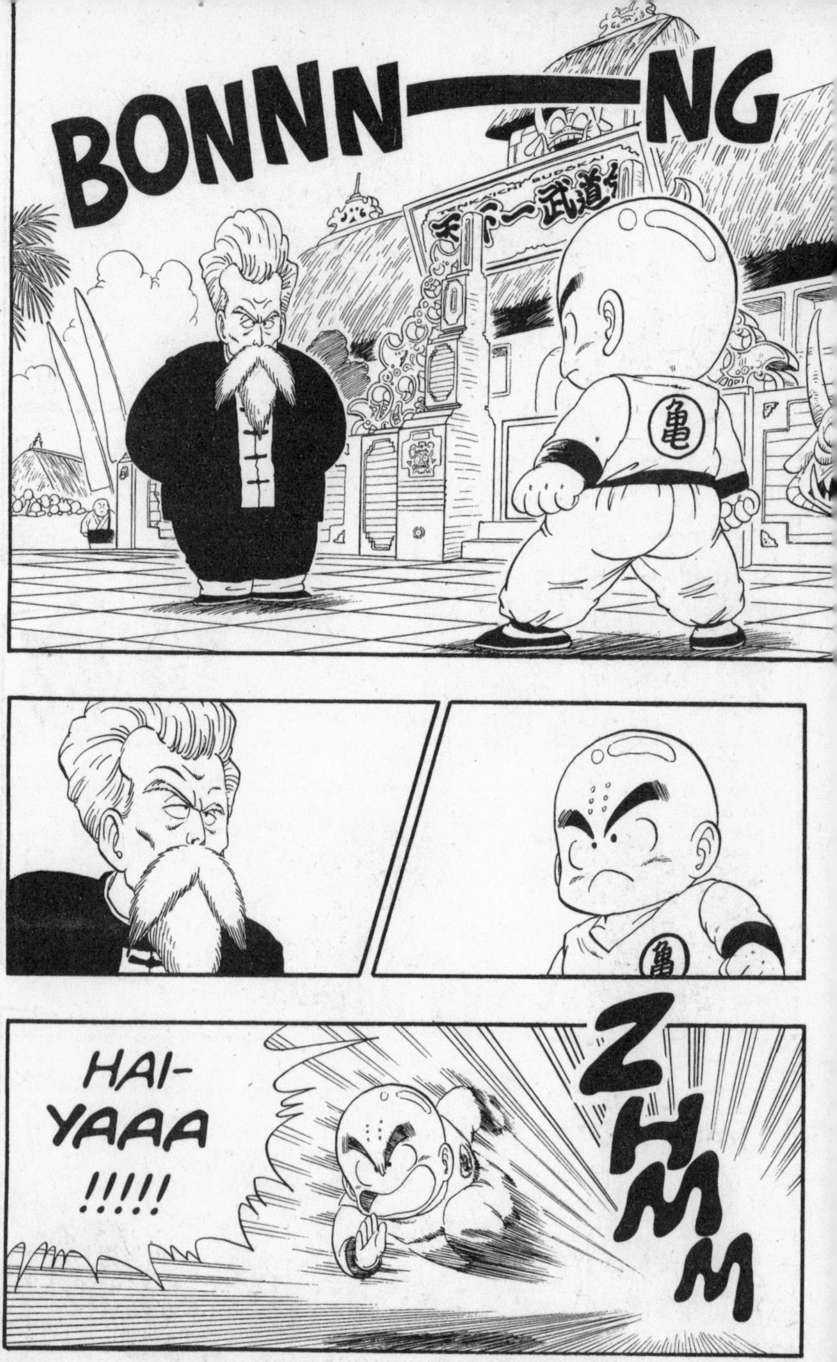
BONNN—NG
TENKAICHI BUDOKAI
ZHMM
HAI-YAAA!!!!!

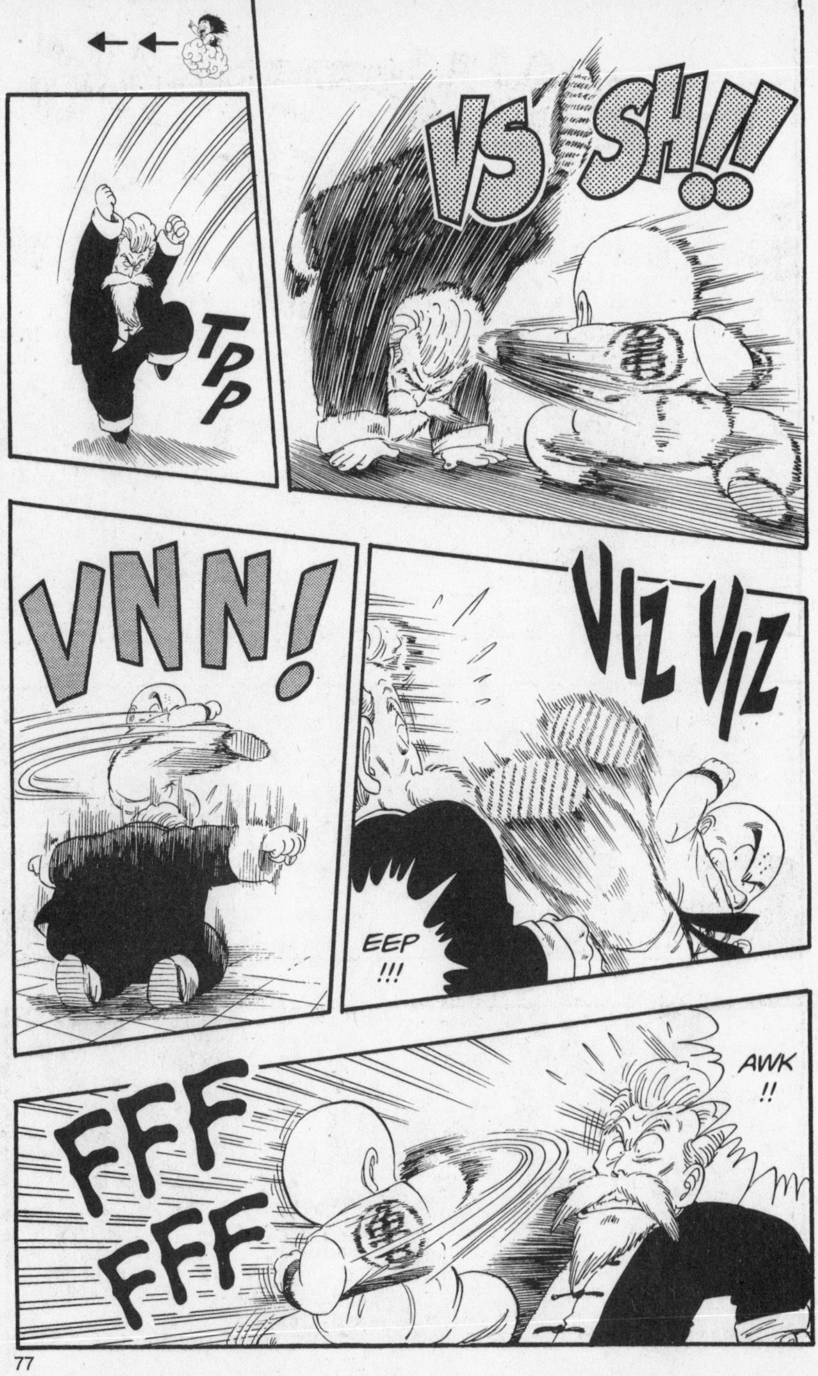

VS SH!!
TPP
VIZ VIZ
EEP !!!
VNN!
AWK !!
FFF FFF

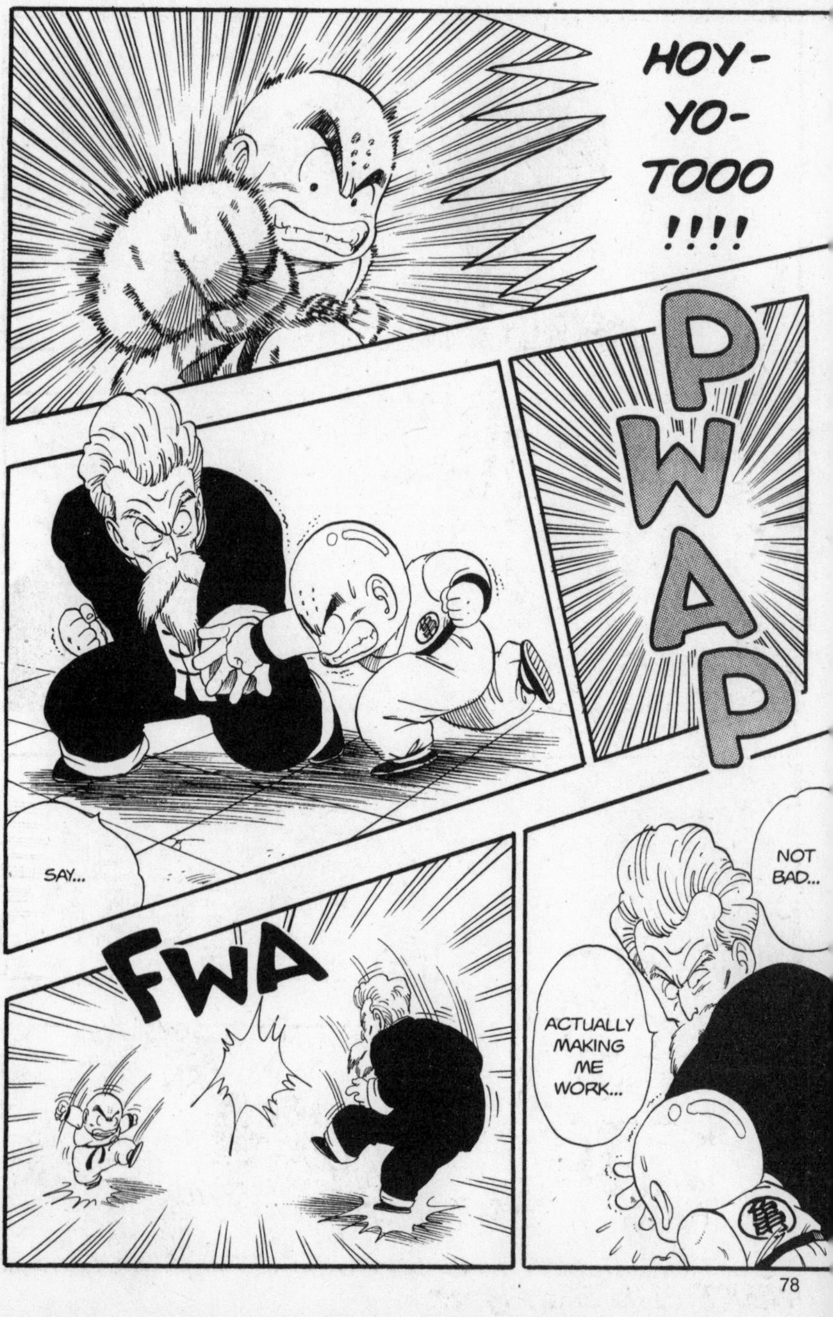
HOY-YO-TOOO!!!!
PWAP
SAY...
NOT BAD...
ACTUALLY MAKING ME WORK...
FWA

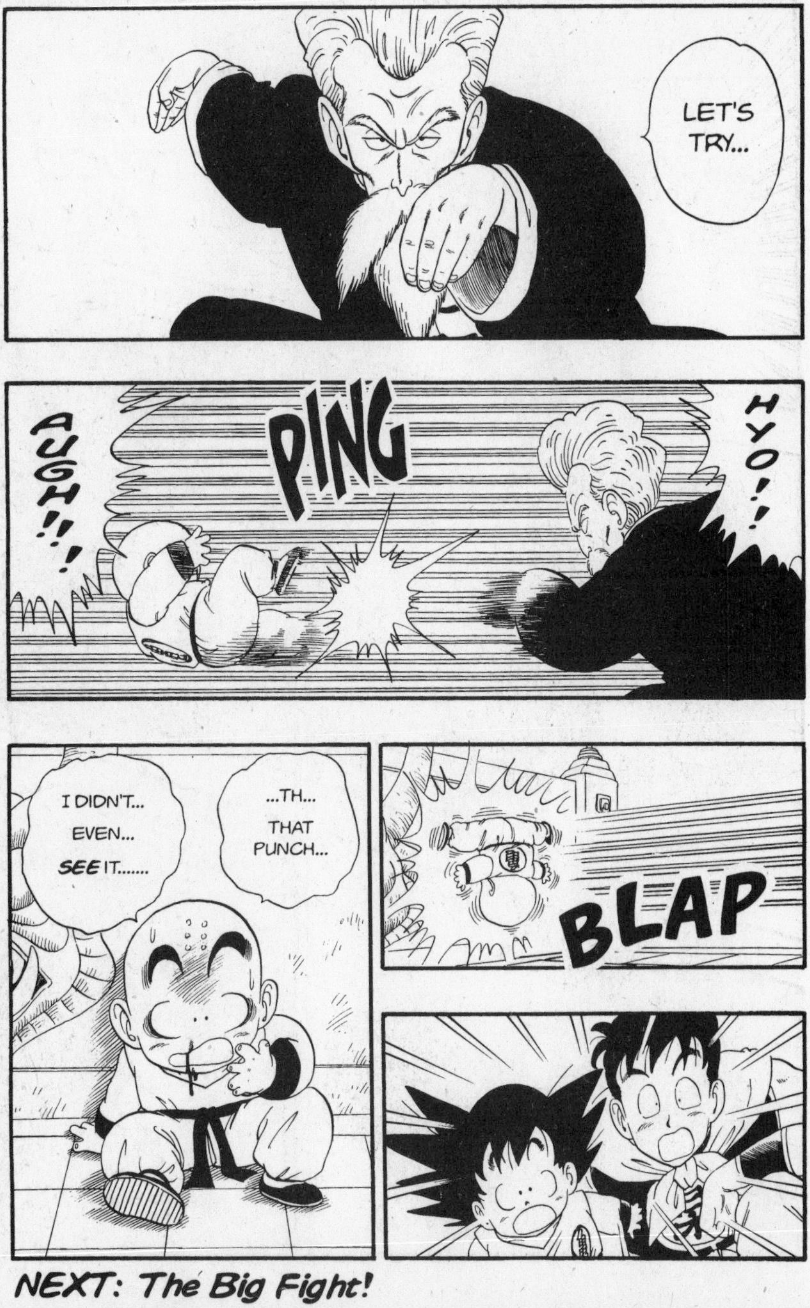
LET'S TRY...
HYO!!
PING
AUGH!!!
BLAP
...TH... THAT PUNCH...
I DIDN'T... EVEN... *SEE* IT.......

NEXT: The Big Fight!

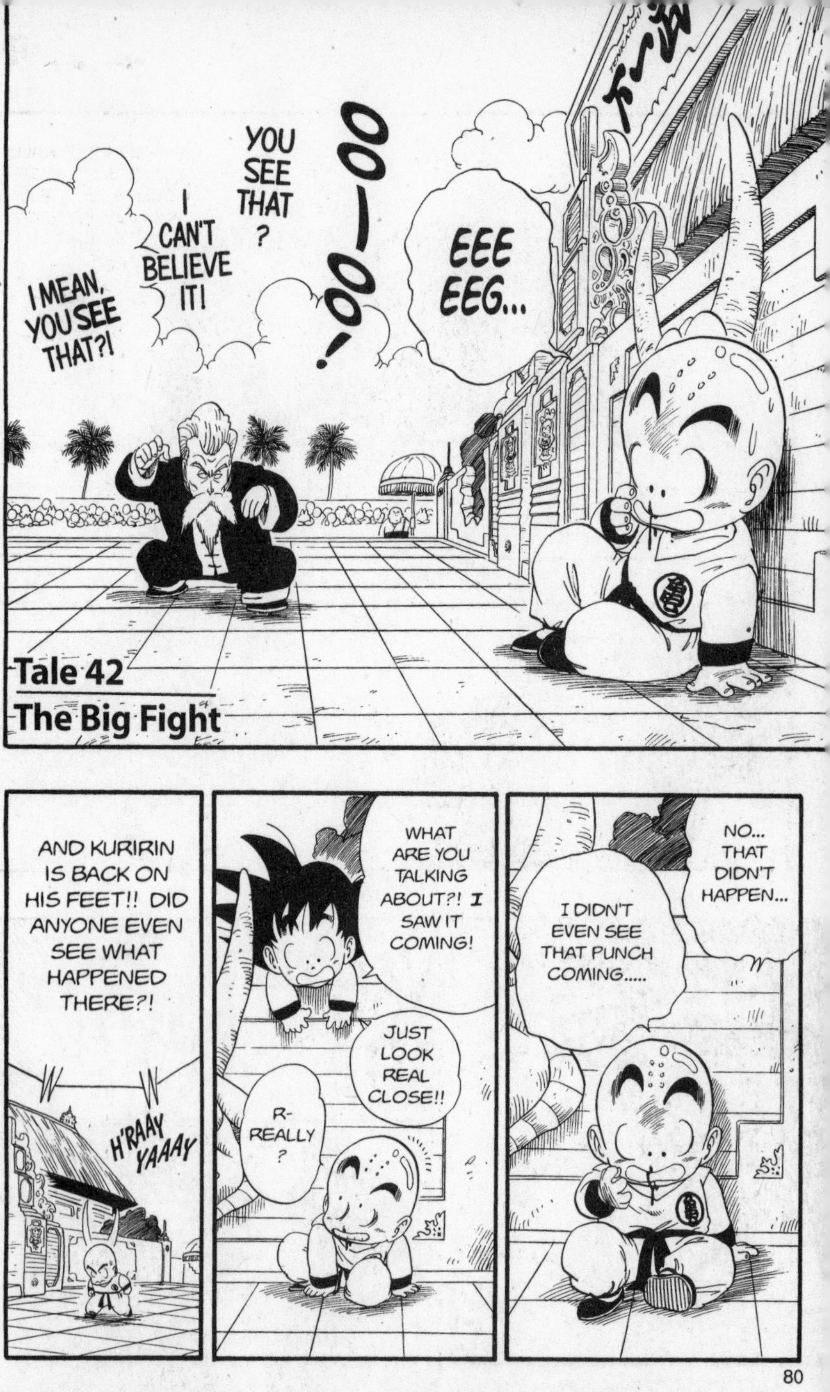
EEE EEG...
OOO-OO!
YOU SEE THAT?
I CAN'T BELIEVE IT!
I MEAN, YOU SEE THAT?!
Tale 42
The Big Fight
NO... THAT DIDN'T HAPPEN...
I DIDN'T EVEN SEE THAT PUNCH COMING.....
WHAT ARE YOU TALKING ABOUT?! I SAW IT COMING!
JUST LOOK REAL CLOSE!!
R-REALLY?
AND KURIRIN IS BACK ON HIS FEET!! DID ANYONE EVEN SEE WHAT HAPPENED THERE?!
H'RAAY YAAAY

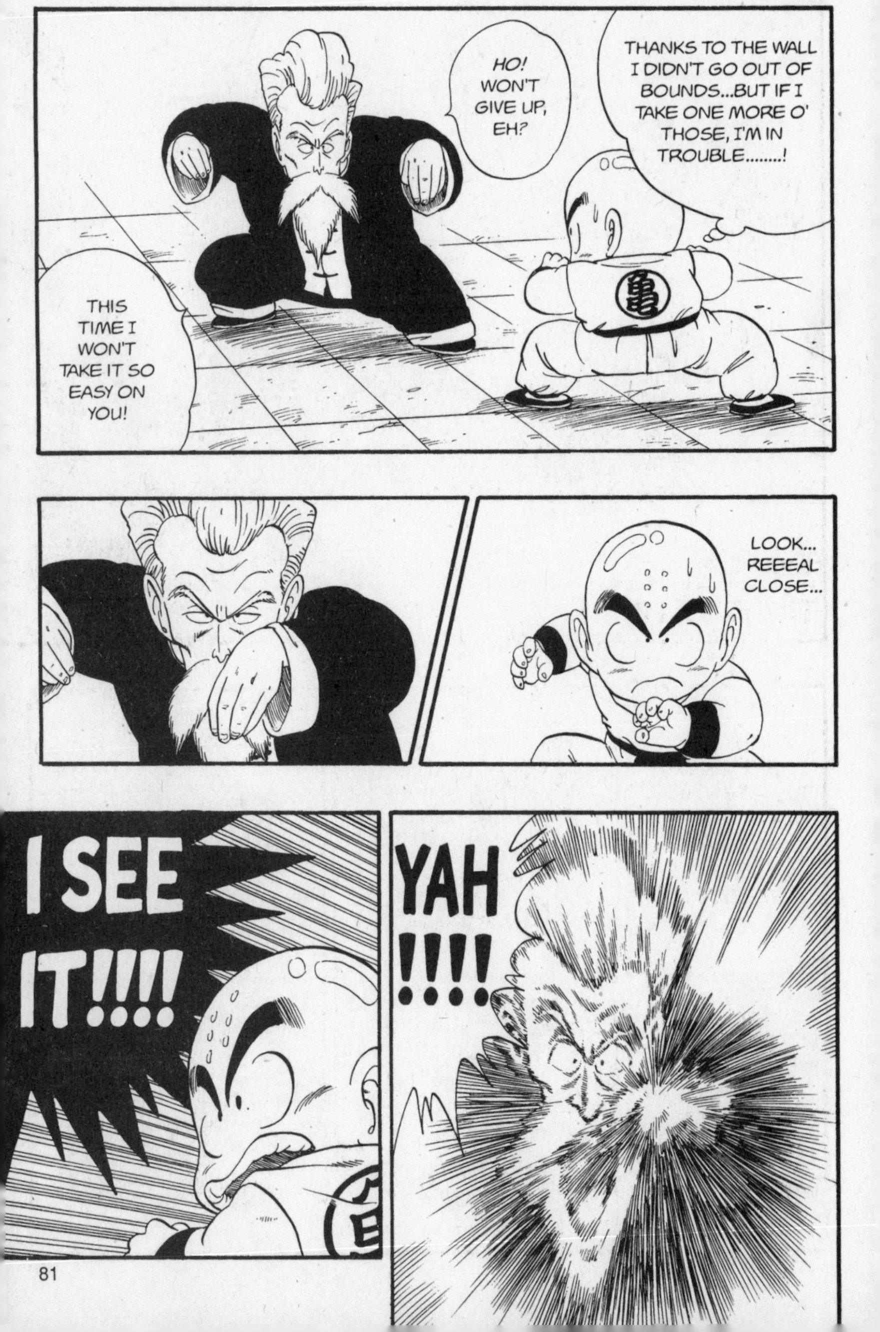
THANKS TO THE WALL I DIDN'T GO OUT OF BOUNDS...BUT IF I TAKE ONE MORE O' THOSE, I'M IN TROUBLE........!
HO! WON'T GIVE UP, EH?
THIS TIME I WON'T TAKE IT SO EASY ON YOU!
LOOK... REEEAL CLOSE...
YAH!!!!
I SEE IT!!!!

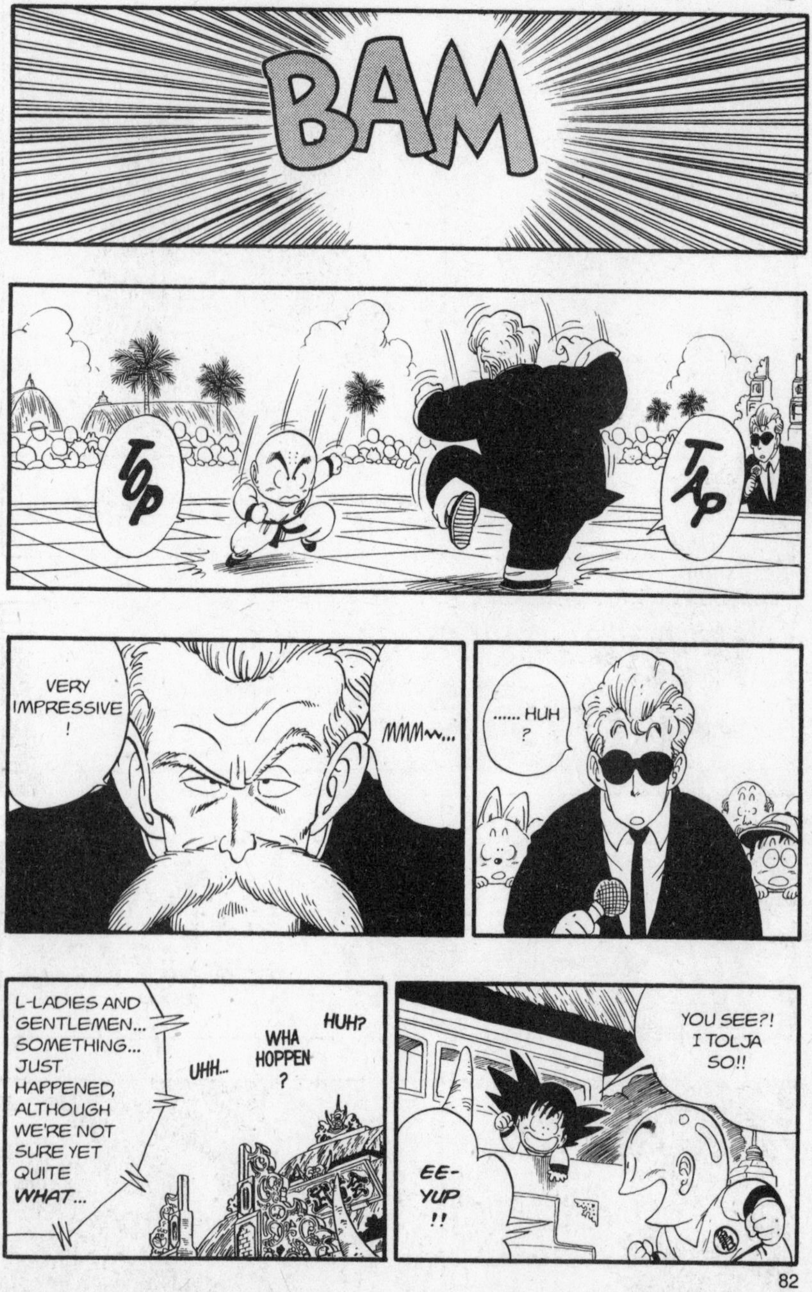

BAM
TAP
TOP
...... HUH ?
MMMm...
VERY IMPRESSIVE !
YOU SEE?! I TOLJA SO!!
EE-YUP !!
HUH?
WHA HOPPEN ?
UHH...
L-LADIES AND GENTLEMEN... SOMETHING... JUST HAPPENED, ALTHOUGH WE'RE NOT SURE YET QUITE WHAT...

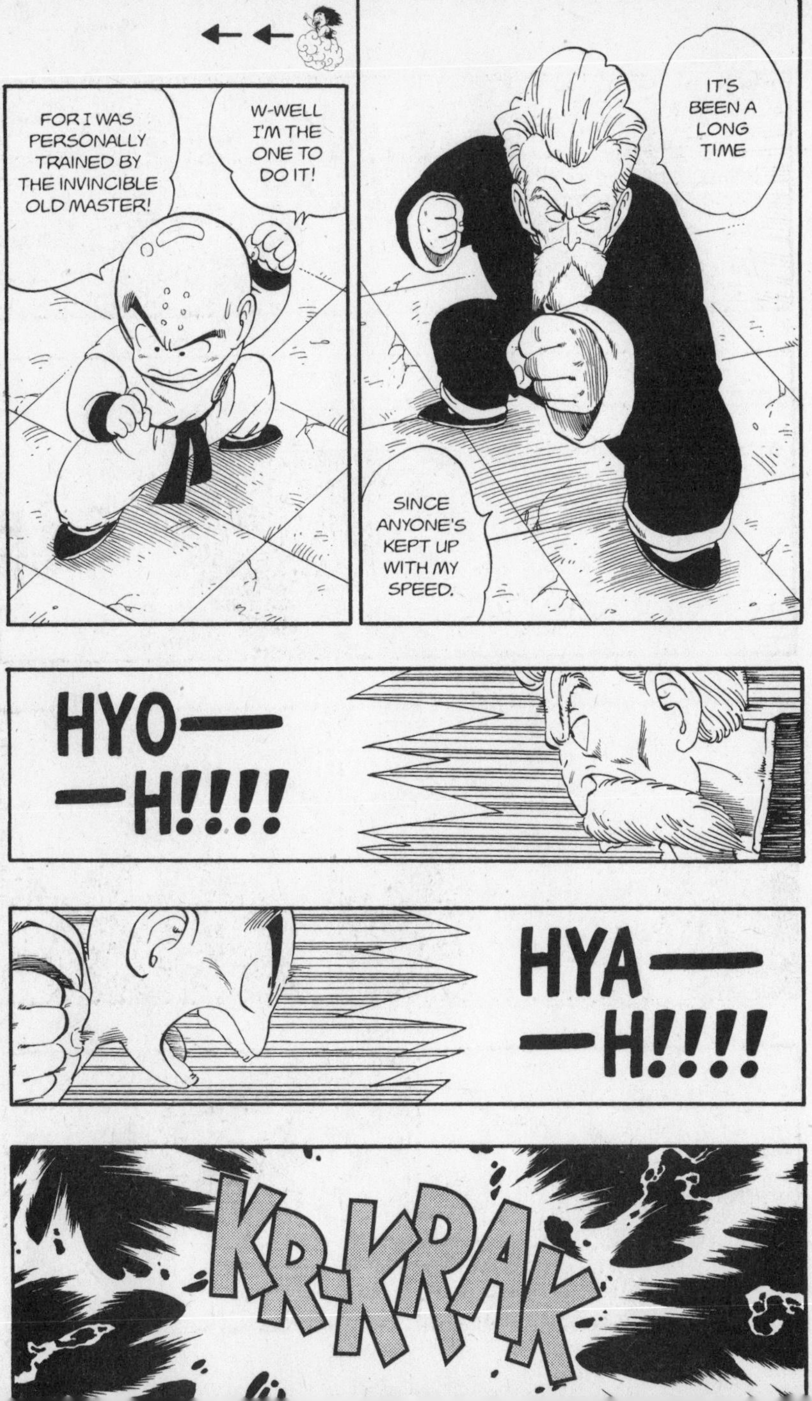
IT'S BEEN A LONG TIME
SINCE ANYONE'S KEPT UP WITH MY SPEED.
W-WELL I'M THE ONE TO DO IT!
FOR I WAS PERSONALLY TRAINED BY THE INVINCIBLE OLD MASTER!
HYO——H!!!!
HYA——H!!!!
KR-KRAK

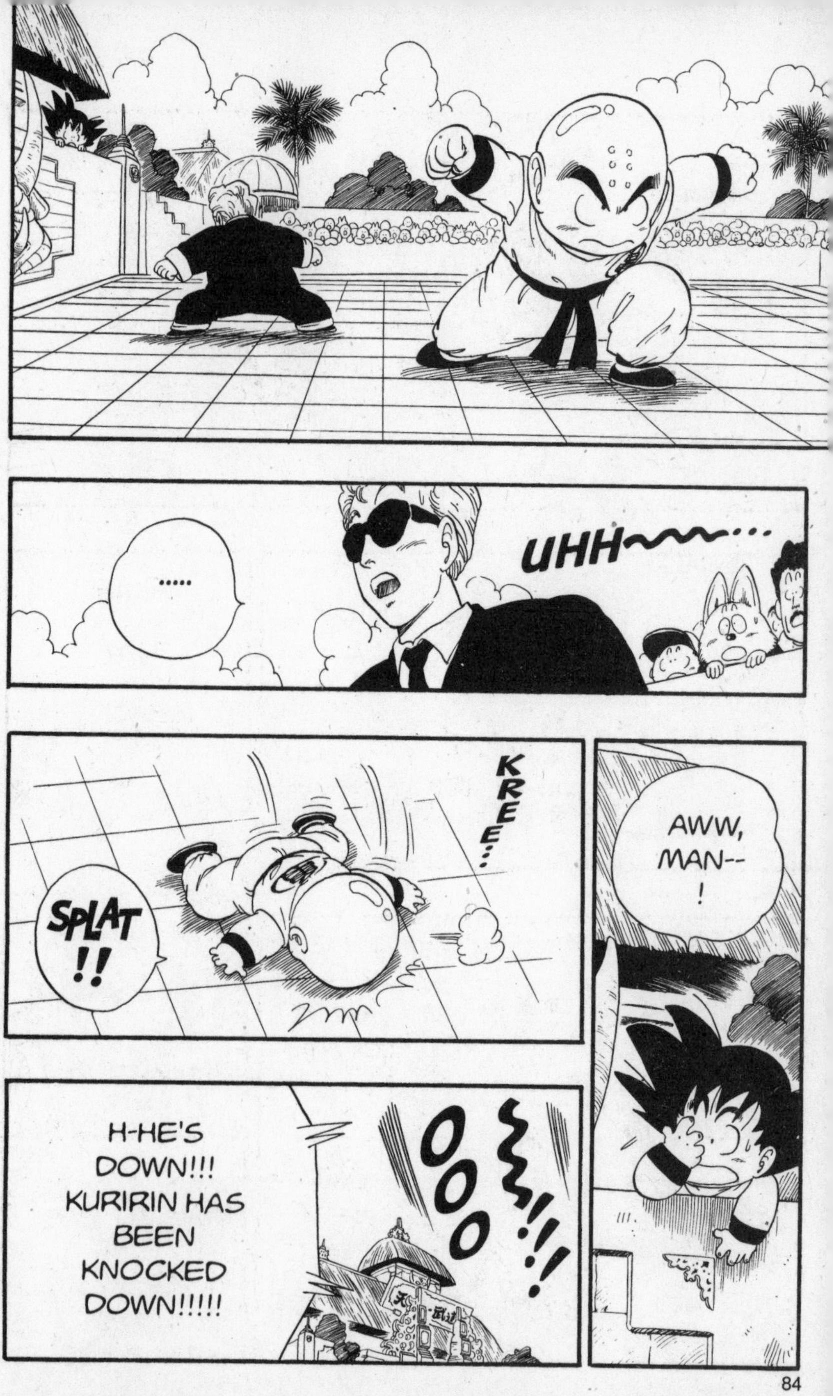
UHH~~~...
.....
AWW, MAN--!
KREE..
SPLAT!!
OOO~!!!
H-HE'S DOWN!!! KURIRIN HAS BEEN KNOCKED DOWN!!!!!

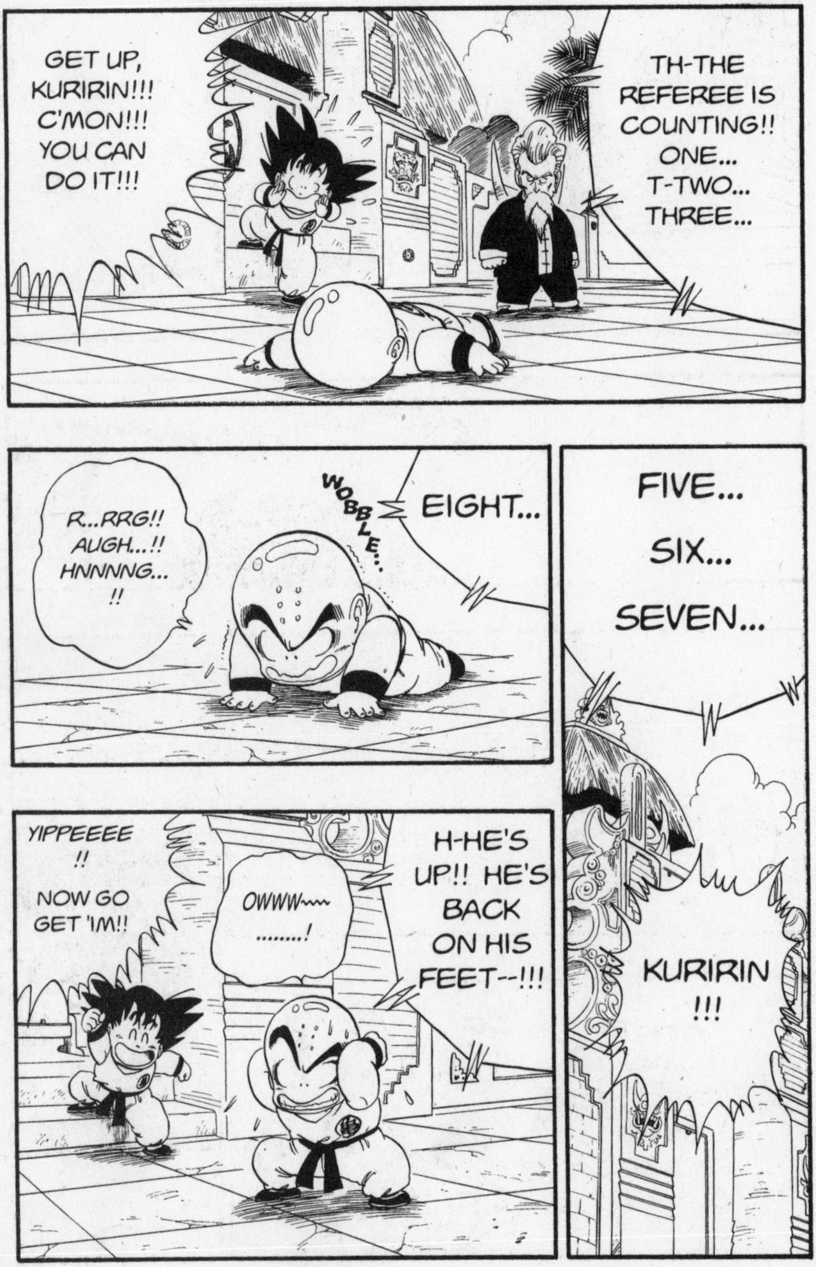
TH-THE REFEREE IS COUNTING!! ONE... T-TWO... THREE...
GET UP, KURIRIN!!! C'MON!!! YOU CAN DO IT!!!
FIVE... SIX... SEVEN...
KURIRIN !!!
EIGHT...
WOBBLE...
R...RRG!! AUGH...!! HNNNNG... !!
H-HE'S UP!! HE'S BACK ON HIS FEET--!!!
OWWW~~~ ....!
YIPPEEEE !! NOW GO GET 'IM!!

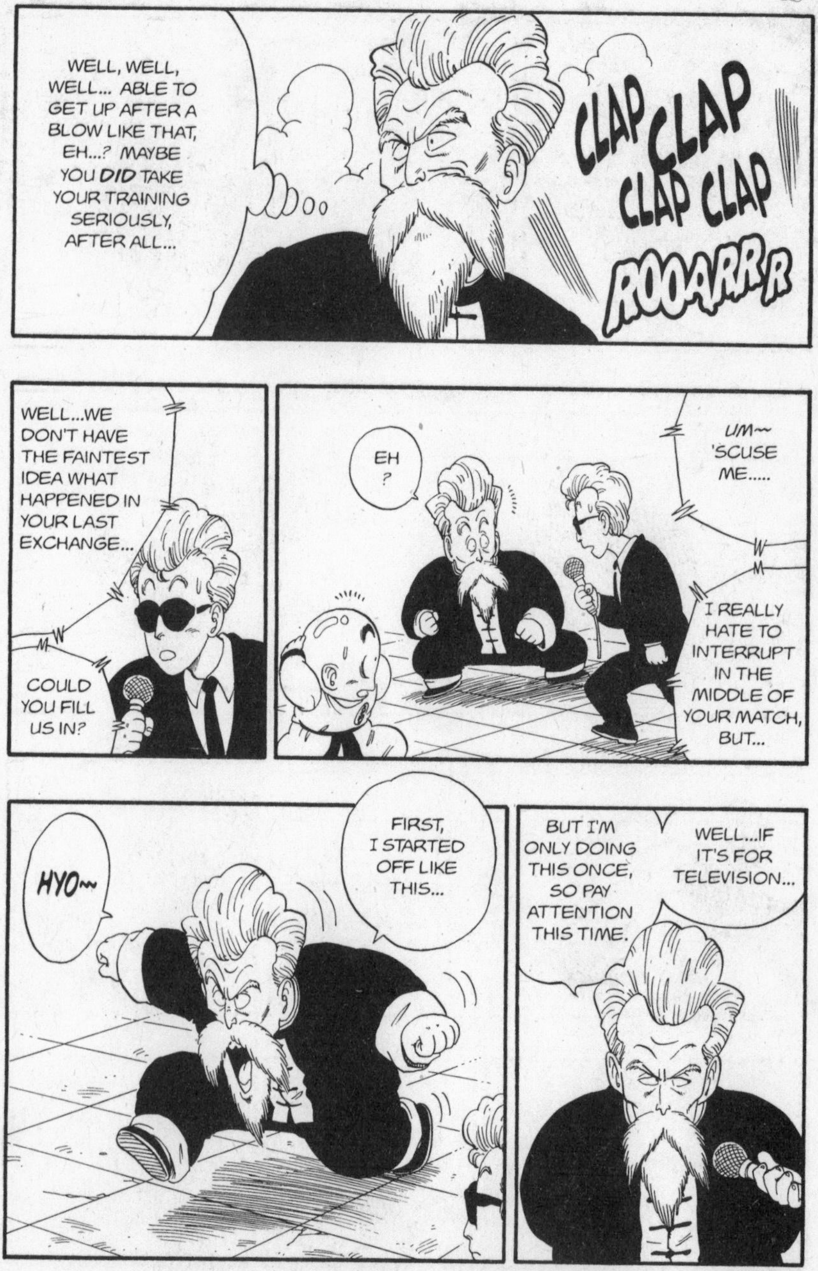
CLAP CLAP
CLAP CLAP
ROOARRR
WELL, WELL, WELL... ABLE TO GET UP AFTER A BLOW LIKE THAT, EH...? MAYBE YOU **DID** TAKE YOUR TRAINING SERIOUSLY, AFTER ALL...
UM~~ 'SCUSE ME.....
I REALLY HATE TO INTERRUPT IN THE MIDDLE OF YOUR MATCH, BUT...
EH ?
WELL...WE DON'T HAVE THE FAINTEST IDEA WHAT HAPPENED IN YOUR LAST EXCHANGE...
COULD YOU FILL US IN?
WELL...IF IT'S FOR TELEVISION...
BUT I'M ONLY DOING THIS ONCE, SO PAY ATTENTION THIS TIME.
FIRST, I STARTED OFF LIKE THIS...
HYO~~

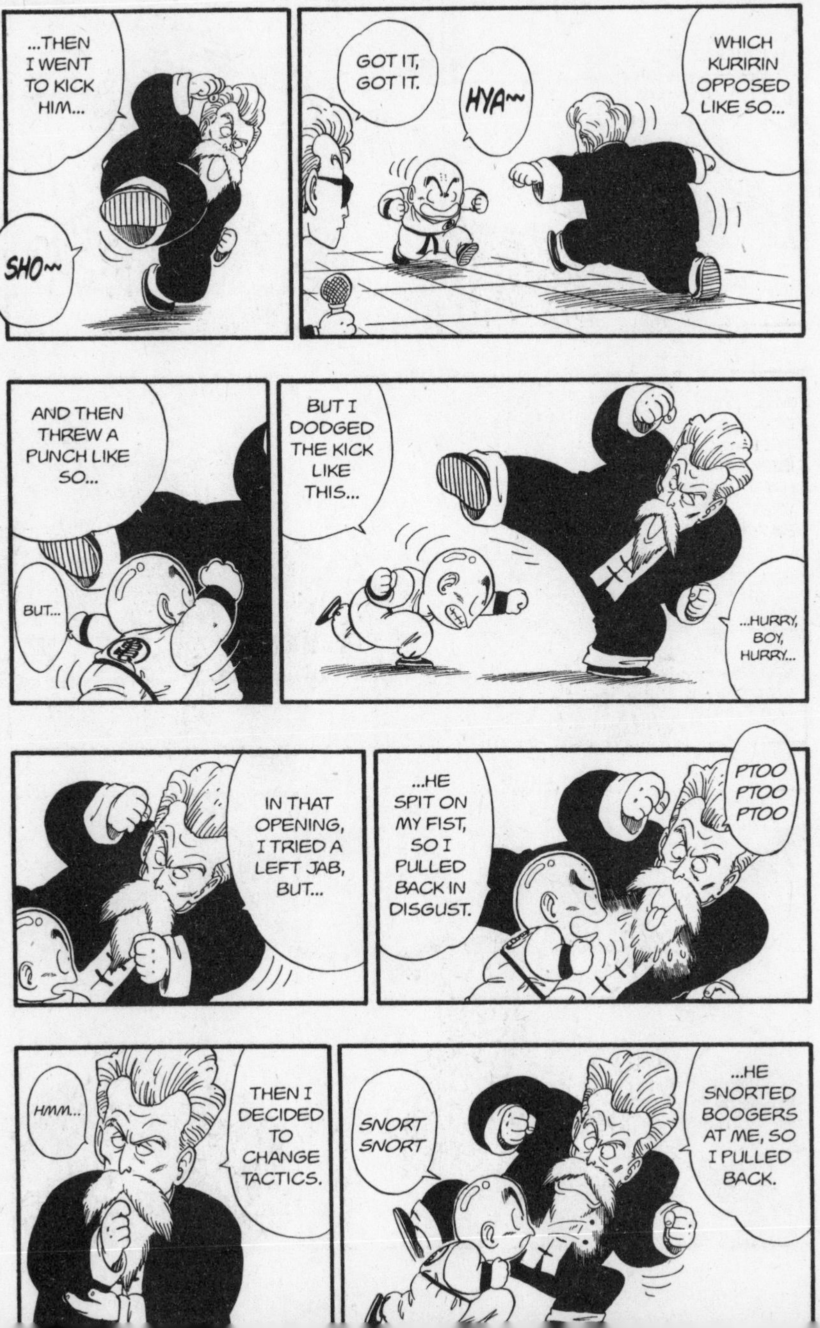
WHICH KURIRIN OPPOSED LIKE SO...
HYA~~
GOT IT, GOT IT.
...THEN I WENT TO KICK HIM...
SHO~~
BUT I DODGED THE KICK LIKE THIS...
...HURRY, BOY, HURRY...
AND THEN THREW A PUNCH LIKE SO...
BUT...
PTOO PTOO PTOO
...HE SPIT ON MY FIST, SO I PULLED BACK IN DISGUST.
IN THAT OPENING, I TRIED A LEFT JAB, BUT...
...HE SNORTED BOOGERS AT ME, SO I PULLED BACK.
SNORT SNORT
THEN I DECIDED TO CHANGE TACTICS.
HMM...

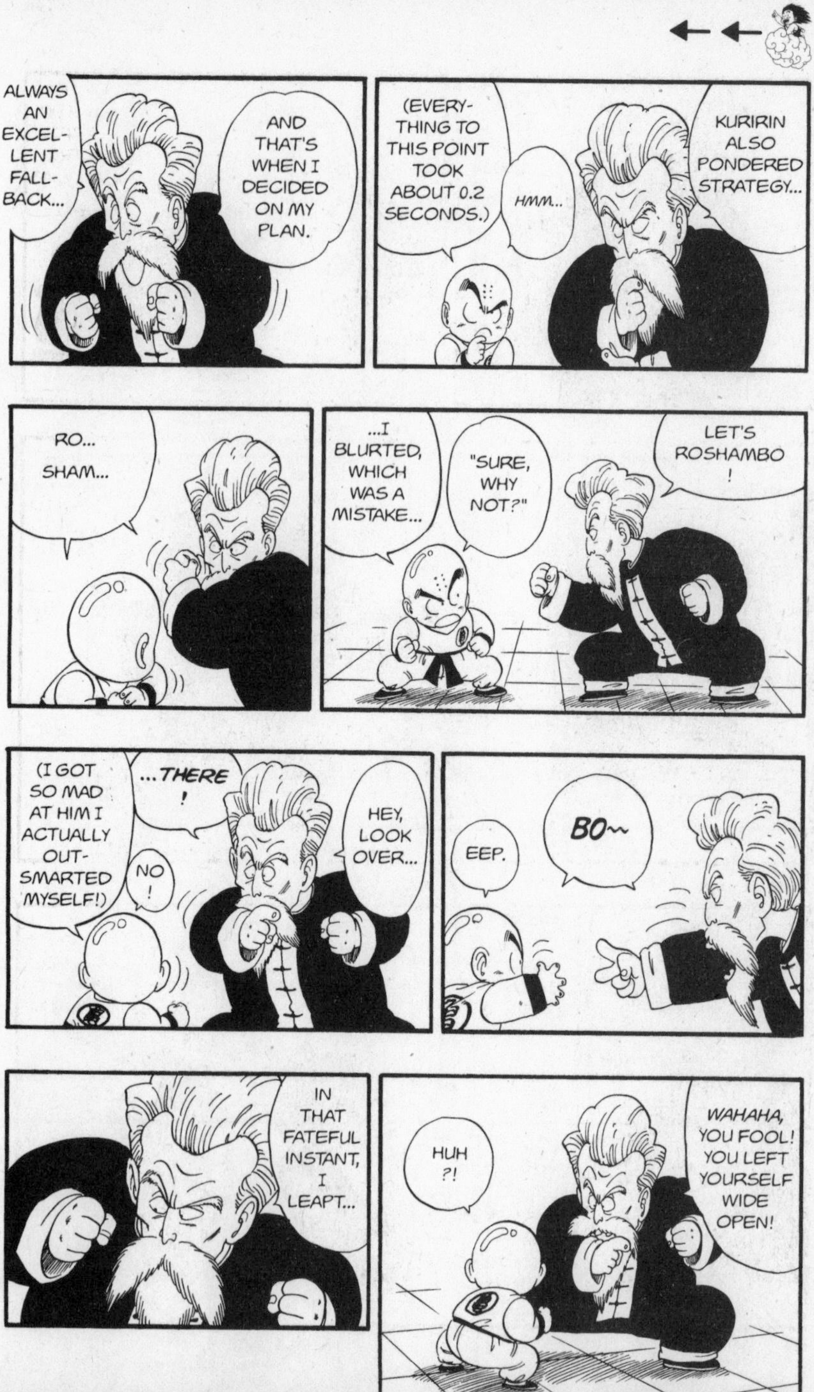
KURIRIN ALSO PONDERED STRATEGY...
HMM...
(EVERYTHING TO THIS POINT TOOK ABOUT 0.2 SECONDS.)
AND THAT'S WHEN I DECIDED ON MY PLAN.
ALWAYS AN EXCELLENT FALLBACK...
LET'S ROSHAMBO!
"SURE, WHY NOT?"
...I BLURTED, WHICH WAS A MISTAKE...
RO... SHAM...
BO~~
EEP.
HEY, LOOK OVER...
...THERE!
NO!
(I GOT SO MAD AT HIM I ACTUALLY OUTSMARTED MYSELF!)
WAHAHA, YOU FOOL! YOU LEFT YOURSELF WIDE OPEN!
HUH?!
IN THAT FATEFUL INSTANT, I LEAPT...

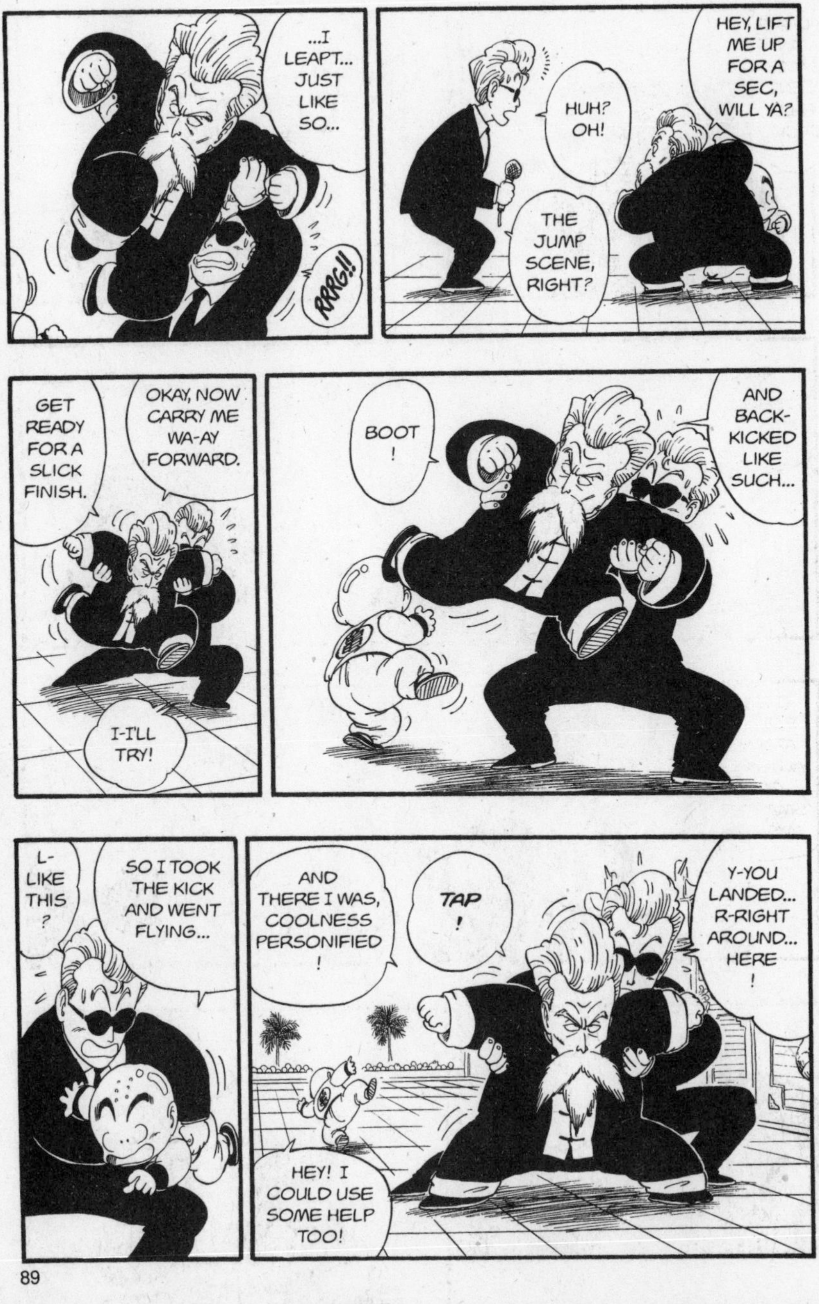
HEY, LIFT ME UP FOR A SEC, WILL YA?
HUH? OH!
THE JUMP SCENE, RIGHT?
...I LEAPT... JUST LIKE SO...
RRRG!!
AND BACK-KICKED LIKE SUCH...
BOOT!
OKAY, NOW CARRY ME WA-AY FORWARD.
GET READY FOR A SLICK FINISH.
I-I'LL TRY!
Y-YOU LANDED... R-RIGHT AROUND... HERE!
TAP!
AND THERE I WAS, COOLNESS PERSONIFIED!
HEY! I COULD USE SOME HELP TOO!
SO I TOOK THE KICK AND WENT FLYING...
L-LIKE THIS?

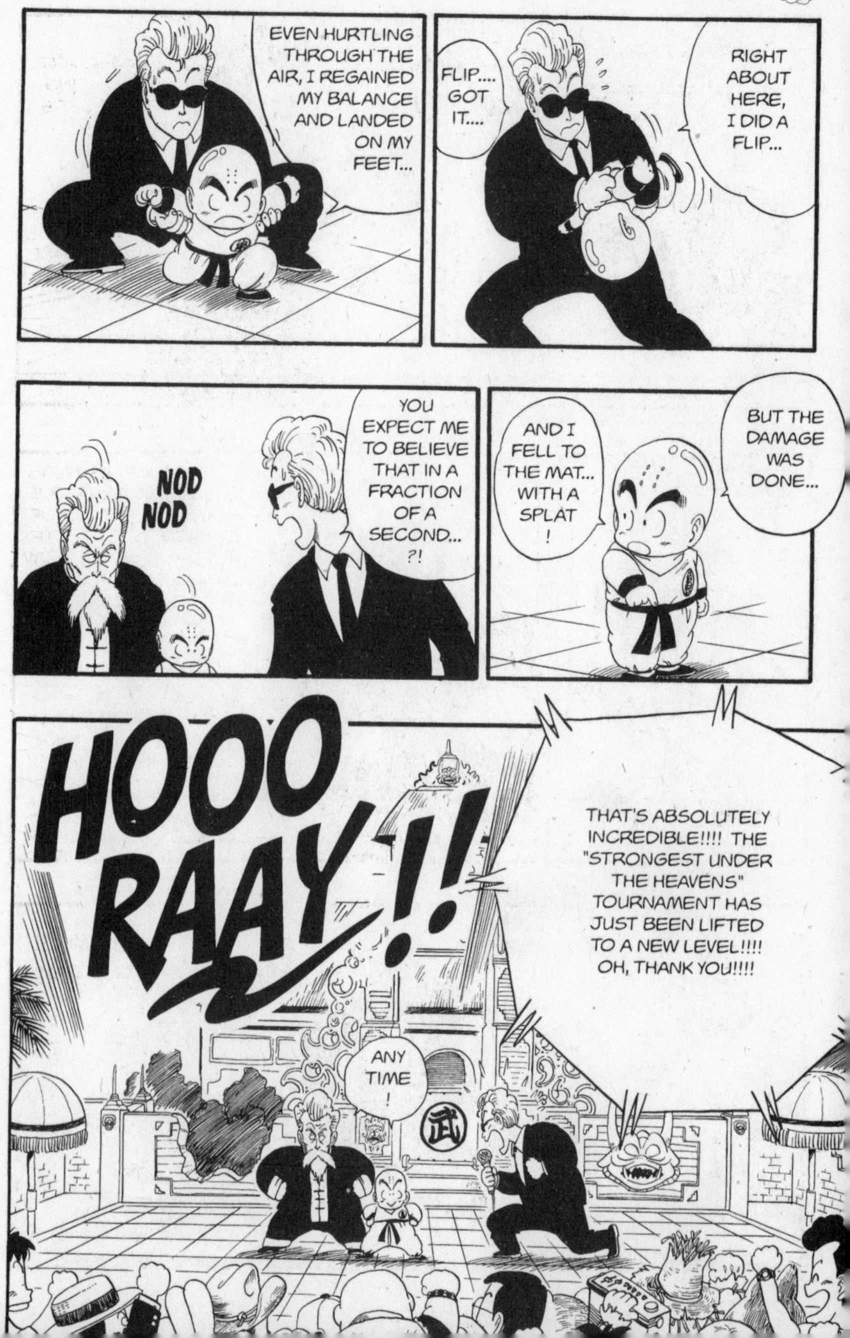
RIGHT ABOUT HERE, I DID A FLIP...
FLIP.... GOT IT....
EVEN HURTLING THROUGH THE AIR, I REGAINED MY BALANCE AND LANDED ON MY FEET...
BUT THE DAMAGE WAS DONE...
AND I FELL TO THE MAT... WITH A SPLAT!
YOU EXPECT ME TO BELIEVE THAT IN A FRACTION OF A SECOND...?!
NOD NOD
THAT'S ABSOLUTELY INCREDIBLE!!!! THE "STRONGEST UNDER THE HEAVENS" TOURNAMENT HAS JUST BEEN LIFTED TO A NEW LEVEL!!!! OH, THANK YOU!!!!
HOOO RAAY!!
ANY TIME!

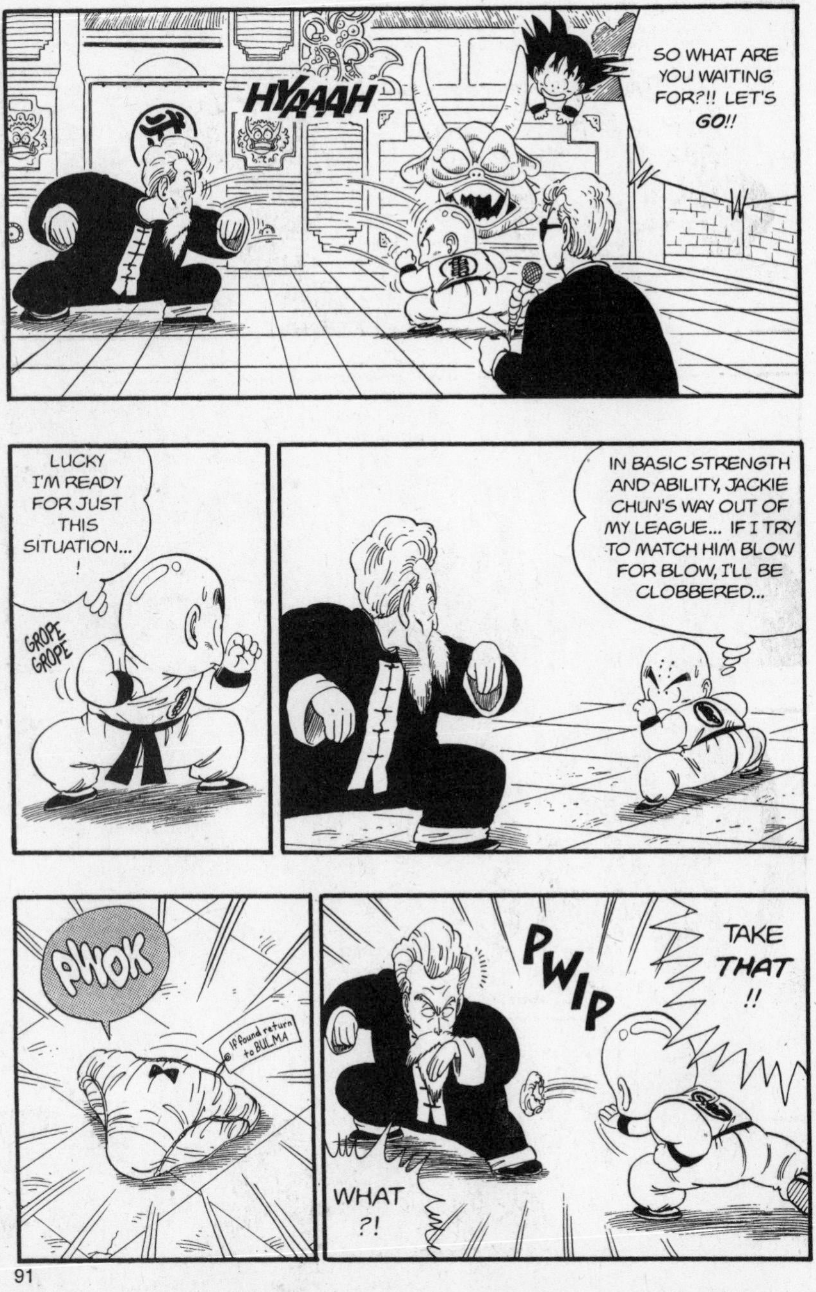
SO WHAT ARE YOU WAITING FOR?!! LET'S GO!!
HYAAAH
IN BASIC STRENGTH AND ABILITY, JACKIE CHUN'S WAY OUT OF MY LEAGUE... IF I TRY TO MATCH HIM BLOW FOR BLOW, I'LL BE CLOBBERED...
LUCKY I'M READY FOR JUST THIS SITUATION... !
GROPE GROPE
TAKE THAT !!
PWIP
WHAT ?!
PWOK
If found return to BULMA

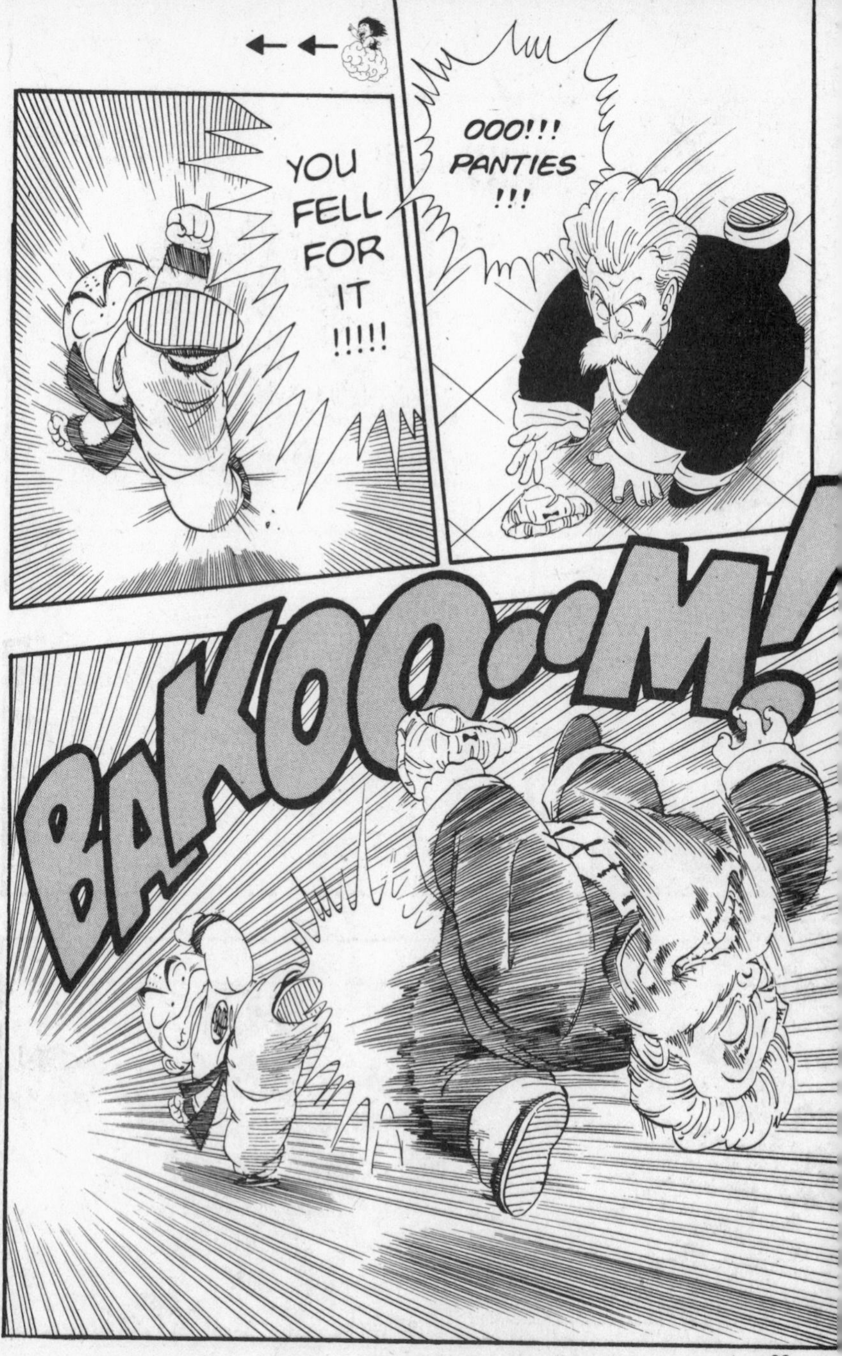
OOO!!! PANTIES !!!
YOU FELL FOR IT !!!!!
BAKOO..M!

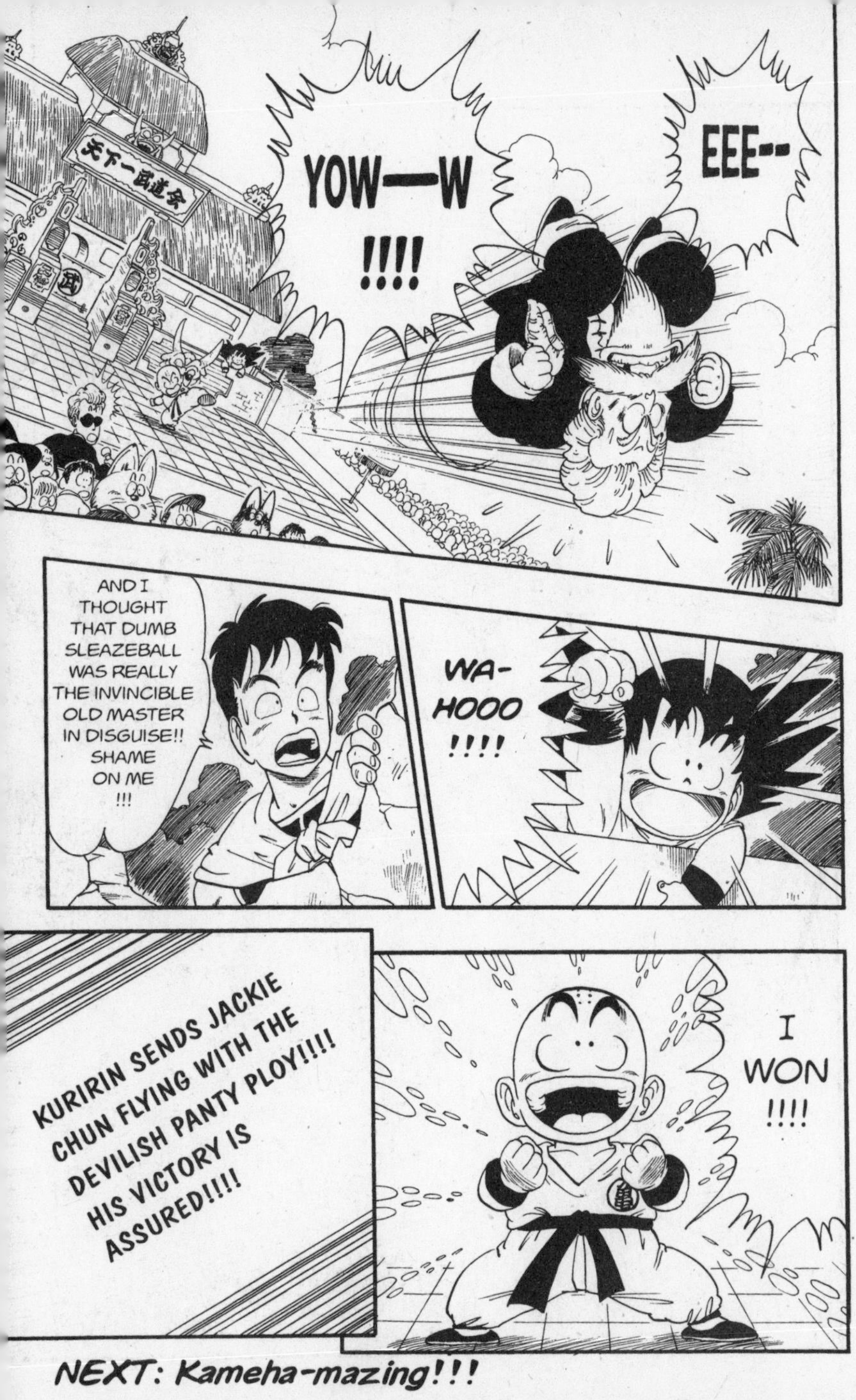
EEE--
YOW—W !!!!
天下一武道会
WA-HOOO !!!!
AND I THOUGHT THAT DUMB SLEAZEBALL WAS REALLY THE INVINCIBLE OLD MASTER IN DISGUISE!! SHAME ON ME !!!
I WON !!!!
KURIRIN SENDS JACKIE CHUN FLYING WITH THE DEVILISH PANTY PLOY!!!! HIS VICTORY IS ASSURED!!!!

NEXT: Kameha-mazing!!!

Tale 43 • The Mysterious Jackie Chun

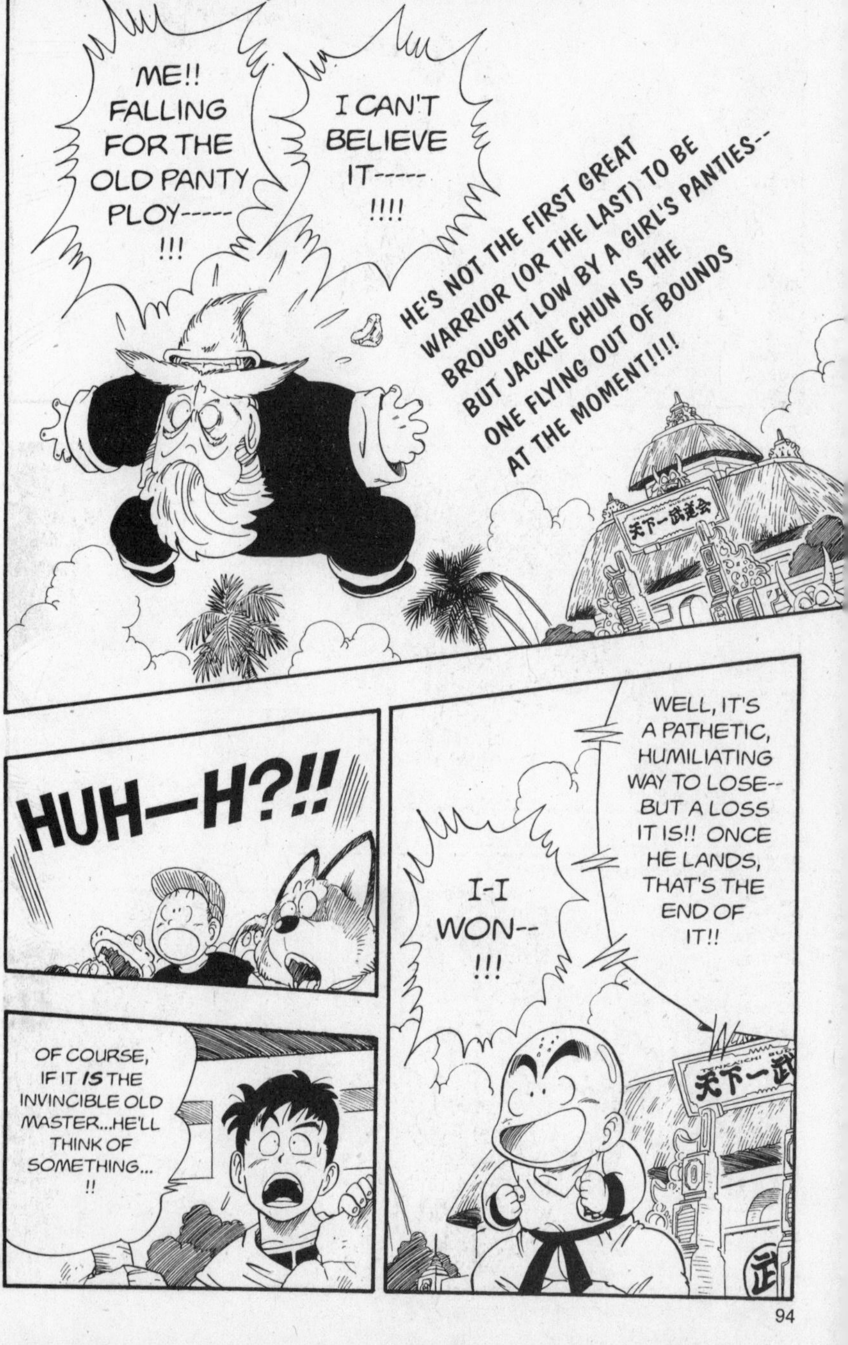
I CAN'T BELIEVE IT----- !!!!
ME!! FALLING FOR THE OLD PANTY PLOY----- !!!
HE'S NOT THE FIRST GREAT WARRIOR (OR THE LAST) TO BE BROUGHT LOW BY A GIRL'S PANTIES-- BUT JACKIE CHUN IS THE ONE FLYING OUT OF BOUNDS AT THE MOMENT!!!!
天下一武道会
WELL, IT'S A PATHETIC, HUMILIATING WAY TO LOSE-- BUT A LOSS IT IS!! ONCE HE LANDS, THAT'S THE END OF IT!!
I-I WON-- !!!
天下一武
HUH--H?!!
OF COURSE, IF IT *IS* THE INVINCIBLE OLD MASTER...HE'LL THINK OF SOMETHING... !!

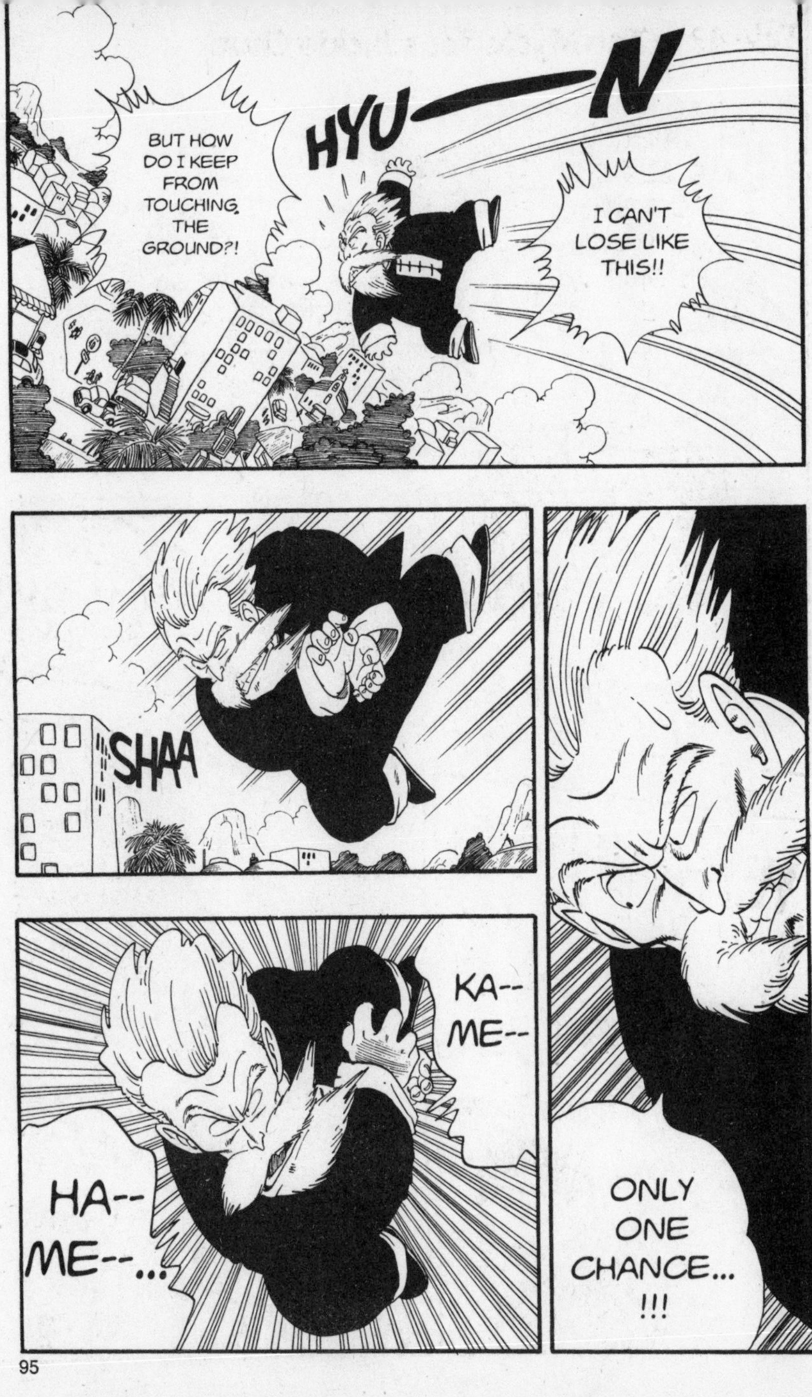
HYU—N
I CAN'T LOSE LIKE THIS!!
BUT HOW DO I KEEP FROM TOUCHING THE GROUND?!
ONLY ONE CHANCE... !!!
SHAA
KA-- ME--
HA-- ME--...

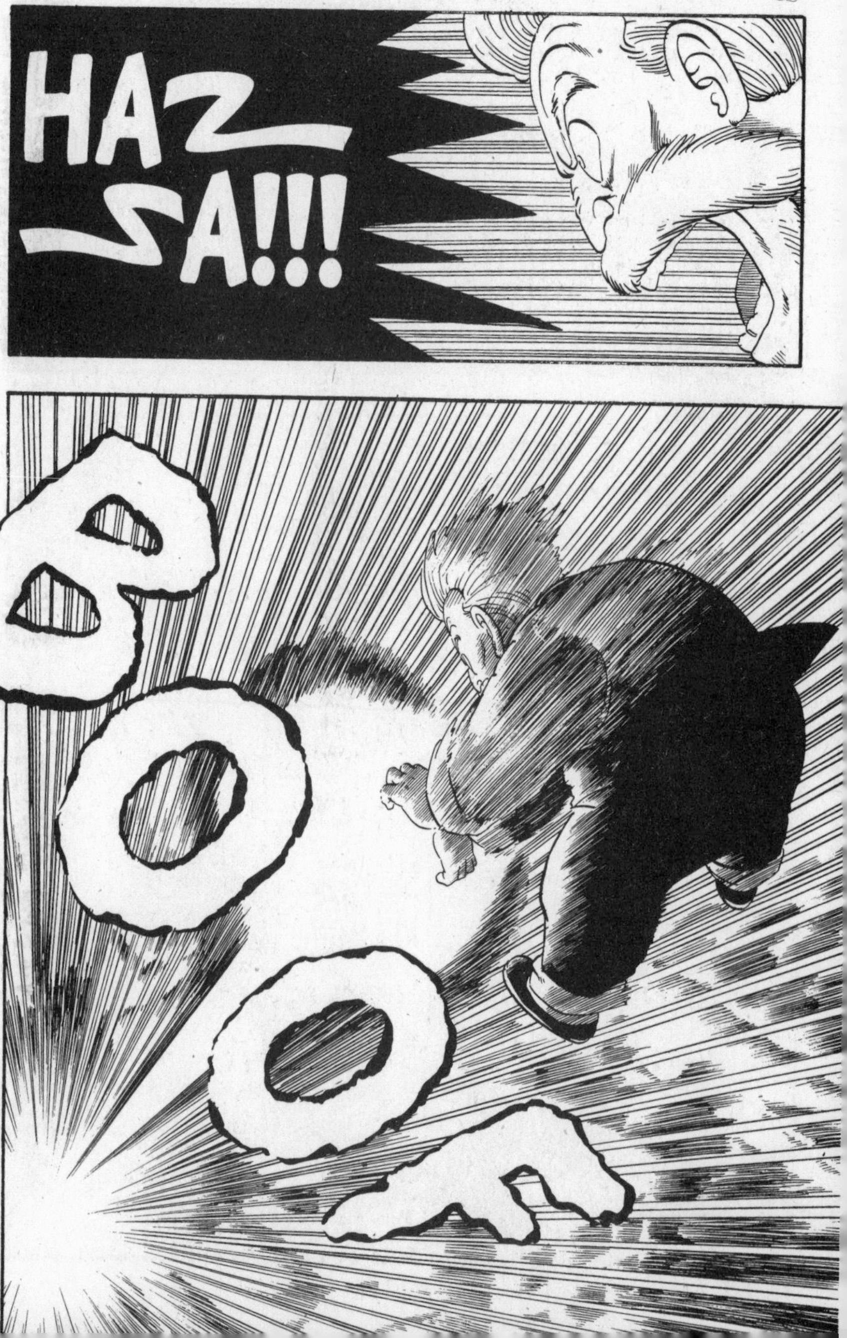
HAZSA!!!
BOO

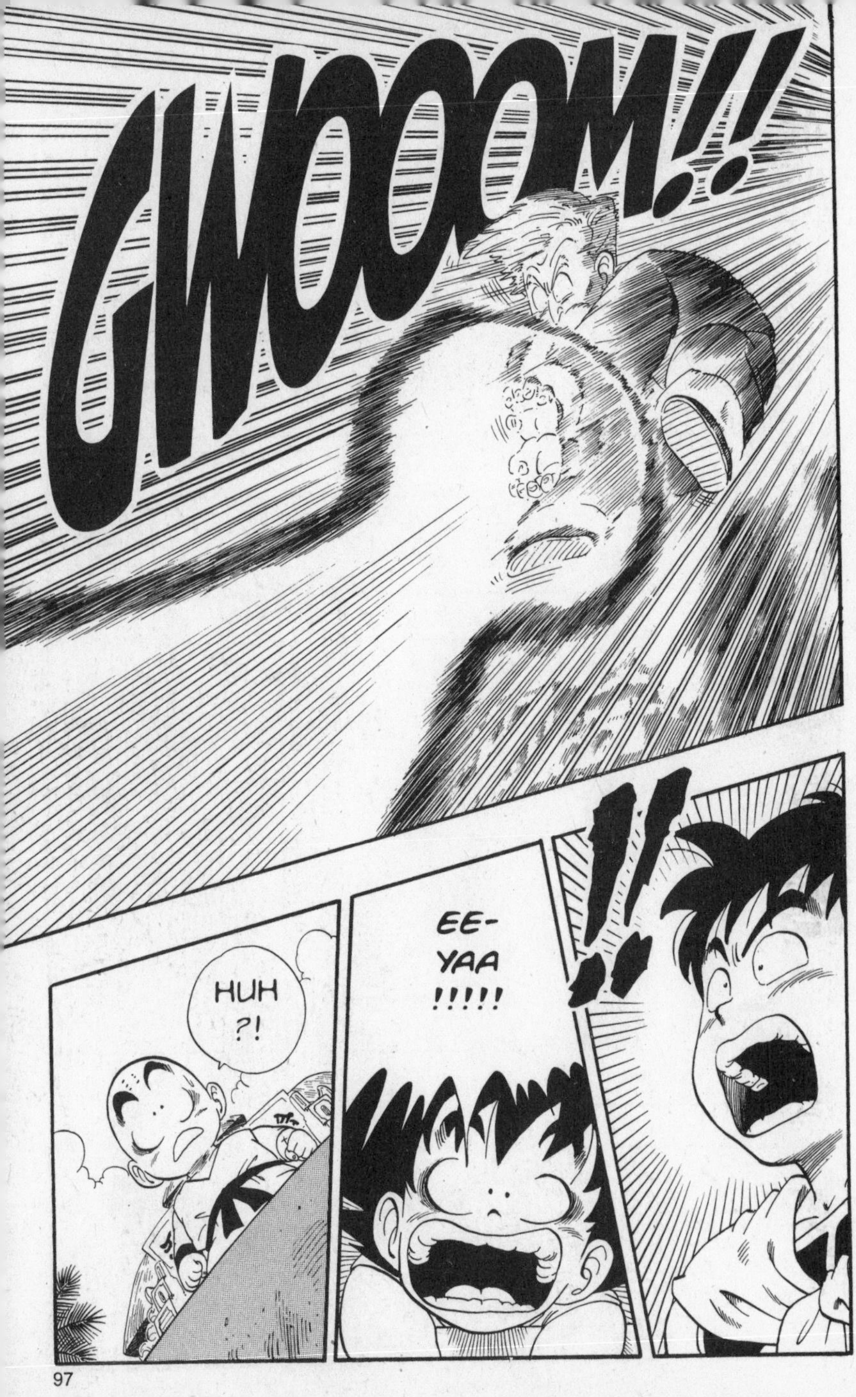
GWOOOM!!
!!
EE-YAA!!!!!
HUH ?!

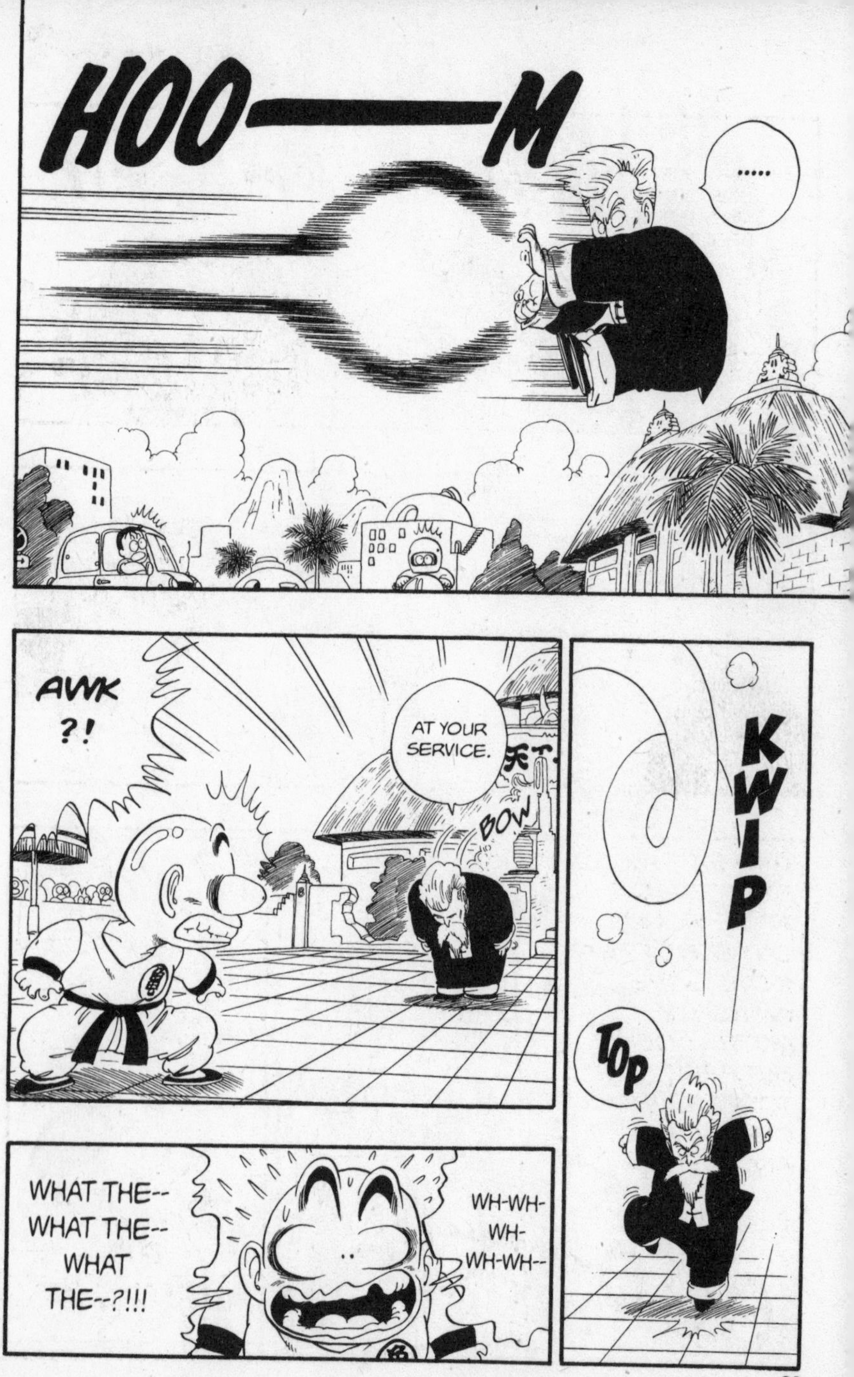
HOO——M
.....
KWIP
TOP
AT YOUR SERVICE.
BOW
AWK ?!
WH-WH-WH-WH-WH--
WHAT THE-- WHAT THE-- WHAT THE--?!!!

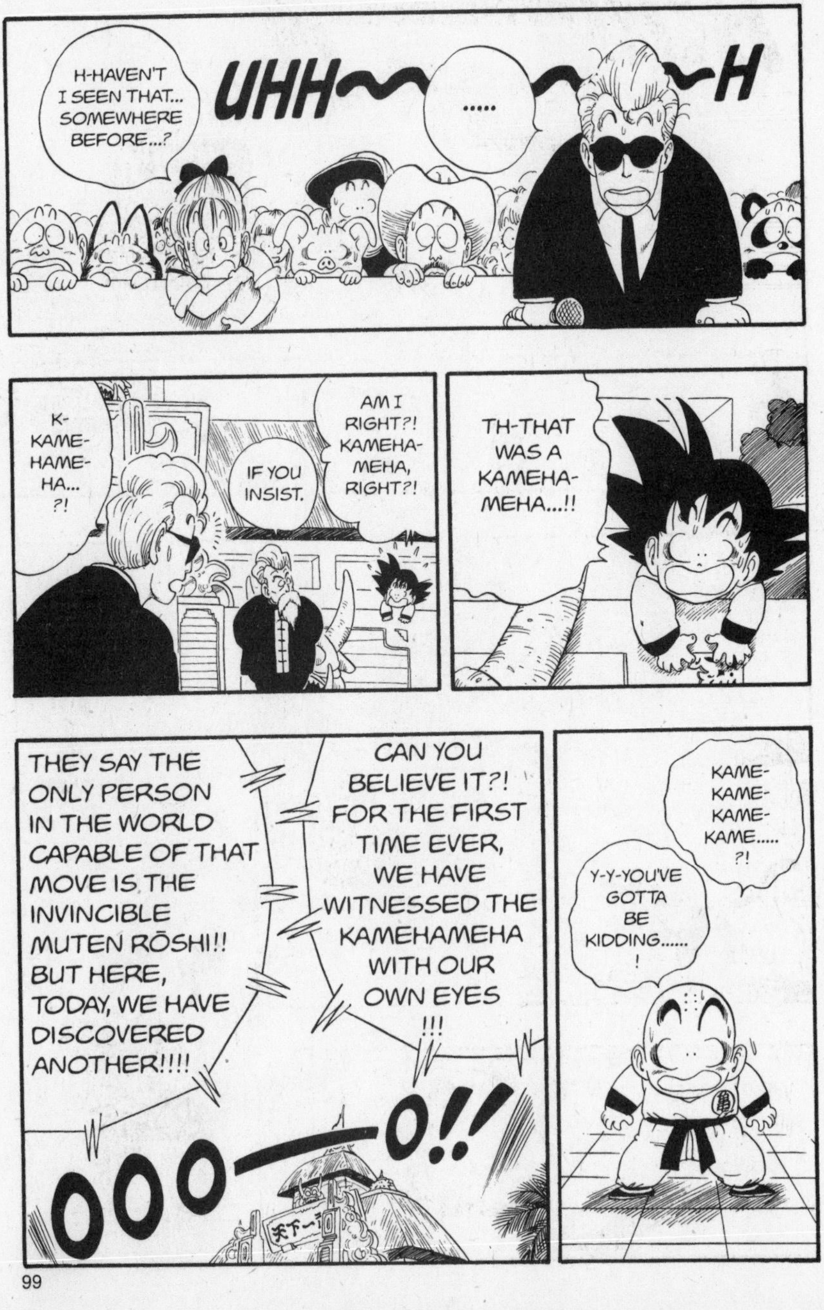
.....
UHH~~~~H
H-HAVEN'T I SEEN THAT... SOMEWHERE BEFORE...?
TH-THAT WAS A KAMEHA-MEHA...!!
AM I RIGHT?! KAMEHA-MEHA, RIGHT?!
IF YOU INSIST.
K-KAME-HAME-HA... ?!
KAME-KAME-KAME-KAME..... ?!
Y-Y-YOU'VE GOTTA BE KIDDING...... !
CAN YOU BELIEVE IT?! FOR THE FIRST TIME EVER, WE HAVE WITNESSED THE KAMEHAMEHA WITH OUR OWN EYES !!!
THEY SAY THE ONLY PERSON IN THE WORLD CAPABLE OF THAT MOVE IS THE INVINCIBLE MUTEN RŌSHI!! BUT HERE, TODAY, WE HAVE DISCOVERED ANOTHER!!!!
OOO—O!!

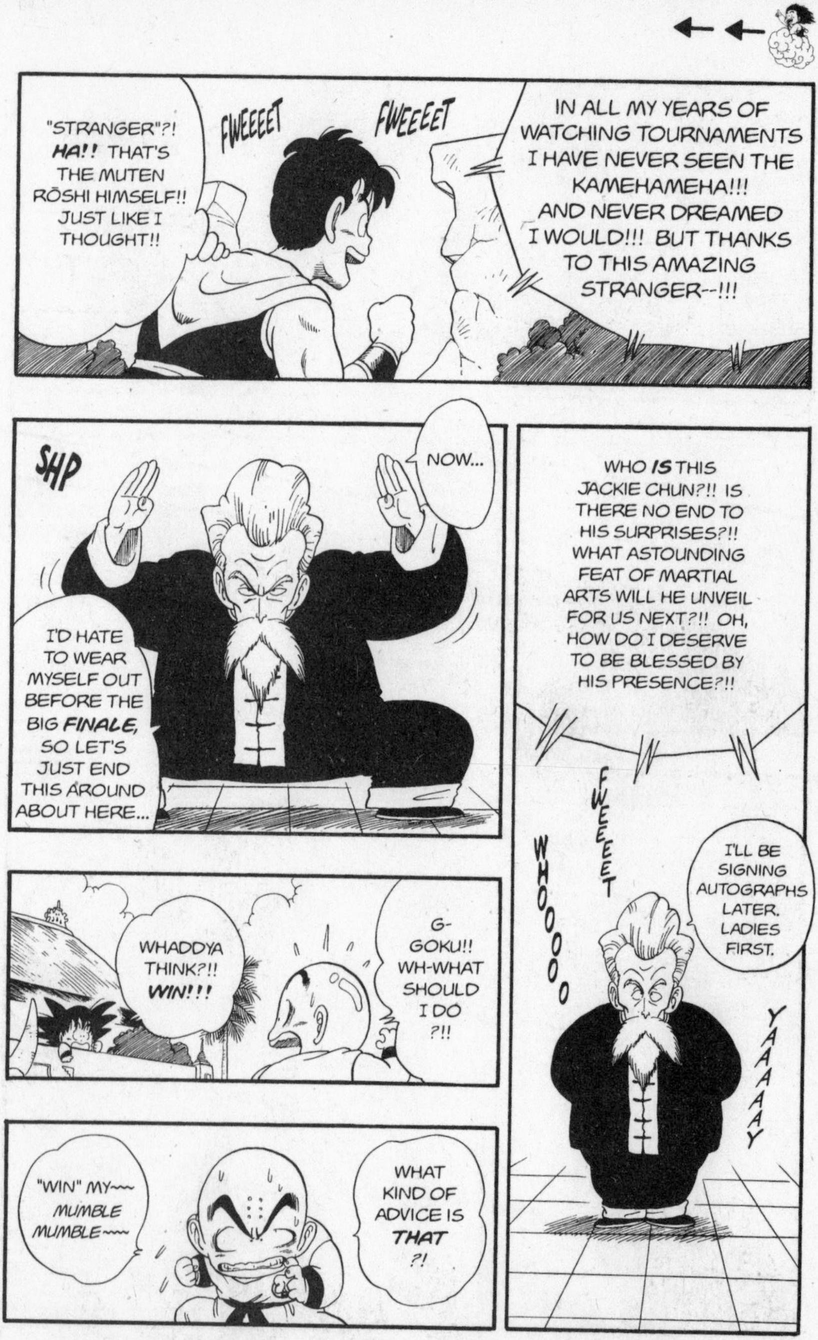

FWEEEEET
FWEEEEET
IN ALL MY YEARS OF WATCHING TOURNAMENTS I HAVE NEVER SEEN THE KAMEHAMEHA!!! AND NEVER DREAMED I WOULD!!! BUT THANKS TO THIS AMAZING STRANGER--!!!
"STRANGER"?! **HA!!** THAT'S THE MUTEN RŌSHI HIMSELF!! JUST LIKE I THOUGHT!!
WHO **IS** THIS JACKIE CHUN?!! IS THERE NO END TO HIS SURPRISES?!! WHAT ASTOUNDING FEAT OF MARTIAL ARTS WILL HE UNVEIL FOR US NEXT?!! OH, HOW DO I DESERVE TO BE BLESSED BY HIS PRESENCE?!!
FWEEEET
WHOOOOOO
I'LL BE SIGNING AUTOGRAPHS LATER. LADIES FIRST.
YAAAAAY
SHP
NOW...
I'D HATE TO WEAR MYSELF OUT BEFORE THE BIG **FINALE**, SO LET'S JUST END THIS AROUND ABOUT HERE...
G-GOKU!! WH-WHAT SHOULD I DO ?!!
WHADDYA THINK?!! **WIN!!!**
WHAT KIND OF ADVICE IS **THAT** ?!
"WIN" MY~~ *MUMBLE MUMBLE*~~

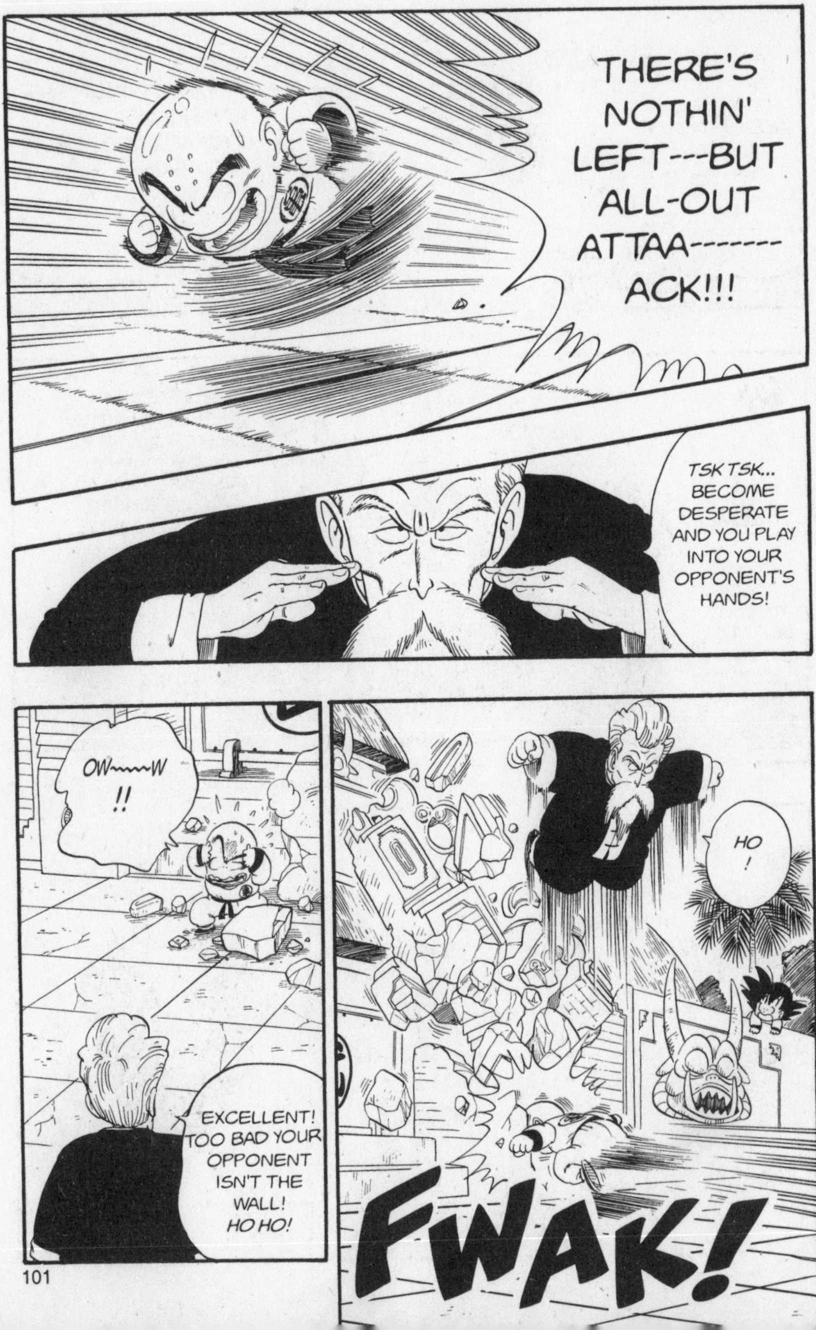
THERE'S NOTHIN' LEFT---BUT ALL-OUT ATTAA-------ACK!!!
TSK TSK... BECOME DESPERATE AND YOU PLAY INTO YOUR OPPONENT'S HANDS!
HO!
FWAK!
OW~~~W!!
EXCELLENT! TOO BAD YOUR OPPONENT ISN'T THE WALL! HO HO!

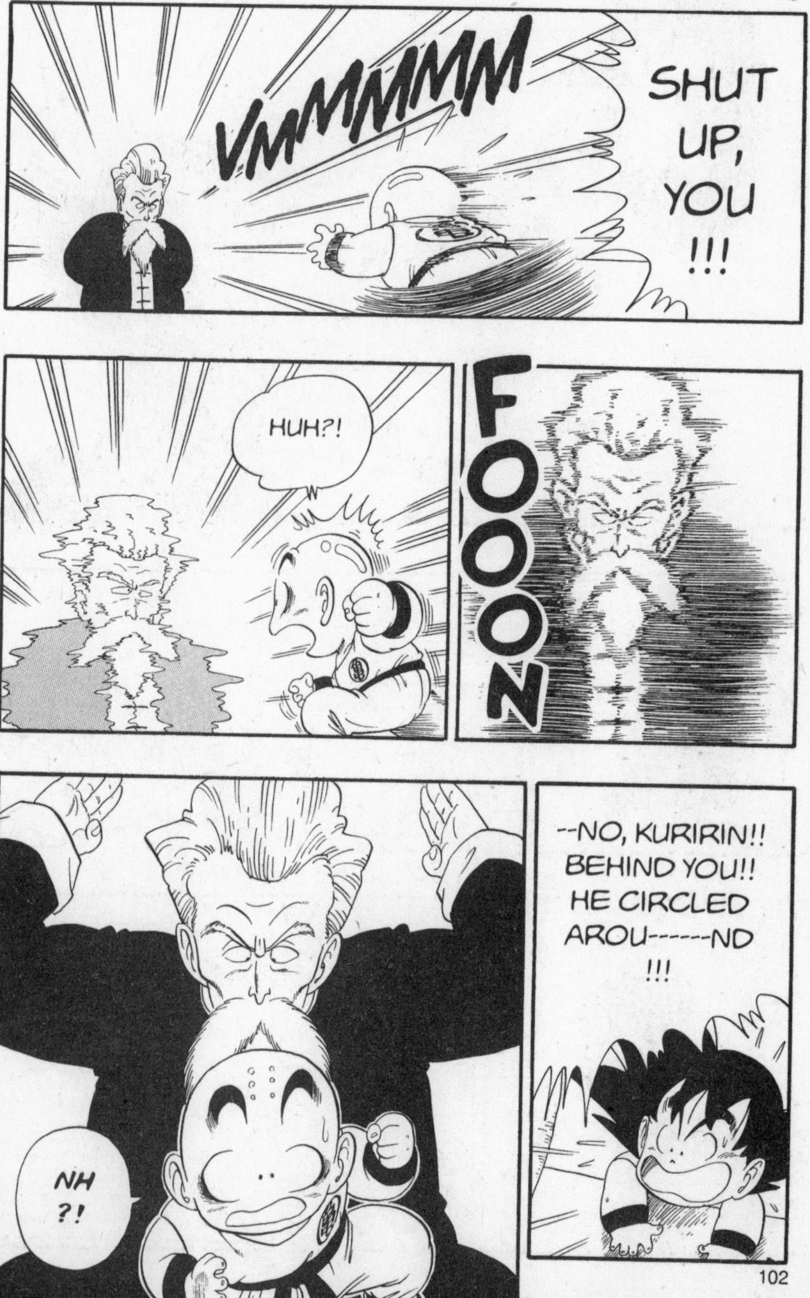
SHUT UP, YOU !!!
VMMMMM
FOOOON
HUH?!
--NO, KURIRIN!! BEHIND YOU!! HE CIRCLED AROU------ND !!!
NH ?!

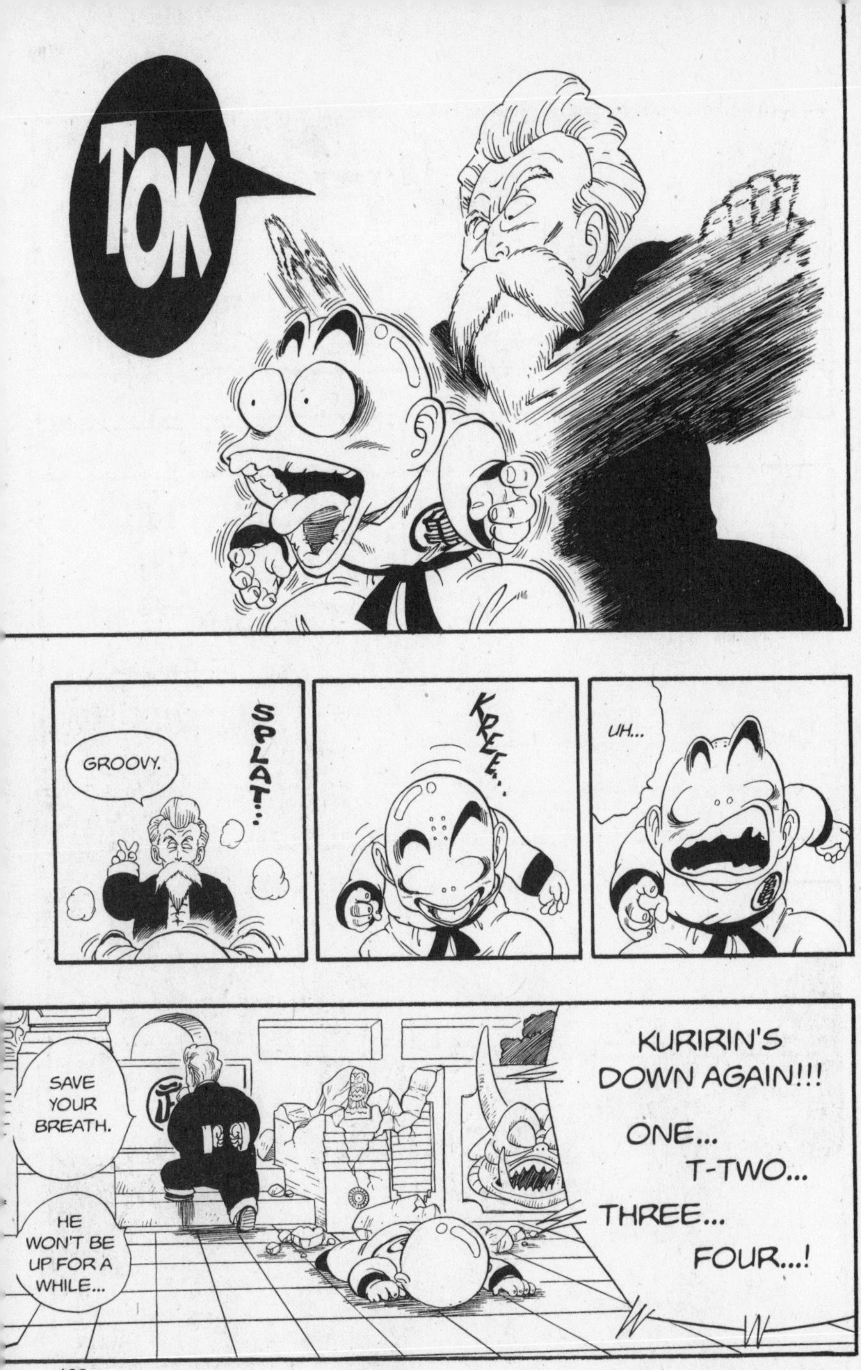
TOK
UH...
KREE...
GROOVY.
SPLAT...
KURIRIN'S DOWN AGAIN!!!
ONE...
T-TWO...
THREE...
FOUR...!
SAVE YOUR BREATH.
HE WON'T BE UP FOR A WHILE...

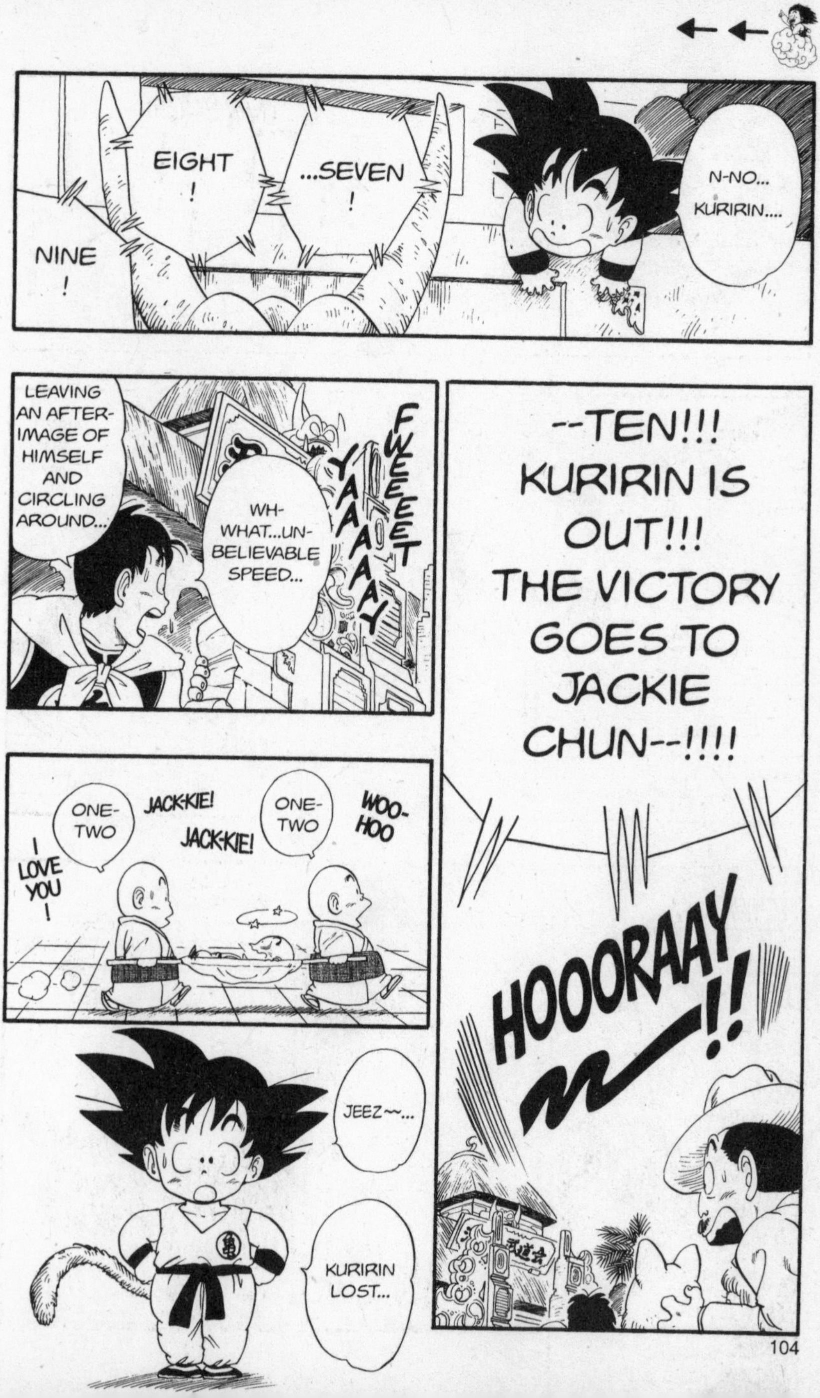
N-NO... KURIRIN....
...SEVEN!
EIGHT!
NINE!
--TEN!!! KURIRIN IS OUT!!! THE VICTORY GOES TO JACKIE CHUN--!!!!
HOOORAAY—!!
FWEEEET
YAAAAAAY
WH-WHAT...UN-BELIEVABLE SPEED...
LEAVING AN AFTER-IMAGE OF HIMSELF AND CIRCLING AROUND...
WOO-HOO
ONE-TWO
JACK-KIE!
JACK-KIE!
ONE-TWO
I LOVE YOU!
JEEZ~...
KURIRIN LOST...

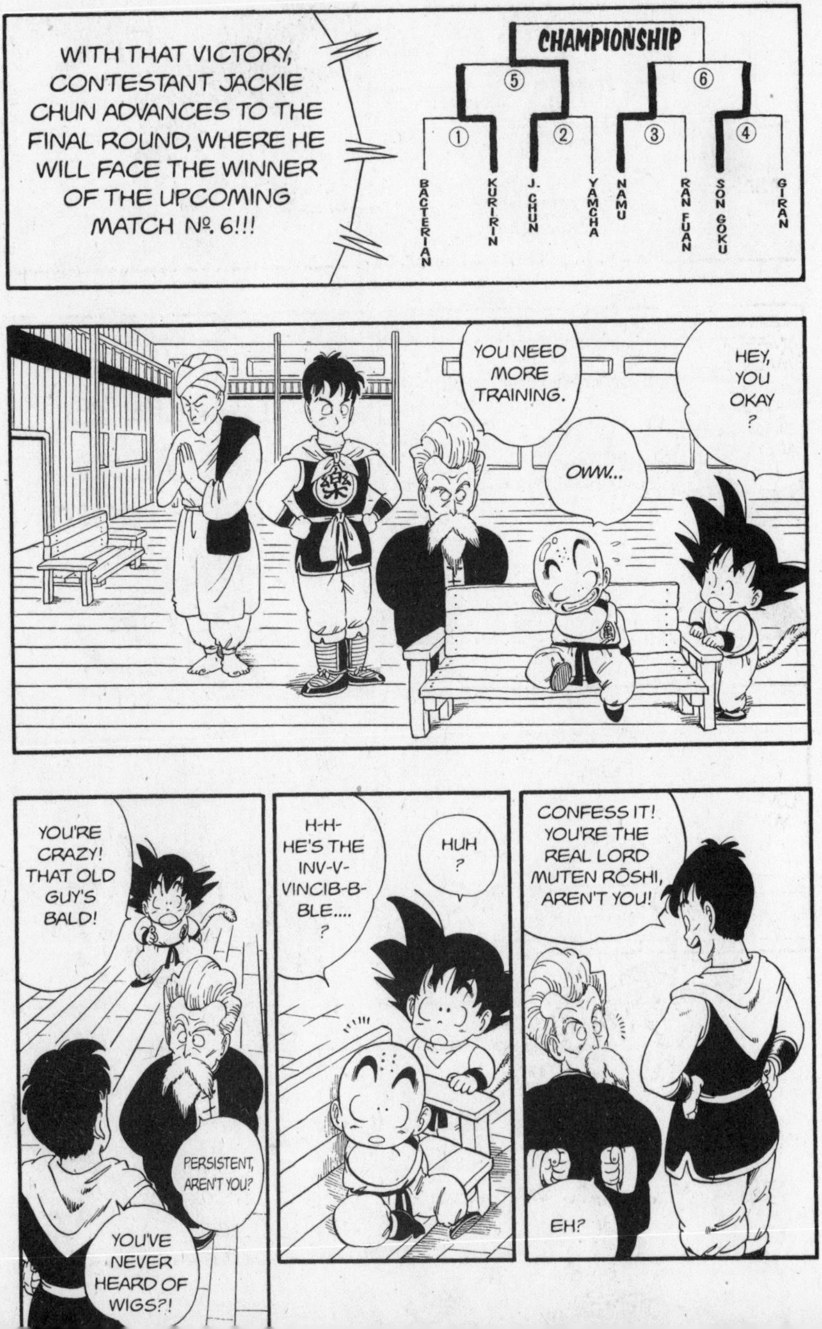
CHAMPIONSHIP
⑤
⑥
①
②
③
④
BACTERIAN
KURIRIN
J. CHUN
YAMCHA
NAMU
RAN FUAN
SON GOKU
GIRAN
WITH THAT VICTORY, CONTESTANT JACKIE CHUN ADVANCES TO THE FINAL ROUND, WHERE HE WILL FACE THE WINNER OF THE UPCOMING MATCH №. 6!!!
HEY, YOU OKAY?
OWW...
YOU NEED MORE TRAINING.
CONFESS IT! YOU'RE THE REAL LORD MUTEN RŌSHI, AREN'T YOU!
EH?
HUH?
H-H-HE'S THE INV-V-VINCIB-B-BLE....?
YOU'RE CRAZY! THAT OLD GUY'S BALD!
PERSISTENT, AREN'T YOU?
YOU'VE NEVER HEARD OF WIGS?!

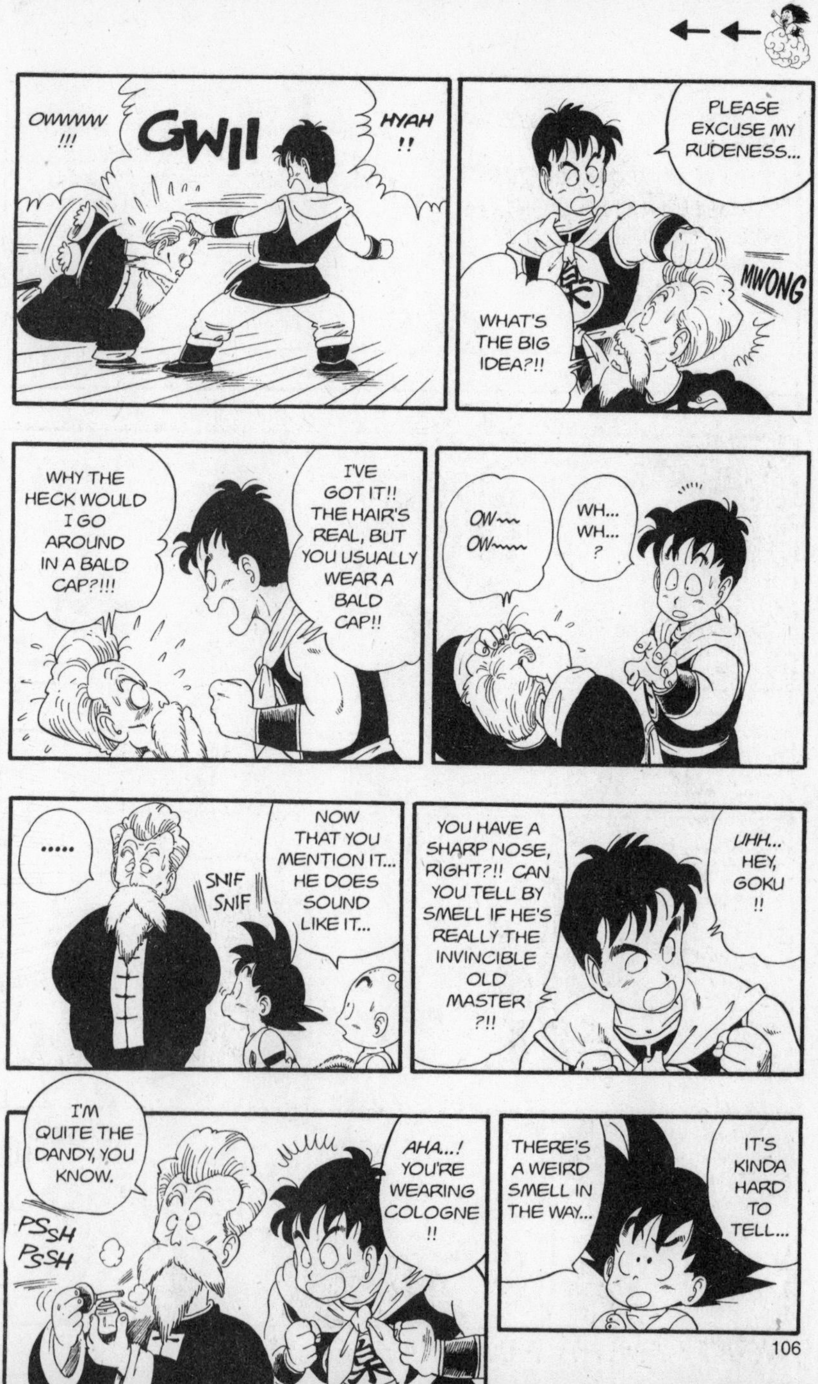
PLEASE EXCUSE MY RUDENESS...
MWONG
WHAT'S THE BIG IDEA?!!
HYAH!!
GWII
OWWWW!!!
WH... WH...?
OW~ OW~
I'VE GOT IT!! THE HAIR'S REAL, BUT YOU USUALLY WEAR A BALD CAP!!
WHY THE HECK WOULD I GO AROUND IN A BALD CAP?!!!
UHH... HEY, GOKU!!
YOU HAVE A SHARP NOSE, RIGHT?!! CAN YOU TELL BY SMELL IF HE'S REALLY THE INVINCIBLE OLD MASTER?!!
NOW THAT YOU MENTION IT... HE DOES SOUND LIKE IT...
SNIF SNIF
......
IT'S KINDA HARD TO TELL...
THERE'S A WEIRD SMELL IN THE WAY...
AHA...! YOU'RE WEARING COLOGNE!!
I'M QUITE THE DANDY, YOU KNOW.
PSSH PSSH

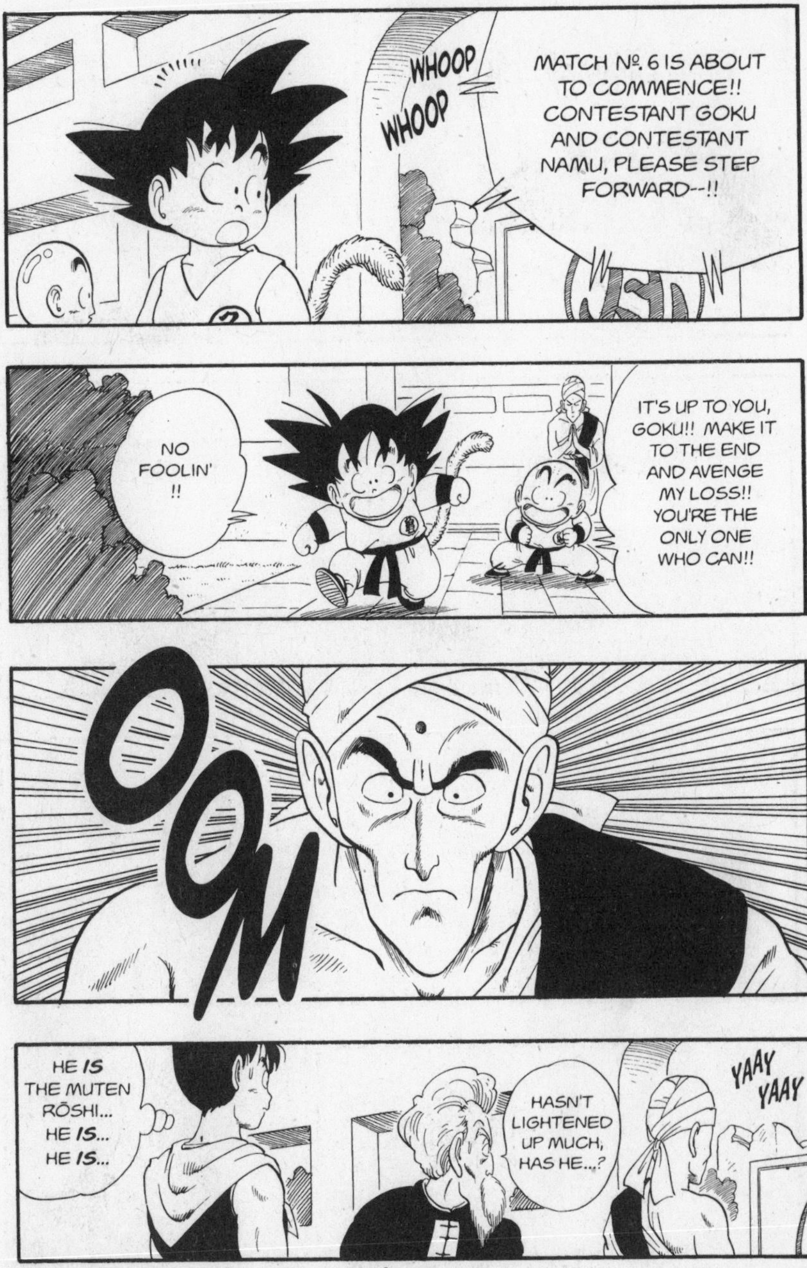
MATCH №. 6 IS ABOUT TO COMMENCE!! CONTESTANT GOKU AND CONTESTANT NAMU, PLEASE STEP FORWARD--!!
WHOOP
WHOOP
IT'S UP TO YOU, GOKU!! MAKE IT TO THE END AND AVENGE MY LOSS!! YOU'RE THE ONLY ONE WHO CAN!!
NO FOOLIN' !!
OOM
YAAY
YAAY
HASN'T LIGHTENED UP MUCH, HAS HE...?
HE *IS* THE MUTEN RŌSHI... HE *IS*... HE *IS*...

***NEXT*: For His People's Sake...!**

DRAGON BALL

Tale 44 • The Name of the Game is Namu

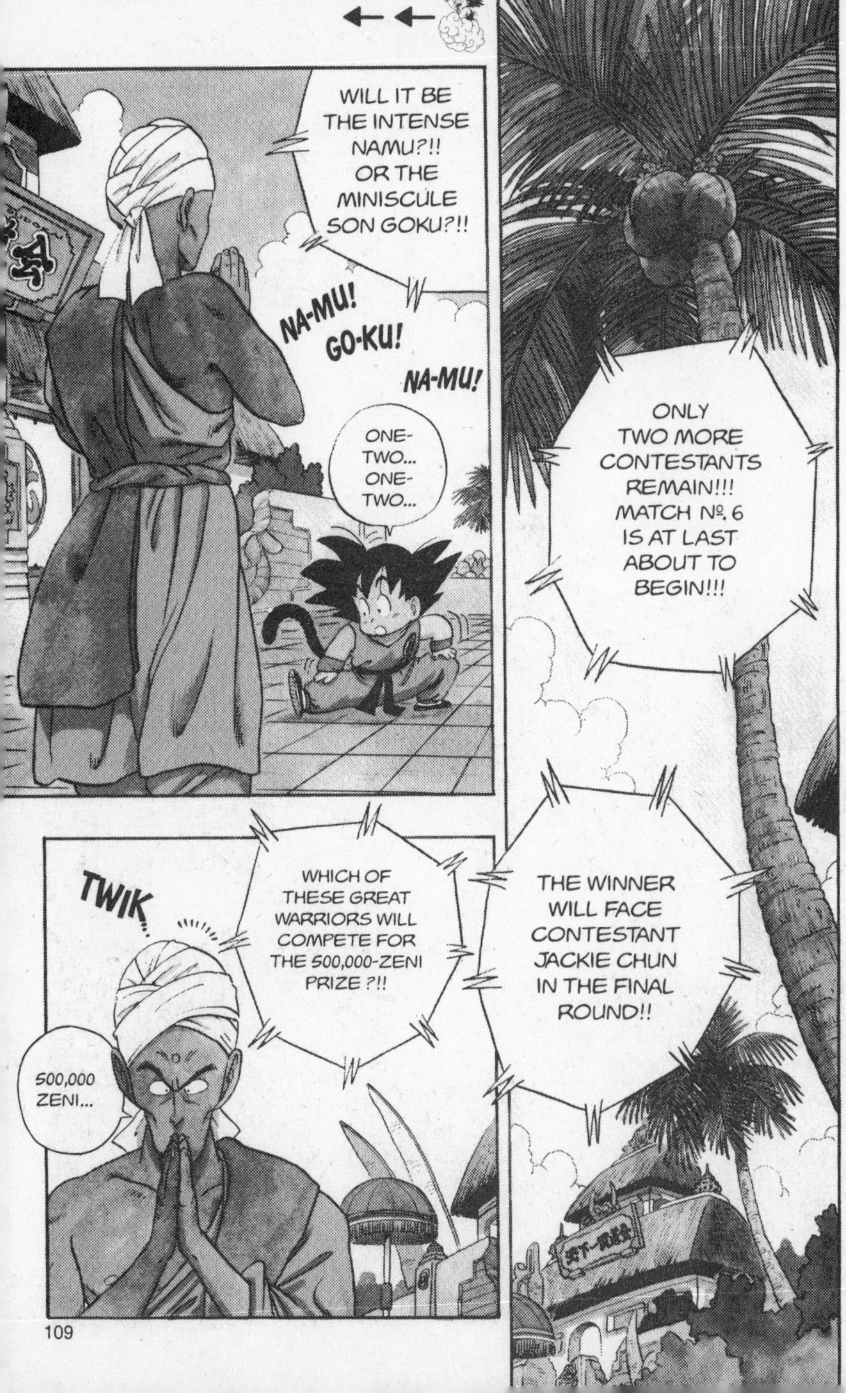
ONLY TWO MORE CONTESTANTS REMAIN!!! MATCH №. 6 IS AT LAST ABOUT TO BEGIN!!!
THE WINNER WILL FACE CONTESTANT JACKIE CHUN IN THE FINAL ROUND!!
WILL IT BE THE INTENSE NAMU?!! OR THE MINISCULE SON GOKU?!!
NA-MU!
GO-KU!
NA-MU!
ONE-TWO... ONE-TWO...
WHICH OF THESE GREAT WARRIORS WILL COMPETE FOR THE 500,000-ZENI PRIZE ?!!
TWIK
500,000 ZENI...

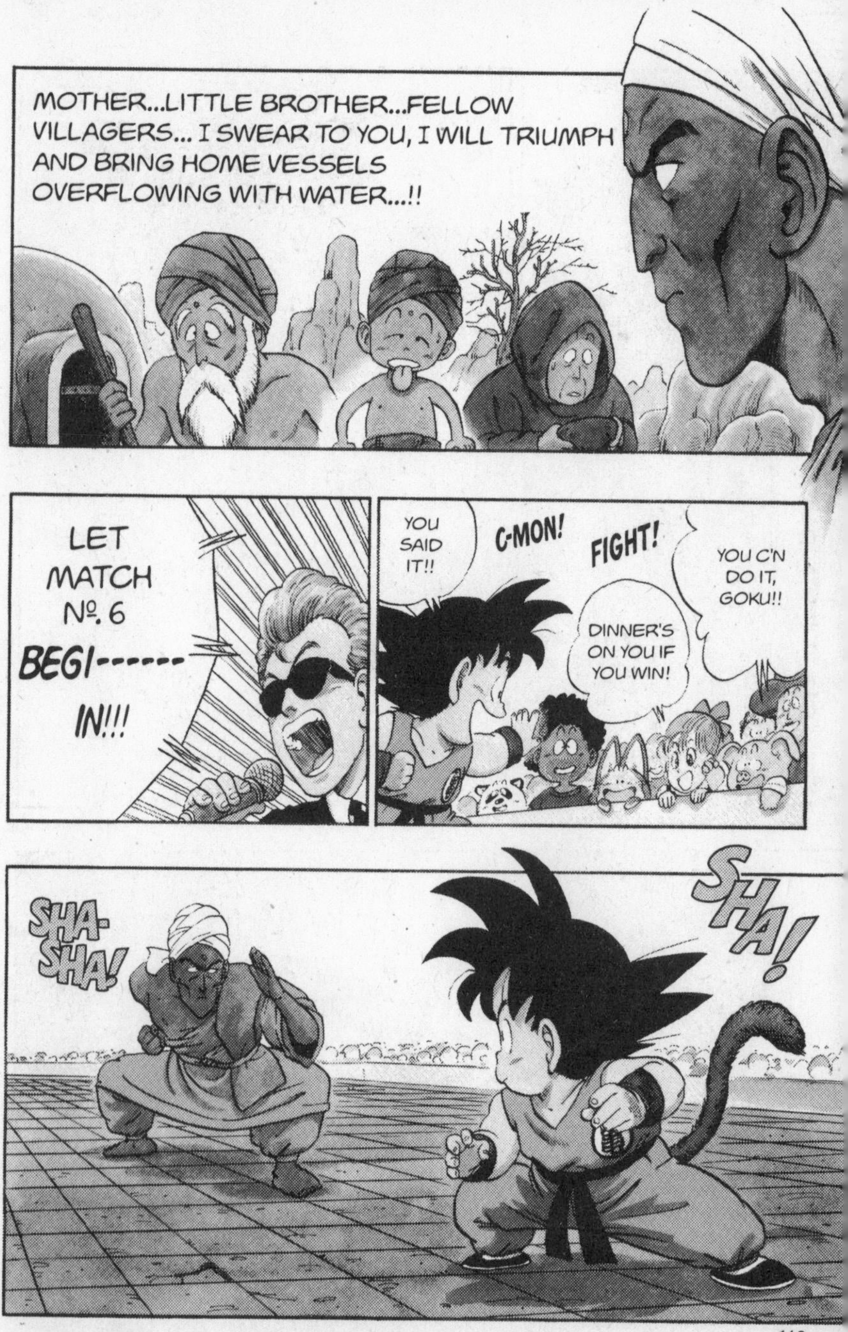
MOTHER...LITTLE BROTHER...FELLOW VILLAGERS... I SWEAR TO YOU, I WILL TRIUMPH AND BRING HOME VESSELS OVERFLOWING WITH WATER...!!
YOU C'N DO IT, GOKU!!
FIGHT!
DINNER'S ON YOU IF YOU WIN!
C-MON!
YOU SAID IT!!
LET MATCH №. 6 BEGI------
IN!!!
SHA!
SHA-SHA!

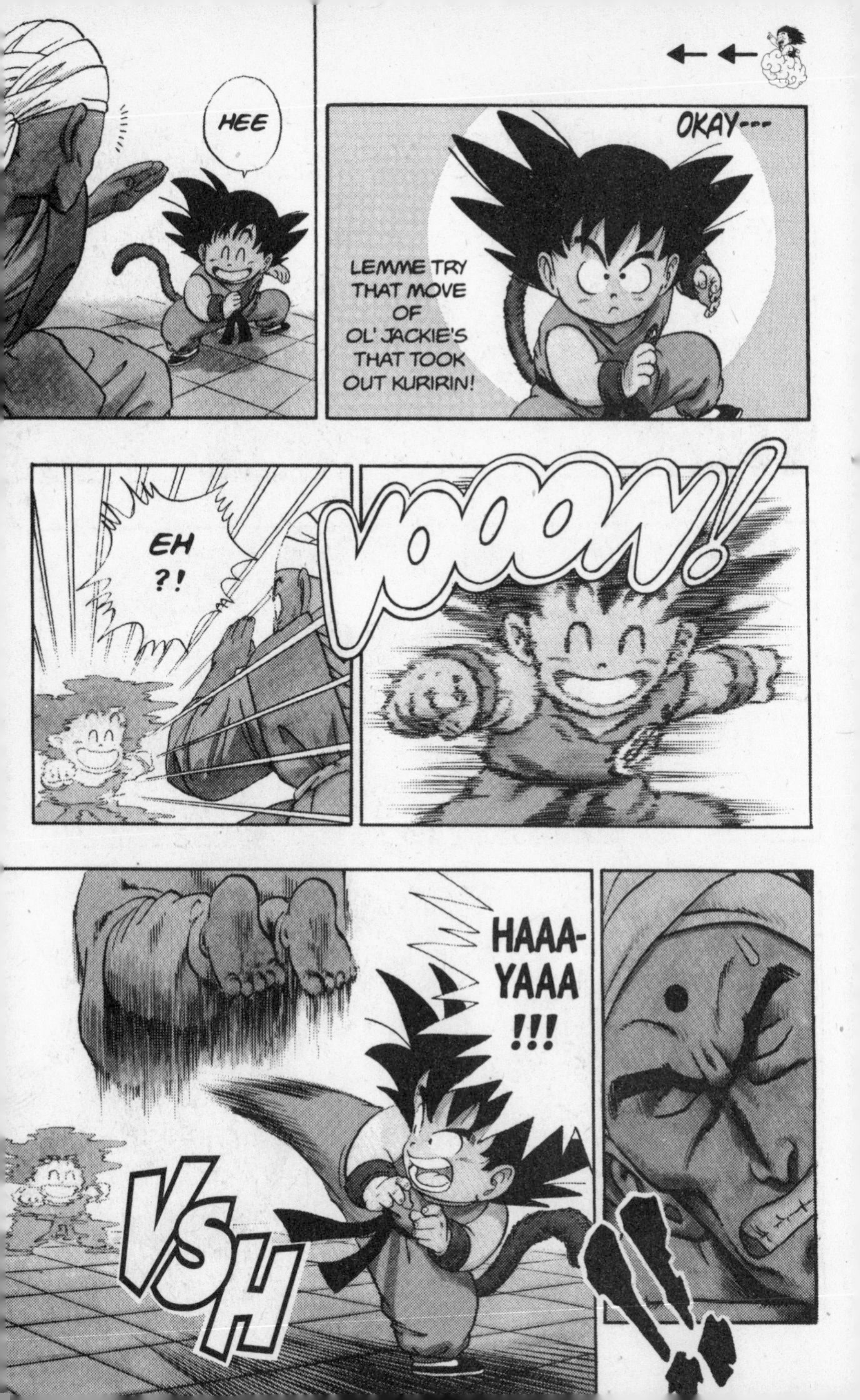
OKAY...
LEMME TRY THAT MOVE OF OL' JACKIE'S THAT TOOK OUT KURIRIN!
HEE
VOOOM!
EH ?!
HAAA-YAAA !!!
VSH
!!

BONUS!

WHEN THIS COMIC RAN IN **SHÔNEN JUMP** MAGAZINE, THERE WAS PROBABLY AN AD ON THIS PAGE!

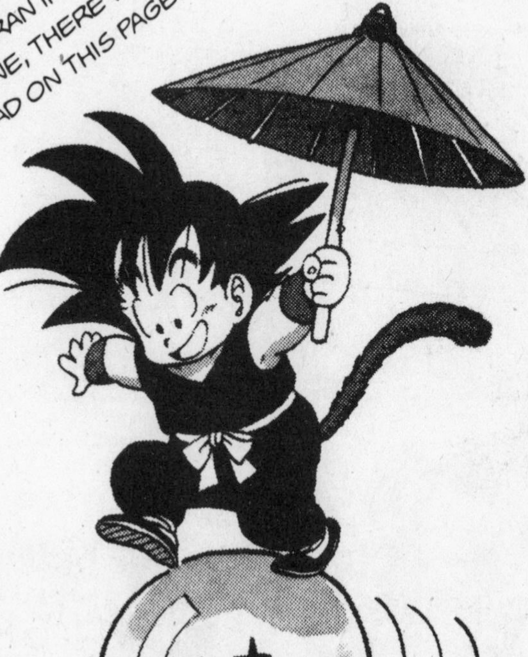

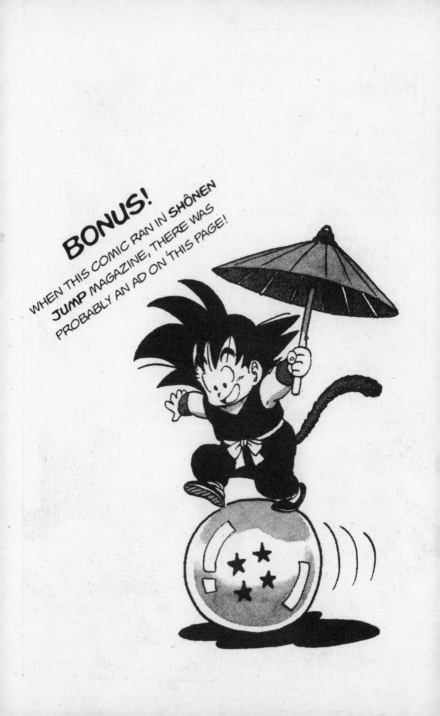

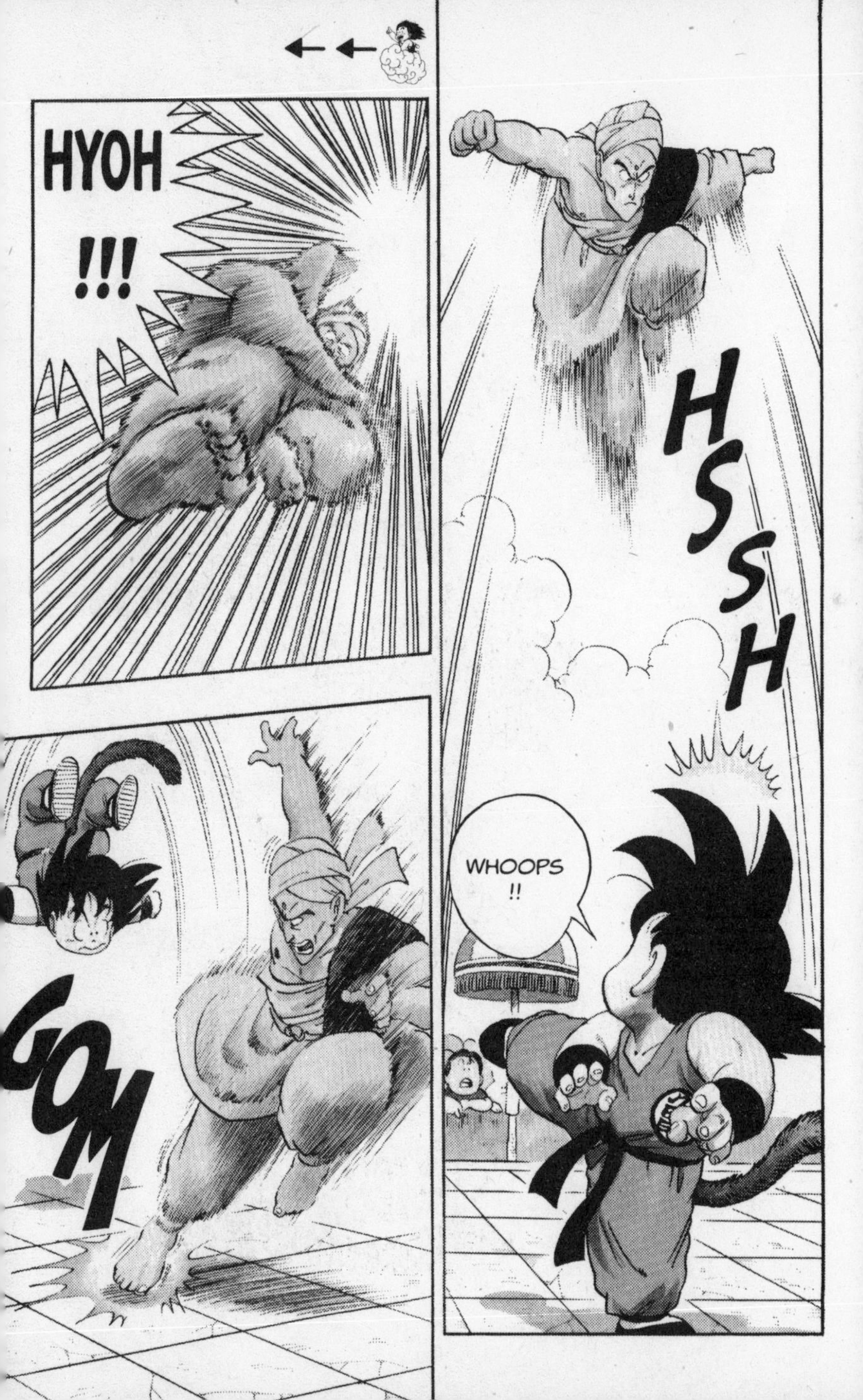
HSSH
WHOOPS !!
HYOH !!!
GOM

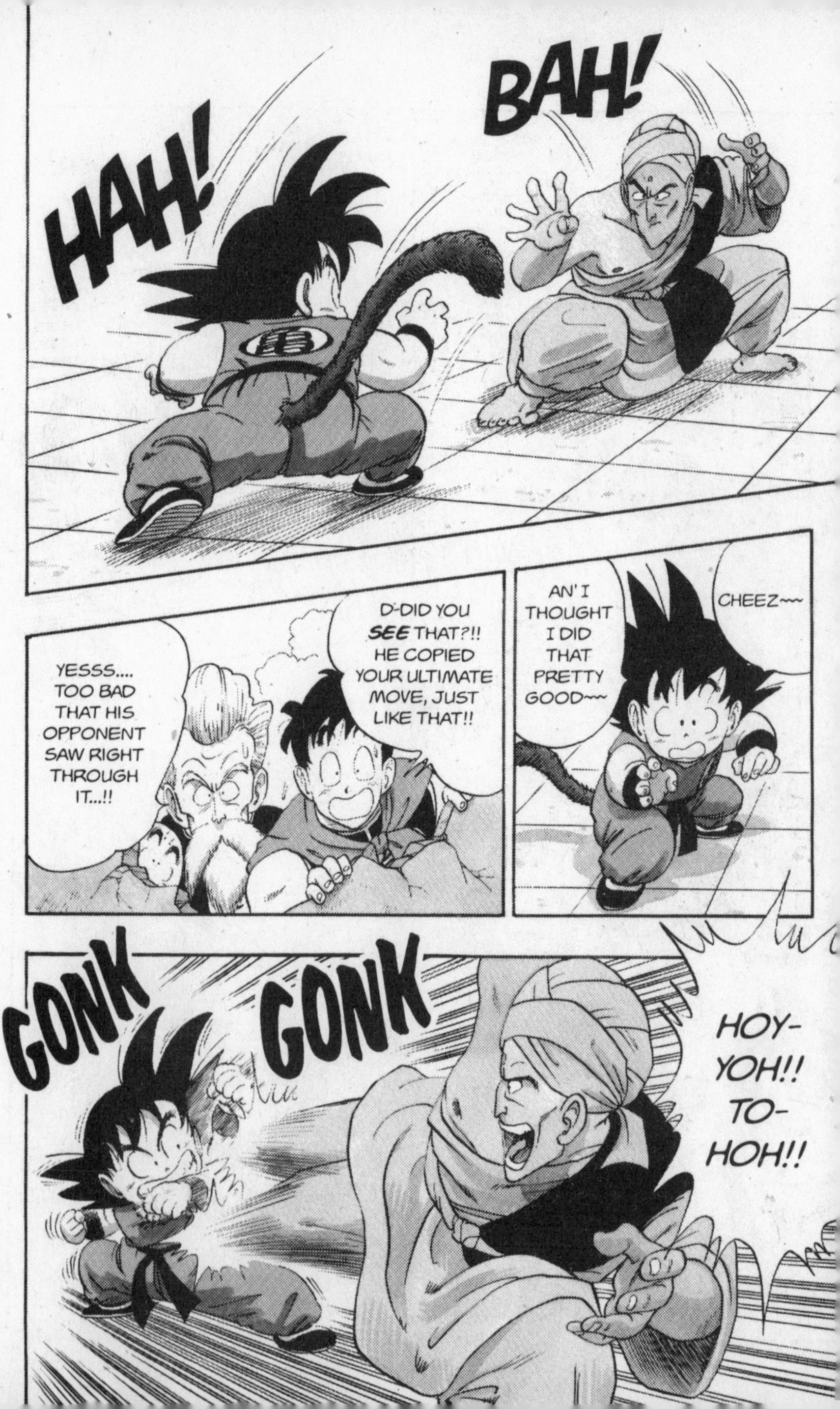
BAH!
HAH!
CHEEZ~~
AN' I THOUGHT I DID THAT PRETTY GOOD~~
D-DID YOU SEE THAT?!! HE COPIED YOUR ULTIMATE MOVE, JUST LIKE THAT!!
YESSS.... TOO BAD THAT HIS OPPONENT SAW RIGHT THROUGH IT...!!
HOY-YOH!! TO-HOH!!
GONK
GONK

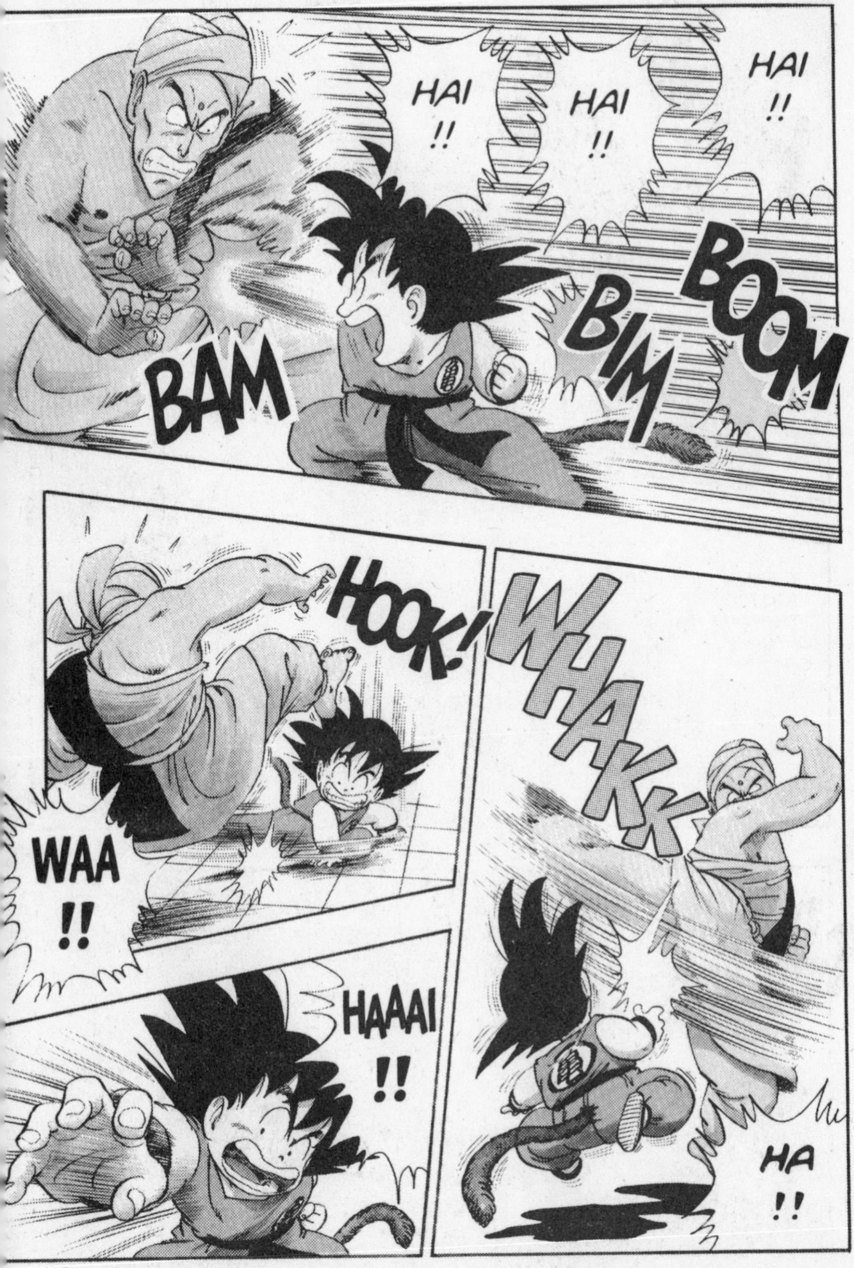
HAI !!
HAI !!
HAI !!
BOOM
BIM
BAM
WHAKK
HA !!
HOOK!
WAA !!
HAAAI !!

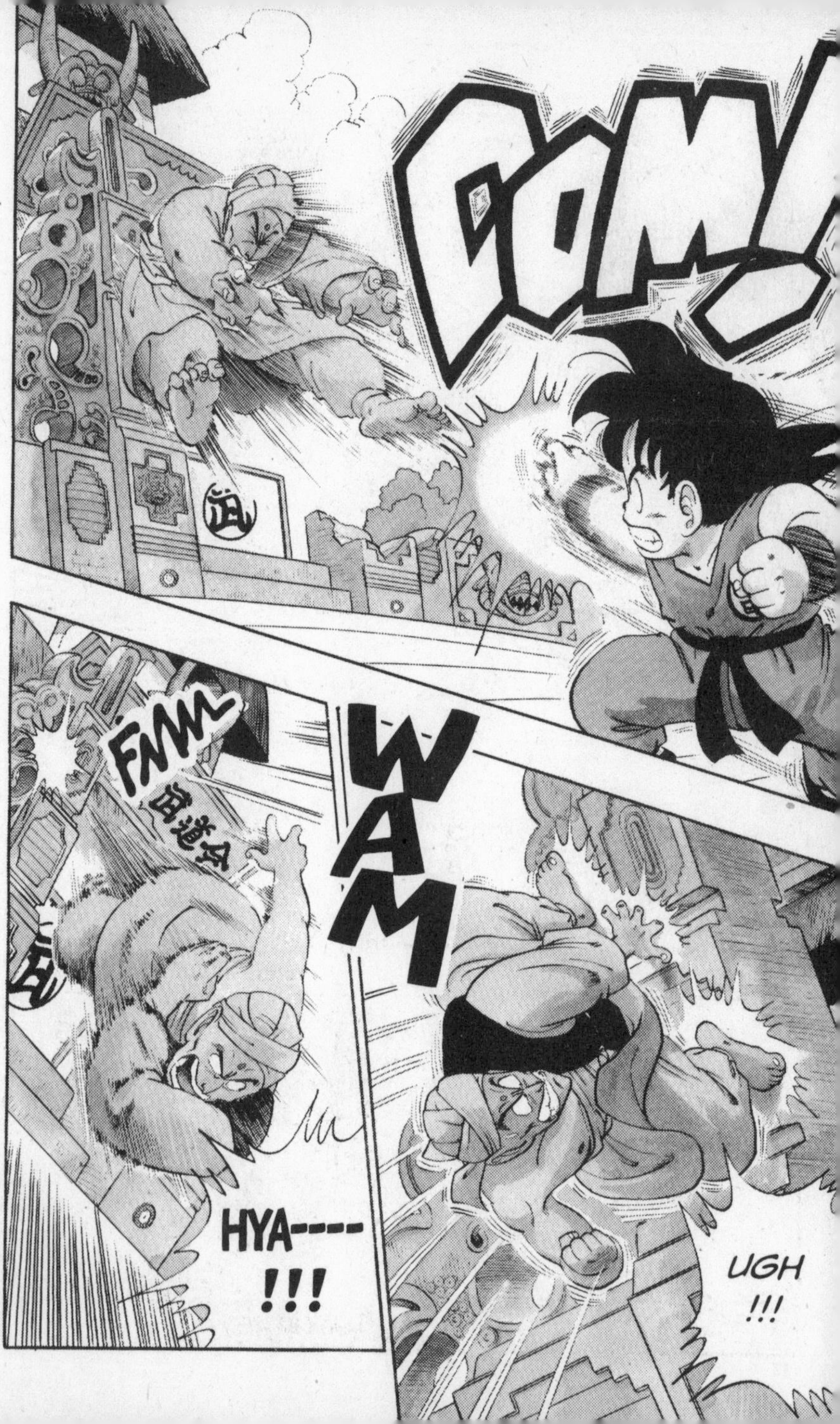

COM
WAM
UGH !!!
FWM
HYA---- !!!

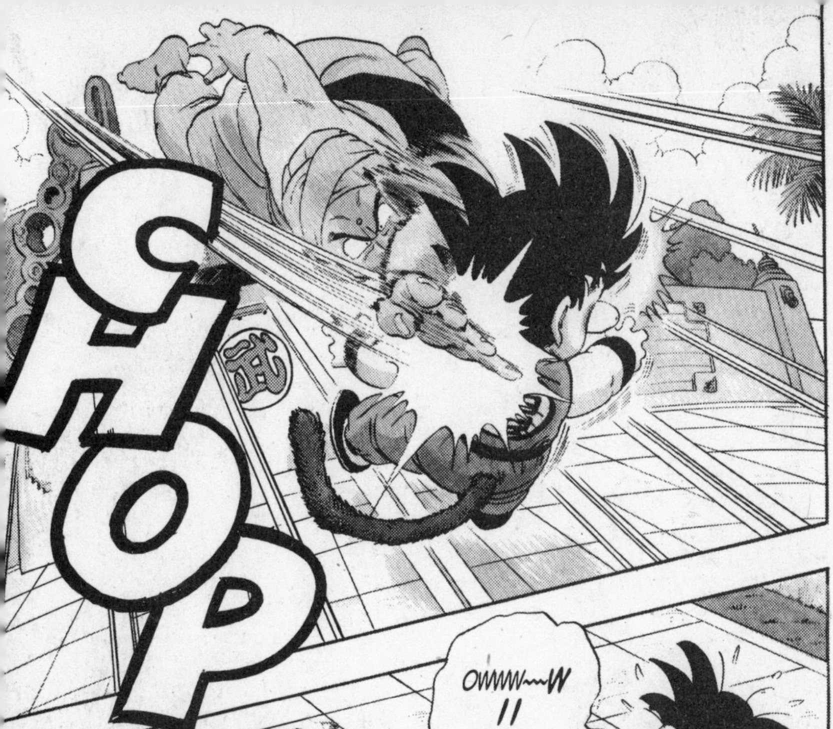
CHOP

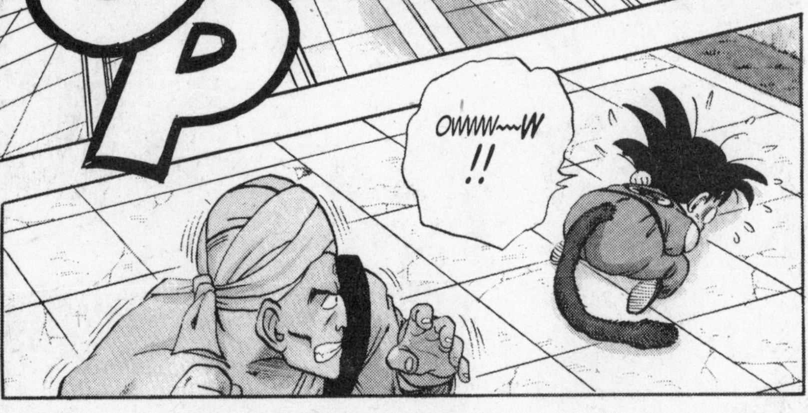
OWWW---W !!

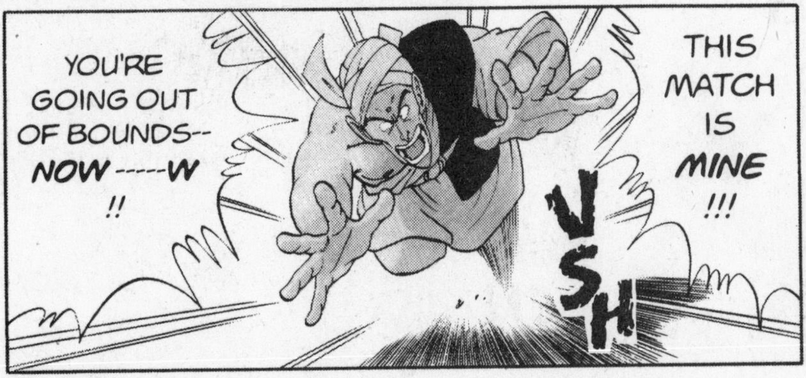
THIS MATCH IS MINE !!!
VSH
YOU'RE GOING OUT OF BOUNDS-- NOW -----W !!

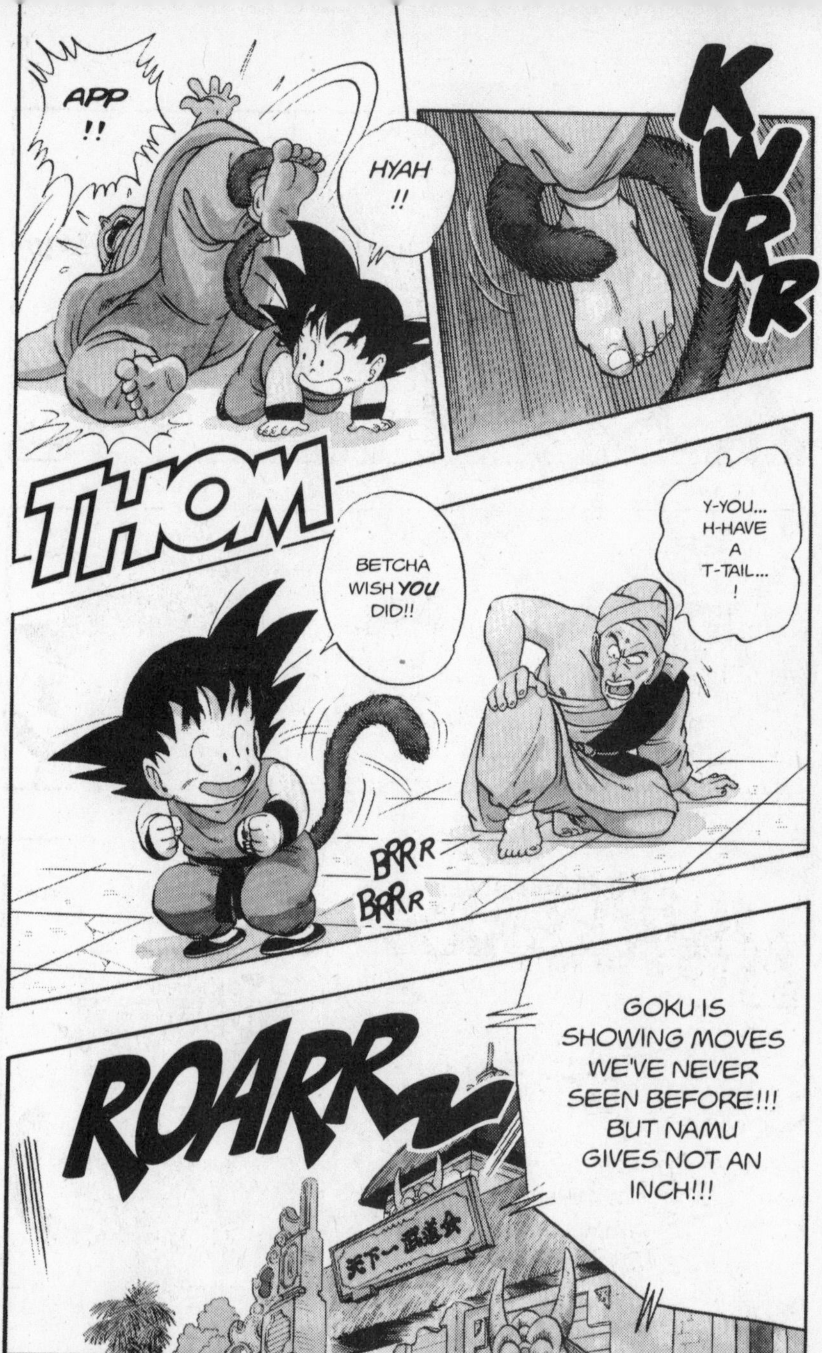
KWRR
APP!!
HYAH!!
THOM
Y-YOU... H-HAVE A T-TAIL...!
BETCHA WISH YOU DID!!
BRRR
BRRR
GOKU IS SHOWING MOVES WE'VE NEVER SEEN BEFORE!!! BUT NAMU GIVES NOT AN INCH!!!
ROARR
天下一武道会

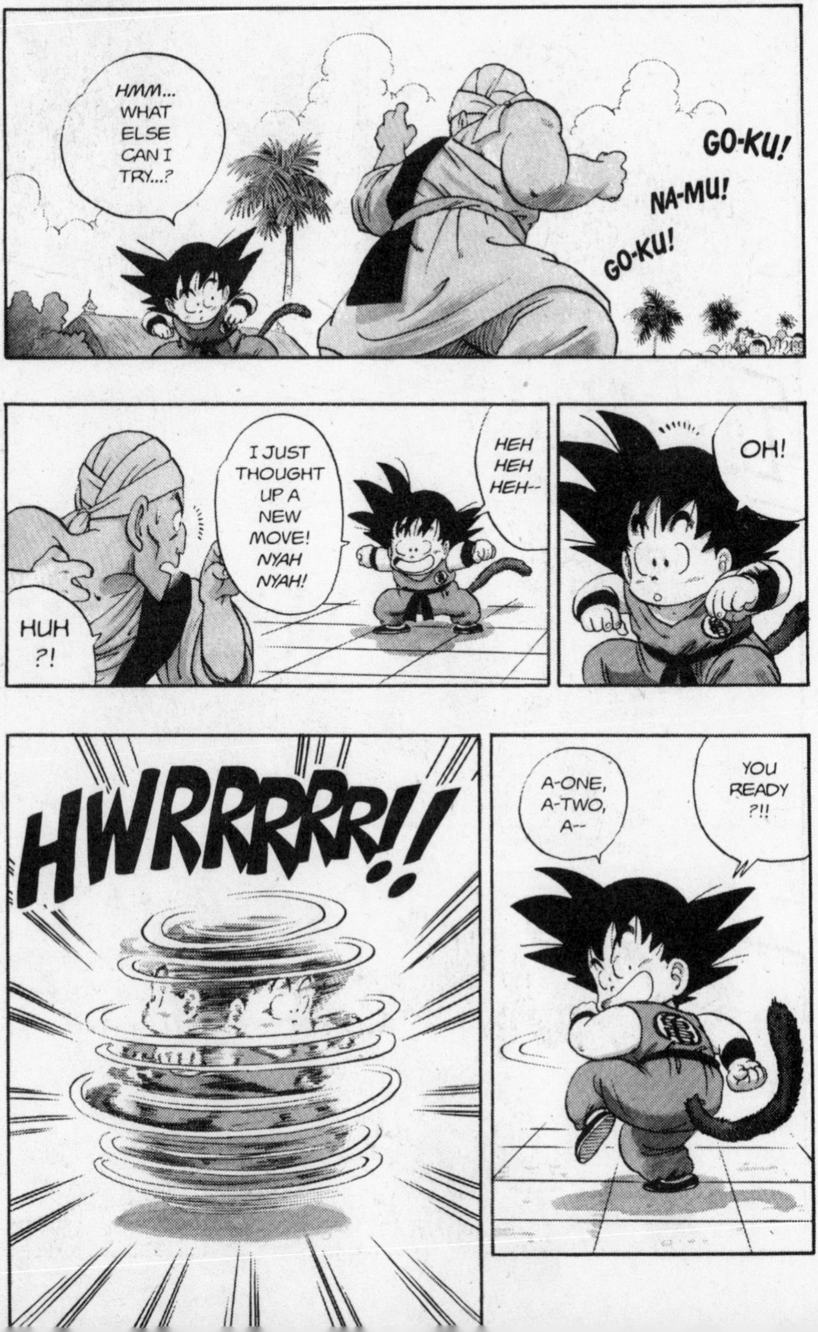
GO-KU!
NA-MU!
GO-KU!
HMM... WHAT ELSE CAN I TRY...?
OH!
HEH HEH HEH--
I JUST THOUGHT UP A NEW MOVE! NYAH NYAH!
HUH ?!
YOU READY ?!!
A-ONE, A-TWO, A--
HWRRRRR!!

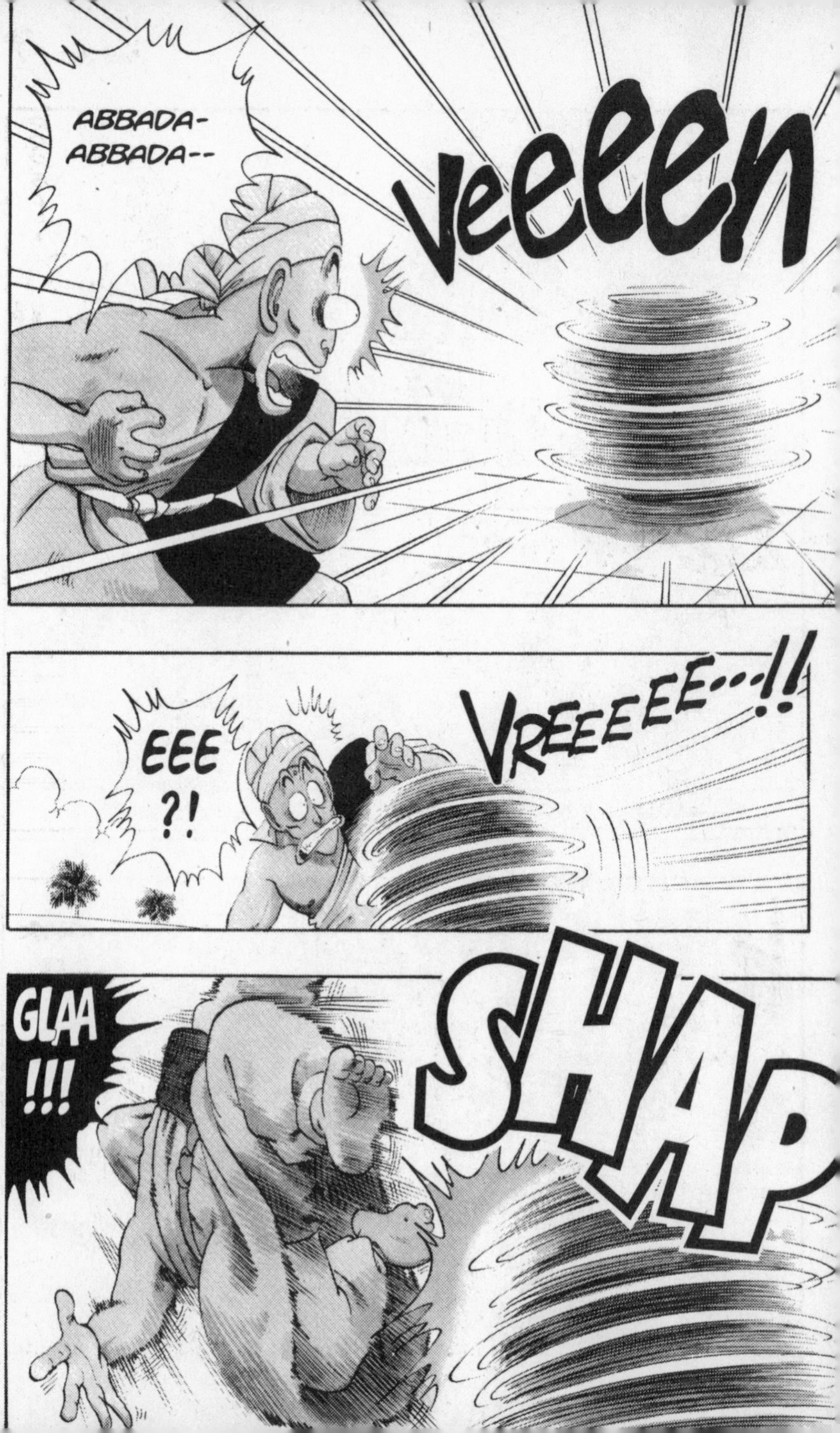
VEEEEN
ABBADA-ABBADA--
VREEEEEE...!!
EEE ?!
SHAP
GLAA !!!

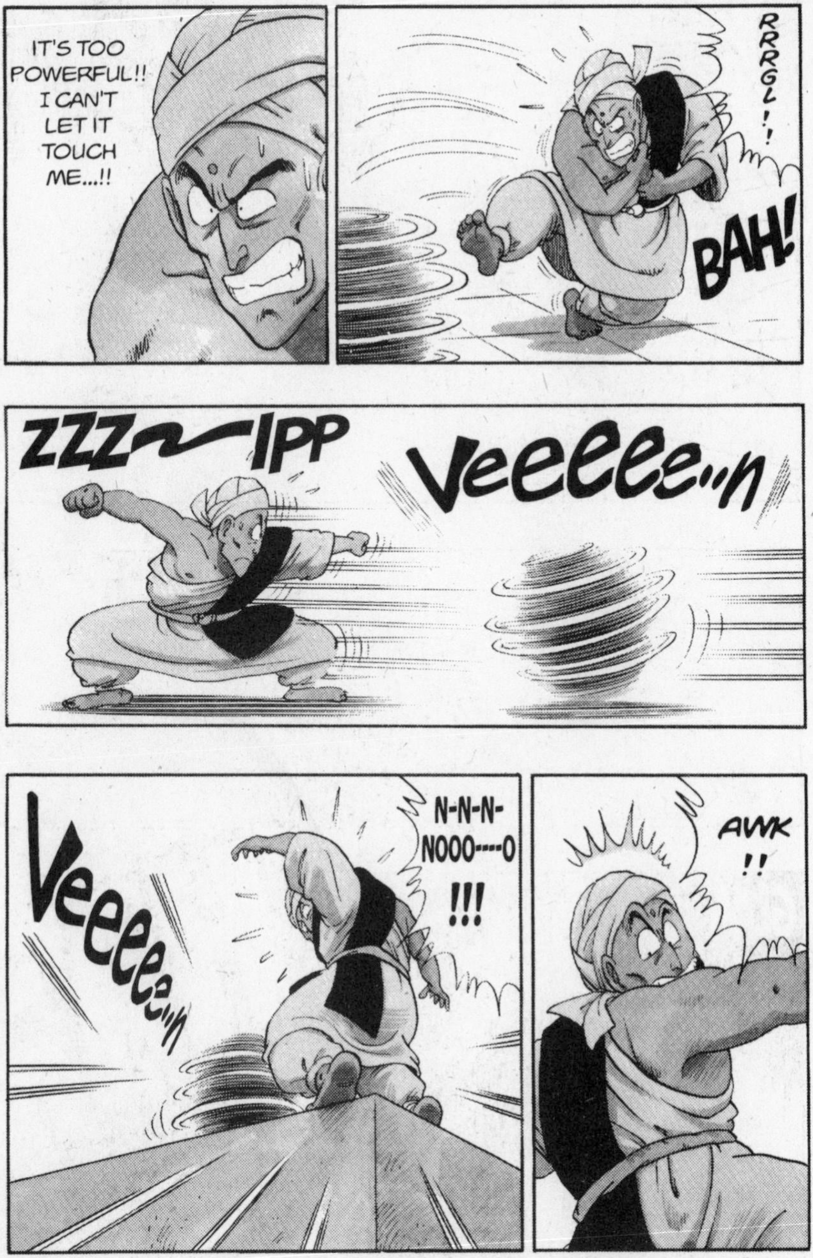
RRRGL!!
BAH!
IT'S TOO POWERFUL!! I CAN'T LET IT TOUCH ME...!!
Veeeee..n
ZZZ~IPP
AWK !!
N-N-N-NOOO----O !!!
Veeeee..n

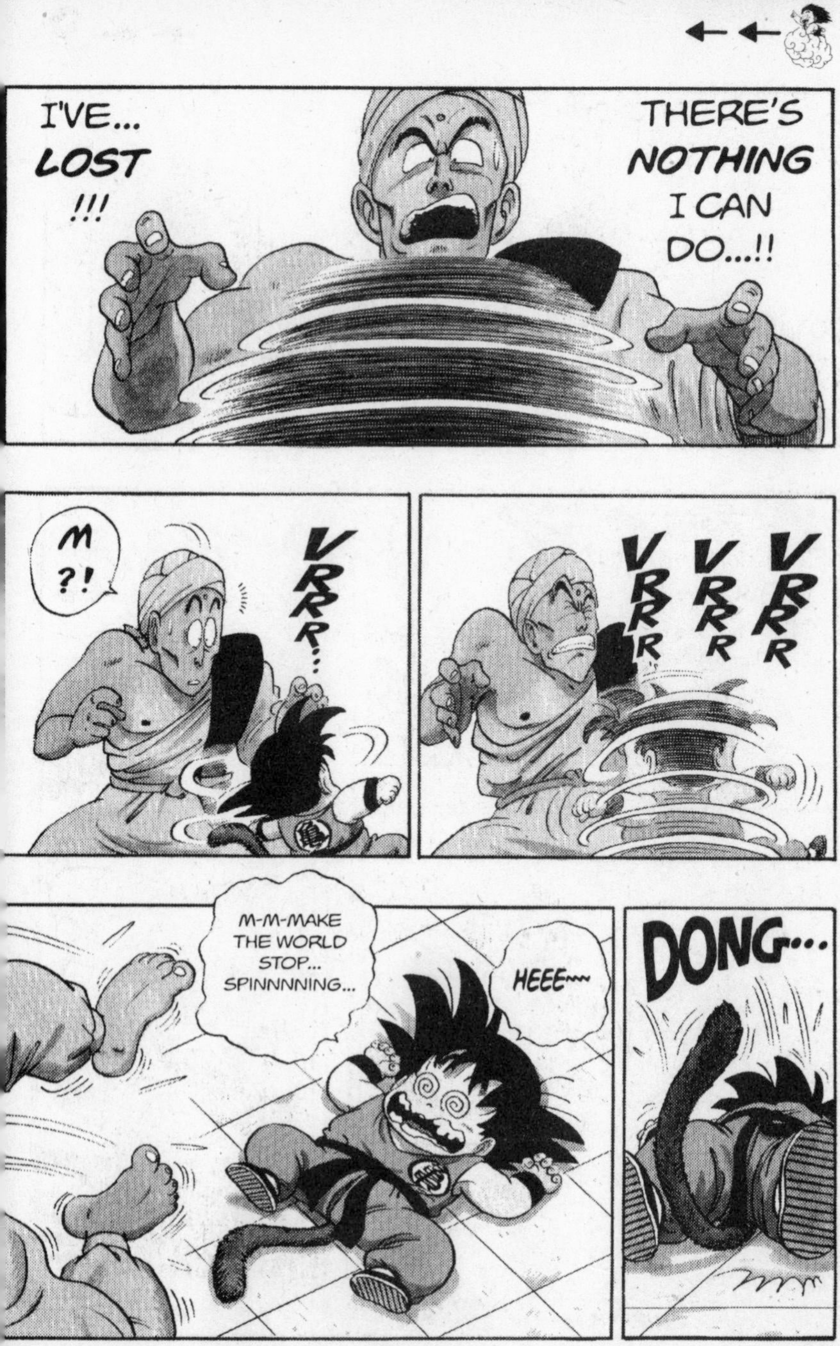
THERE'S NOTHING I CAN DO...!!
I'VE... LOST !!!
VRRRR VRRR VRRR
VRRR...
M ?!
DONG...
HEEE~~
M-M-MAKE THE WORLD STOP... SPINNNNING...

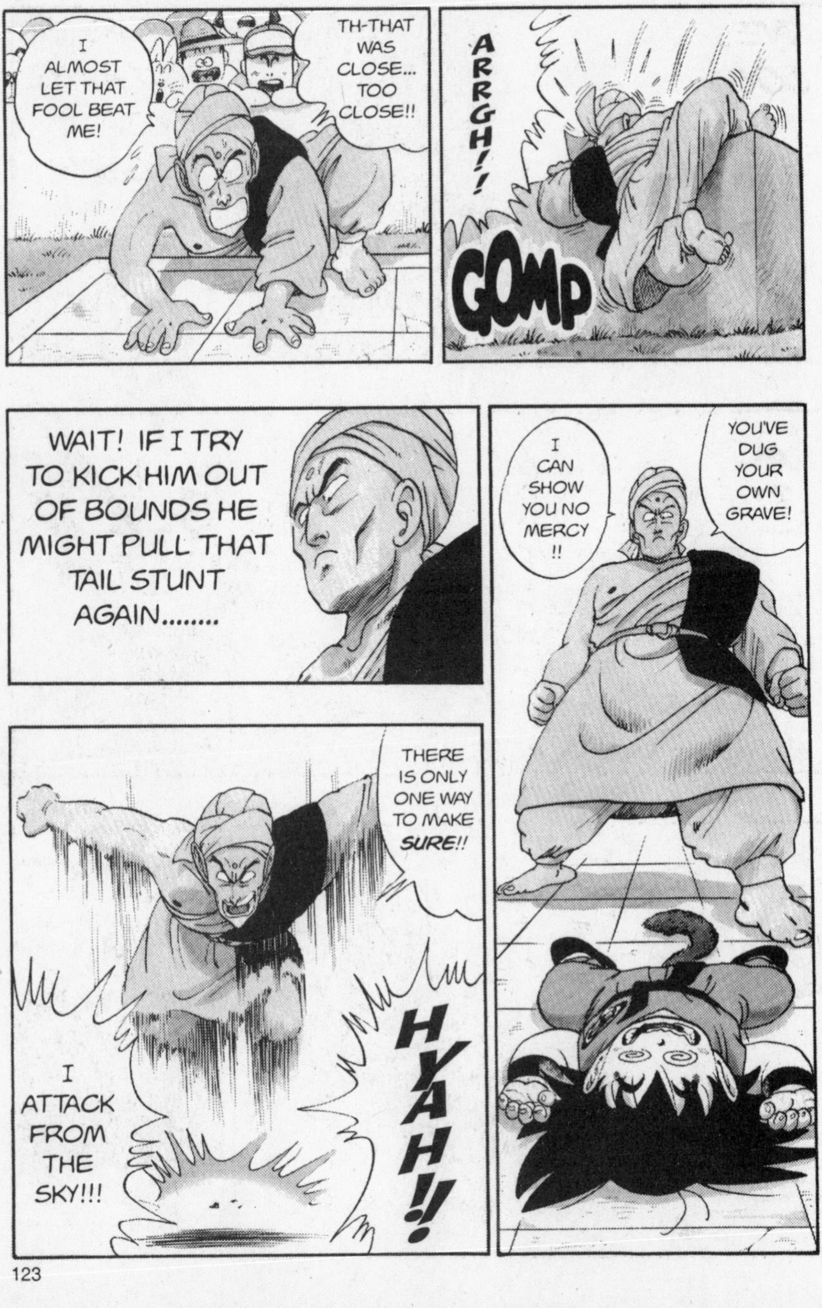
ARRGH!!
GOMP
TH-THAT WAS CLOSE... TOO CLOSE!!
I ALMOST LET THAT FOOL BEAT ME!
YOU'VE DUG YOUR OWN GRAVE!
I CAN SHOW YOU NO MERCY!!
WAIT! IF I TRY TO KICK HIM OUT OF BOUNDS HE MIGHT PULL THAT TAIL STUNT AGAIN........
THERE IS ONLY ONE WAY TO MAKE *SURE!!*
HYAH!!
I ATTACK FROM THE SKY!!!

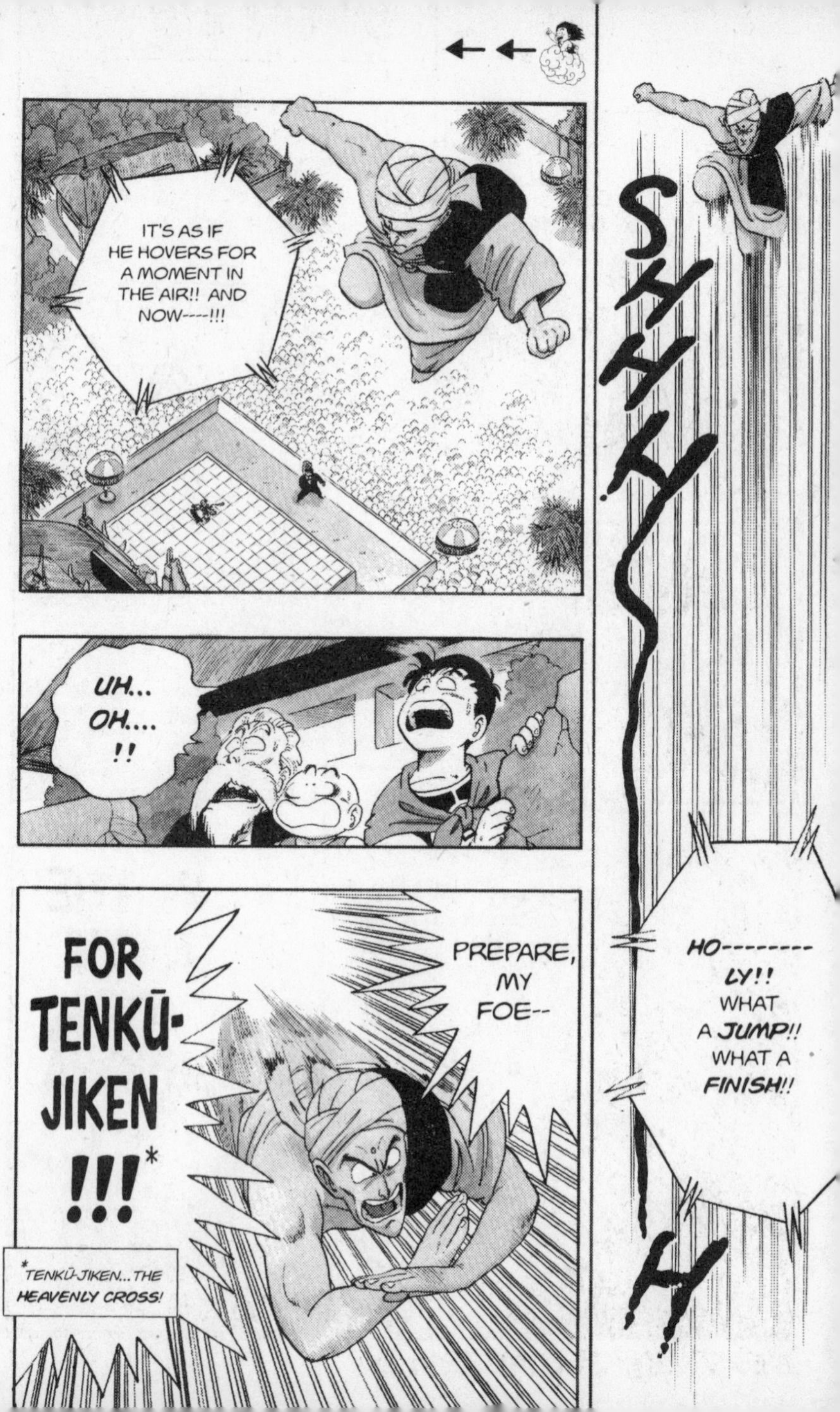
SHYYYYYY
HO---------LY!! WHAT A JUMP!! WHAT A FINISH!!
IT'S AS IF HE HOVERS FOR A MOMENT IN THE AIR!! AND NOW----!!!
UH... OH.... !!
PREPARE, MY FOE--
FOR TENKŪ-JIKEN!!!*
*TENKŪ-JIKEN...THE HEAVENLY CROSS!

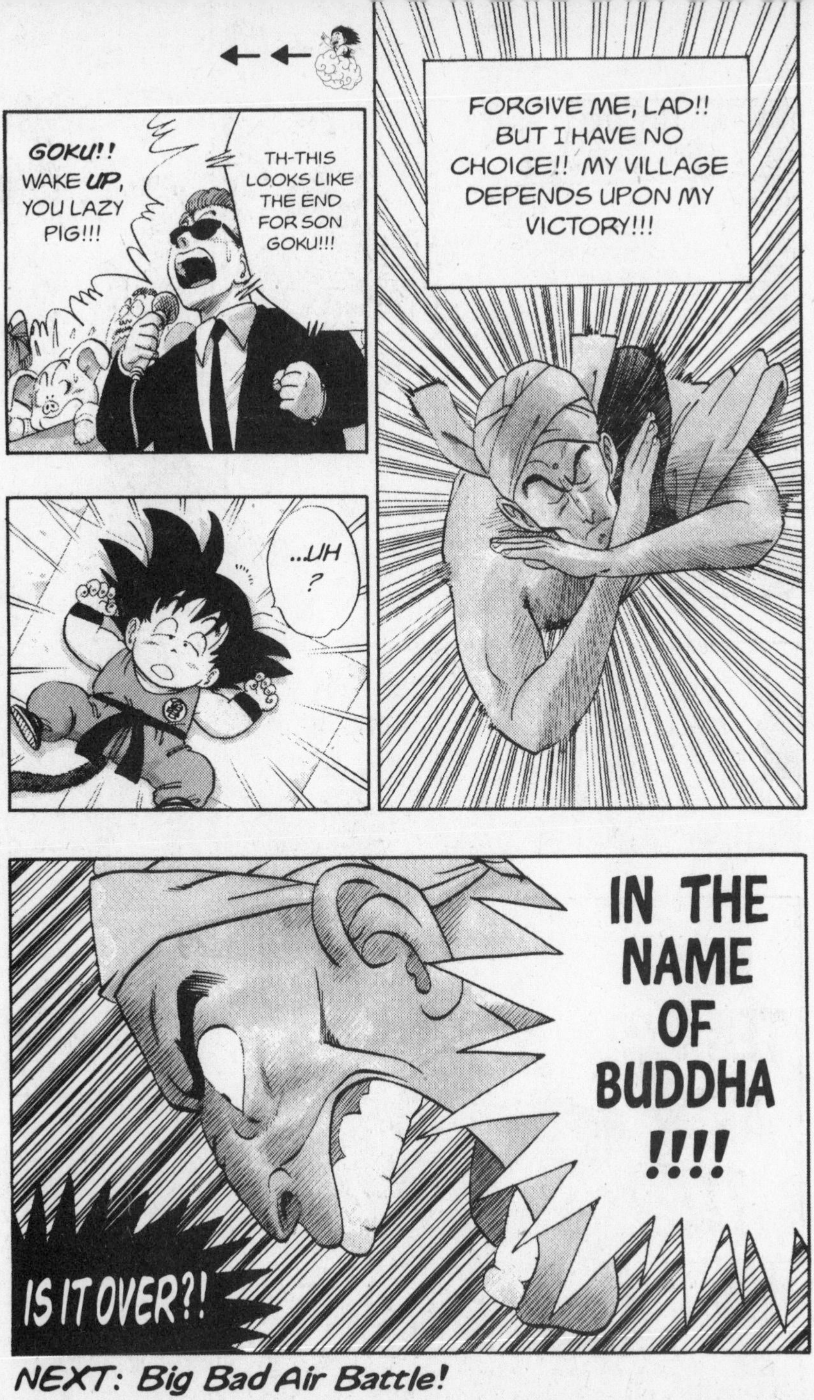

FORGIVE ME, LAD!! BUT I HAVE NO CHOICE!! MY VILLAGE DEPENDS UPON MY VICTORY!!!
TH-THIS LOOKS LIKE THE END FOR SON GOKU!!!
GOKU!! WAKE UP, YOU LAZY PIG!!!
..UH ?
IN THE NAME OF BUDDHA !!!!
IS IT OVER?!

NEXT: Big Bad Air Battle!

Tale 45
Taking the Air

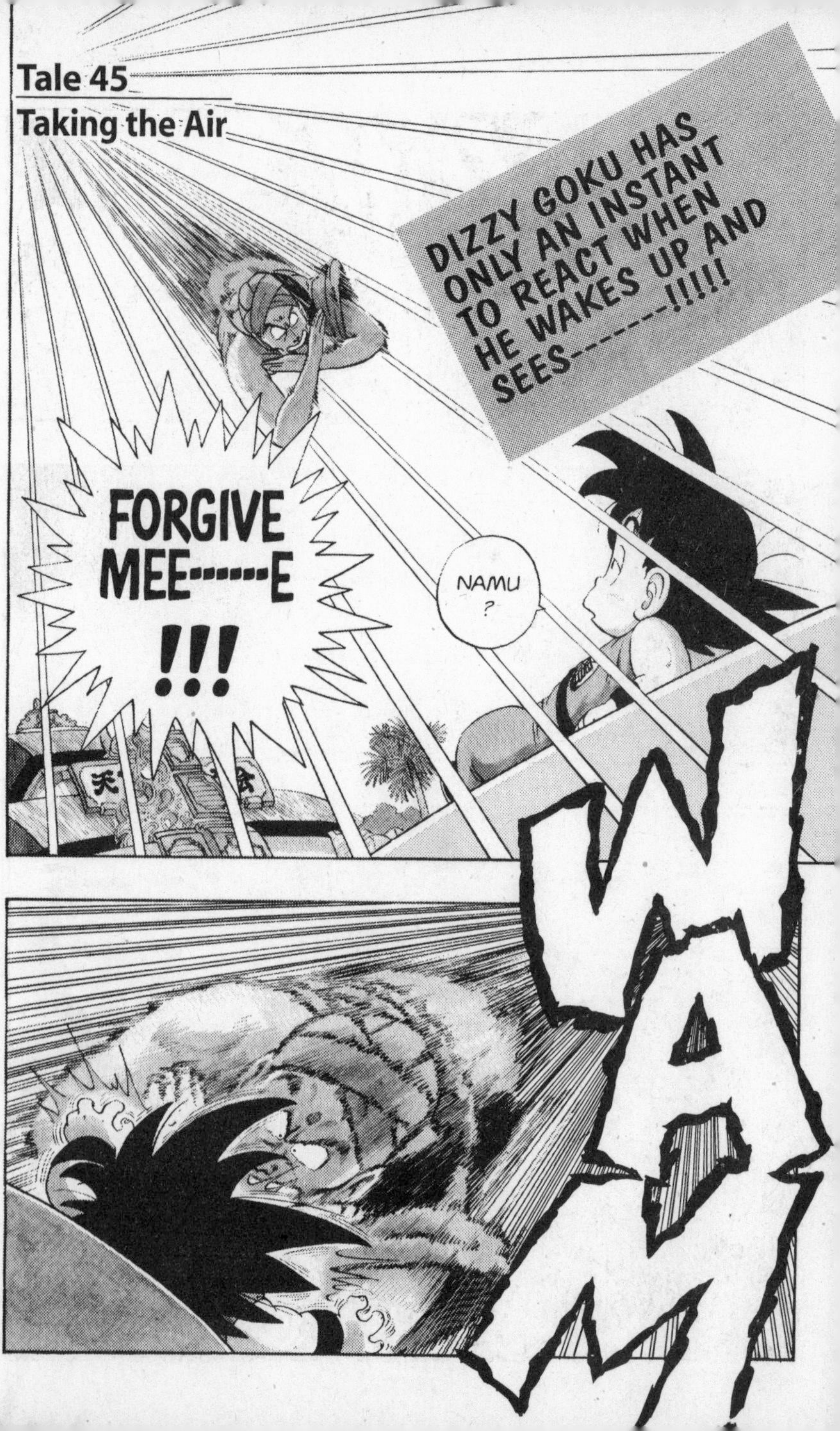
DIZZY GOKU HAS ONLY AN INSTANT TO REACT WHEN HE WAKES UP AND SEES--------!!!!!
NAMU ?
FORGIVE MEE------E !!!
WA

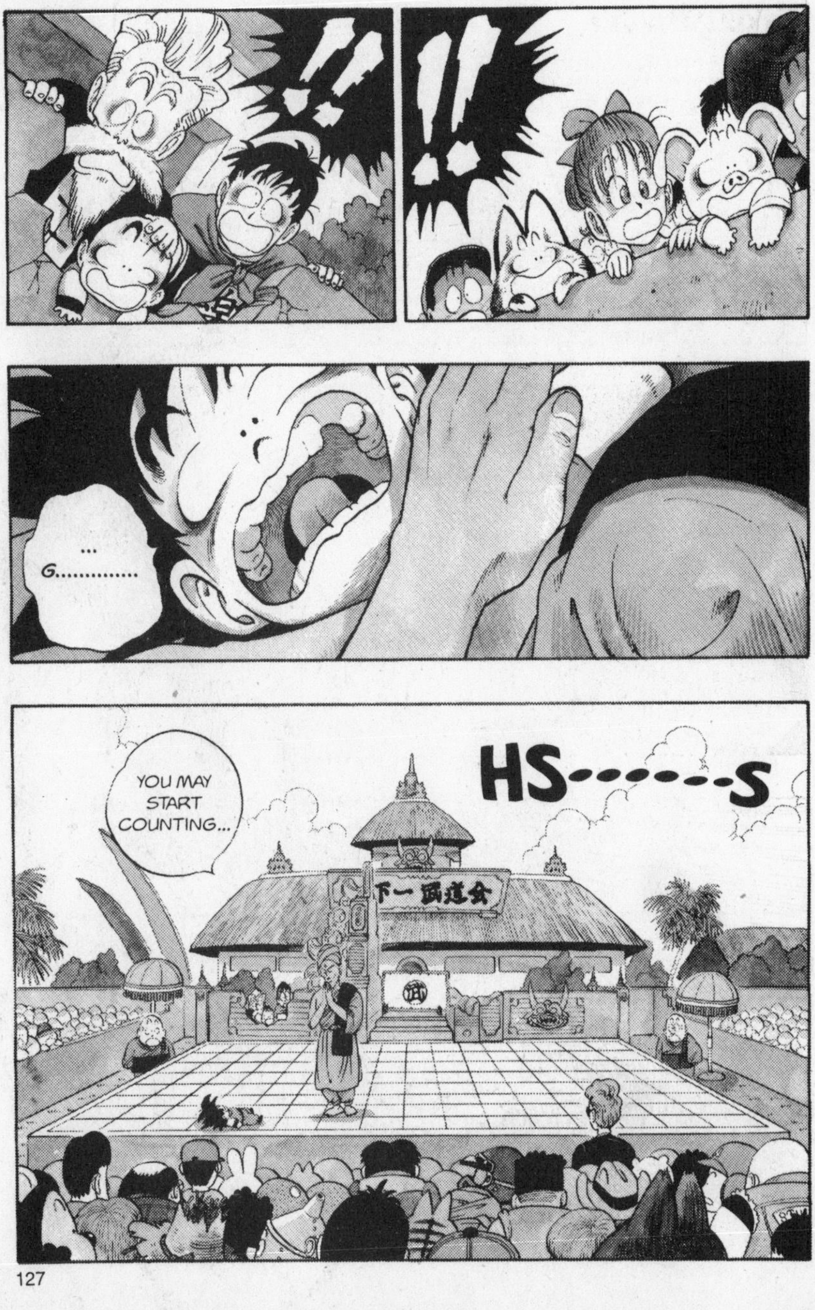
...
G.............
HS------S
YOU MAY START COUNTING...

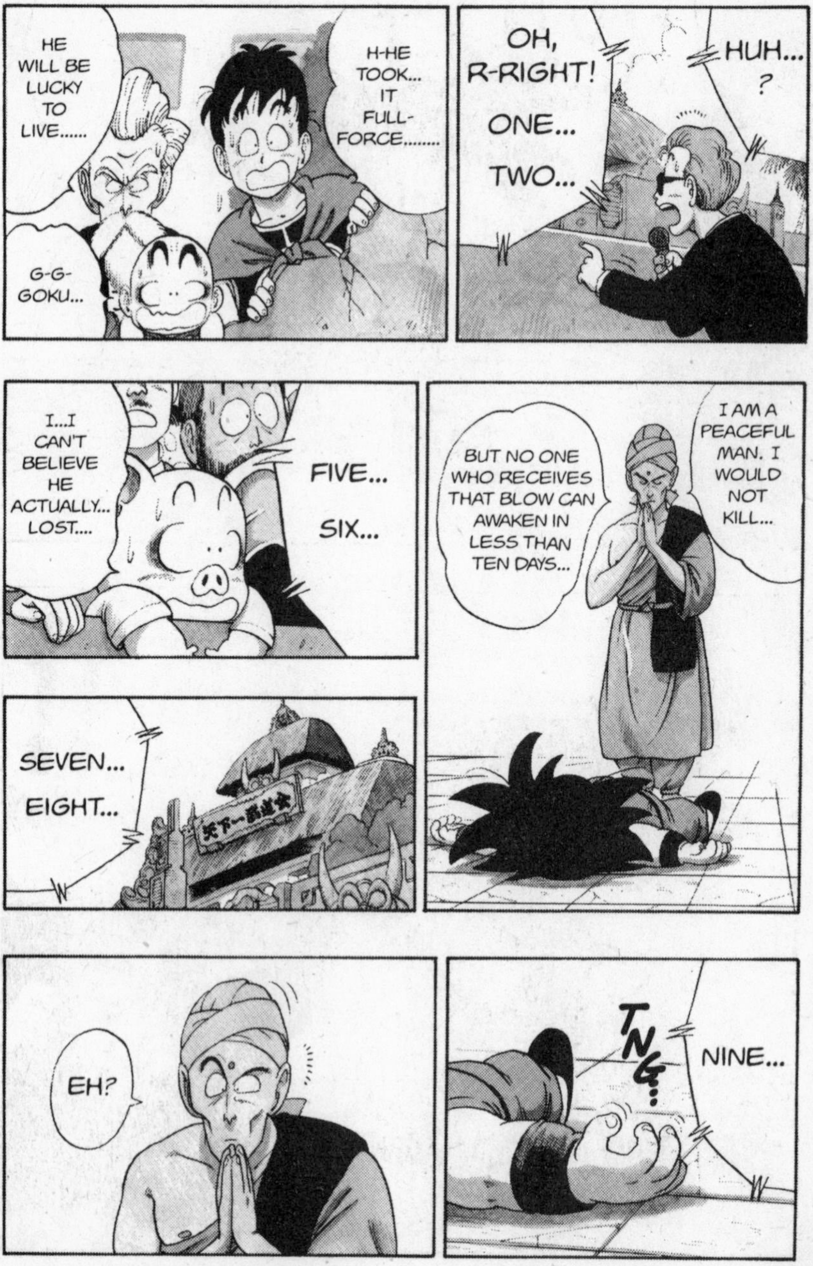
HUH...?
OH, R-RIGHT! ONE... TWO...
H-HE TOOK... IT FULL-FORCE.......
HE WILL BE LUCKY TO LIVE......
G-G-GOKU...
I AM A PEACEFUL MAN. I WOULD NOT KILL...
BUT NO ONE WHO RECEIVES THAT BLOW CAN AWAKEN IN LESS THAN TEN DAYS...
FIVE... SIX...
I...I CAN'T BELIEVE HE ACTUALLY... LOST....
SEVEN... EIGHT...
NINE...
TNG...
EH?

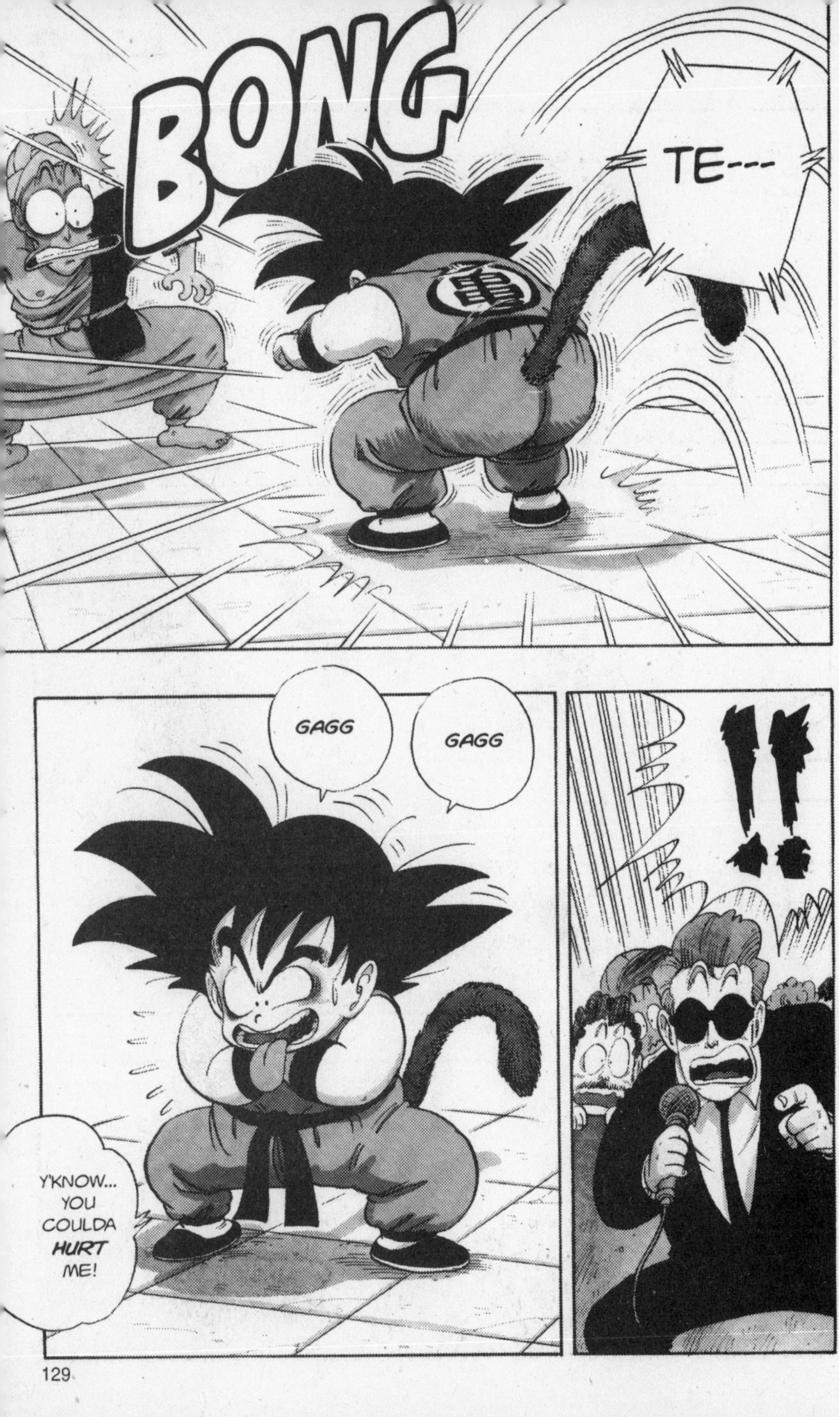
TE---
BONG
!!
GAGG
GAGG
Y'KNOW... YOU COULDA **HURT** ME!

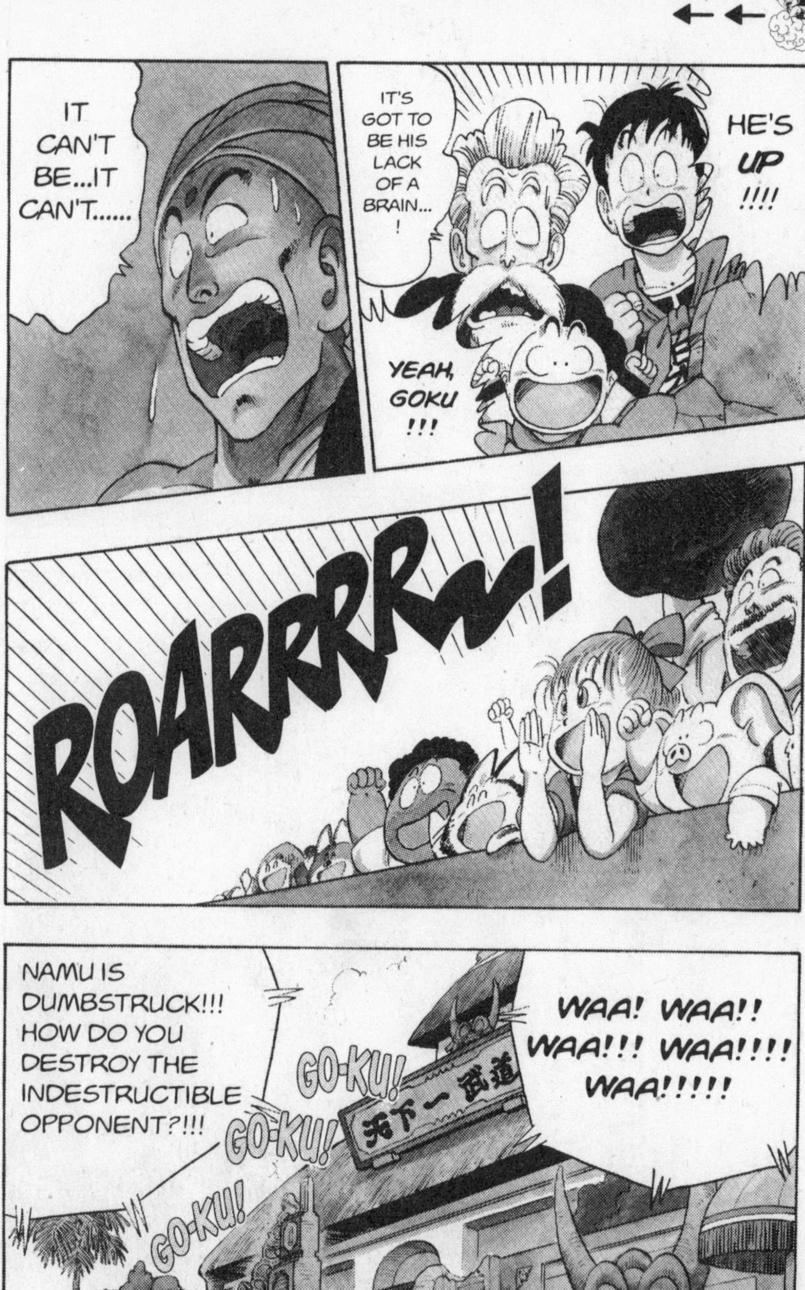
HE'S *UP* !!!!
IT'S GOT TO BE HIS LACK OF A BRAIN... !
YEAH, GOKU !!!
IT CAN'T BE...IT CAN'T......
ROARRRRW!
WAA! WAA!! WAA!!! WAA!!!! WAA!!!!!
GO-KU!
GO-KU!
GO-KU!
NAMU IS DUMBSTRUCK!!! HOW DO YOU DESTROY THE INDESTRUCTIBLE OPPONENT?!!!

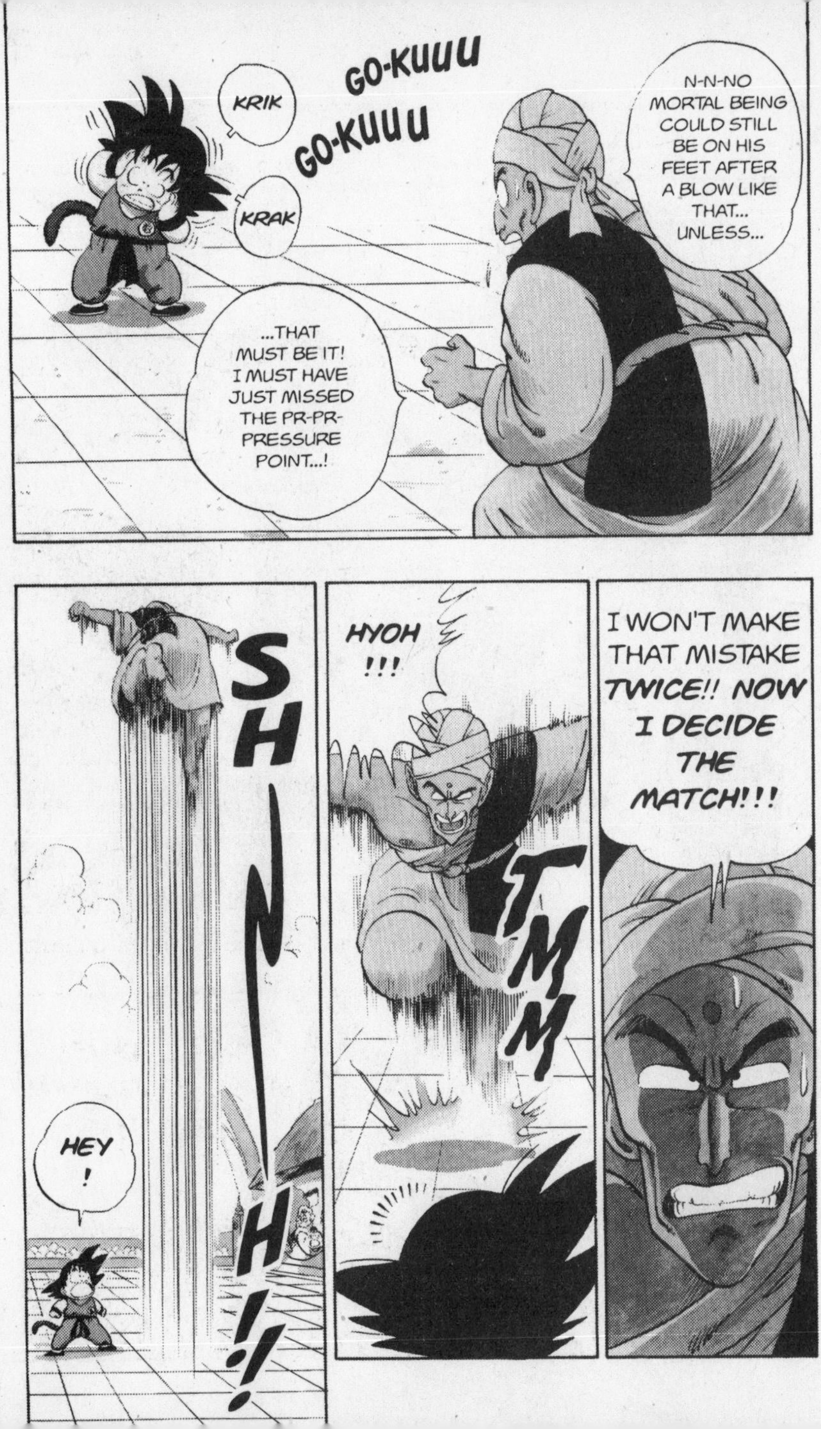
N-N-NO MORTAL BEING COULD STILL BE ON HIS FEET AFTER A BLOW LIKE THAT... UNLESS...
GO-KUUU
GO-KUUU
KRIK
KRAK
...THAT MUST BE IT! I MUST HAVE JUST MISSED THE PR-PR-PRESSURE POINT...!
I WON'T MAKE THAT MISTAKE TWICE!! NOW I DECIDE THE MATCH!!!
HYOH!!!
TMM
SHHH!!!
HEY!

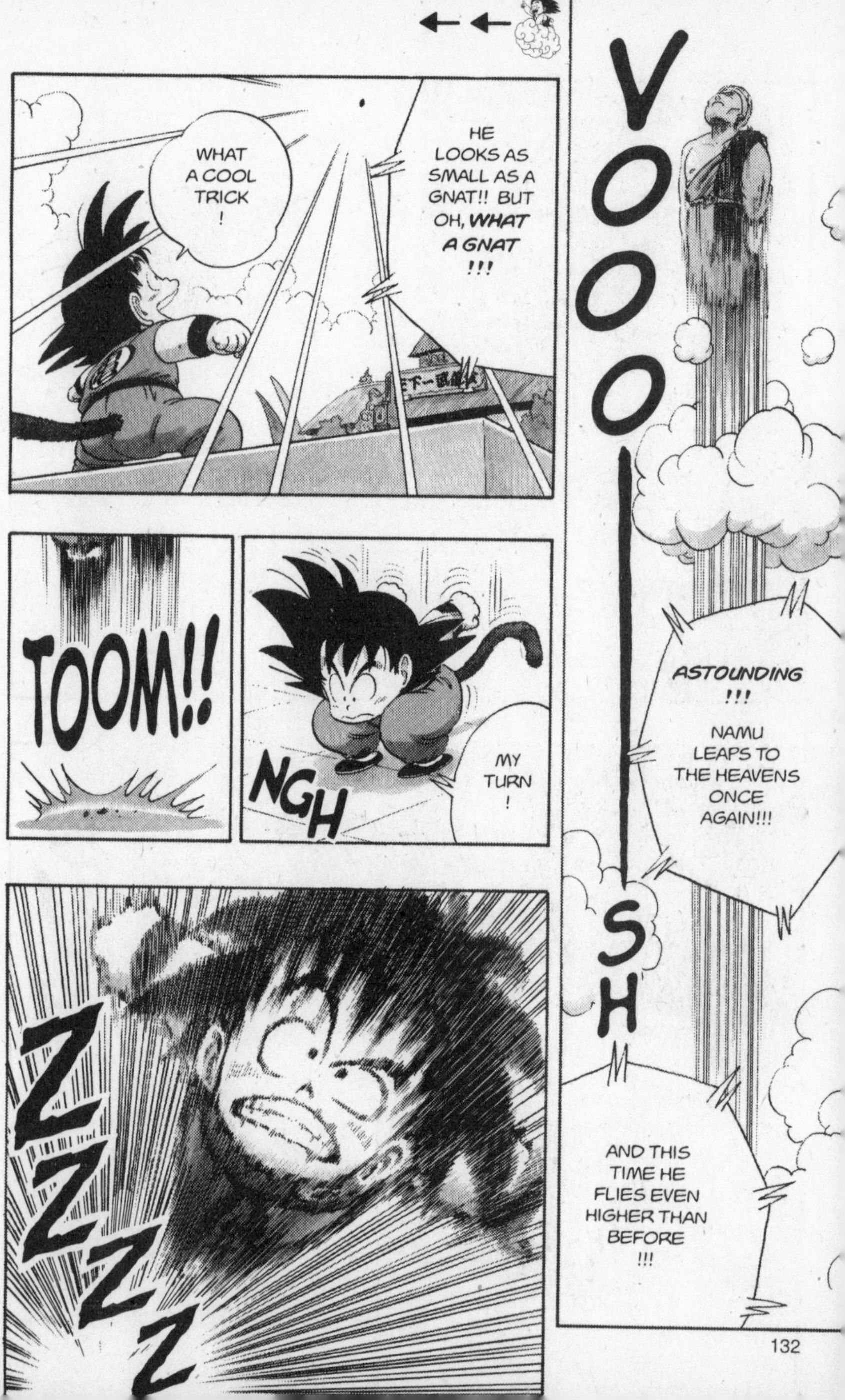
VOOOO—SH
ASTOUNDING!!! NAMU LEAPS TO THE HEAVENS ONCE AGAIN!!!
AND THIS TIME HE FLIES EVEN HIGHER THAN BEFORE!!!
HE LOOKS AS SMALL AS A GNAT!! BUT OH, WHAT A GNAT!!!
WHAT A COOL TRICK!
MY TURN!
NGH
TOOM!!
ZZZZZ

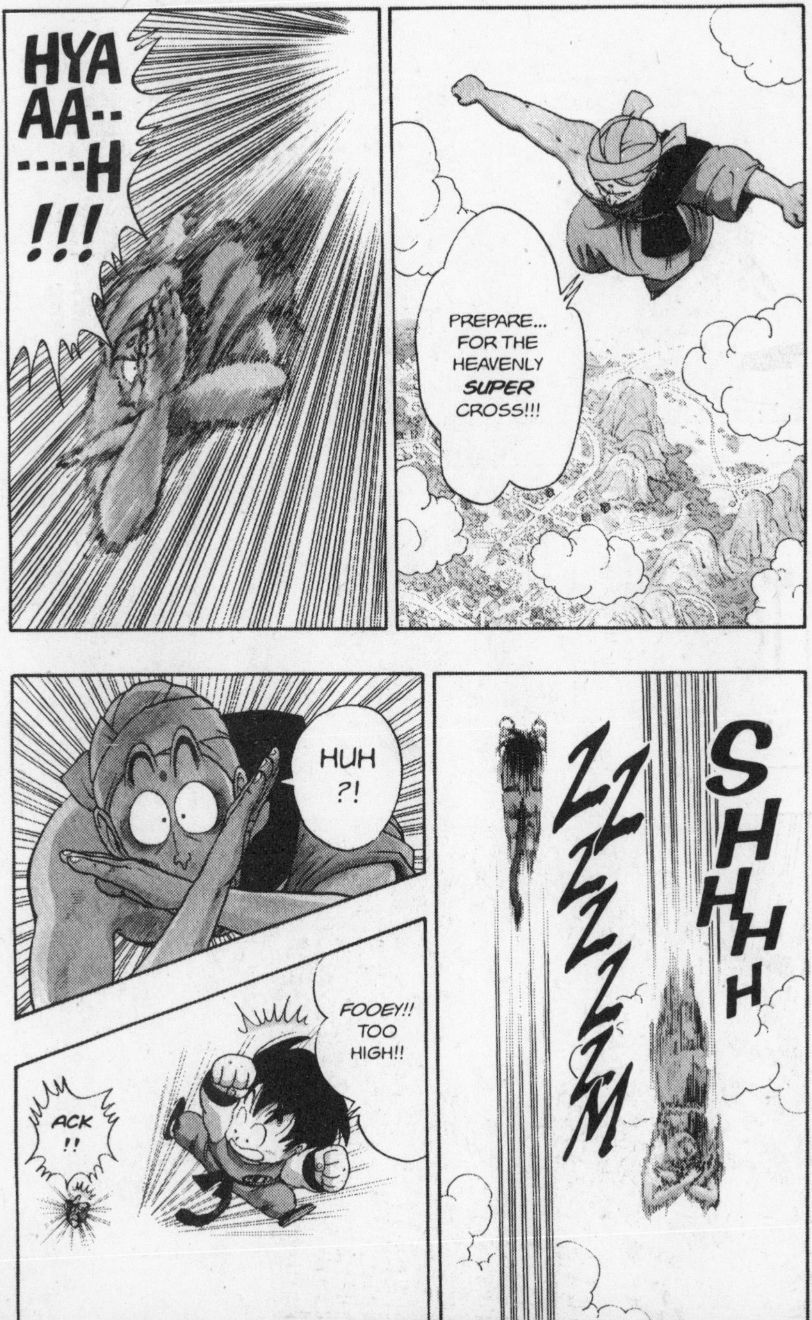
PREPARE... FOR THE HEAVENLY SUPER CROSS!!!
HYAAA-----H!!!
SHHHHH
ZZZZZZM
HUH?!
FOOEY!! TOO HIGH!!
ACK!!

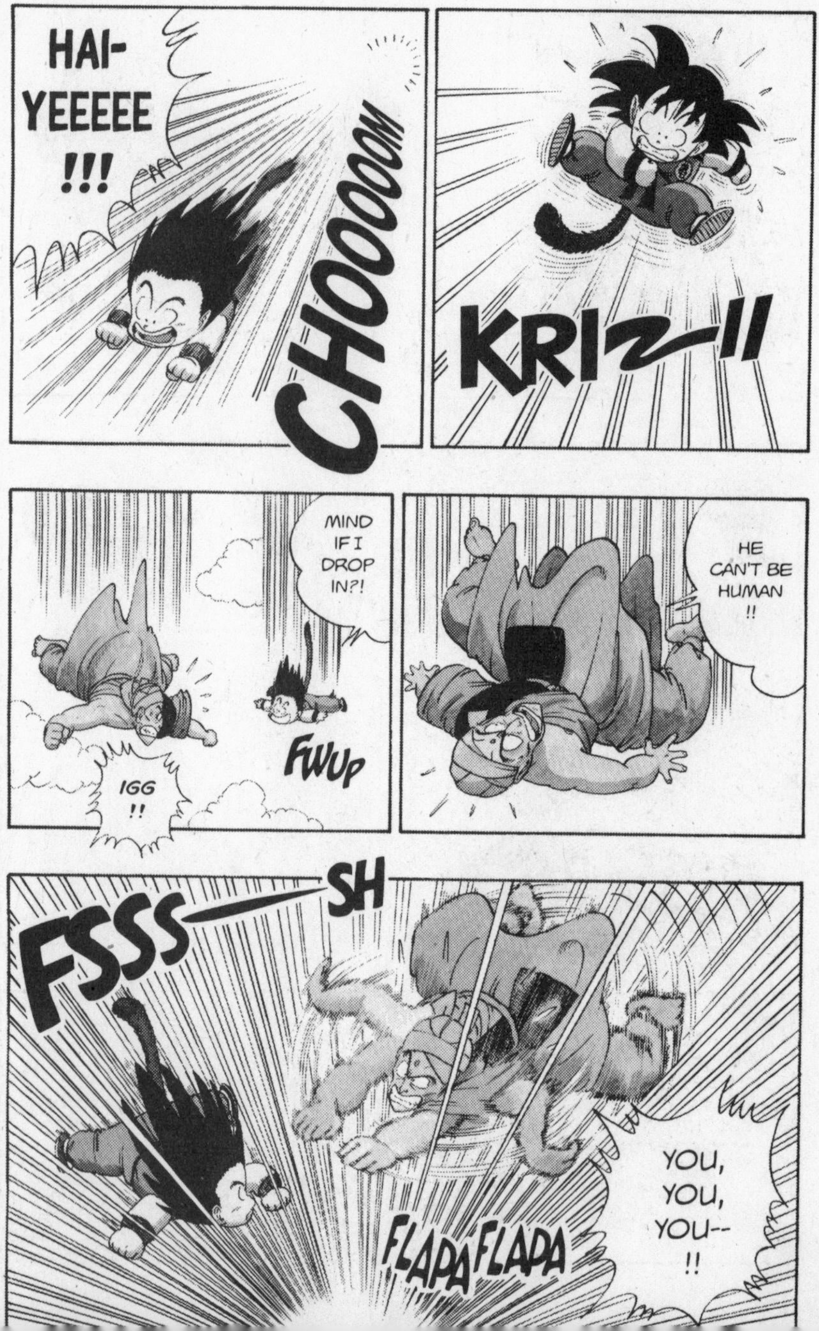
KRI~!!
HAI-YEEEEE!!!
CHOOOOOM
HE CAN'T BE HUMAN!!
MIND IF I DROP IN?!
FWUP
IGG!!
FSSS—SH
YOU, YOU, YOU--!!
FLAPA FLAPA

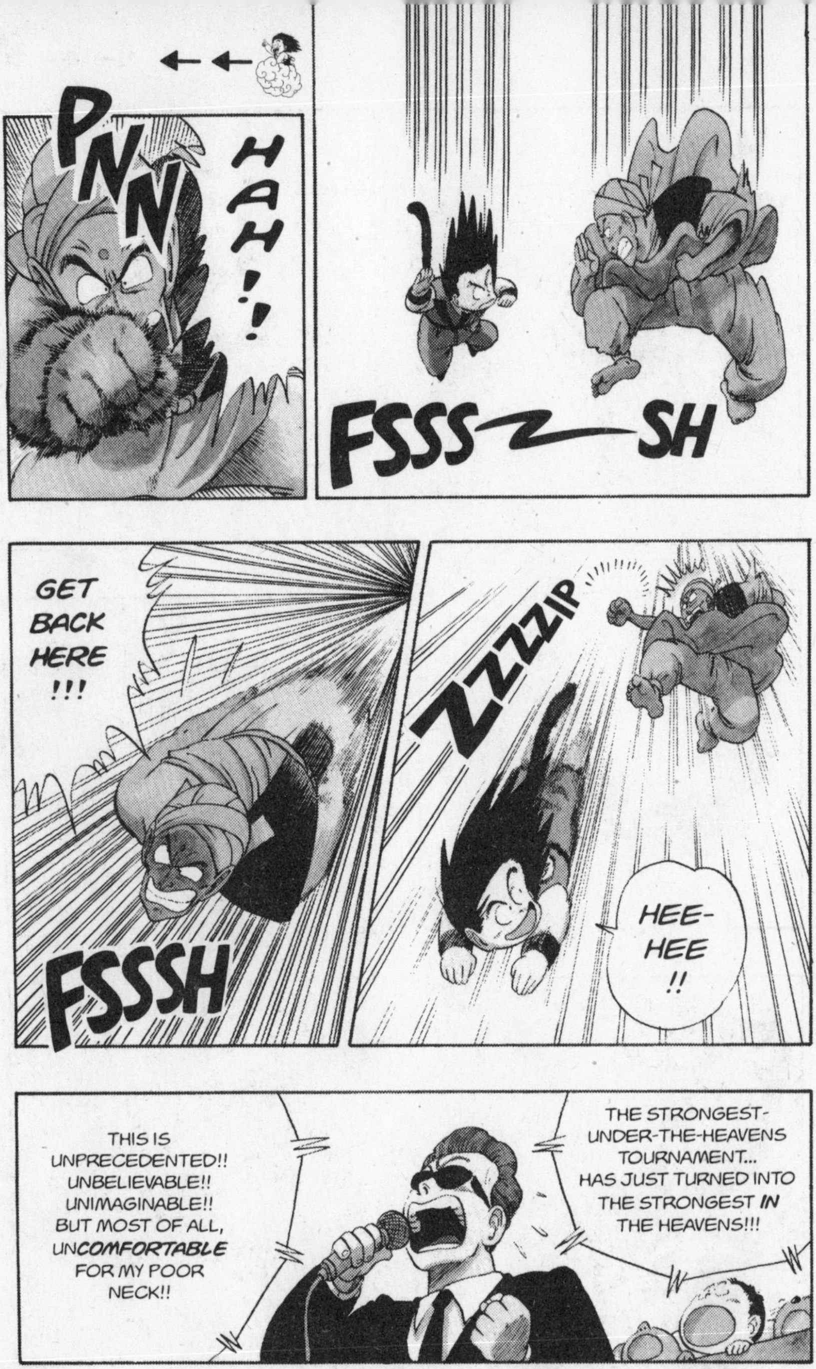
FSSS—SH
PNN
HAH!!
ZZZZZIP
HEE-HEE!!
GET BACK HERE!!!
FSSSH
THE STRONGEST-UNDER-THE-HEAVENS TOURNAMENT... HAS JUST TURNED INTO THE STRONGEST IN THE HEAVENS!!!
THIS IS UNPRECEDENTED!! UNBELIEVABLE!! UNIMAGINABLE!! BUT MOST OF ALL, UNCOMFORTABLE FOR MY POOR NECK!!

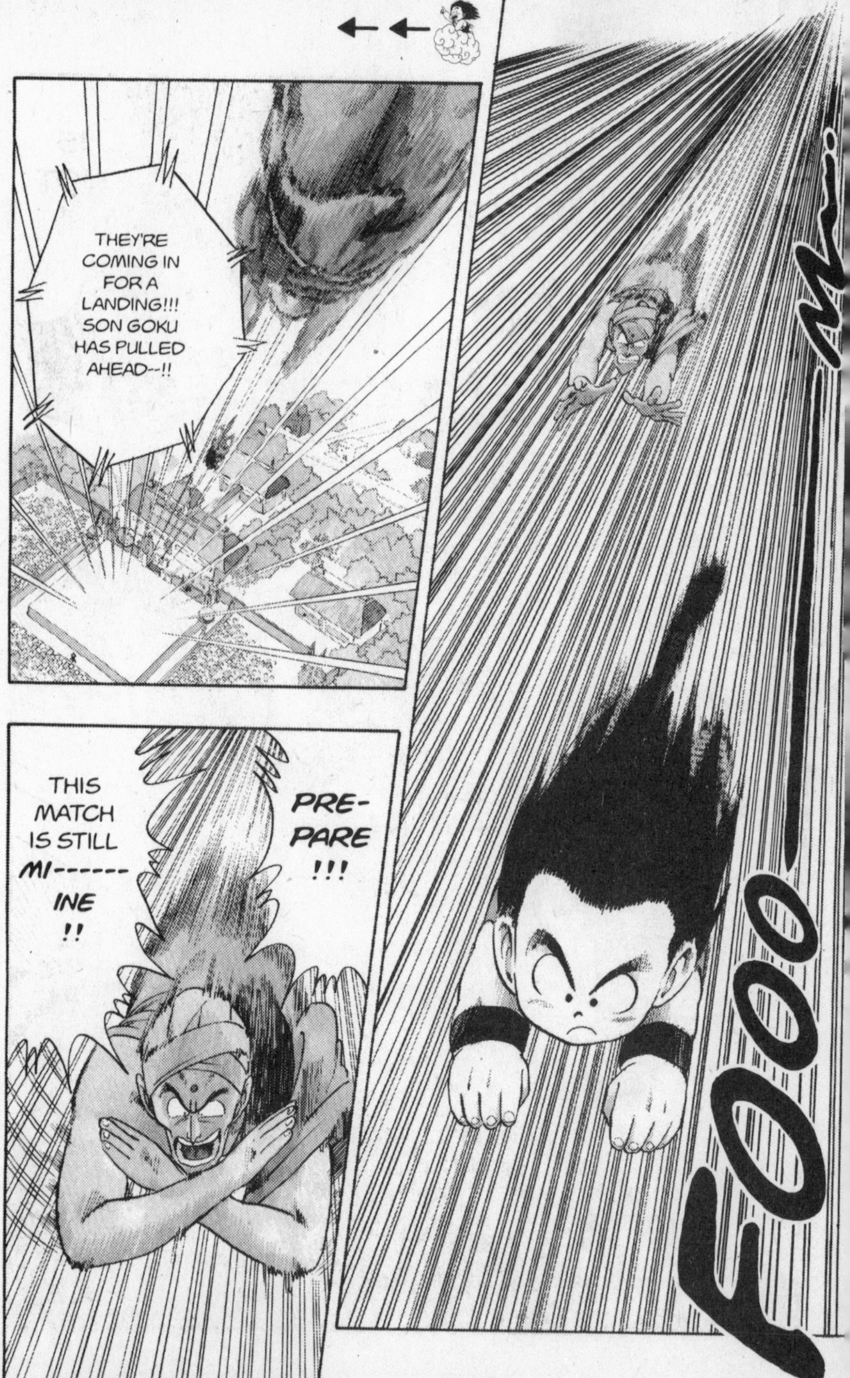

FOOO——M…
THEY'RE COMING IN FOR A LANDING!!! SON GOKU HAS PULLED AHEAD--!!
PRE-PARE !!!
THIS MATCH IS STILL MI------INE !!

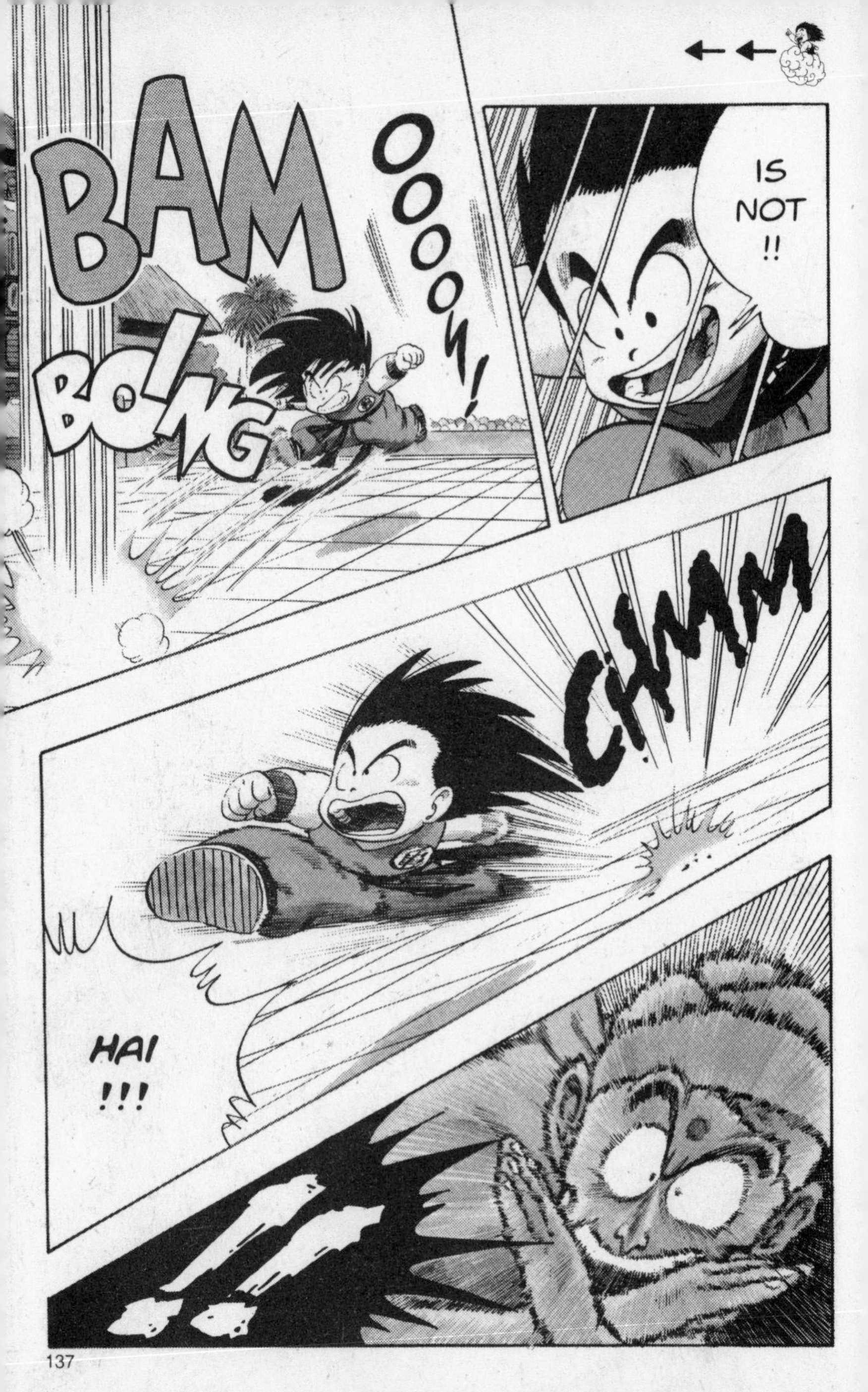
IS NOT !!
BAM
BOING
OOOOOH!
CHAM
HAI !!!

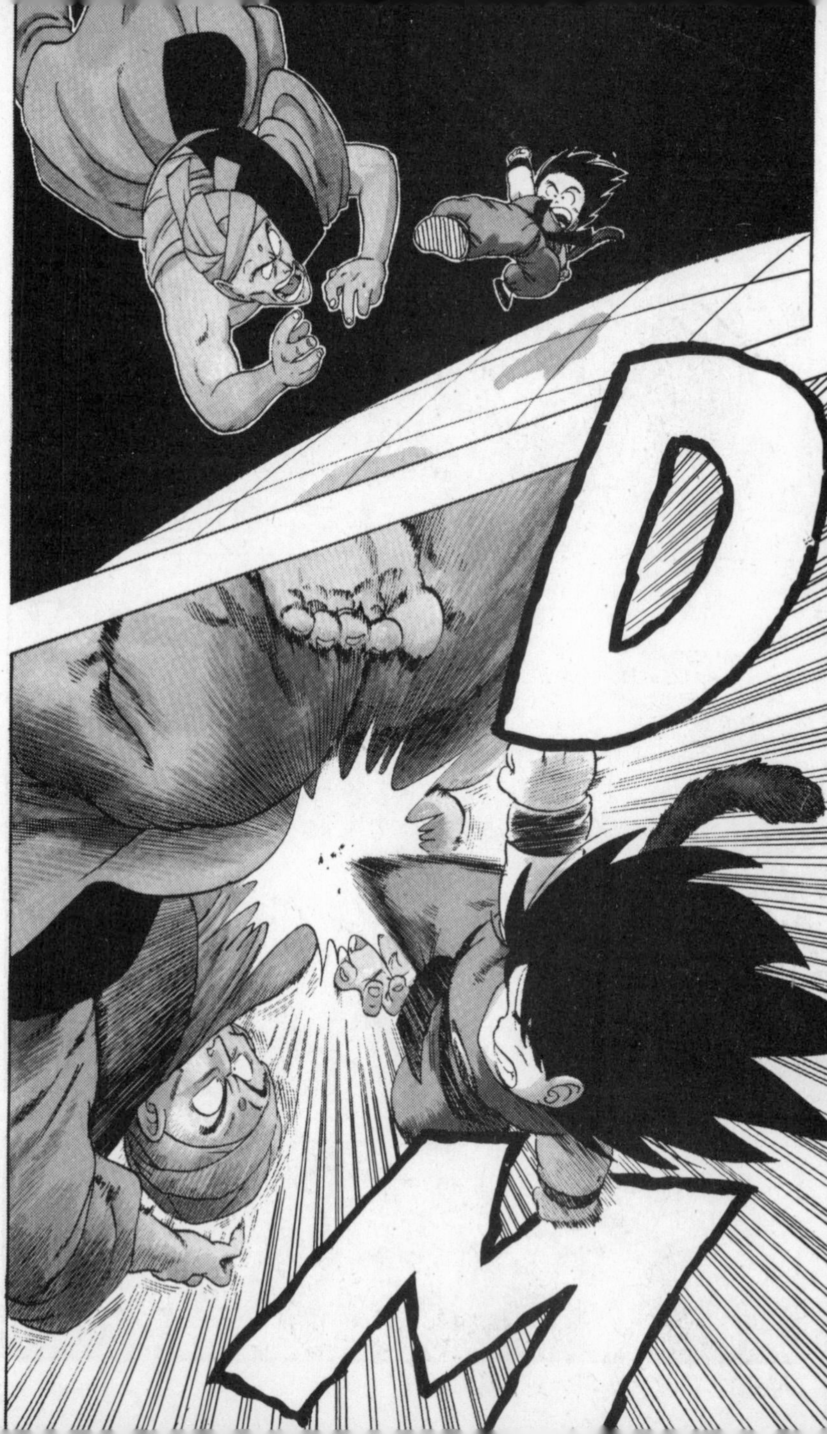

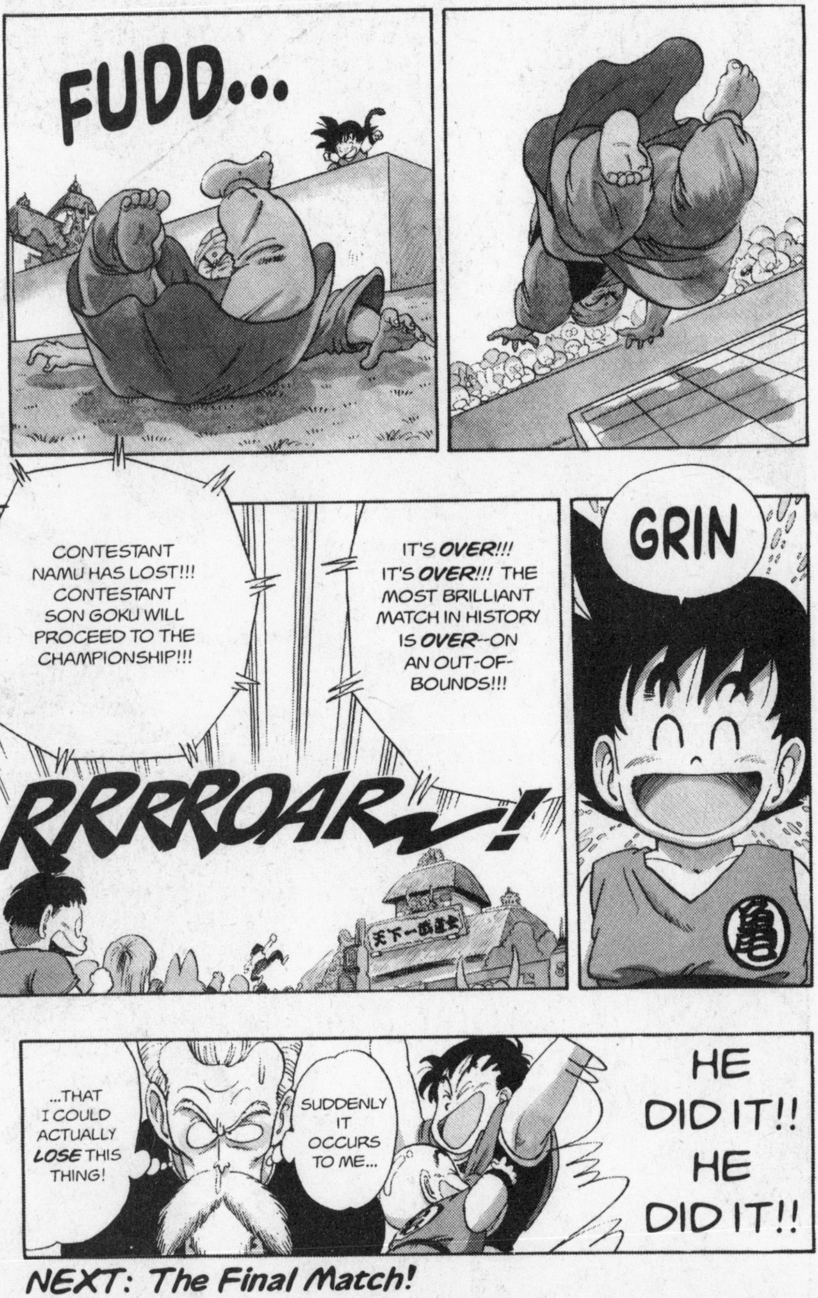
FUDD...
GRIN
IT'S OVER!!! IT'S OVER!!! THE MOST BRILLIANT MATCH IN HISTORY IS OVER--ON AN OUT-OF-BOUNDS!!!
CONTESTANT NAMU HAS LOST!!! CONTESTANT SON GOKU WILL PROCEED TO THE CHAMPIONSHIP!!!
RRRROAR!
HE DID IT!! HE DID IT!!
SUDDENLY IT OCCURS TO ME...
...THAT I COULD ACTUALLY LOSE THIS THING!

NEXT: The Final Match!

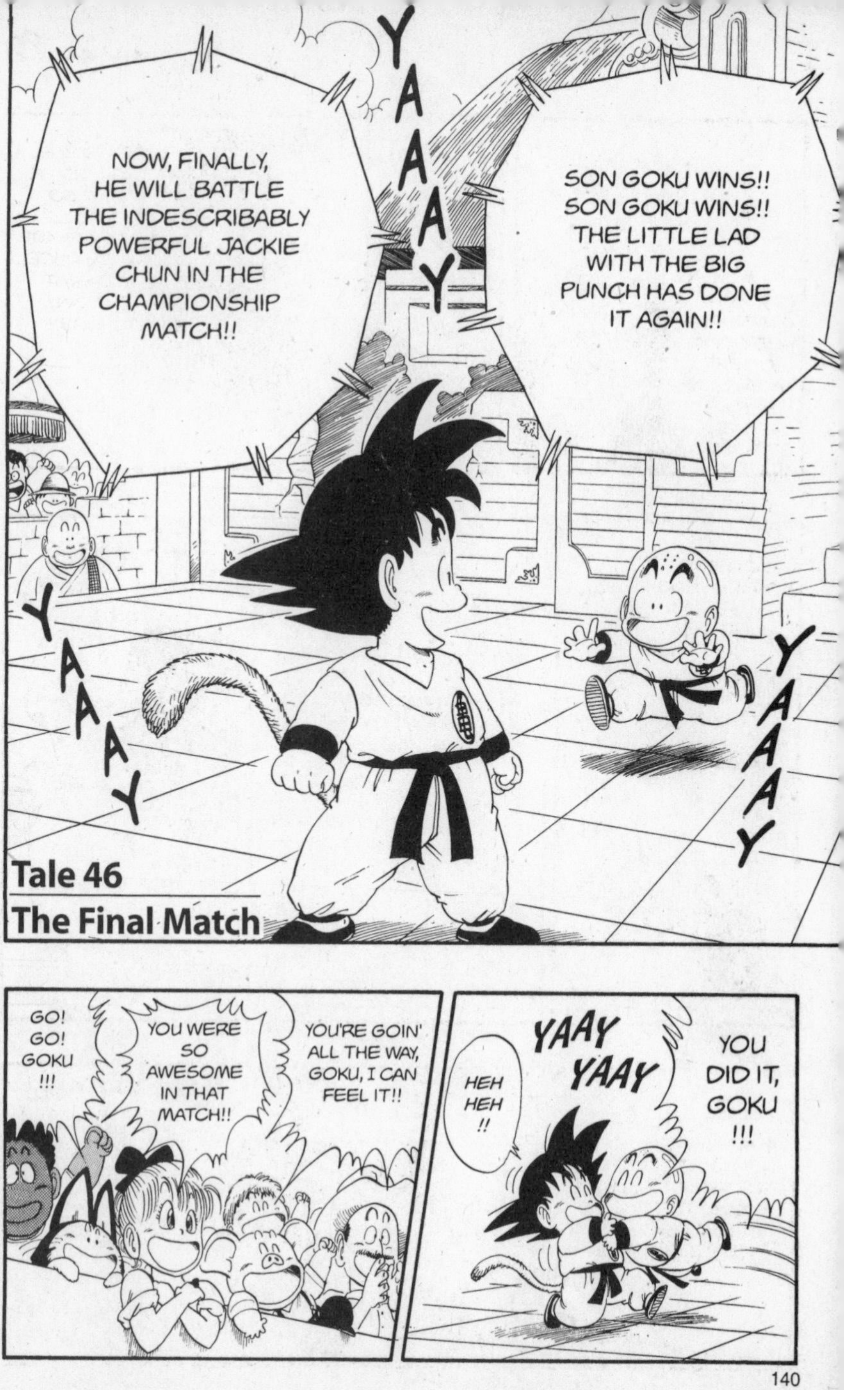
SON GOKU WINS!! SON GOKU WINS!! THE LITTLE LAD WITH THE BIG PUNCH HAS DONE IT AGAIN!!
YAAAY
NOW, FINALLY, HE WILL BATTLE THE INDESCRIBABLY POWERFUL JACKIE CHUN IN THE CHAMPIONSHIP MATCH!!
YAAAAY
YAAAY
Tale 46
The Final Match
YOU DID IT, GOKU !!!
YAAY YAAY
HEH HEH !!
YOU'RE GOIN' ALL THE WAY, GOKU, I CAN FEEL IT!!
YOU WERE SO AWESOME IN THAT MATCH!!
GO! GO! GOKU !!!

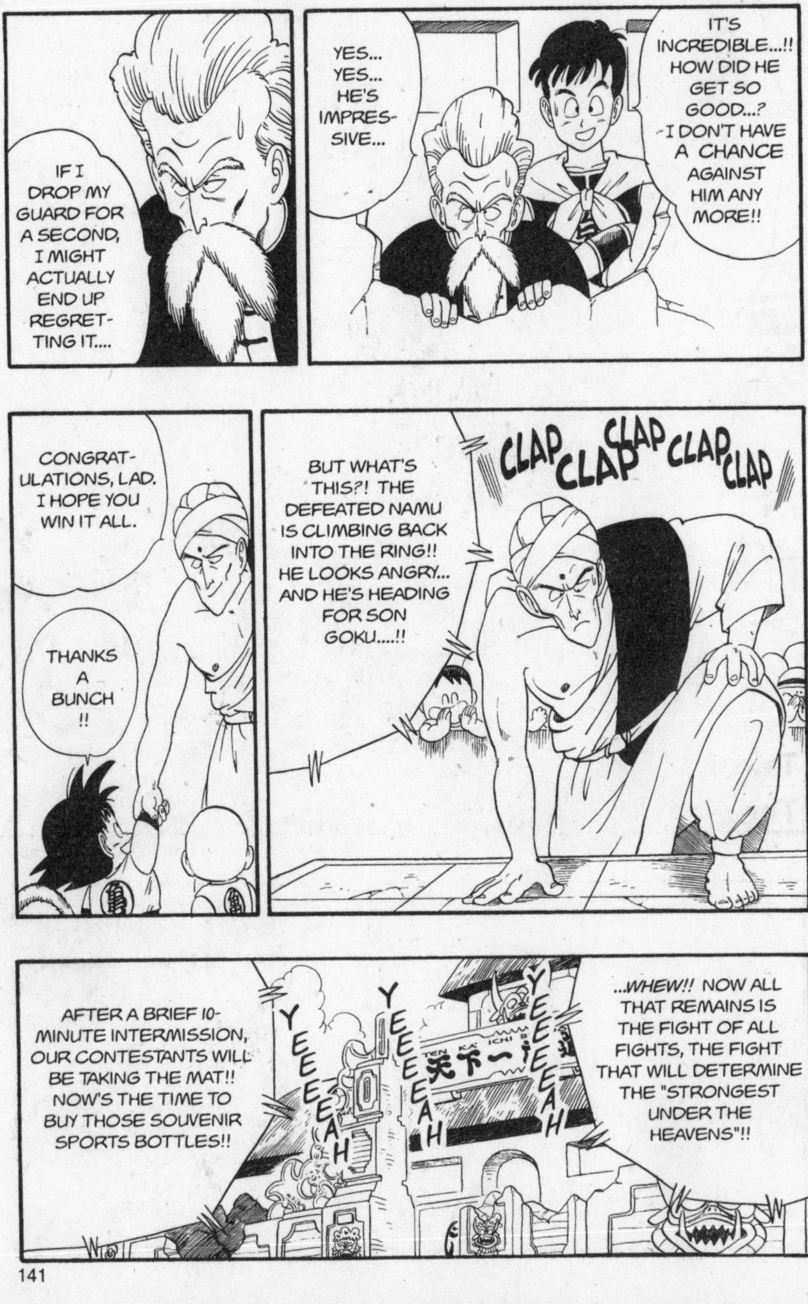

IT'S INCREDIBLE...!! HOW DID HE GET SO GOOD...? I DON'T HAVE A CHANCE AGAINST HIM ANY MORE!!
YES... YES... HE'S IMPRES-SIVE...
IF I DROP MY GUARD FOR A SECOND, I MIGHT ACTUALLY END UP REGRET-TING IT....
CLAP CLAP CLAP CLAP CLAP
BUT WHAT'S THIS?! THE DEFEATED NAMU IS CLIMBING BACK INTO THE RING!! HE LOOKS ANGRY... AND HE'S HEADING FOR SON GOKU....!!
CONGRAT-ULATIONS, LAD. I HOPE YOU WIN IT ALL.
THANKS A BUNCH !!
...WHEW!! NOW ALL THAT REMAINS IS THE FIGHT OF ALL FIGHTS, THE FIGHT THAT WILL DETERMINE THE "STRONGEST UNDER THE HEAVENS"!!
YEEEEAH
YEEEEAH
YEEEEAH
AFTER A BRIEF 10-MINUTE INTERMISSION, OUR CONTESTANTS WILL BE TAKING THE MAT!! NOW'S THE TIME TO BUY THOSE SOUVENIR SPORTS BOTTLES!!

LEAVING? NOT EVEN GOING TO WATCH OUR MATCH?

I WISH I COULD...BUT I CANNOT AFFORD TO DALLY HERE...

YADA YADA

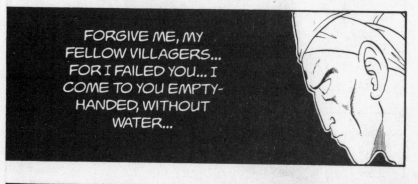

FORGIVE ME, MY FELLOW VILLAGERS... FOR I FAILED YOU... I COME TO YOU EMPTY-HANDED, WITHOUT WATER...

PAP

CATCH.

HEY, NAMU. TAKE THIS WITH YOU.

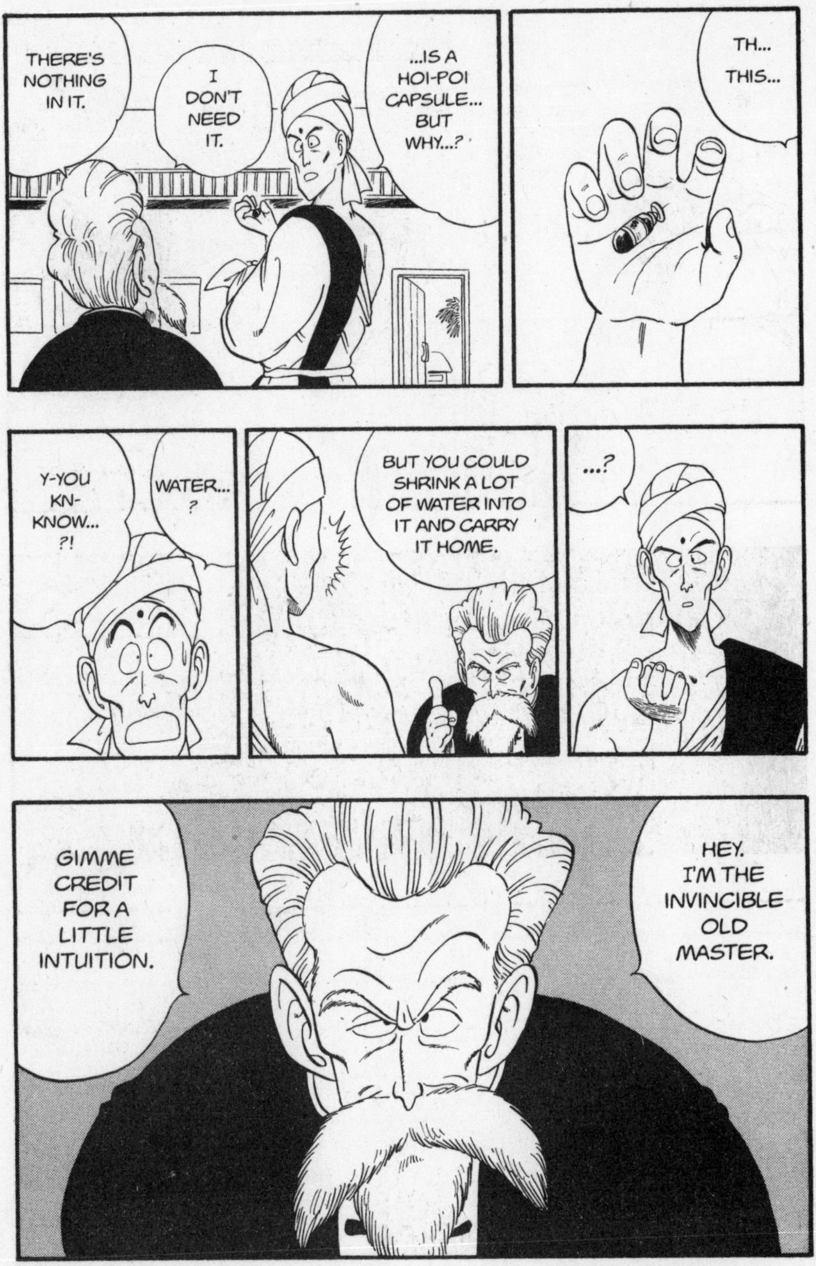
TH... THIS...
...IS A HOI-POI CAPSULE... BUT WHY...?
I DON'T NEED IT.
THERE'S NOTHING IN IT.
...?
BUT YOU COULD SHRINK A LOT OF WATER INTO IT AND CARRY IT HOME.
WATER...?
Y-YOU KN-KNOW...?!
HEY. I'M THE INVINCIBLE OLD MASTER.
GIMME CREDIT FOR A LITTLE INTUITION.

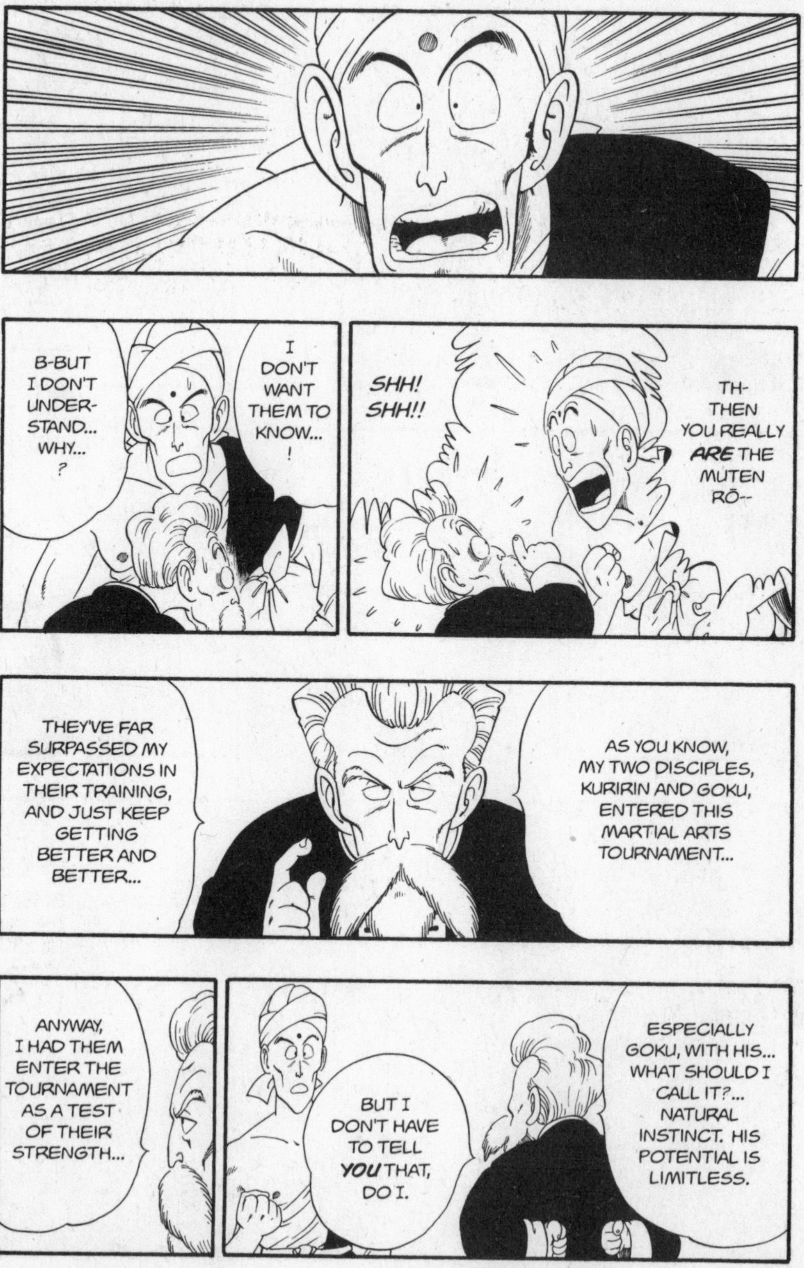
TH- THEN YOU REALLY *ARE* THE MŪTEN RŌ--
SHH! SHH!!
I DON'T WANT THEM TO KNOW... !
B-BUT I DON'T UNDERSTAND... WHY... ?
AS YOU KNOW, MY TWO DISCIPLES, KURIRIN AND GOKU, ENTERED THIS MARTIAL ARTS TOURNAMENT...
THEY'VE FAR SURPASSED MY EXPECTATIONS IN THEIR TRAINING, AND JUST KEEP GETTING BETTER AND BETTER...
ESPECIALLY GOKU, WITH HIS... WHAT SHOULD I CALL IT?... NATURAL INSTINCT. HIS POTENTIAL IS LIMITLESS.
BUT I DON'T HAVE TO TELL *YOU* THAT, DO I.
ANYWAY, I HAD THEM ENTER THE TOURNAMENT AS A TEST OF THEIR STRENGTH...

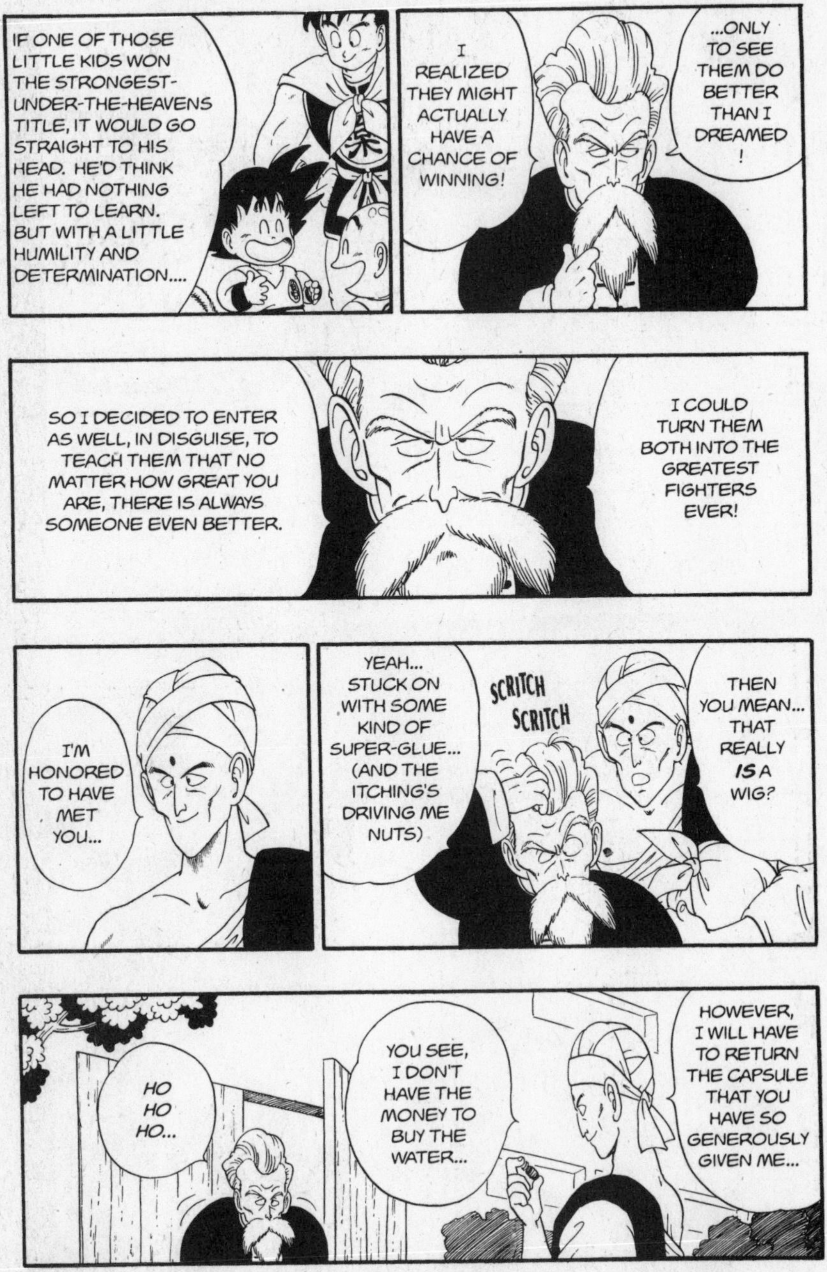
...ONLY TO SEE THEM DO BETTER THAN I DREAMED!
I REALIZED THEY MIGHT ACTUALLY HAVE A CHANCE OF WINNING!
IF ONE OF THOSE LITTLE KIDS WON THE STRONGEST-UNDER-THE-HEAVENS TITLE, IT WOULD GO STRAIGHT TO HIS HEAD. HE'D THINK HE HAD NOTHING LEFT TO LEARN. BUT WITH A LITTLE HUMILITY AND DETERMINATION....
I COULD TURN THEM BOTH INTO THE GREATEST FIGHTERS EVER!
SO I DECIDED TO ENTER AS WELL, IN DISGUISE, TO TEACH THEM THAT NO MATTER HOW GREAT YOU ARE, THERE IS ALWAYS SOMEONE EVEN BETTER.
THEN YOU MEAN... THAT REALLY *IS* A WIG?
SCRITCH SCRITCH
YEAH... STUCK ON WITH SOME KIND OF SUPER-GLUE... (AND THE ITCHING'S DRIVING ME NUTS)
I'M HONORED TO HAVE MET YOU...
HOWEVER, I WILL HAVE TO RETURN THE CAPSULE THAT YOU HAVE SO GENEROUSLY GIVEN ME...
YOU SEE, I DON'T HAVE THE MONEY TO BUY THE WATER...
HO HO HO...

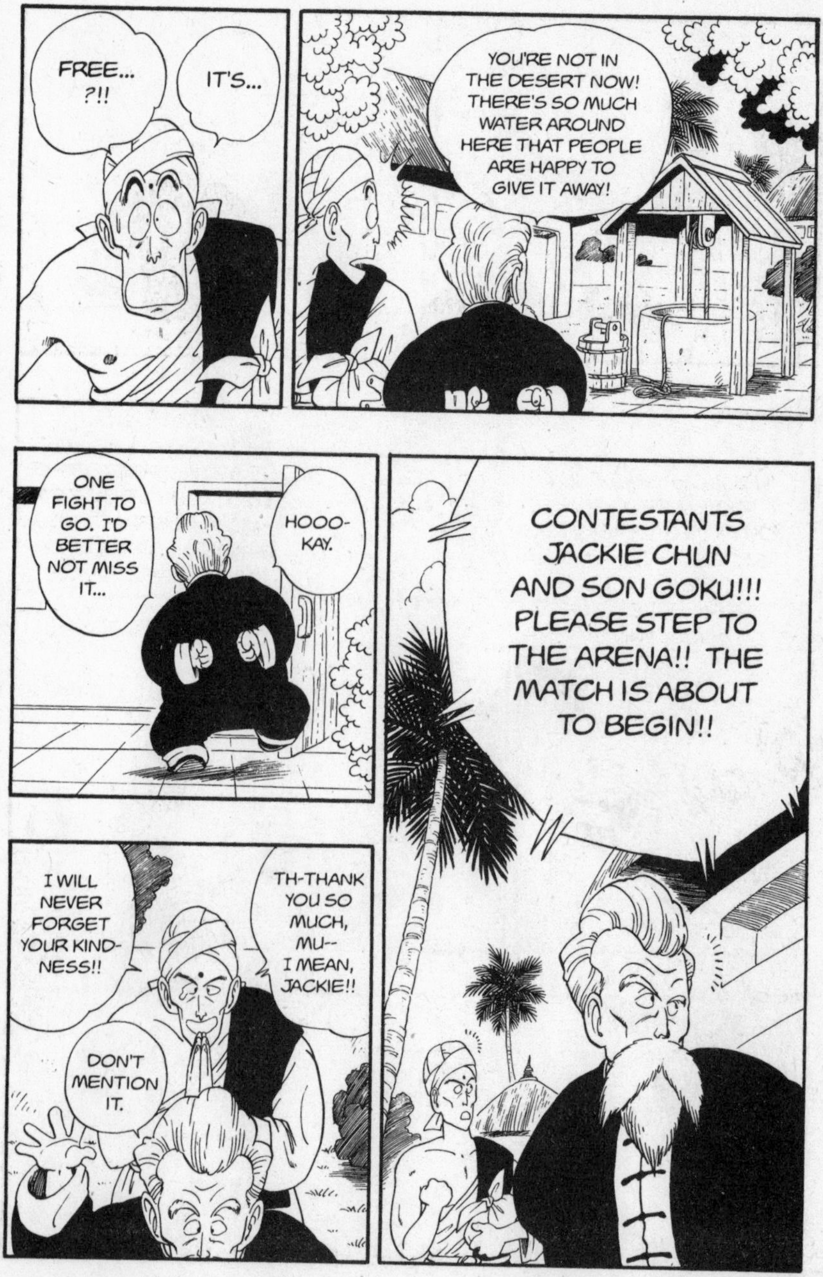

YOU'RE NOT IN THE DESERT NOW! THERE'S SO MUCH WATER AROUND HERE THAT PEOPLE ARE HAPPY TO GIVE IT AWAY!
IT'S...
FREE... ?!!
CONTESTANTS JACKIE CHUN AND SON GOKU!!! PLEASE STEP TO THE ARENA!! THE MATCH IS ABOUT TO BEGIN!!
HOOO-KAY.
ONE FIGHT TO GO. I'D BETTER NOT MISS IT...
TH-THANK YOU SO MUCH, MU-- I MEAN, JACKIE!!
I WILL NEVER FORGET YOUR KIND-NESS!!
DON'T MENTION IT.

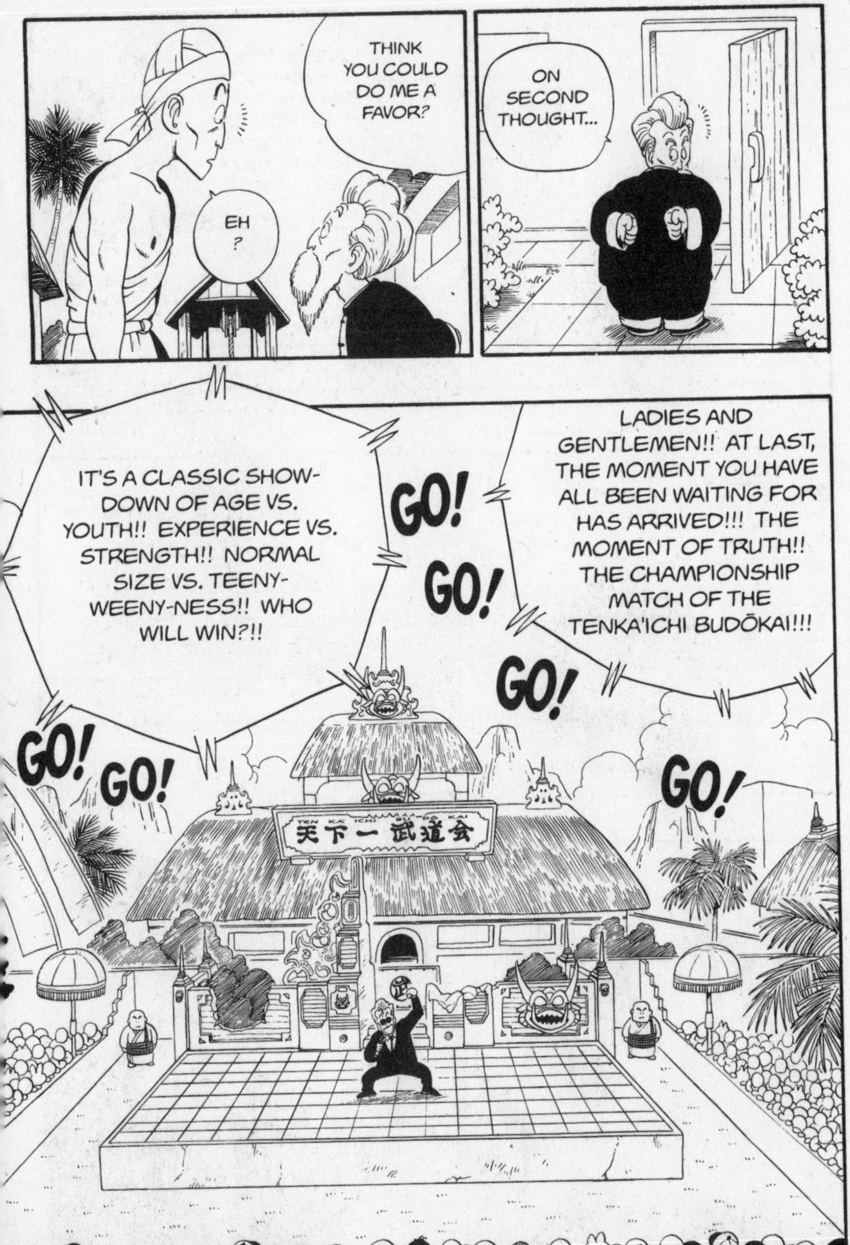
ON SECOND THOUGHT...
THINK YOU COULD DO ME A FAVOR?
EH ?
LADIES AND GENTLEMEN!! AT LAST, THE MOMENT YOU HAVE ALL BEEN WAITING FOR HAS ARRIVED!!! THE MOMENT OF TRUTH!! THE CHAMPIONSHIP MATCH OF THE TENKA'ICHI BUDŌKAI!!!
IT'S A CLASSIC SHOW-DOWN OF AGE VS. YOUTH!! EXPERIENCE VS. STRENGTH!! NORMAL SIZE VS. TEENY-WEENY-NESS!! WHO WILL WIN?!!
GO!
GO!
GO!
GO!
GO!
GO!
天下一武道会

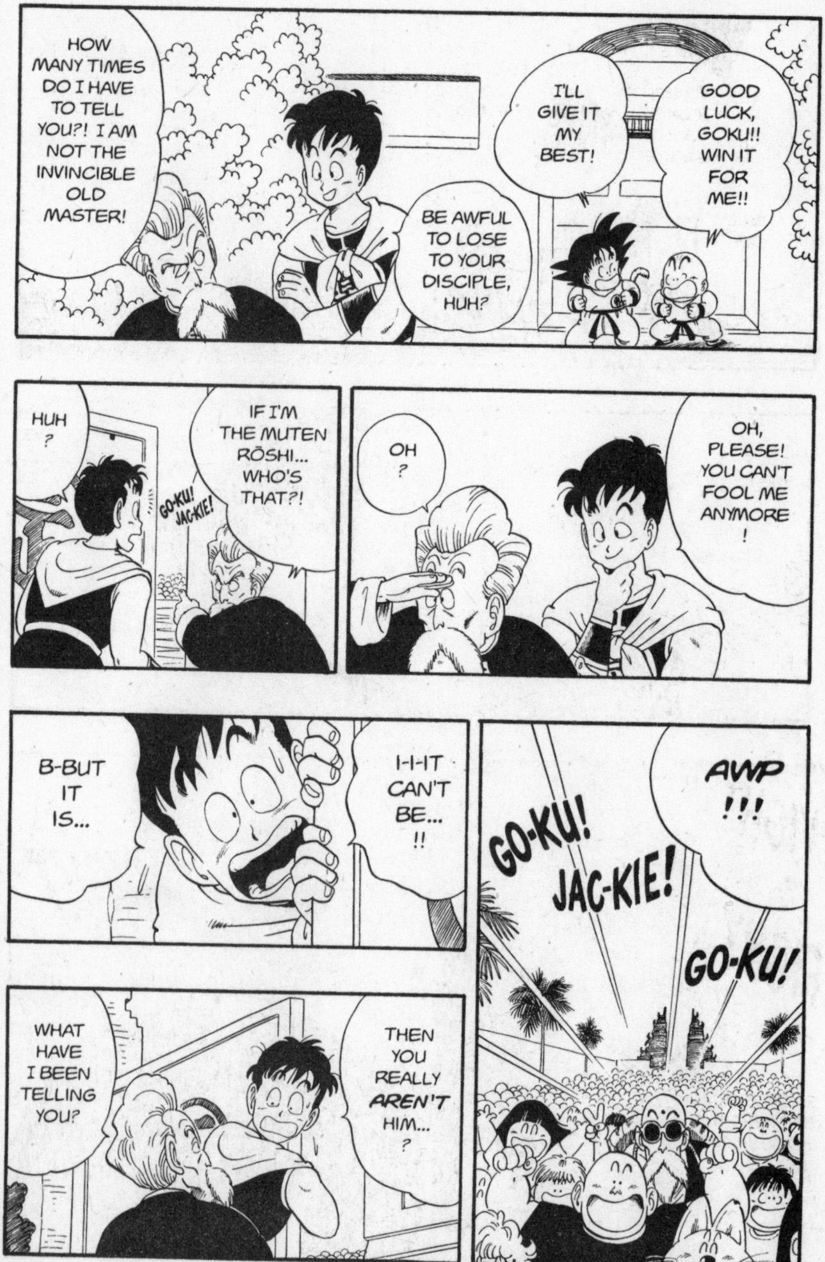
GOOD LUCK, GOKU!! WIN IT FOR ME!!
I'LL GIVE IT MY BEST!
BE AWFUL TO LOSE TO YOUR DISCIPLE, HUH?
HOW MANY TIMES DO I HAVE TO TELL YOU?! I AM NOT THE INVINCIBLE OLD MASTER!
OH, PLEASE! YOU CAN'T FOOL ME ANYMORE!
OH?
IF I'M THE MUTEN RŌSHI... WHO'S THAT?!
GO-KU! JAC-KIE!
HUH?
AWP!!!
GO-KU!
JAC-KIE!
GO-KU!
I-I-IT CAN'T BE...!!
B-BUT IT IS...
THEN YOU REALLY *AREN'T* HIM...?
WHAT HAVE I BEEN TELLING YOU?

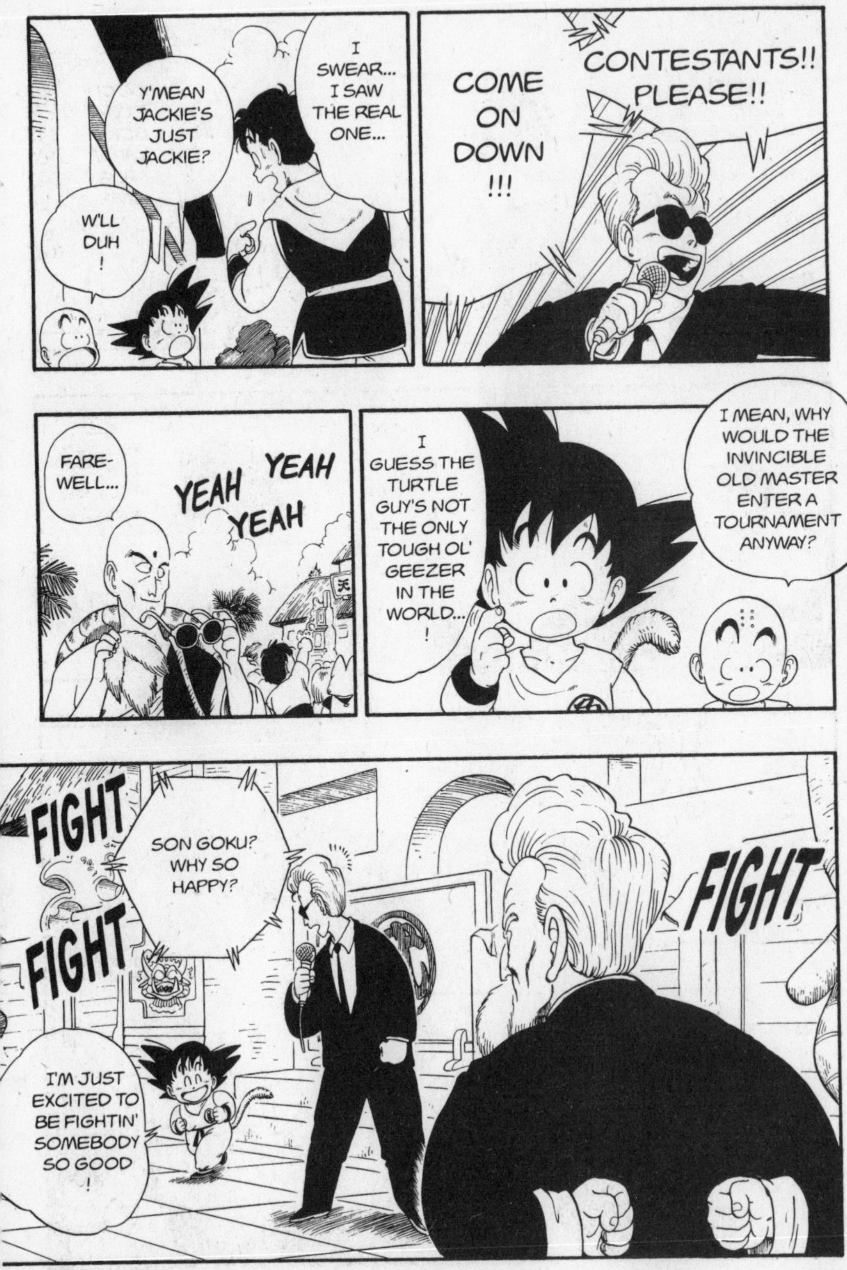
CONTESTANTS!! PLEASE!!
COME ON DOWN!!!
I SWEAR... I SAW THE REAL ONE...
Y'MEAN JACKIE'S JUST JACKIE?
W'LL DUH!
I MEAN, WHY WOULD THE INVINCIBLE OLD MASTER ENTER A TOURNAMENT ANYWAY?
I GUESS THE TURTLE GUY'S NOT THE ONLY TOUGH OL' GEEZER IN THE WORLD...!
YEAH
YEAH
YEAH
FARE-WELL...
FIGHT
SON GOKU? WHY SO HAPPY?
FIGHT
FIGHT
I'M JUST EXCITED TO BE FIGHTIN' SOMEBODY SO GOOD!

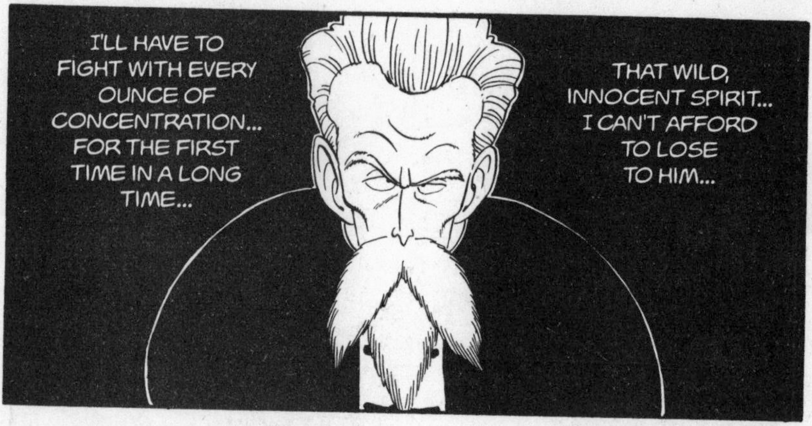
THAT WILD, INNOCENT SPIRIT... I CAN'T AFFORD TO LOSE TO HIM...
I'LL HAVE TO FIGHT WITH EVERY OUNCE OF CONCENTRATION... FOR THE FIRST TIME IN A LONG TIME...

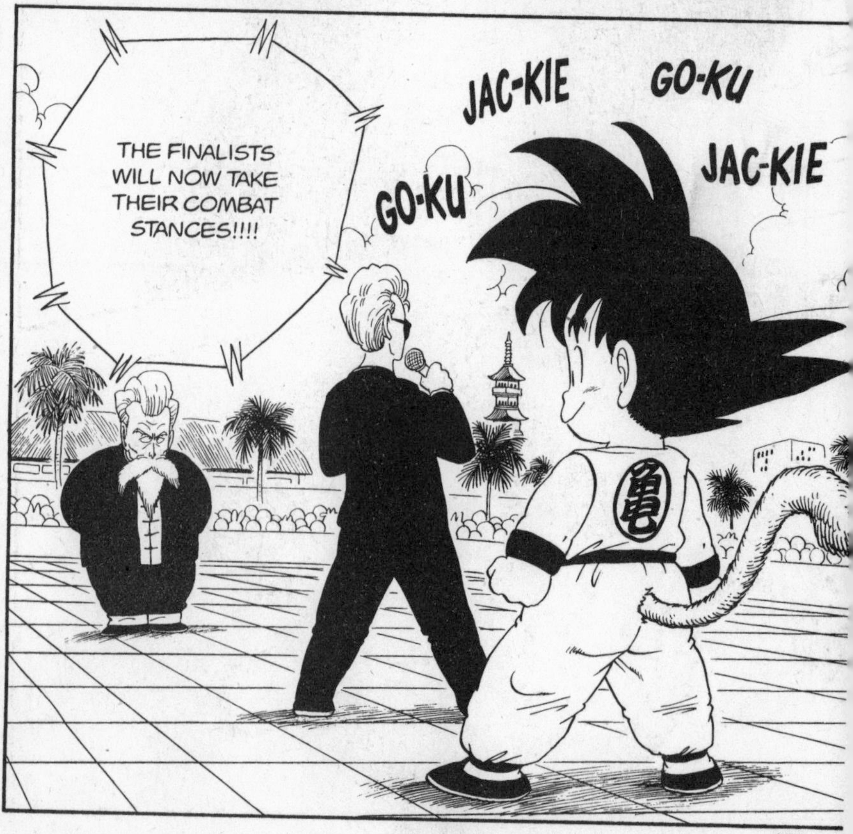
GO-KU
JAC-KIE
JAC-KIE
GO-KU
THE FINALISTS WILL NOW TAKE THEIR COMBAT STANCES!!!!

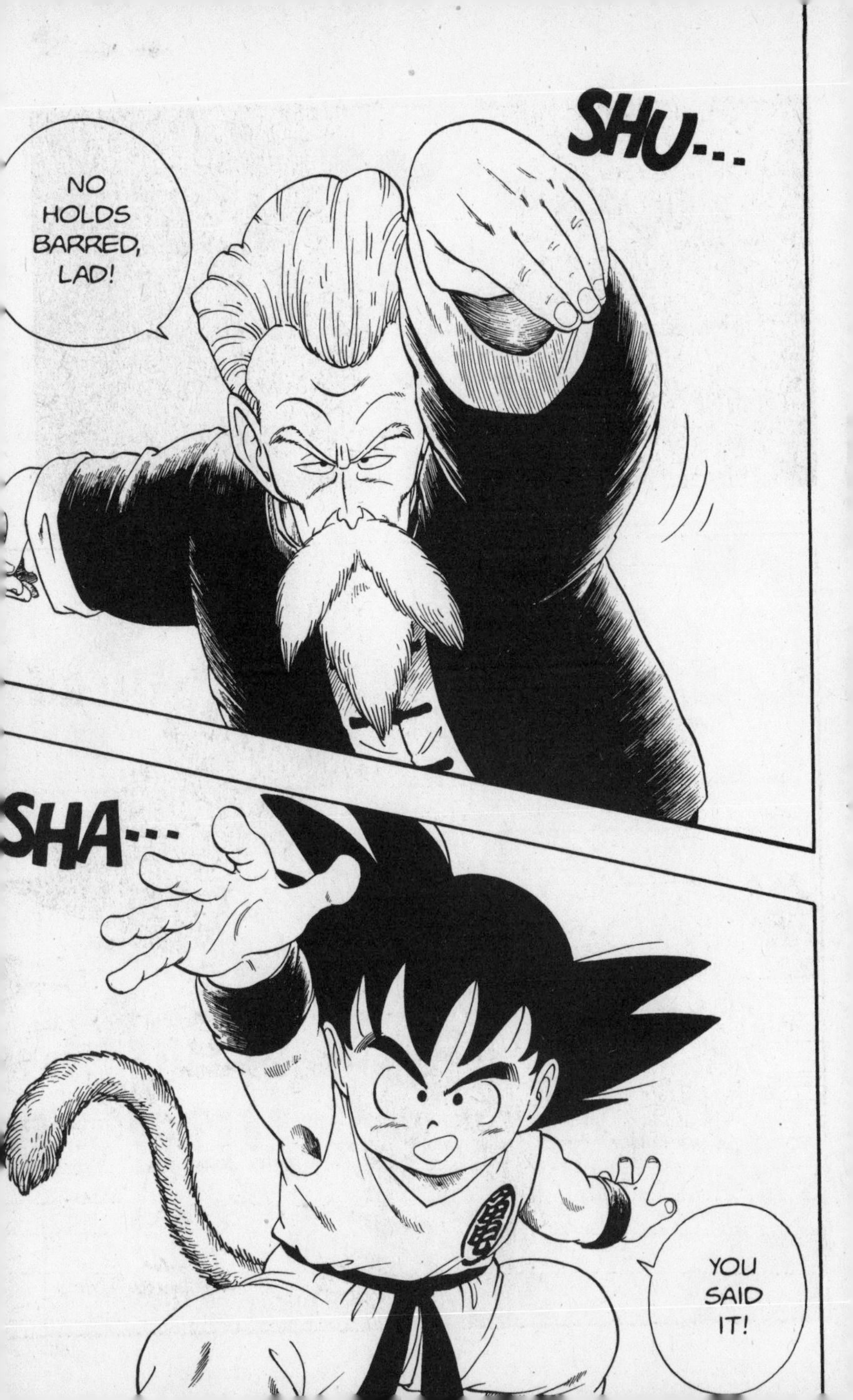
SHU...
NO HOLDS BARRED, LAD!
SHA...
YOU SAID IT!

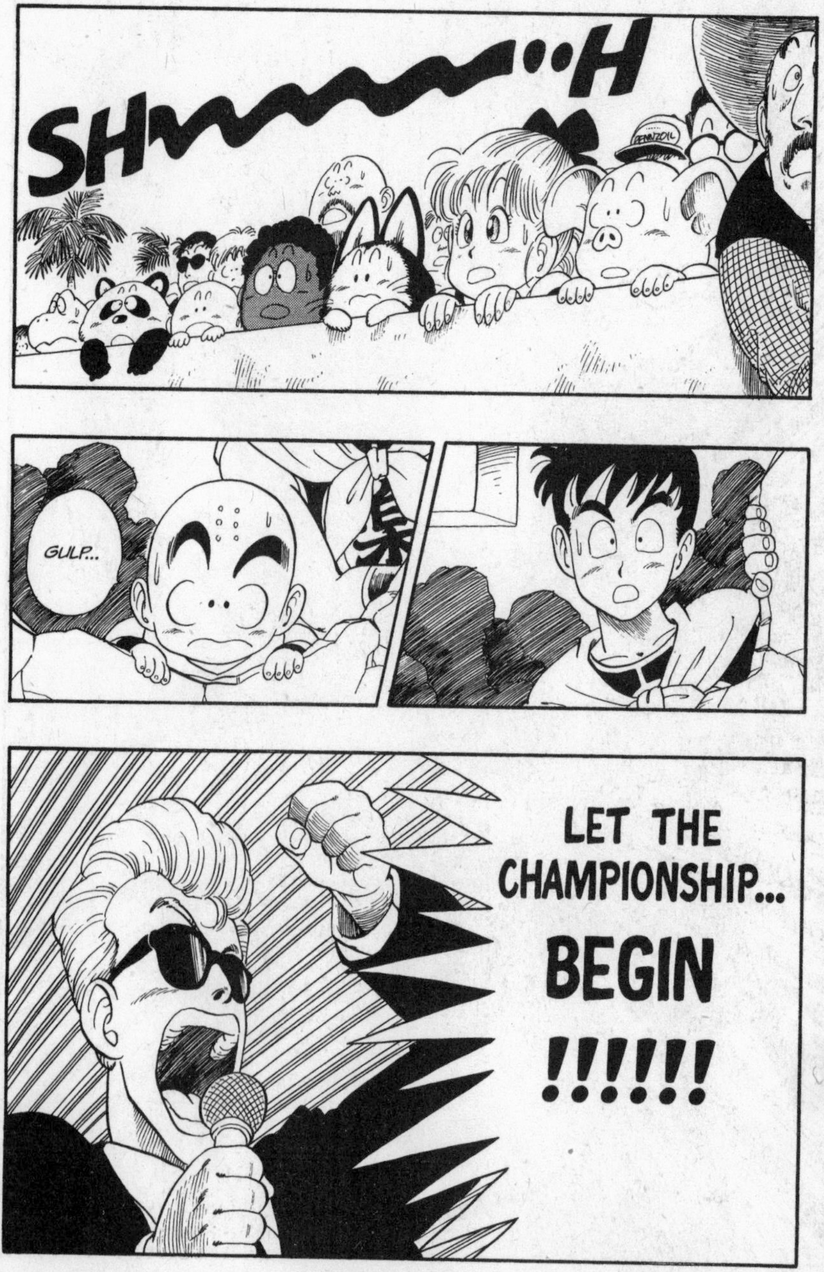
SH~~~H
GULP...
LET THE CHAMPIONSHIP... BEGIN !!!!!!

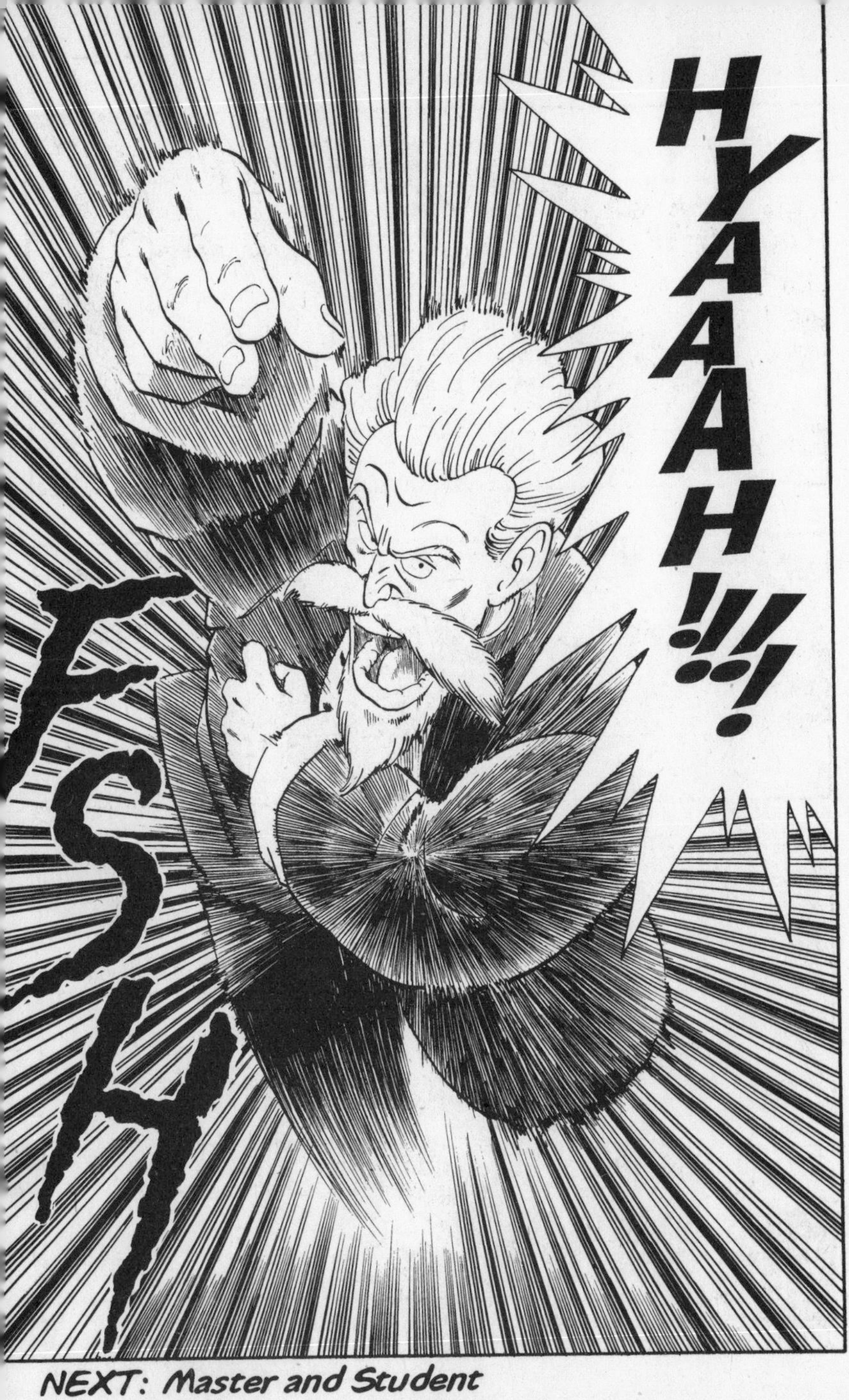
HYAAAH!!!!
FSH
NEXT: Master and Student

Tale 47 • The Kamehameha

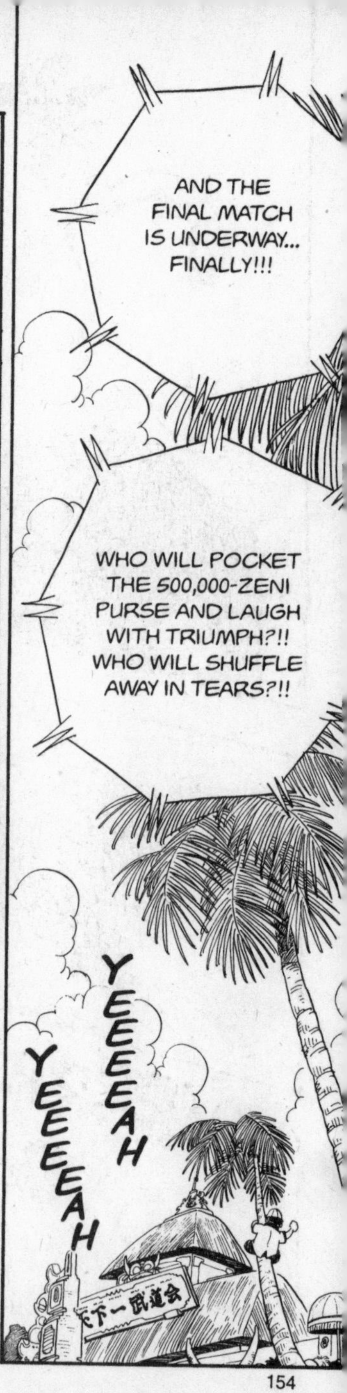
AND THE FINAL MATCH IS UNDERWAY... FINALLY!!!
WHO WILL POCKET THE 500,000-ZENI PURSE AND LAUGH WITH TRIUMPH?!! WHO WILL SHUFFLE AWAY IN TEARS?!!
YEEEEAH
YEEEEAH
天下一武道会

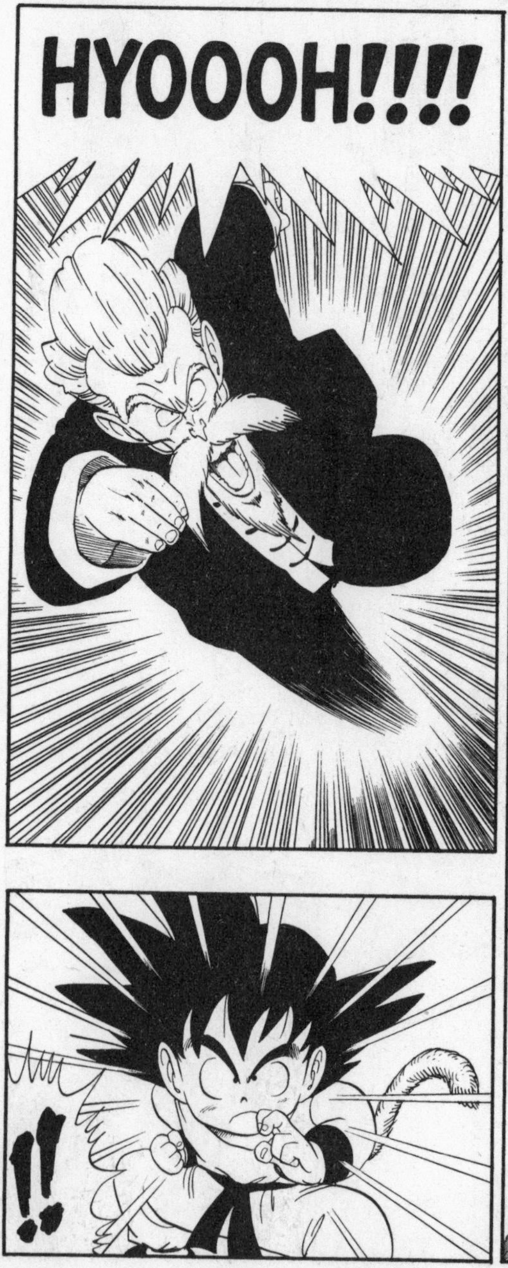
HYOOOH!!!!
!!

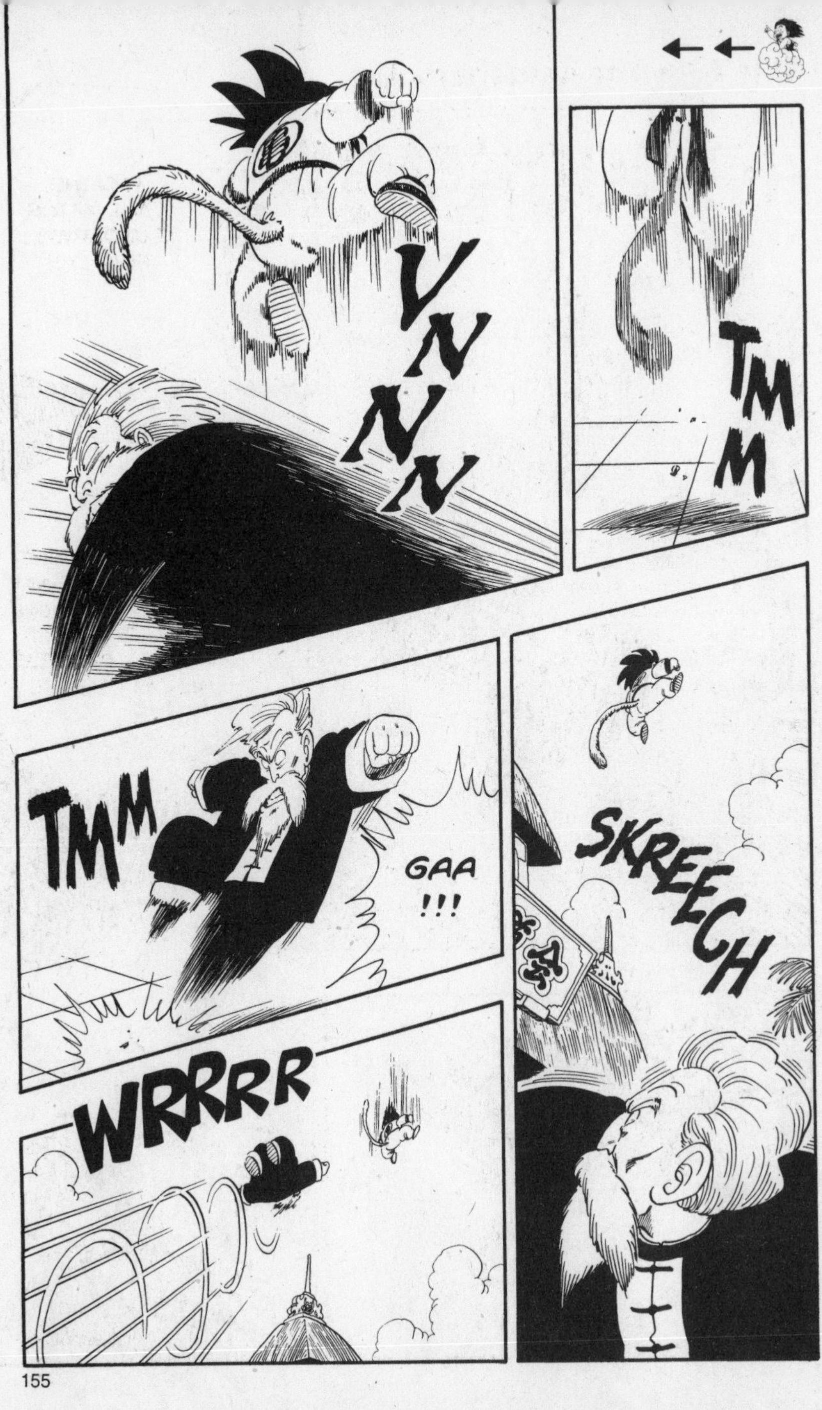
TMM
VNNN
SKREECH
TMM
GAA !!!
WRRRR

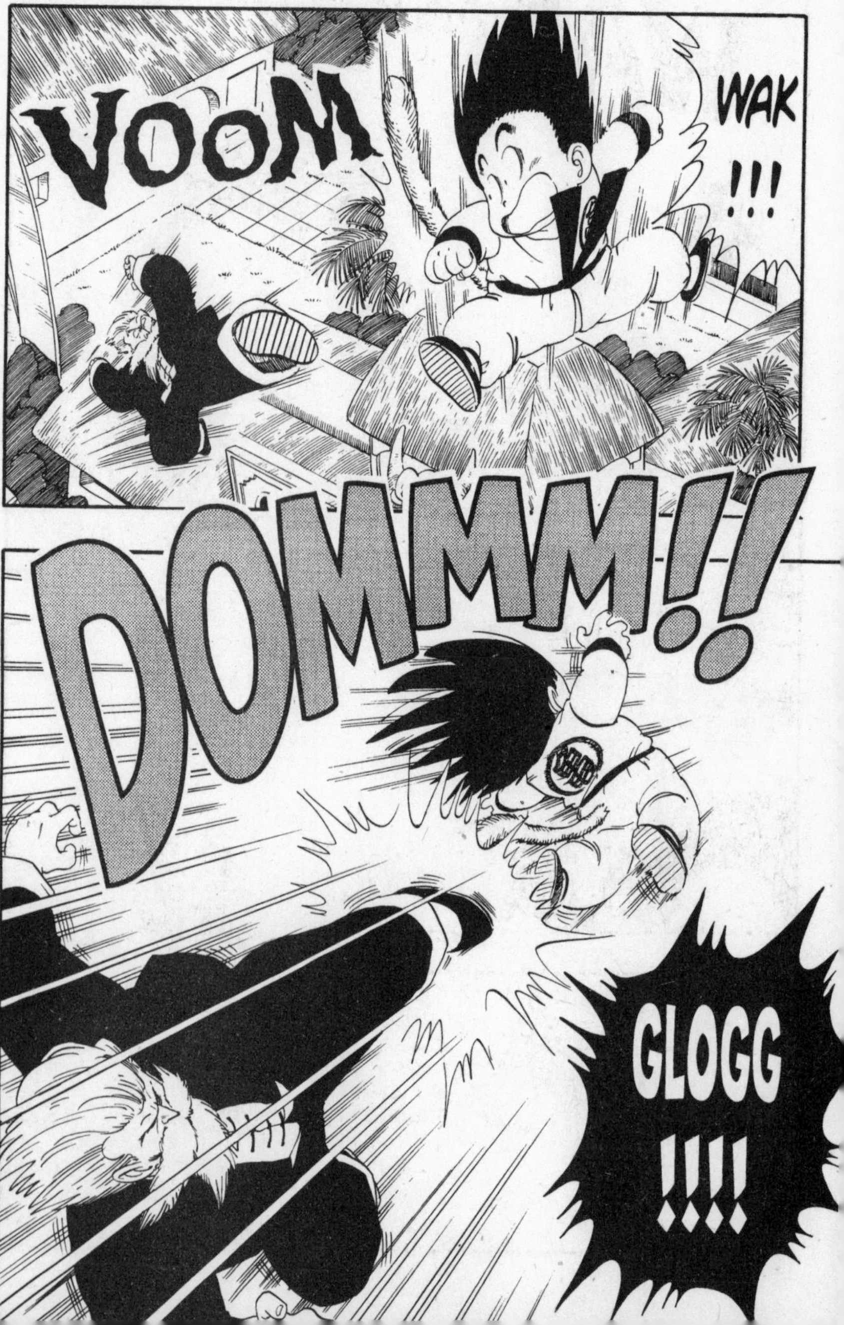
WAK!!!
VOOM
DOMMM!!
GLOGG!!!!

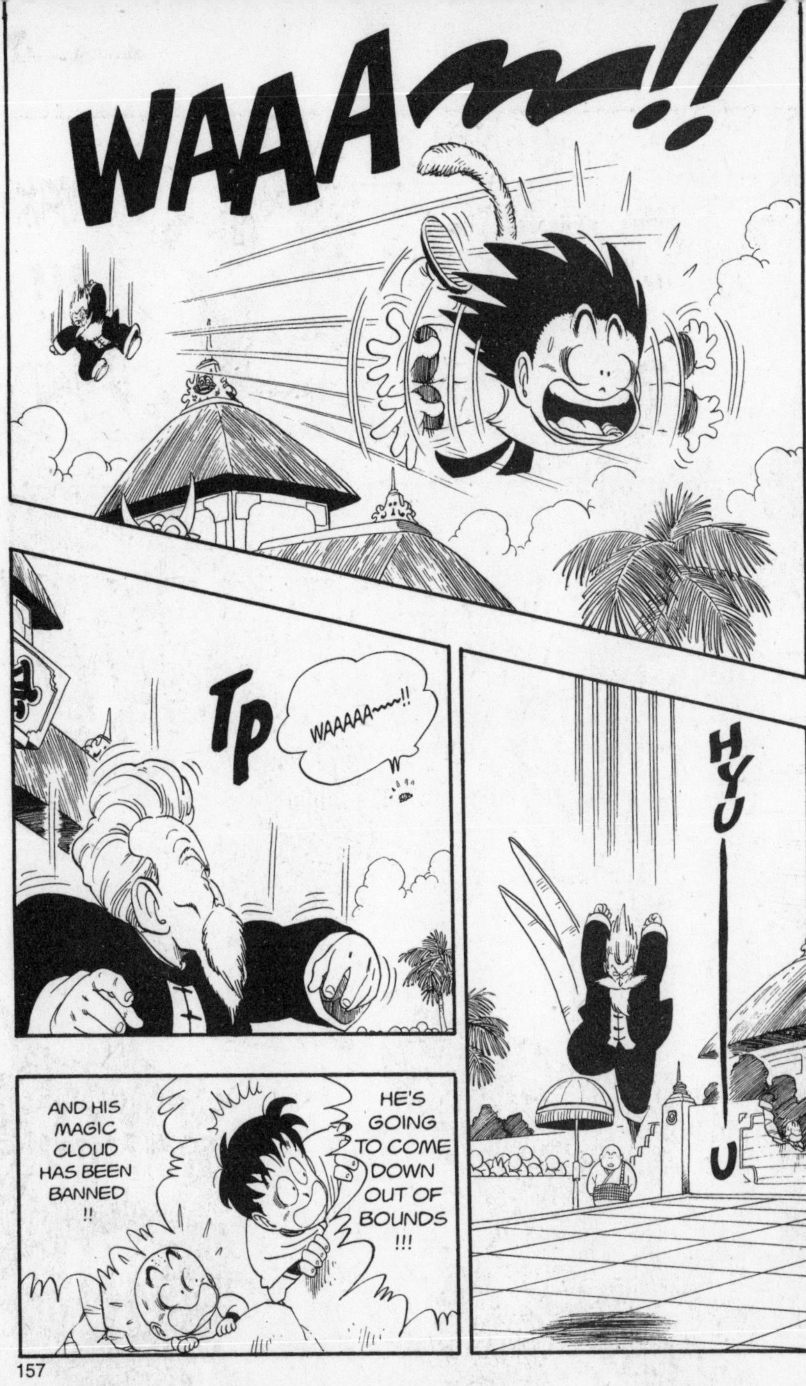
WAAAM!!
HYU
U
Tp
WAAAAA~~!!
HE'S GOING TO COME DOWN OUT OF BOUNDS !!!
AND HIS MAGIC CLOUD HAS BEEN BANNED !!

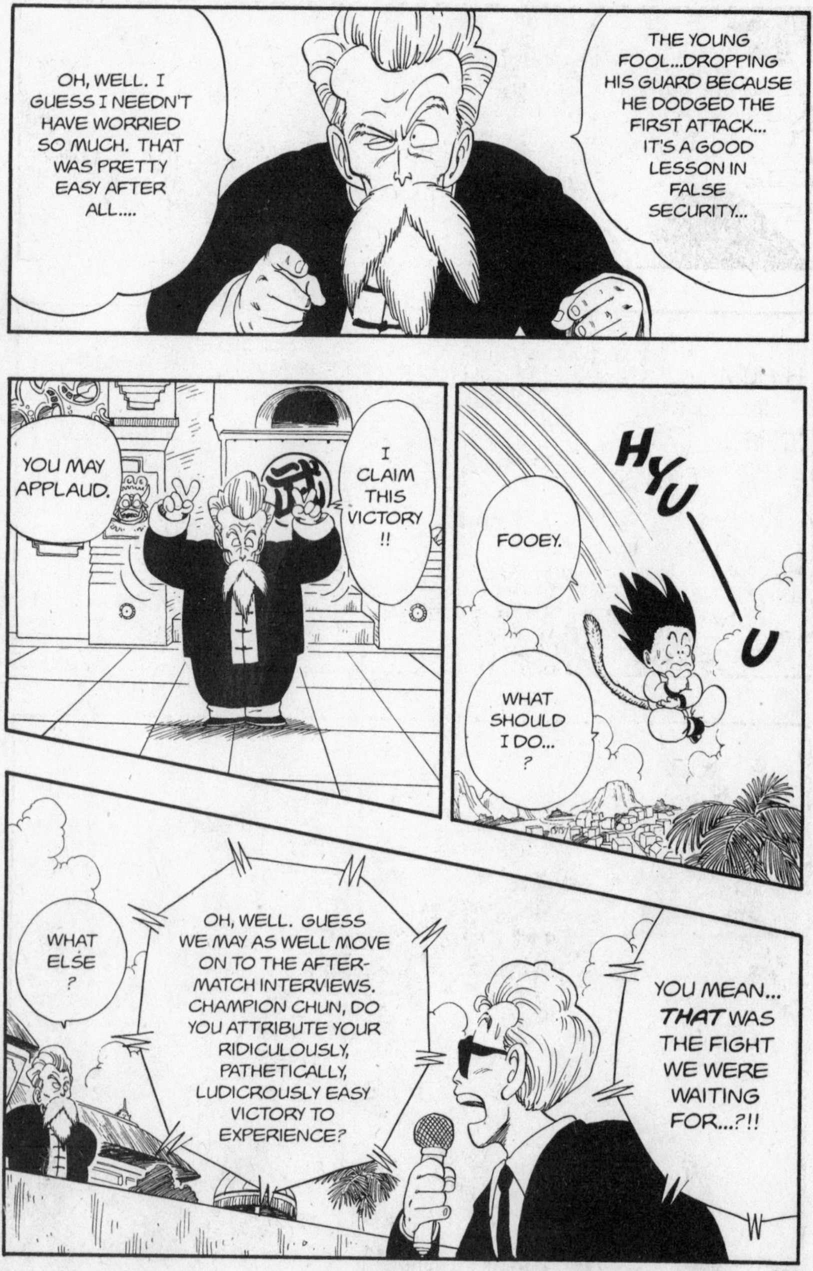
THE YOUNG FOOL...DROPPING HIS GUARD BECAUSE HE DODGED THE FIRST ATTACK... IT'S A GOOD LESSON IN FALSE SECURITY...
OH, WELL. I GUESS I NEEDN'T HAVE WORRIED SO MUCH. THAT WAS PRETTY EASY AFTER ALL....
HYU—U
FOOEY.
WHAT SHOULD I DO...?
I CLAIM THIS VICTORY!!
YOU MAY APPLAUD.
YOU MEAN... *THAT* WAS THE FIGHT WE WERE WAITING FOR...?!!
OH, WELL. GUESS WE MAY AS WELL MOVE ON TO THE AFTER-MATCH INTERVIEWS. CHAMPION CHUN, DO YOU ATTRIBUTE YOUR RIDICULOUSLY, PATHETICALLY, LUDICROUSLY EASY VICTORY TO EXPERIENCE?
WHAT ELSE?

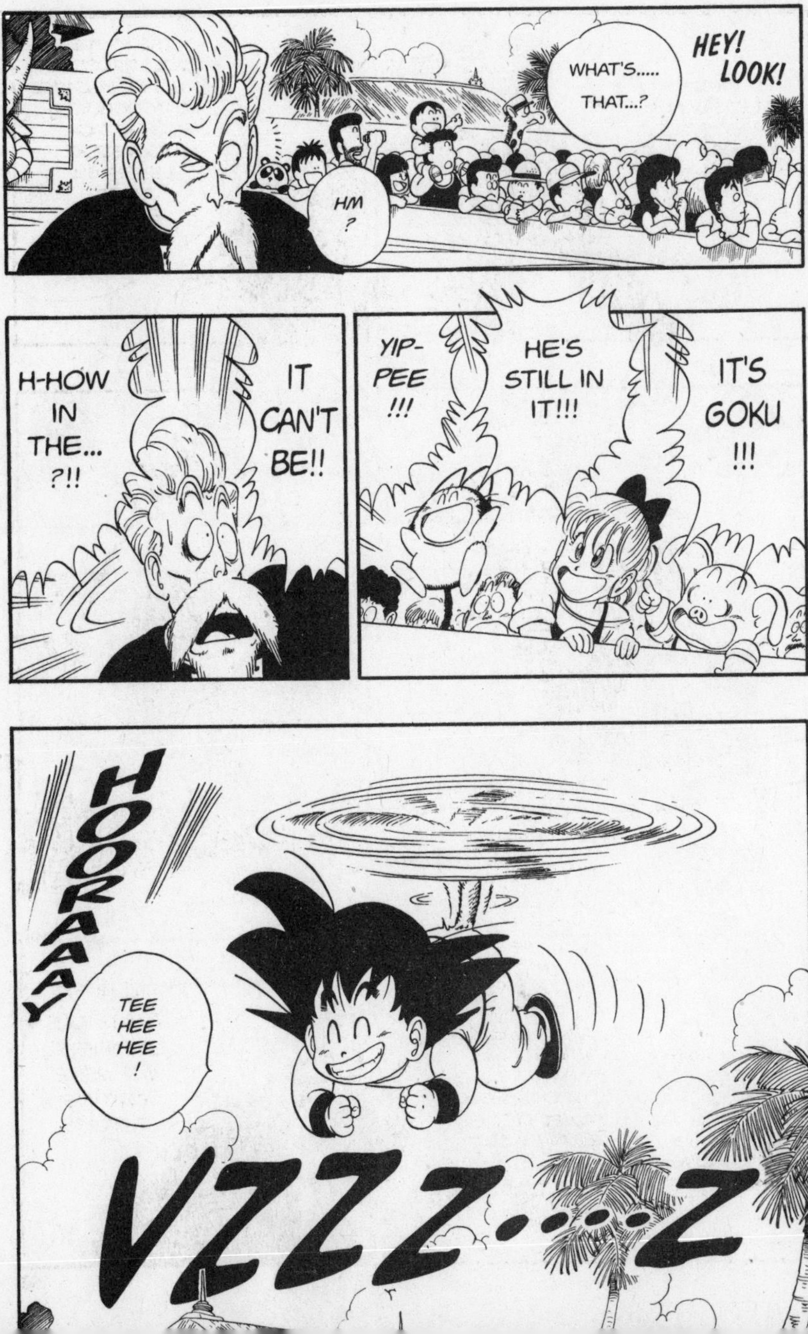
HEY! LOOK!
WHAT'S..... THAT...?
HM ?
IT'S GOKU !!!
HE'S STILL IN IT!!!
YIP-PEE !!!
IT CAN'T BE!!
H-HOW IN THE... ?!!
HOORAAAY
TEE HEE HEE !
VZZZ...Z

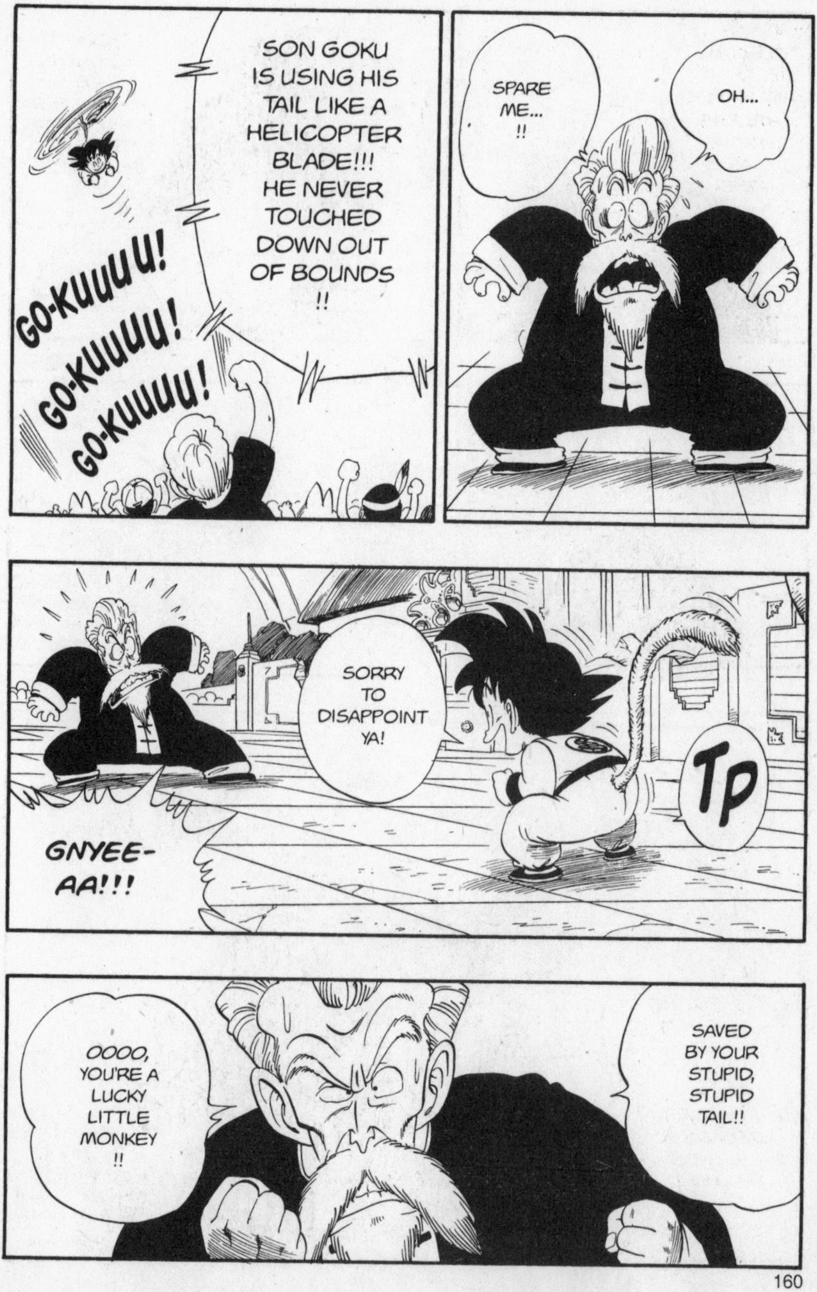
OH...
SPARE ME... !!
SON GOKU IS USING HIS TAIL LIKE A HELICOPTER BLADE!!! HE NEVER TOUCHED DOWN OUT OF BOUNDS !!
GO-KUUUU!
GO-KUUUU!
GO-KUUUU!
Tp
SORRY TO DISAPPOINT YA!
GNYEE-AA!!!
SAVED BY YOUR STUPID, STUPID TAIL!!
OOOO, YOU'RE A LUCKY LITTLE MONKEY !!

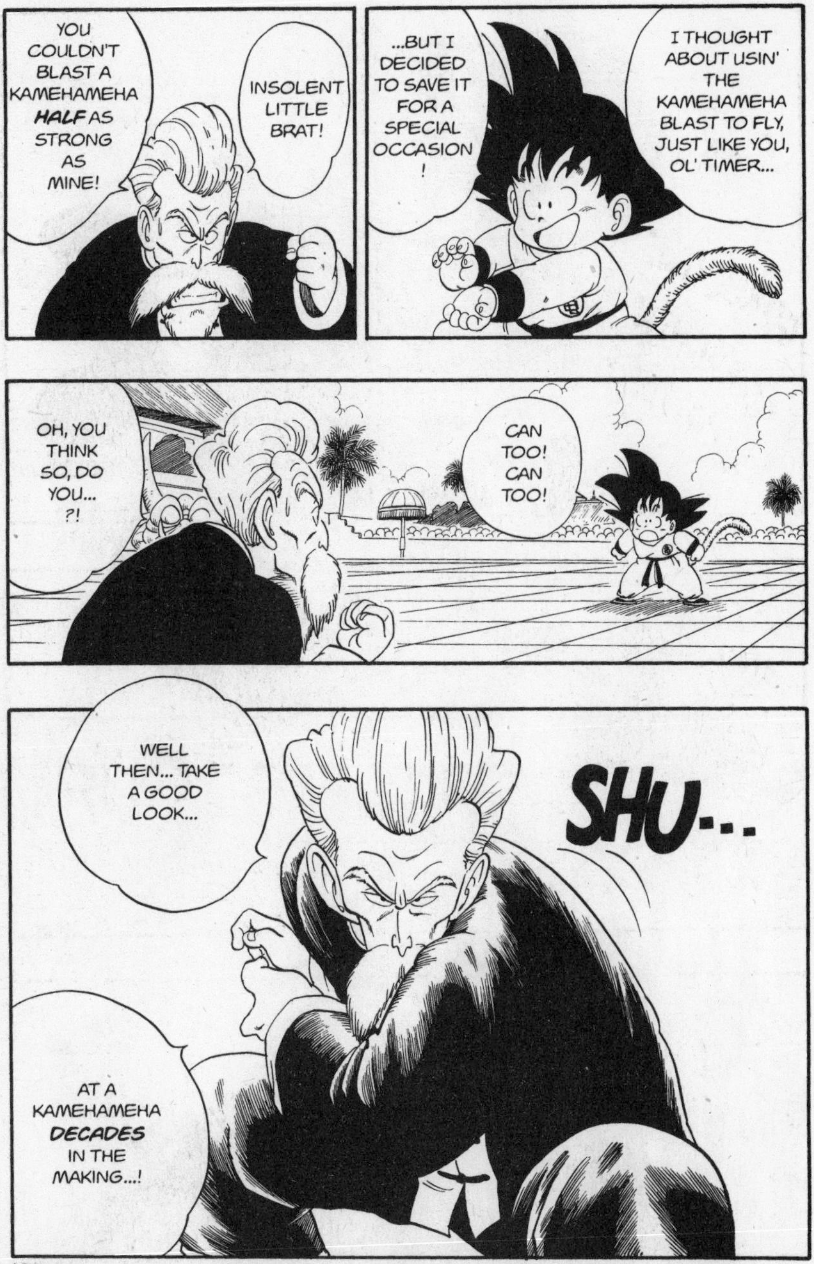
I THOUGHT ABOUT USIN' THE KAMEHAMEHA BLAST TO FLY, JUST LIKE YOU, OL' TIMER...
...BUT I DECIDED TO SAVE IT FOR A SPECIAL OCCASION!
INSOLENT LITTLE BRAT!
YOU COULDN'T BLAST A KAMEHAMEHA HALF AS STRONG AS MINE!
CAN TOO! CAN TOO!
OH, YOU THINK SO, DO YOU...?!
SHU...
WELL THEN... TAKE A GOOD LOOK...
AT A KAMEHAMEHA DECADES IN THE MAKING...!

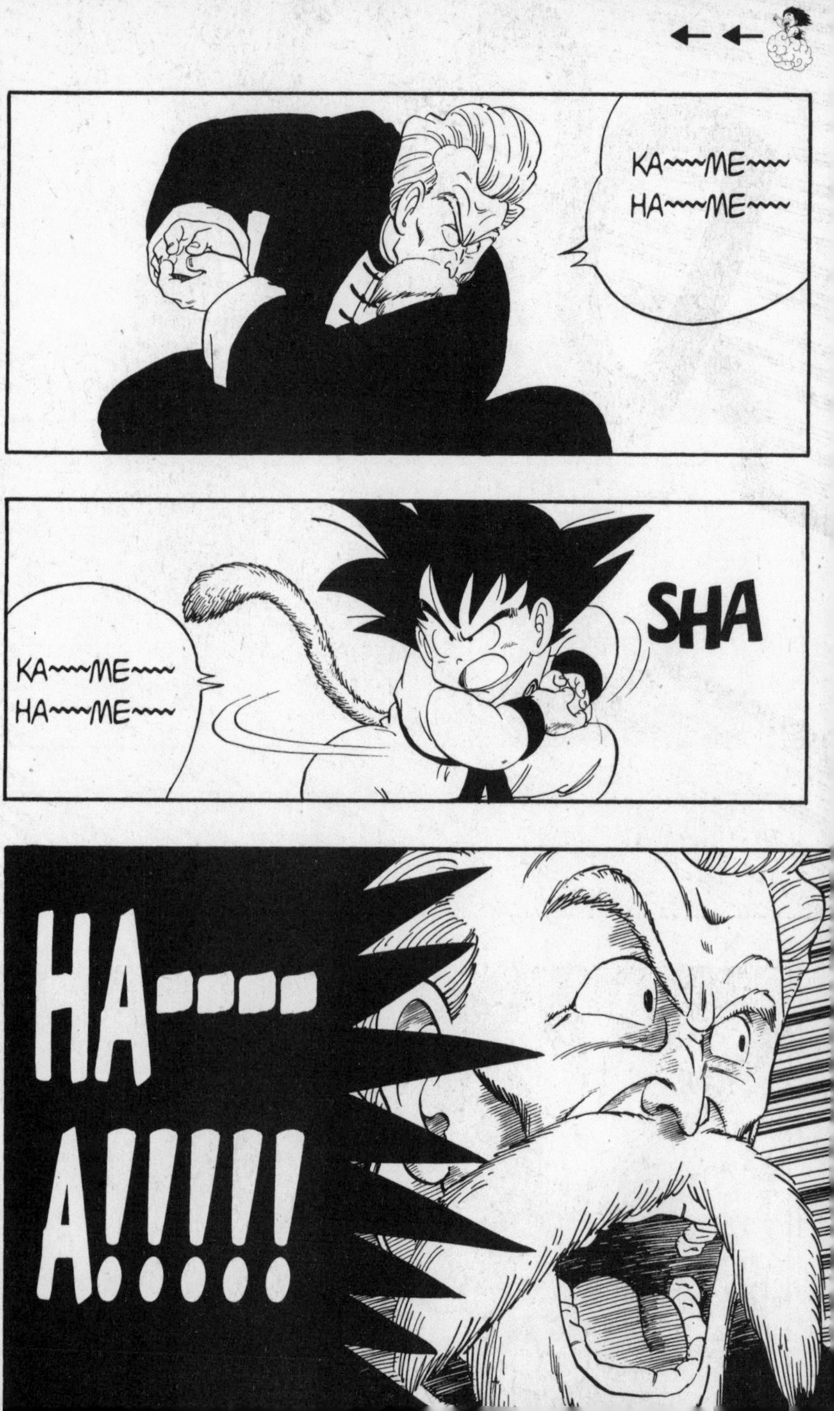
KA~~~ME~~~ HA~~~ME~~~
SHA
KA~~~ME~~~ HA~~~ME~~~
HA----A!!!!!

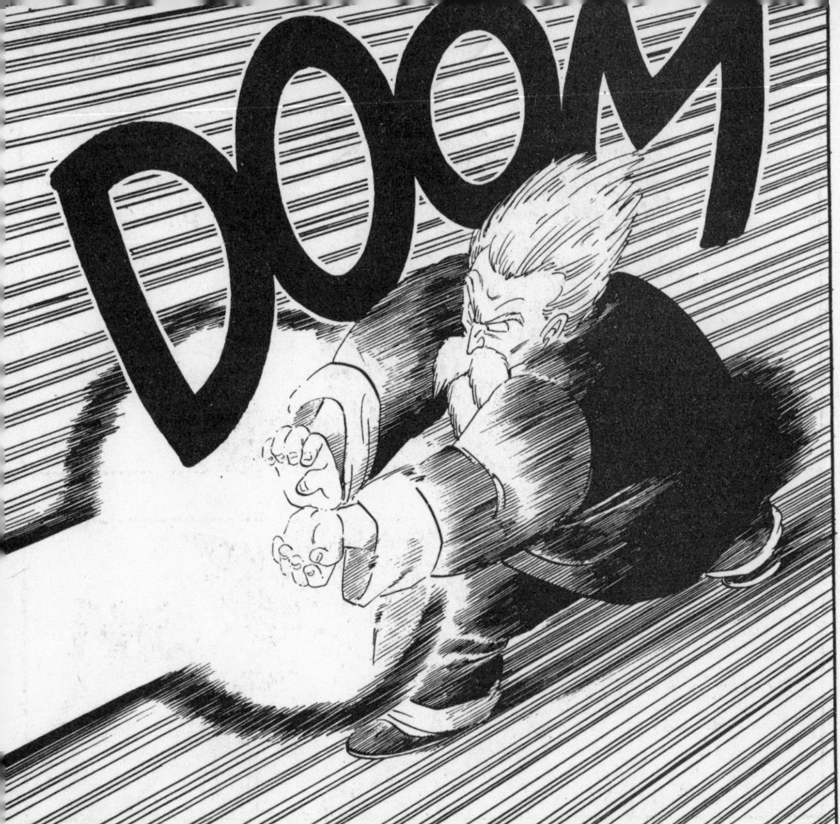
DOOM
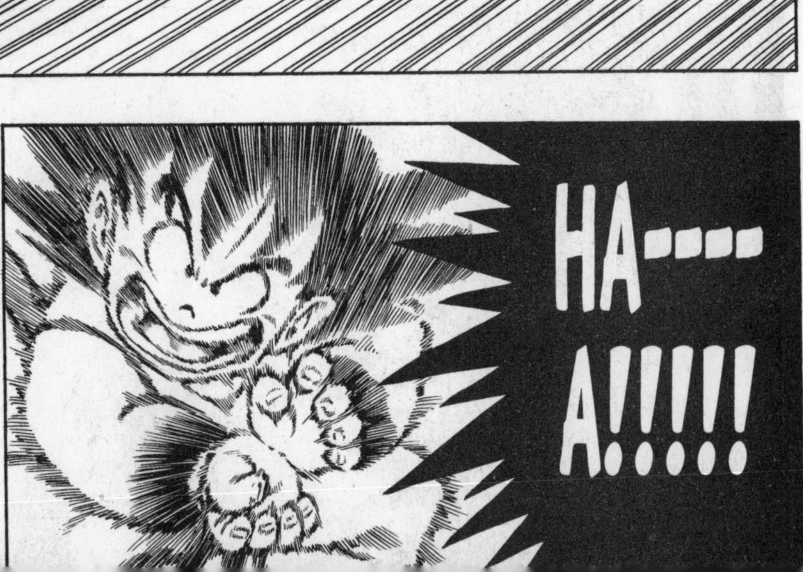
HA----
A!!!!!

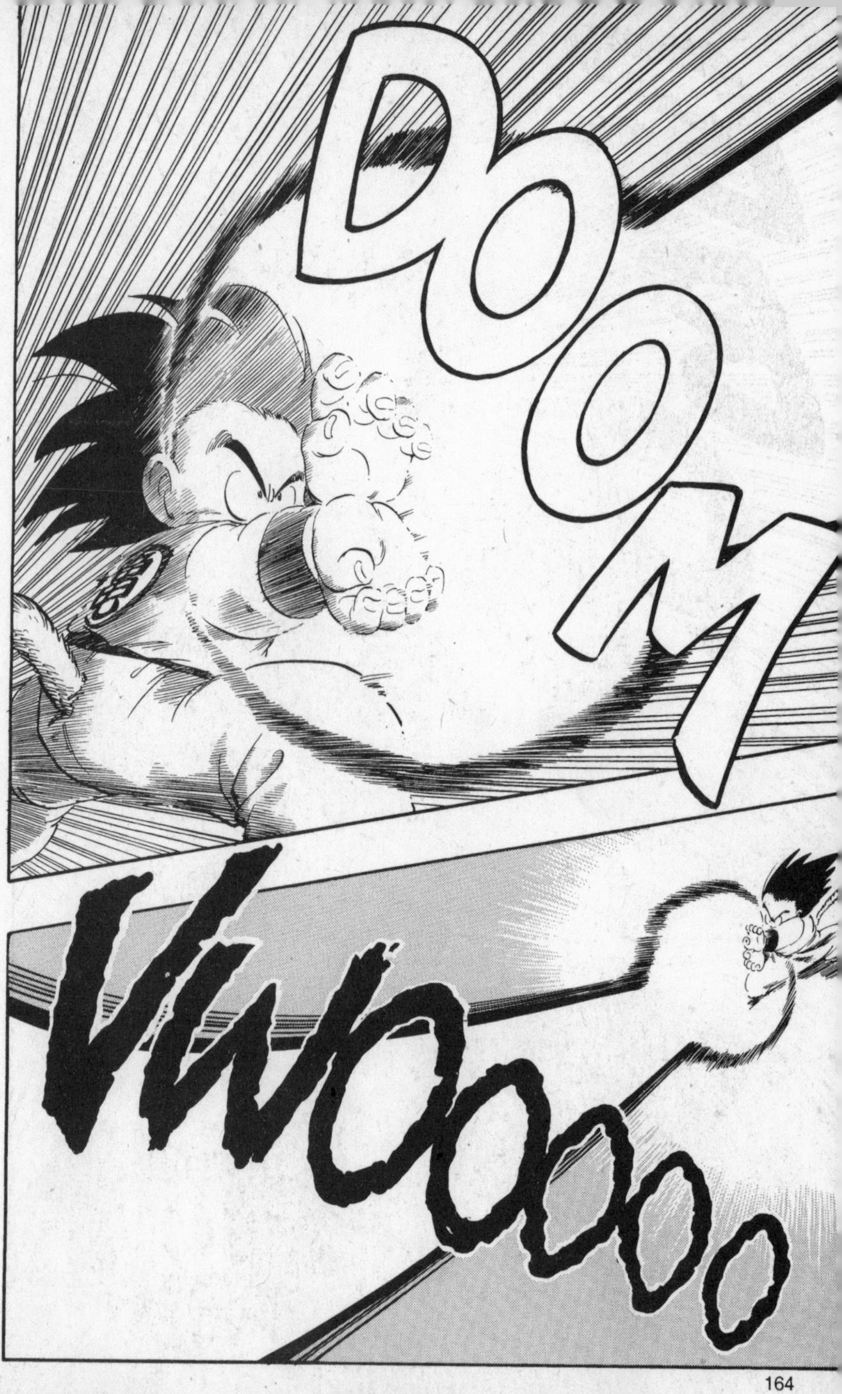
DOOOM
VWOOOOO

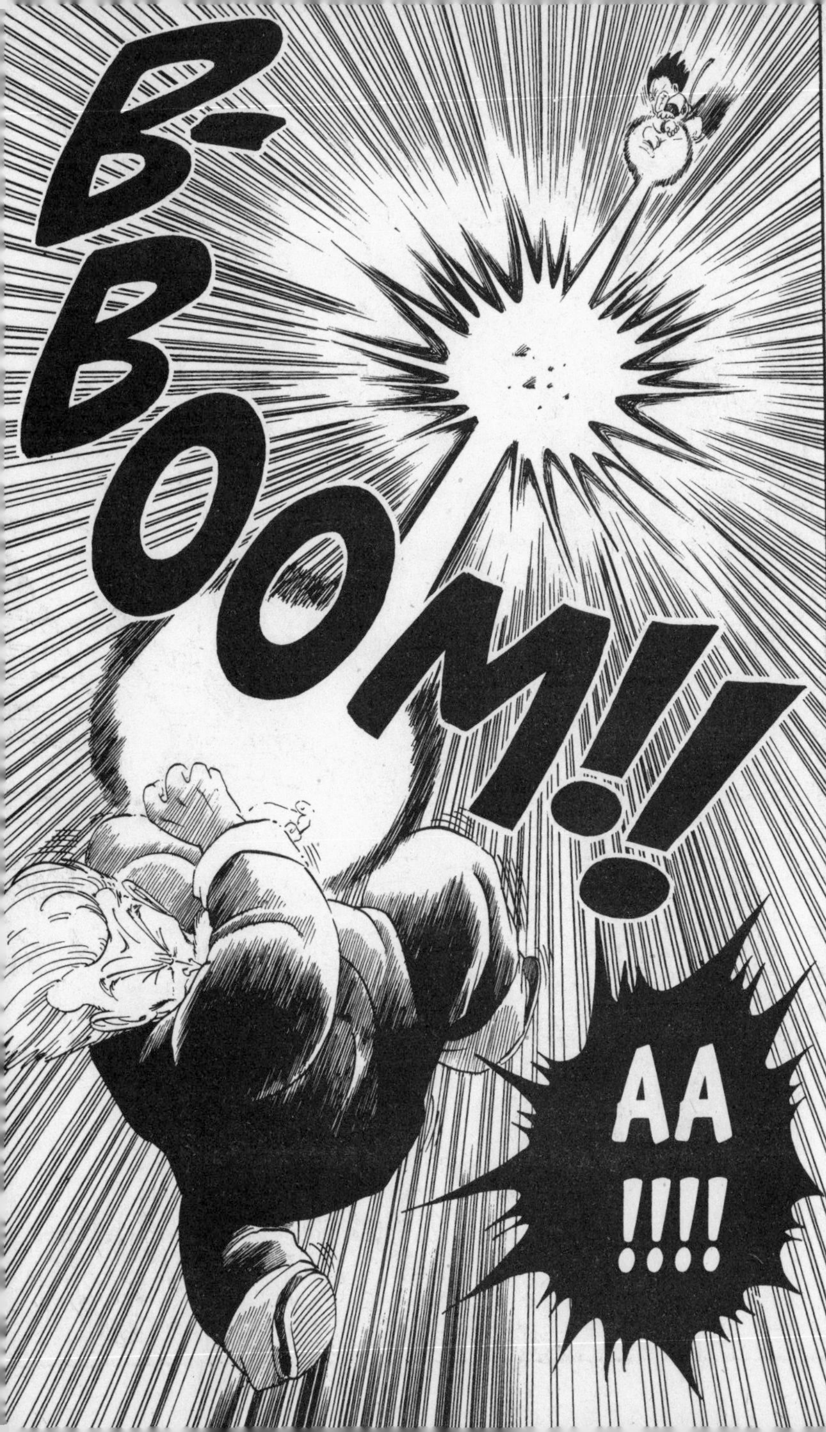
B-BOOM!!
AA
!!!!

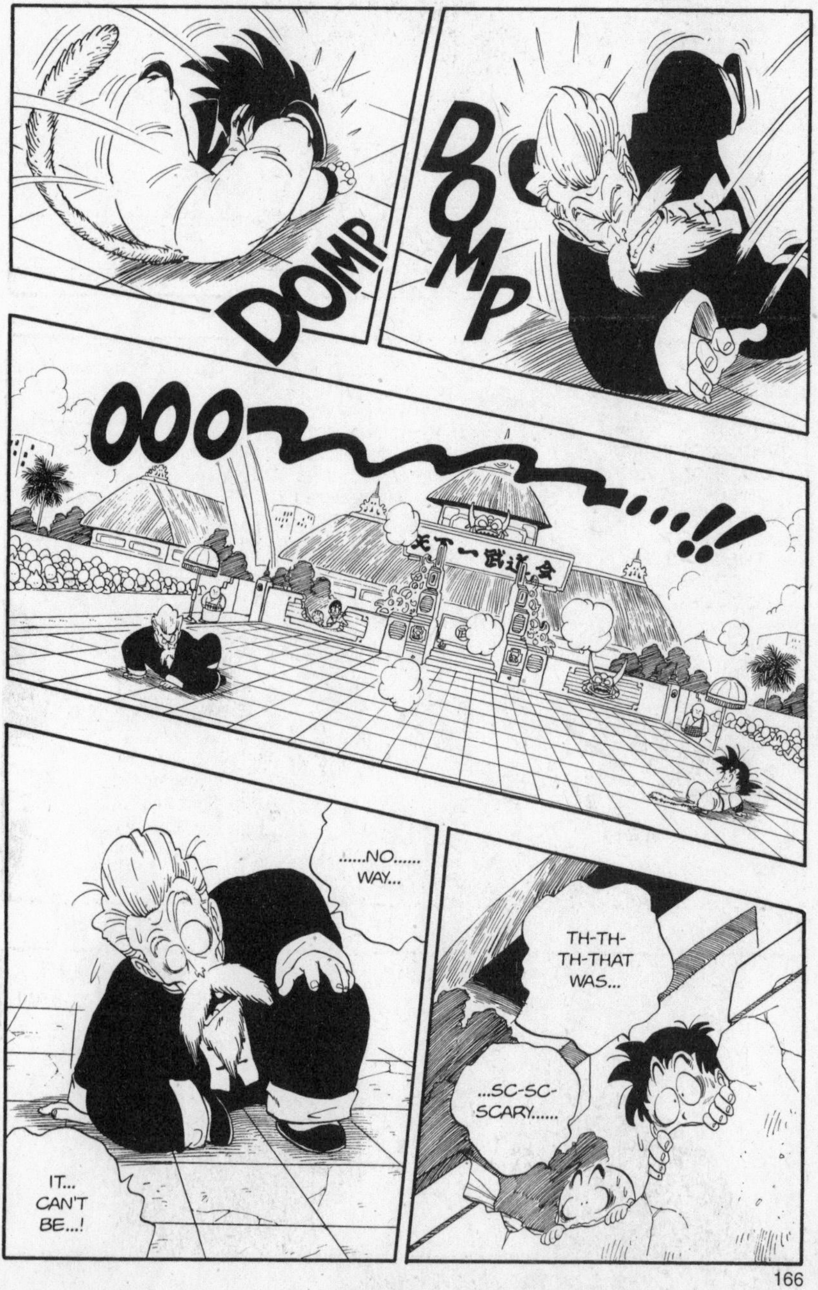
DOMP
DOMP
OOO~~~...!!
TH-TH-
TH-THAT
WAS...
...SC-SC-
SCARY......
......NO......
WAY...
IT...
CAN'T
BE...!

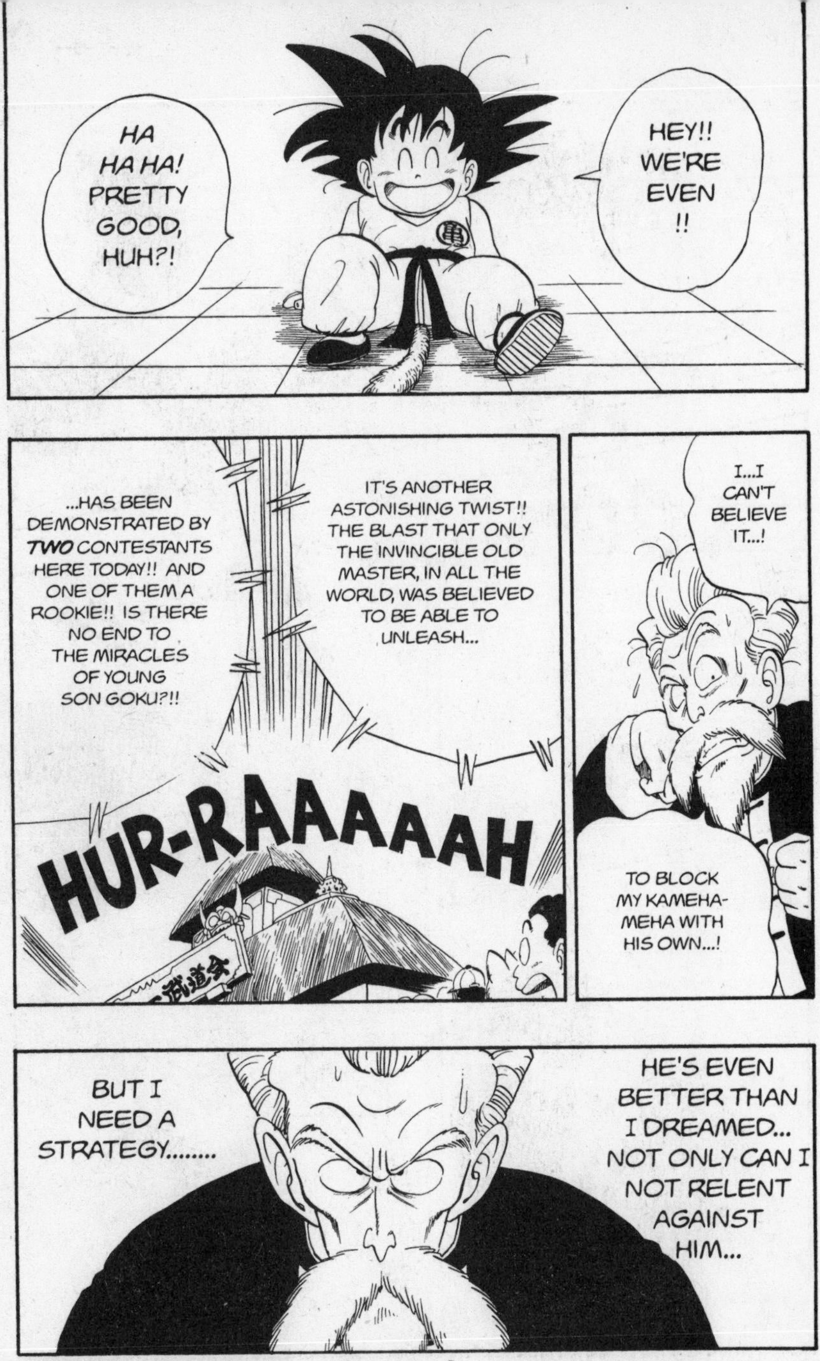
HEY!! WE'RE EVEN !!
HA HA HA! PRETTY GOOD, HUH?!
I...I CAN'T BELIEVE IT...!
TO BLOCK MY KAMEHA-MEHA WITH HIS OWN...!
IT'S ANOTHER ASTONISHING TWIST!! THE BLAST THAT ONLY THE INVINCIBLE OLD MASTER, IN ALL THE WORLD, WAS BELIEVED TO BE ABLE TO UNLEASH...
...HAS BEEN DEMONSTRATED BY *TWO* CONTESTANTS HERE TODAY!! AND ONE OF THEM A ROOKIE!! IS THERE NO END TO THE MIRACLES OF YOUNG SON GOKU?!!
HUR-RAAAAAH
HE'S EVEN BETTER THAN I DREAMED... NOT ONLY CAN I NOT RELENT AGAINST HIM...
BUT I NEED A STRATEGY........

NEXT*: *One Lucky Monkey!

Tale 48
One Lucky Monkey

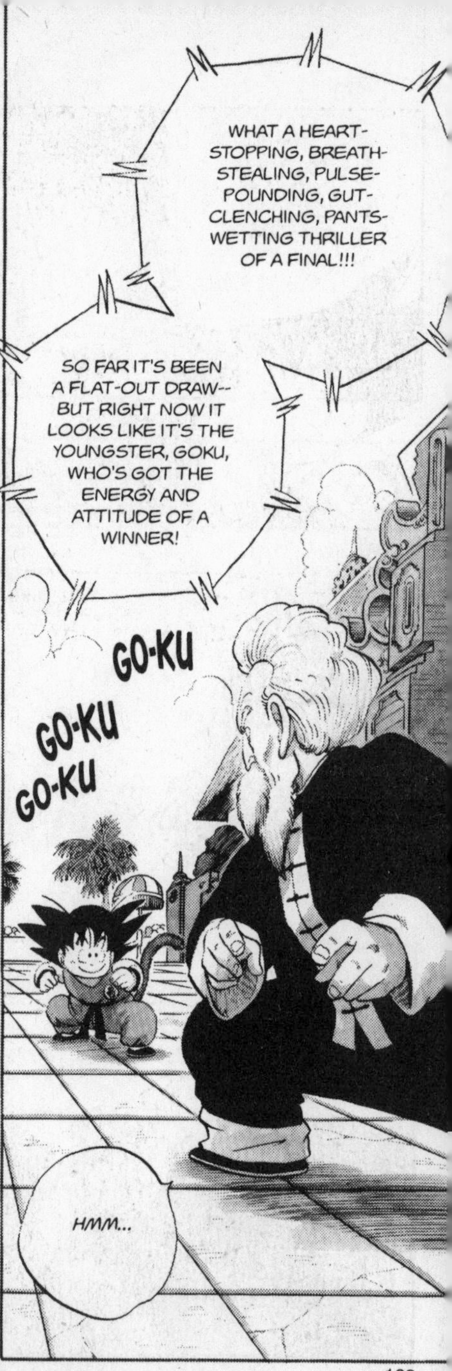

WHAT A HEART-STOPPING, BREATH-STEALING, PULSE-POUNDING, GUT-CLENCHING, PANTS-WETTING THRILLER OF A FINAL!!!
SO FAR IT'S BEEN A FLAT-OUT DRAW-- BUT RIGHT NOW IT LOOKS LIKE IT'S THE YOUNGSTER, GOKU, WHO'S GOT THE ENERGY AND ATTITUDE OF A WINNER!
GO-KU
GO-KU
GO-KU
HMM...

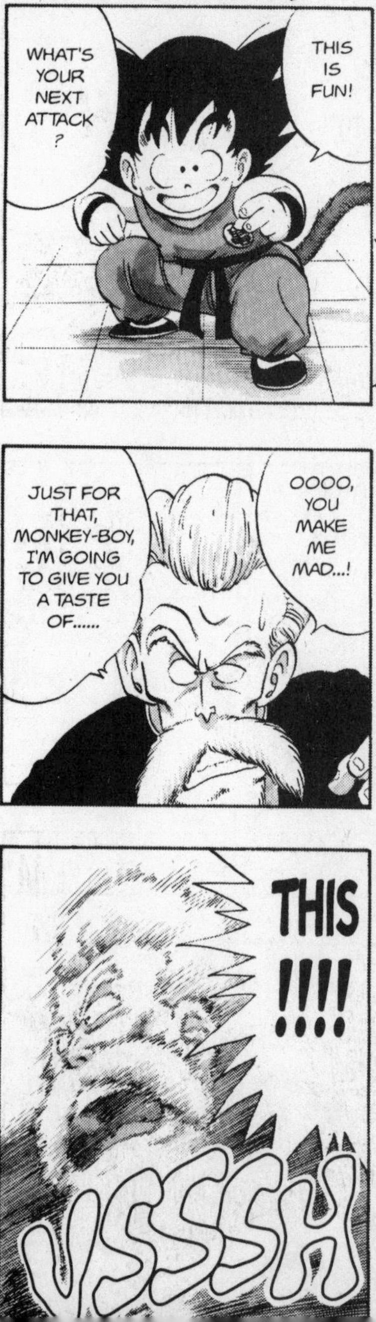

THIS IS FUN!
WHAT'S YOUR NEXT ATTACK ?
OOOO, YOU MAKE ME MAD...!
JUST FOR THAT, MONKEY-BOY, I'M GOING TO GIVE YOU A TASTE OF......
THIS !!!!
VSSSH

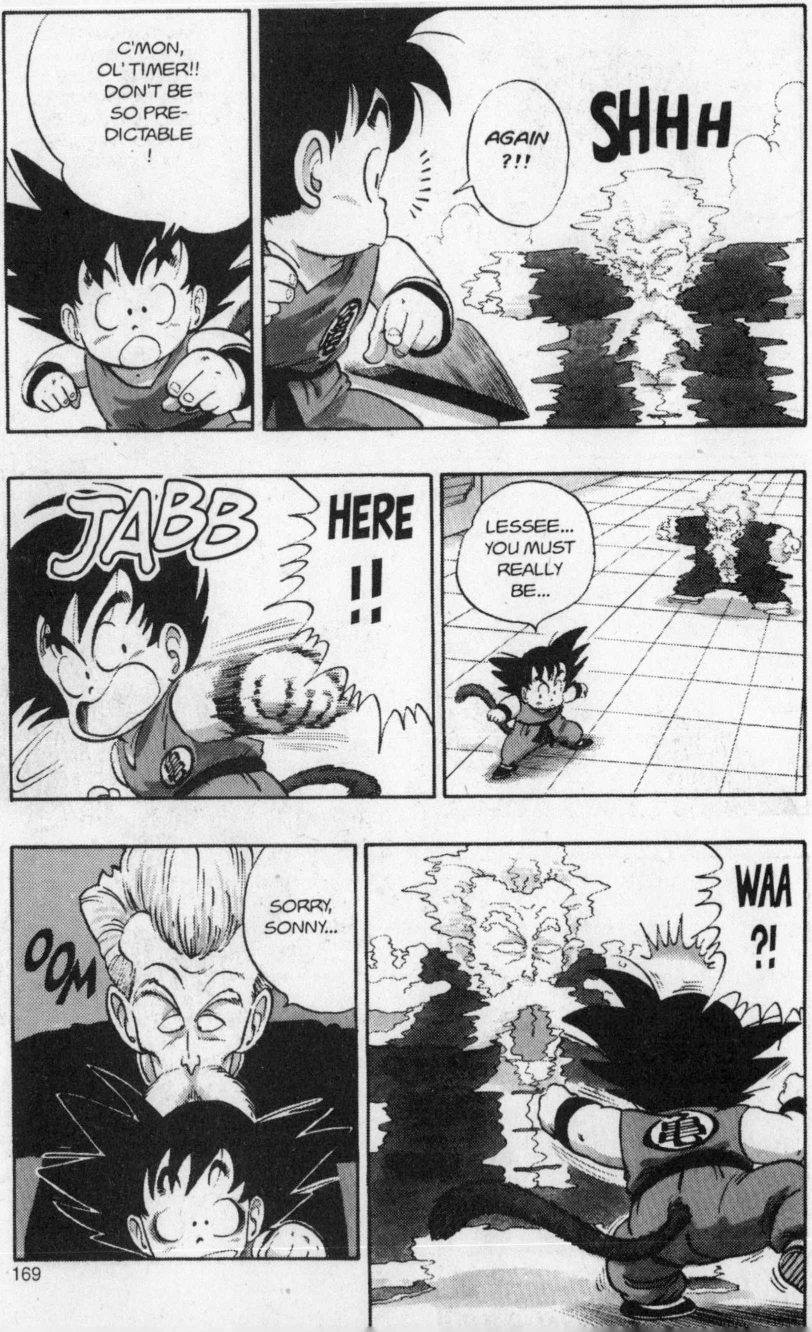
AGAIN ?!!
SHHH
C'MON, OL' TIMER!! DON'T BE SO PRE-DICTABLE !
LESSEE... YOU MUST REALLY BE...
JABB
HERE !!
WAA ?!
SORRY, SONNY...
OOM

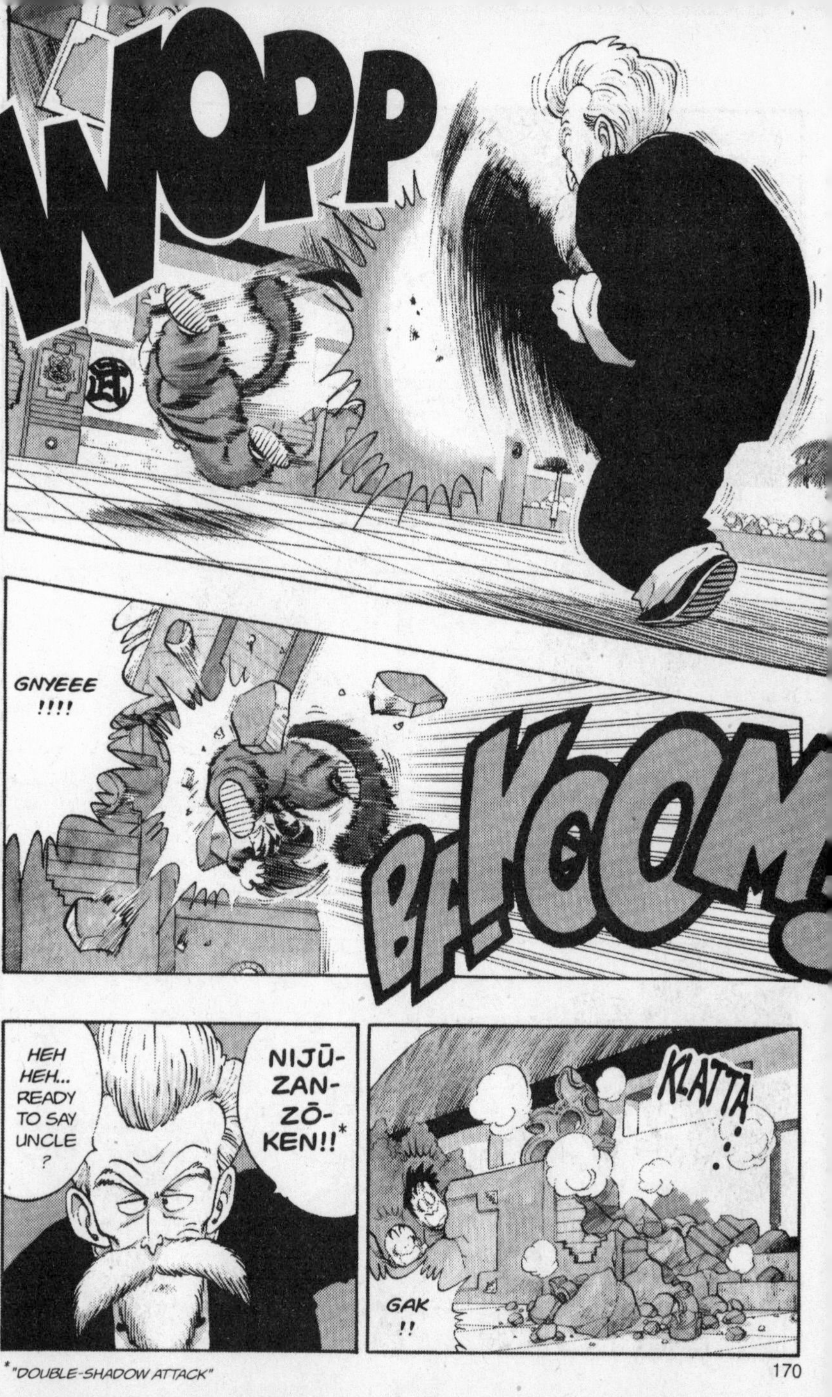
WOPP
BA-KOOM!
GNYEEE !!!!
KLATTA
GAK !!
NIJŪ-ZAN-ZŌ-KEN!!*
HEH HEH... READY TO SAY UNCLE ?

*"DOUBLE-SHADOW ATTACK"

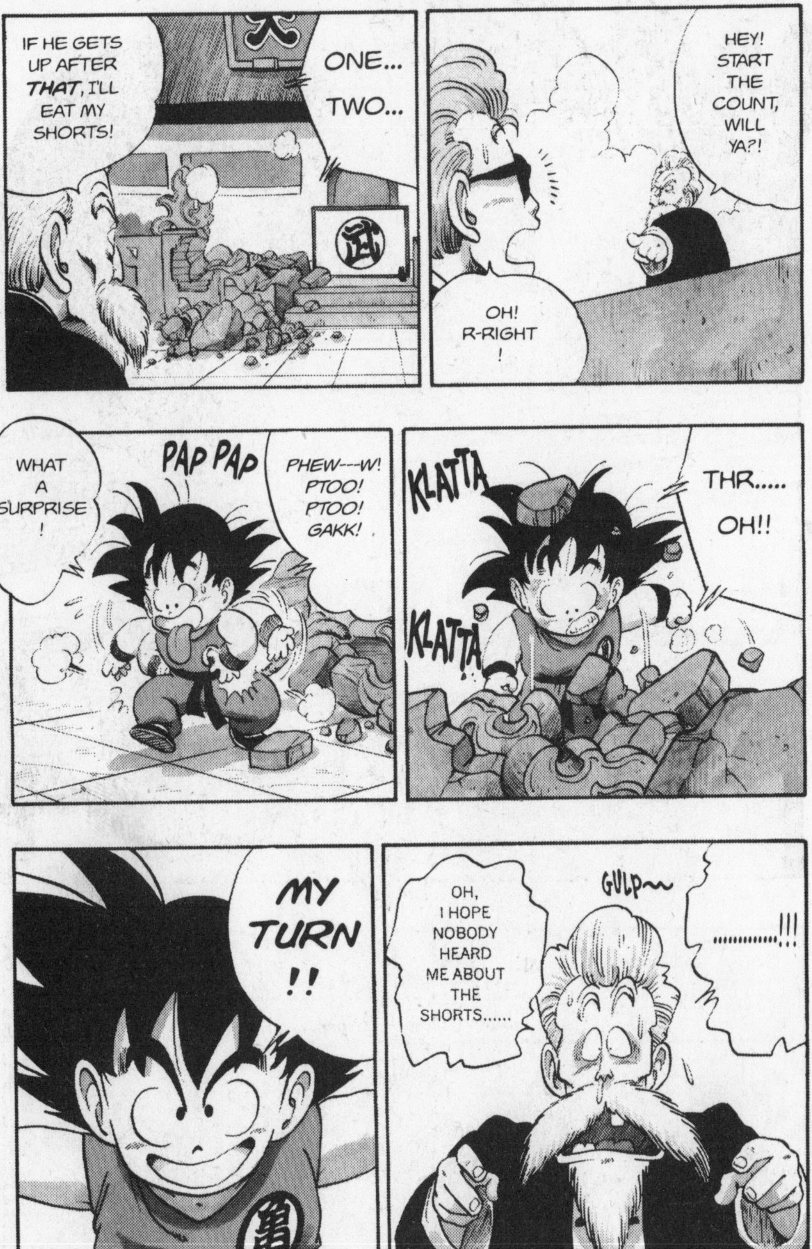
HEY! START THE COUNT, WILL YA?!
OH! R-RIGHT!
ONE...
TWO...
IF HE GETS UP AFTER THAT, I'LL EAT MY SHORTS!
THR.....
OH!!
KLATTA
KLATTA
PHEW---W! PTOO! PTOO! GAKK!
PAP PAP
WHAT A SURPRISE!
............!!!
GULP~~
OH, I HOPE NOBODY HEARD ME ABOUT THE SHORTS......
MY TURN!!

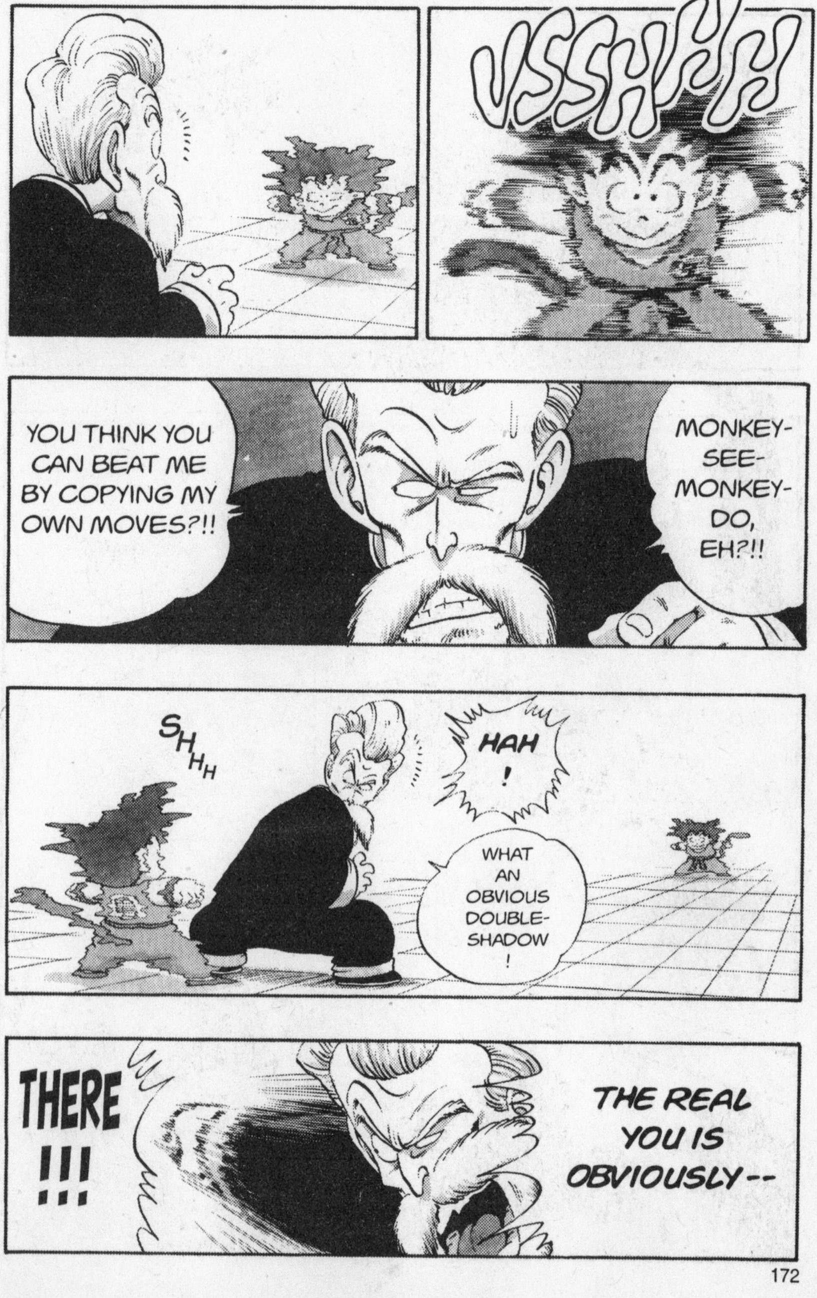
VSSHHHH
MONKEY-SEE-MONKEY-DO, EH?!!
YOU THINK YOU CAN BEAT ME BY COPYING MY OWN MOVES?!!
HAH!
WHAT AN OBVIOUS DOUBLE-SHADOW!
SHHH
THE REAL YOU IS OBVIOUSLY--
THERE!!!

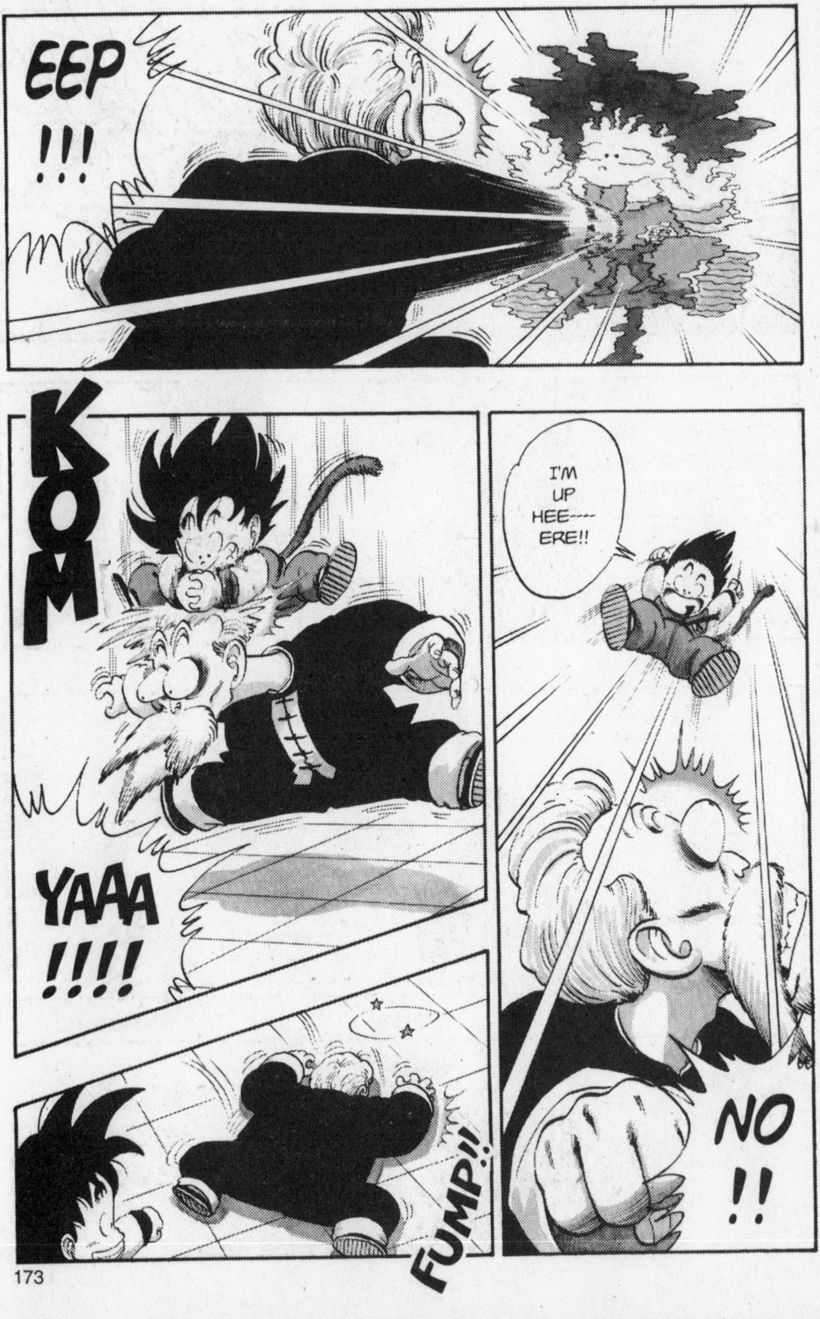
EEP!!!
I'M UP HEE---- ERE!!
NO!!
KOM
YAAA!!!!
FUMP!!

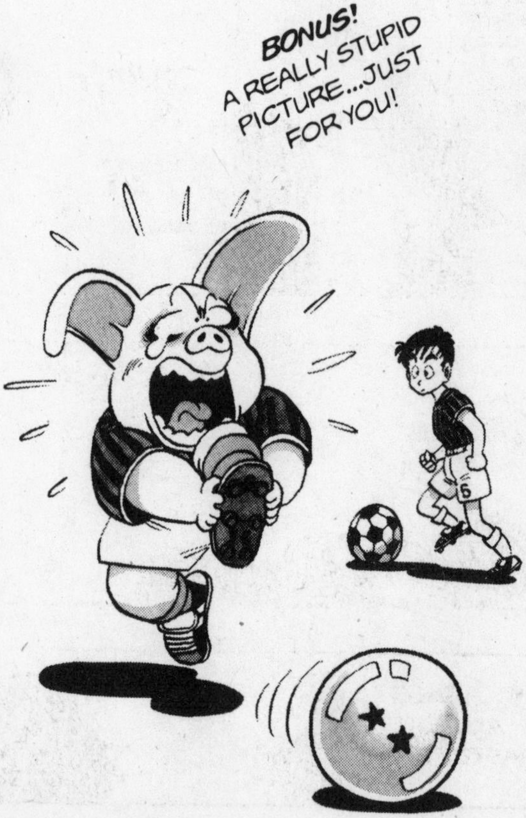
BONUS!
A REALLY STUPID
PICTURE...JUST
FOR YOU!

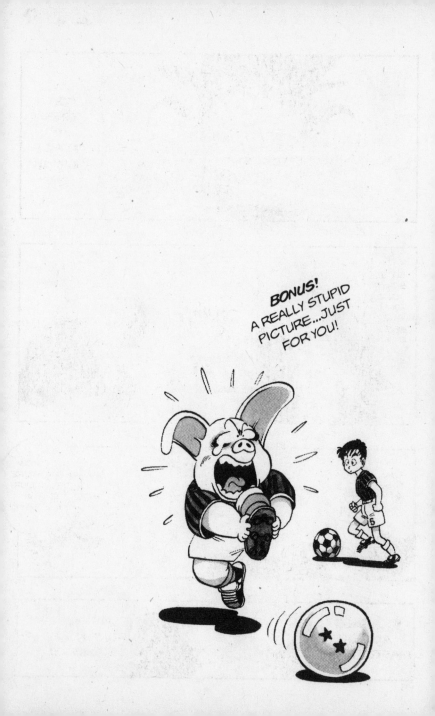

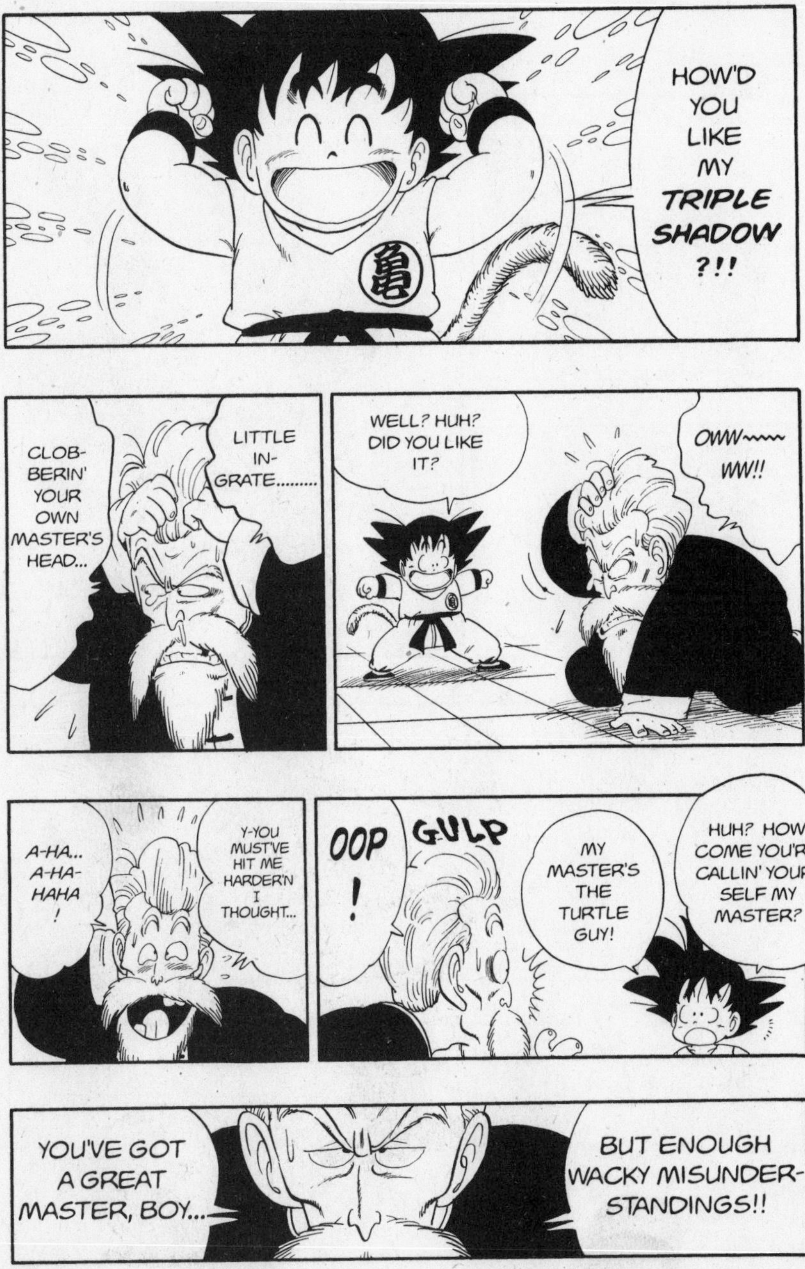
HOW'D YOU LIKE MY TRIPLE SHADOW ?!!
OWW~~~~WW!!
WELL? HUH? DID YOU LIKE IT?
LITTLE IN-GRATE.........
CLOB-BERIN' YOUR OWN MASTER'S HEAD...
HUH? HOW COME YOU'RE CALLIN' YOUR-SELF MY MASTER?
MY MASTER'S THE TURTLE GUY!
GULP
OOP !
Y-YOU MUST'VE HIT ME HARDER'N I THOUGHT...
A-HA... A-HA-HAHA !
BUT ENOUGH WACKY MISUNDER-STANDINGS!!
YOU'VE GOT A GREAT MASTER, BOY...

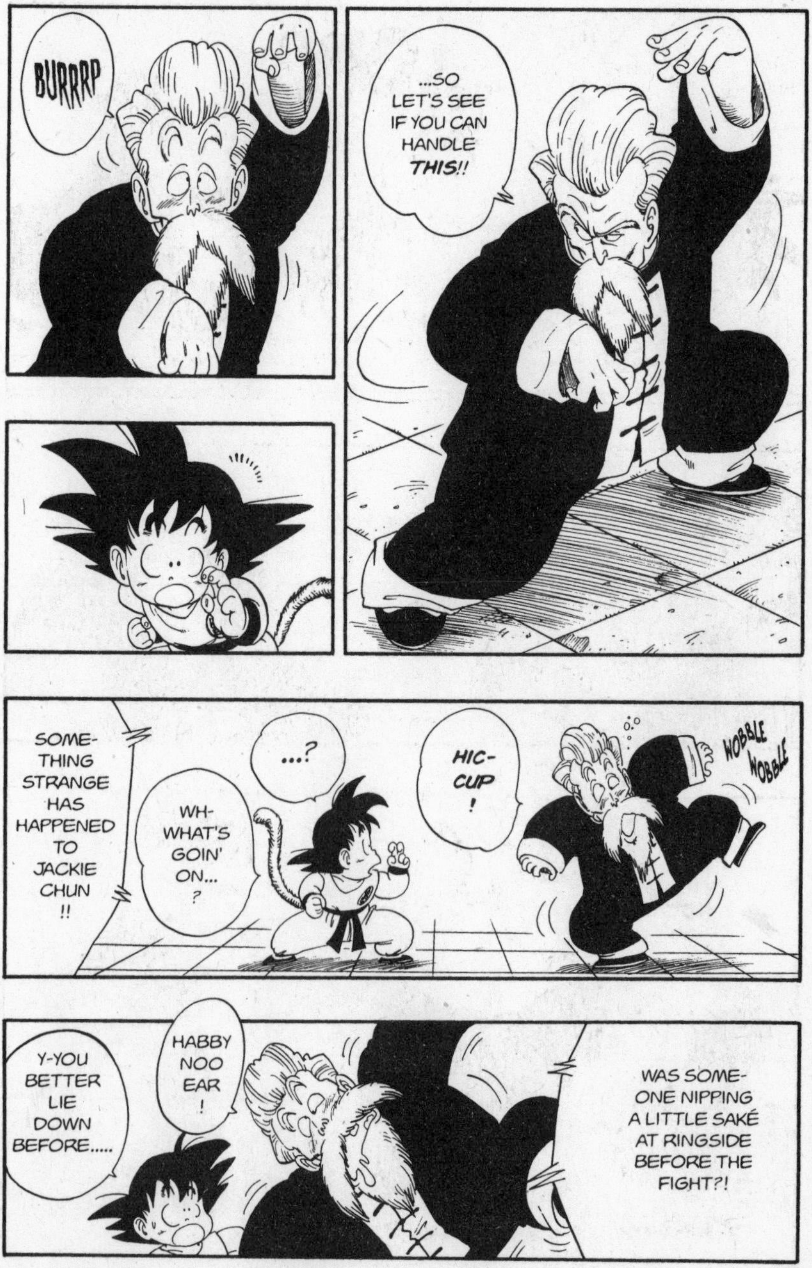
...SO LET'S SEE IF YOU CAN HANDLE **THIS!!**
BURRRP
WOBBLE WOBBLE
HIC-CUP!
...?
WH-WHAT'S GOIN' ON...?
SOME-THING STRANGE HAS HAPPENED TO JACKIE CHUN!!
WAS SOME-ONE NIPPING A LITTLE SAKÉ AT RINGSIDE BEFORE THE FIGHT?!
HABBY NOO EAR!
Y-YOU BETTER LIE DOWN BEFORE.....

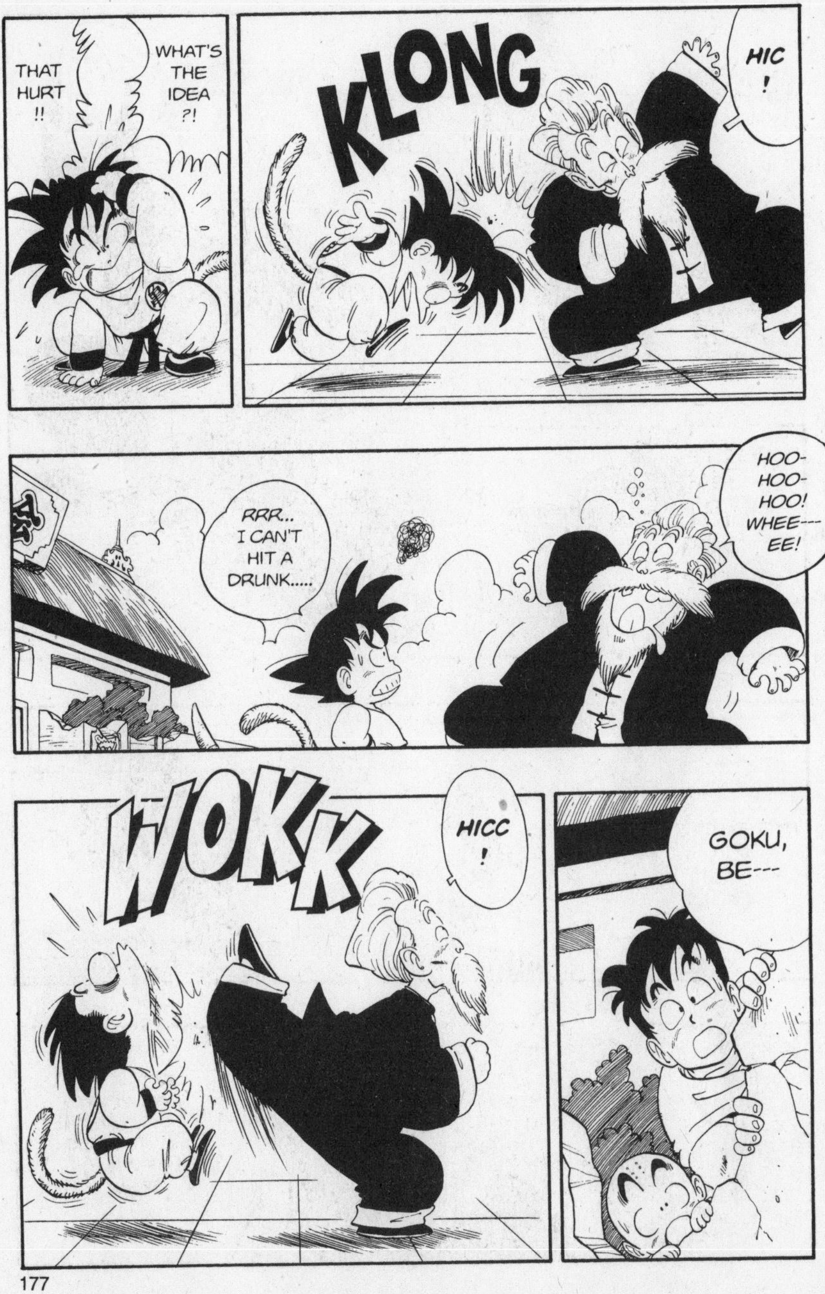
HIC!
KLONG
WHAT'S THE IDEA?!
THAT HURT!!
HOO-HOO-HOO! WHEEE---EE!
RRR... I CAN'T HIT A DRUNK.....
GOKU, BE---
HICC!
WOKK

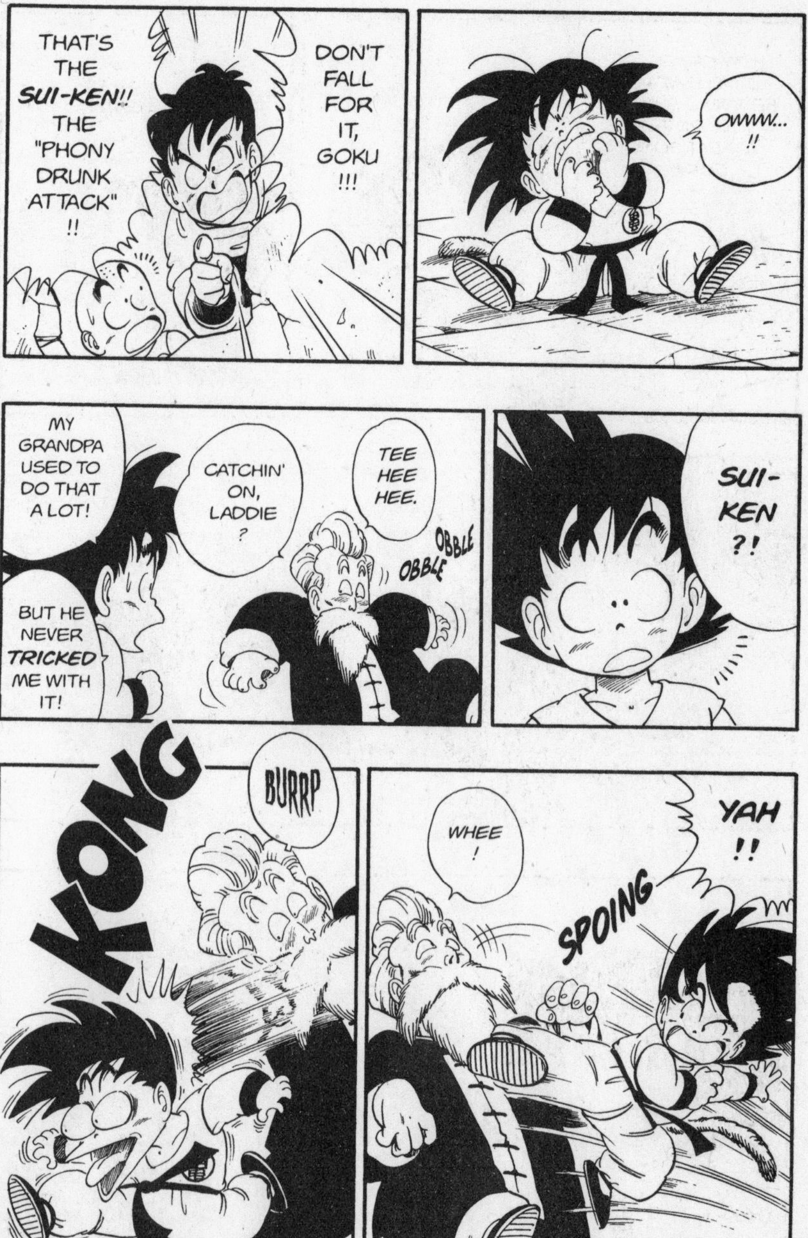
OWWW... !!
DON'T FALL FOR IT, GOKU !!!
THAT'S THE **SUI-KEN!!** THE "PHONY DRUNK ATTACK" !!
SUI-KEN ?!
TEE HEE HEE.
OBBLE OBBLE
CATCHIN' ON, LADDIE ?
MY GRANDPA USED TO DO THAT A LOT!
BUT HE NEVER **TRICKED** ME WITH IT!
YAH !!
WHEE !
SPOING
BURRP
KONG

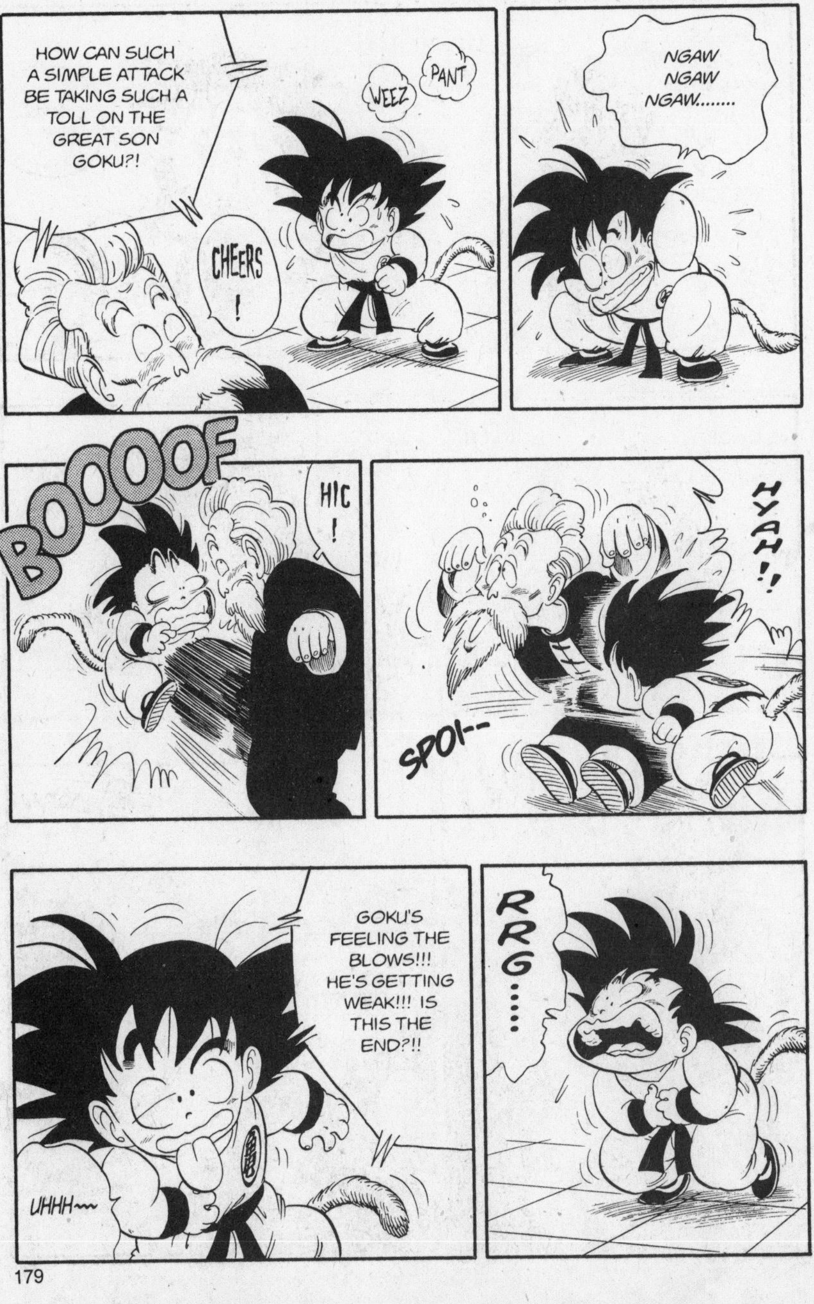
NGAW NGAW NGAW........
PANT
WEEZ
HOW CAN SUCH A SIMPLE ATTACK BE TAKING SUCH A TOLL ON THE GREAT SON GOKU?!
CHEERS !
HYAH!!
SPOI--
HIC !
BOOOOF
RRG....
GOKU'S FEELING THE BLOWS!!! HE'S GETTING WEAK!!! IS THIS THE END?!!
UHHH~~

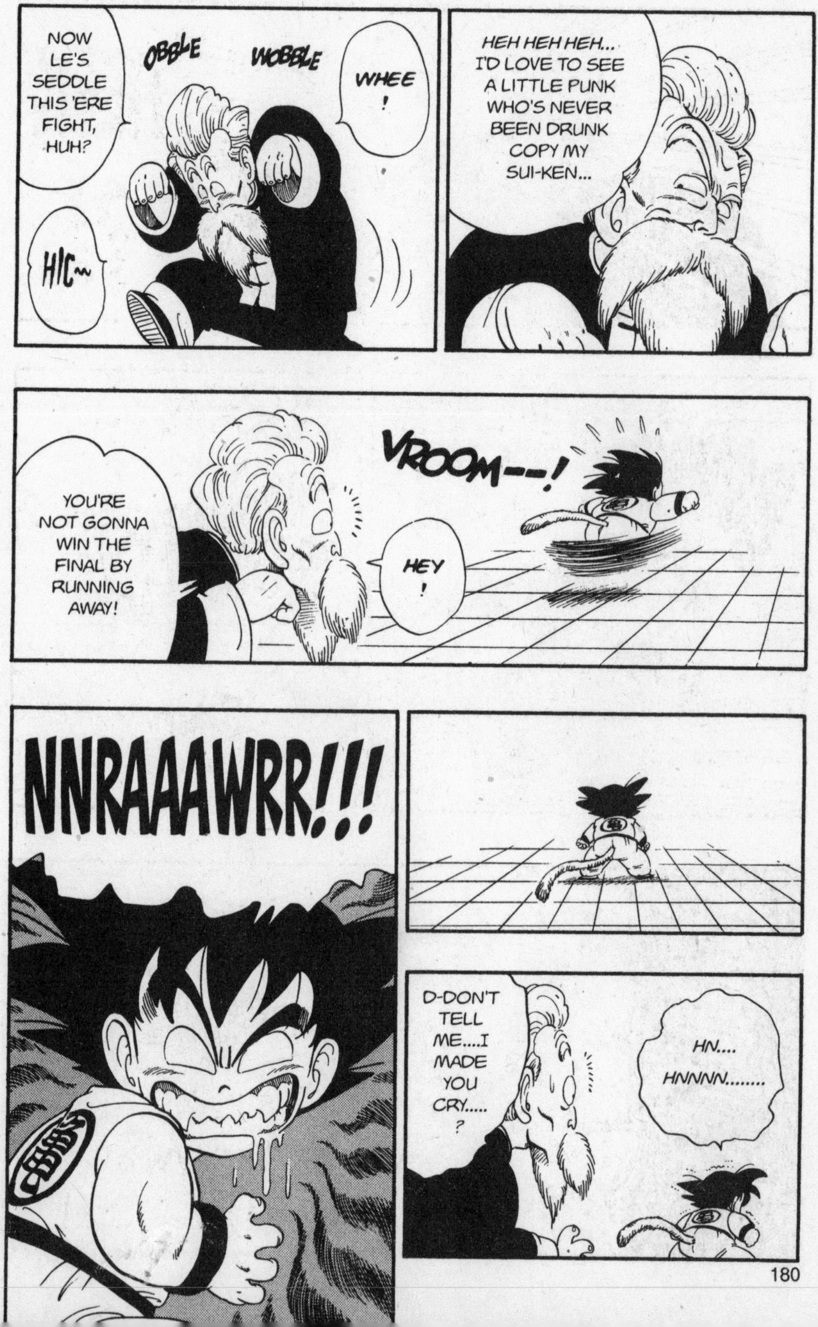
HEH HEH HEH... I'D LOVE TO SEE A LITTLE PUNK WHO'S NEVER BEEN DRUNK COPY MY SUI-KEN...
WHEE !
WOBBLE
OBBLE
NOW LE'S SEDDLE THIS 'ERE FIGHT, HUH?
HIC~
VROOM--!
HEY !
YOU'RE NOT GONNA WIN THE FINAL BY RUNNING AWAY!
HN.... HNNNN........
D-DON'T TELL ME....I MADE YOU CRY..... ?
NNRAAAWRR!!!

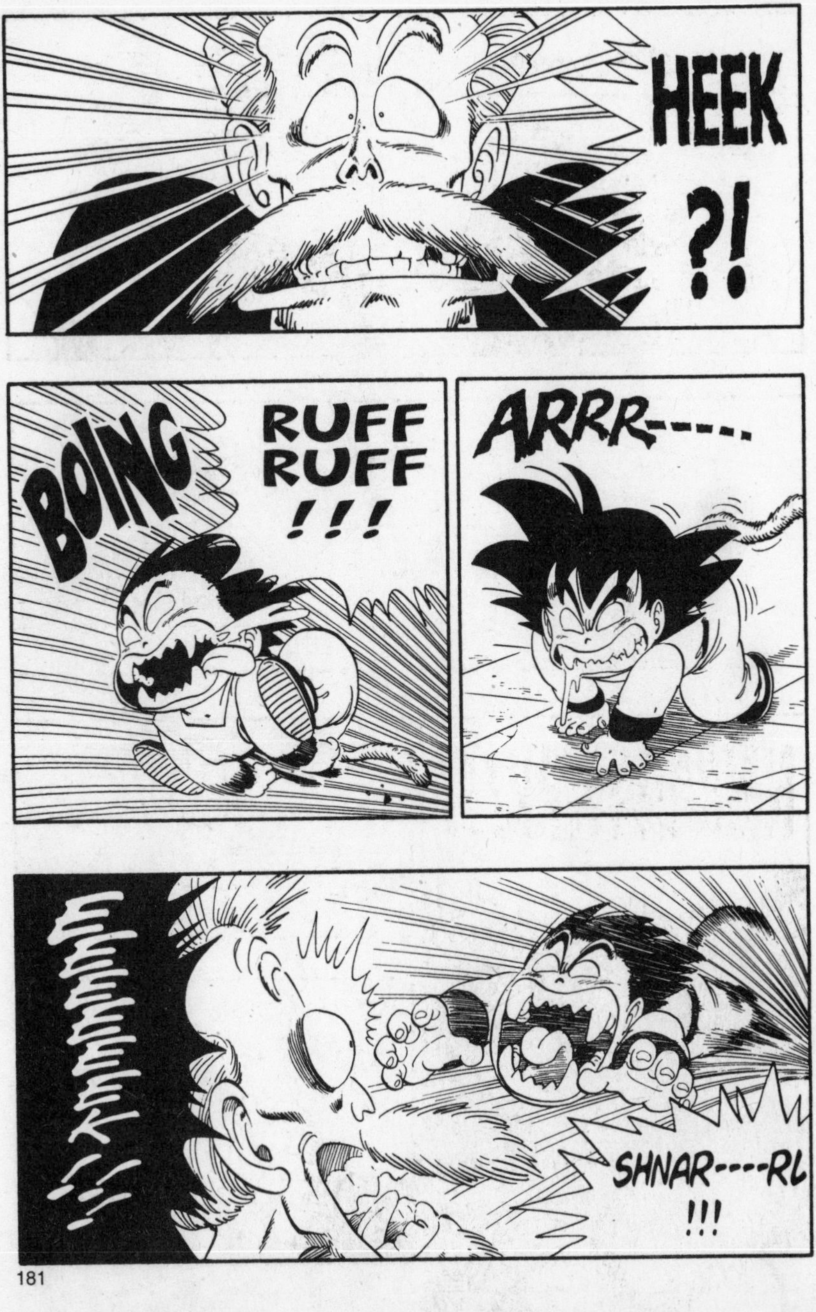
HEEK ?!
ARRR-----
BOING
RUFF RUFF !!!
SHNAR----RL !!!
EEEEEEK!!!

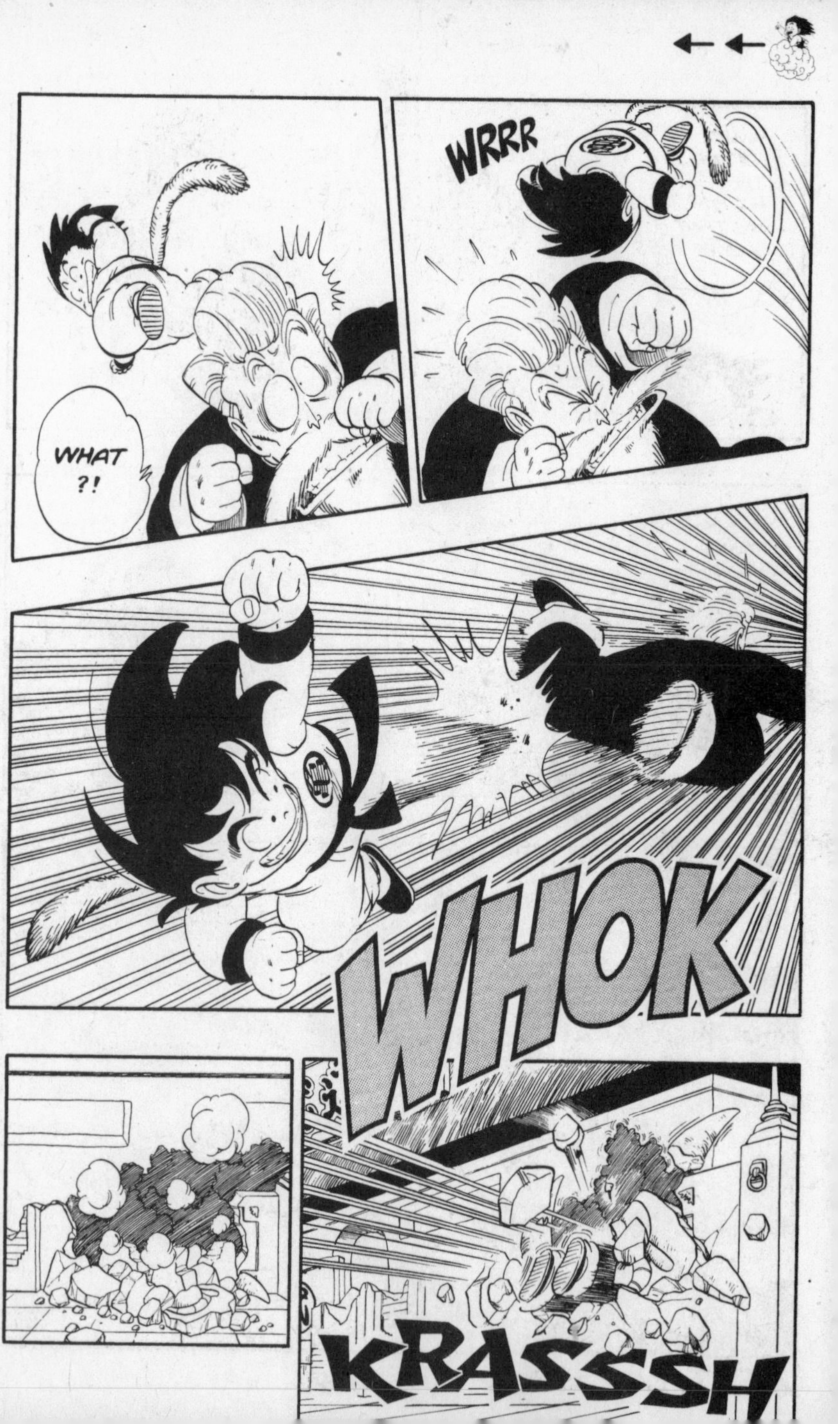
WRRR
WHAT ?!
WHOK
KRASSSH

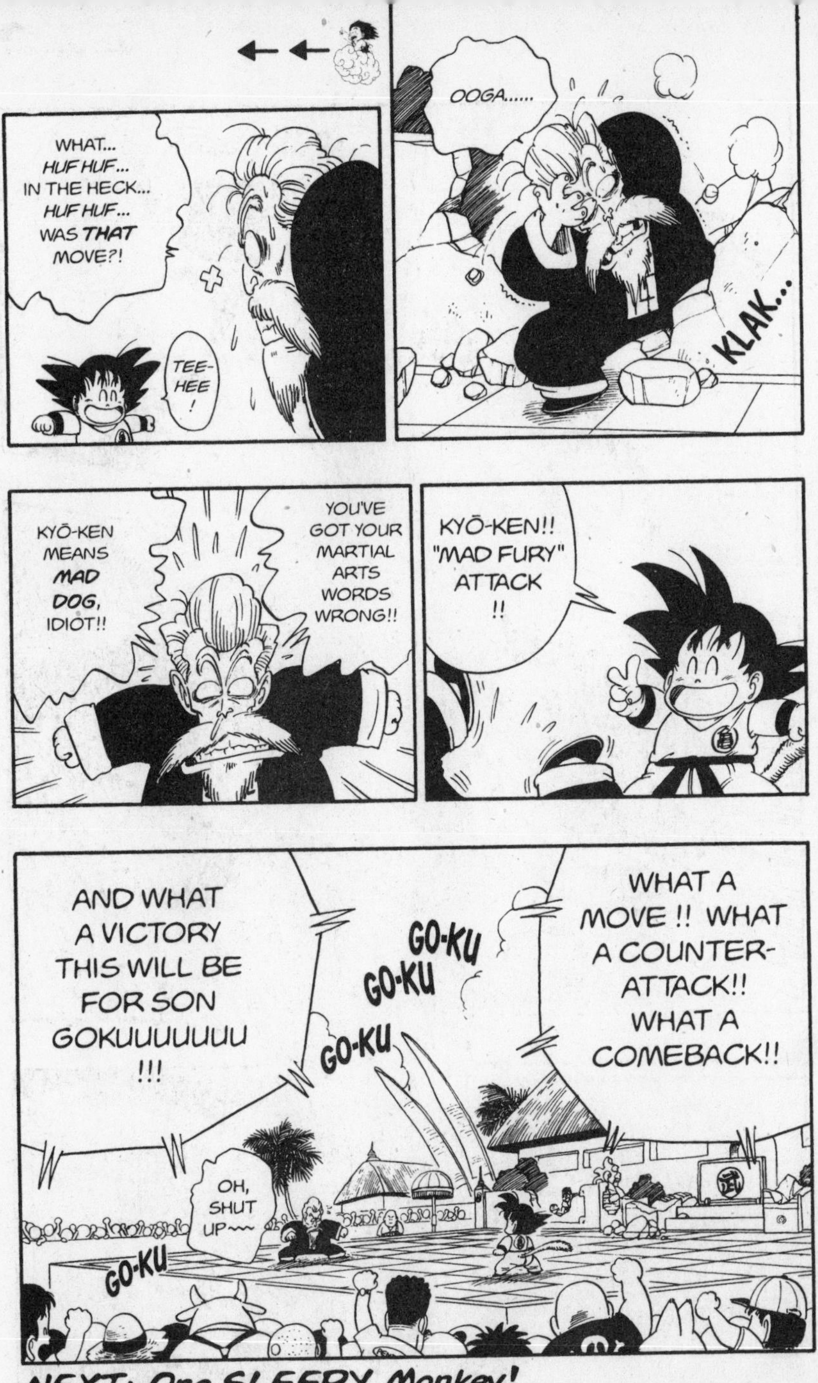

OOGA......
KLAK...
WHAT... HUF HUF... IN THE HECK... HUF HUF... WAS THAT MOVE?!
TEE-HEE!
KYŌ-KEN!! "MAD FURY" ATTACK!!
YOU'VE GOT YOUR MARTIAL ARTS WORDS WRONG!!
KYŌ-KEN MEANS MAD DOG, IDIOT!!
WHAT A MOVE!! WHAT A COUNTER-ATTACK!! WHAT A COMEBACK!!
GO-KU
GO-KU
GO-KU
AND WHAT A VICTORY THIS WILL BE FOR SON GOKUUUUUUU!!!
OH, SHUT UP~~~
GO-KU

NEXT: One SLEEPY Monkey!

Title Page Gallery

Here are some of the chapter title pages which were used when **Dragon Ball Vol. 4** was originally published in Japan in 1986 in **Weekly Shonen Jump** magazine.

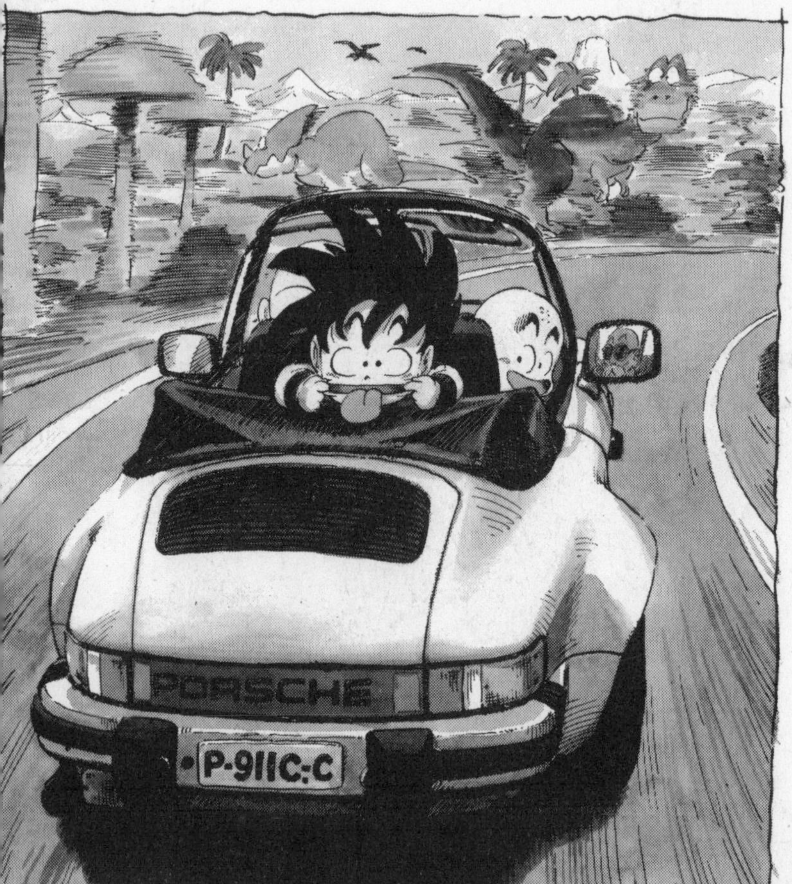
PORSCHE
P-911C:C

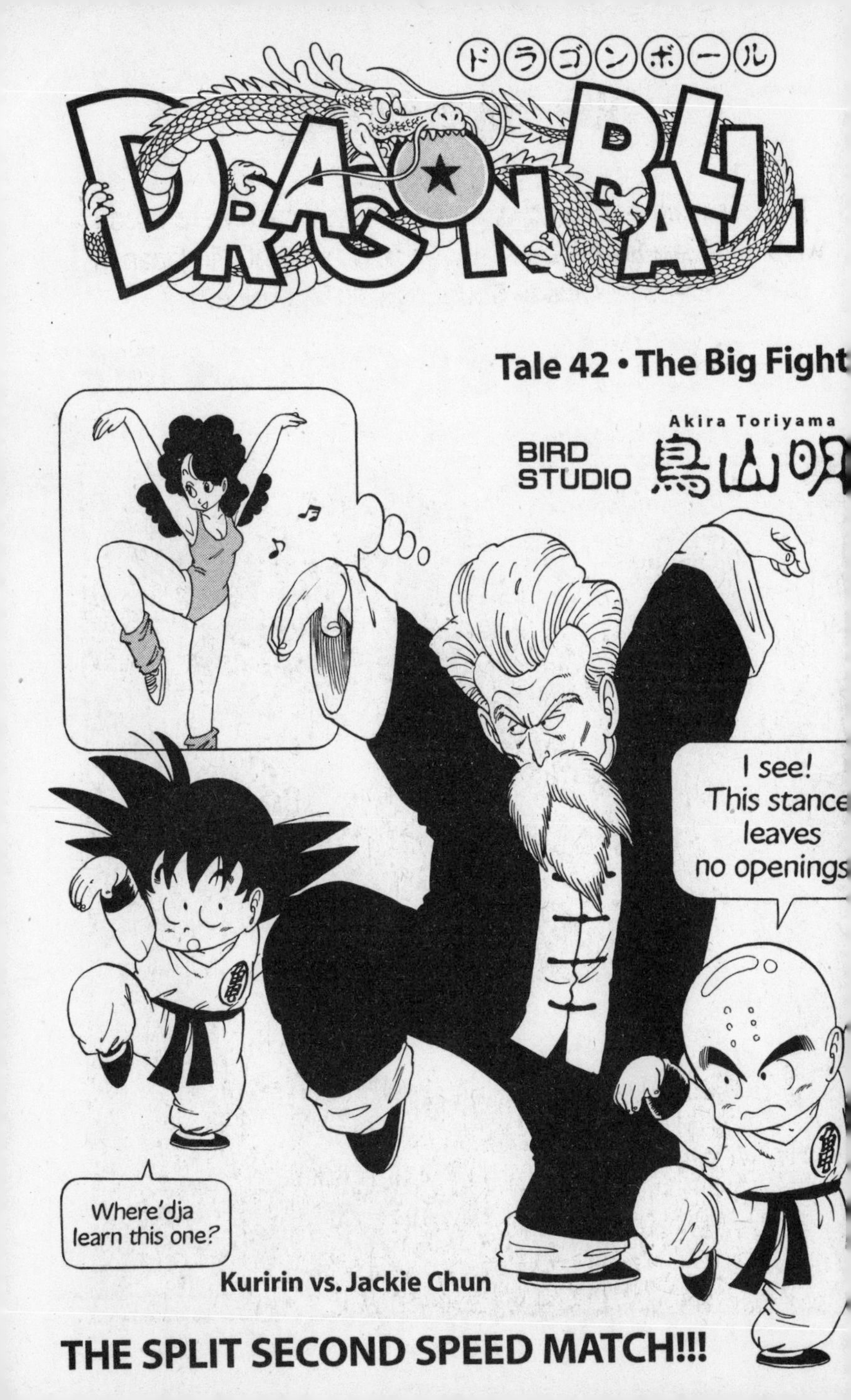

ドラゴンボール
DRAGON BALL
Tale 42 • The Big Fight
Akira Toriyama
BIRD STUDIO 鳥山明
I see! This stance leaves no openings
Where'dja learn this one?
Kuririn vs. Jackie Chun
THE SPLIT SECOND SPEED MATCH!!!

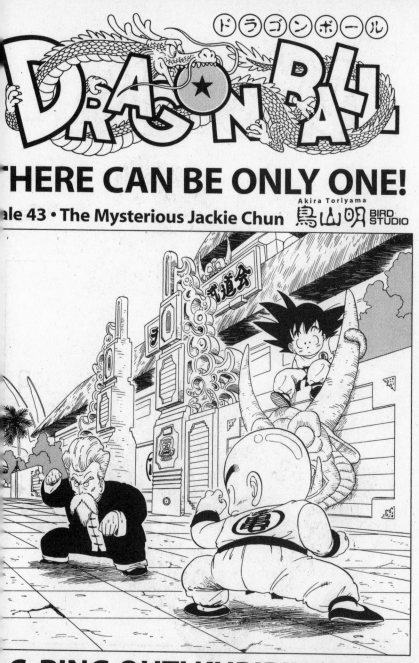

ドラゴン・ボール

DRAGON BALL

THERE CAN BE ONLY ONE!

ale 43 • The Mysterious Jackie Chun 鳥山明 Akira Toriyama BIRD STUDIO

.C. RING OUT! KURIRIN WINS!?

ドラゴンボール

DRAGON BALL

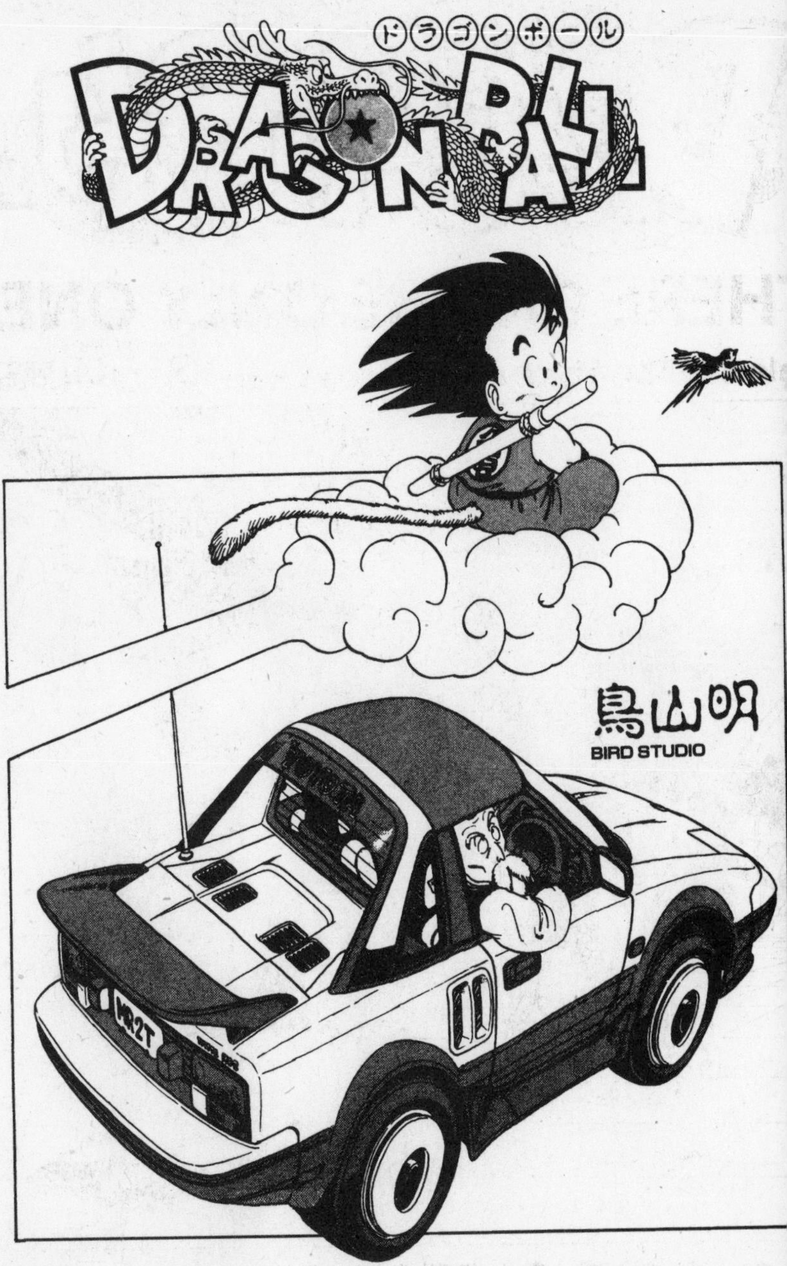
MR2T

鳥山明
BIRD STUDIO

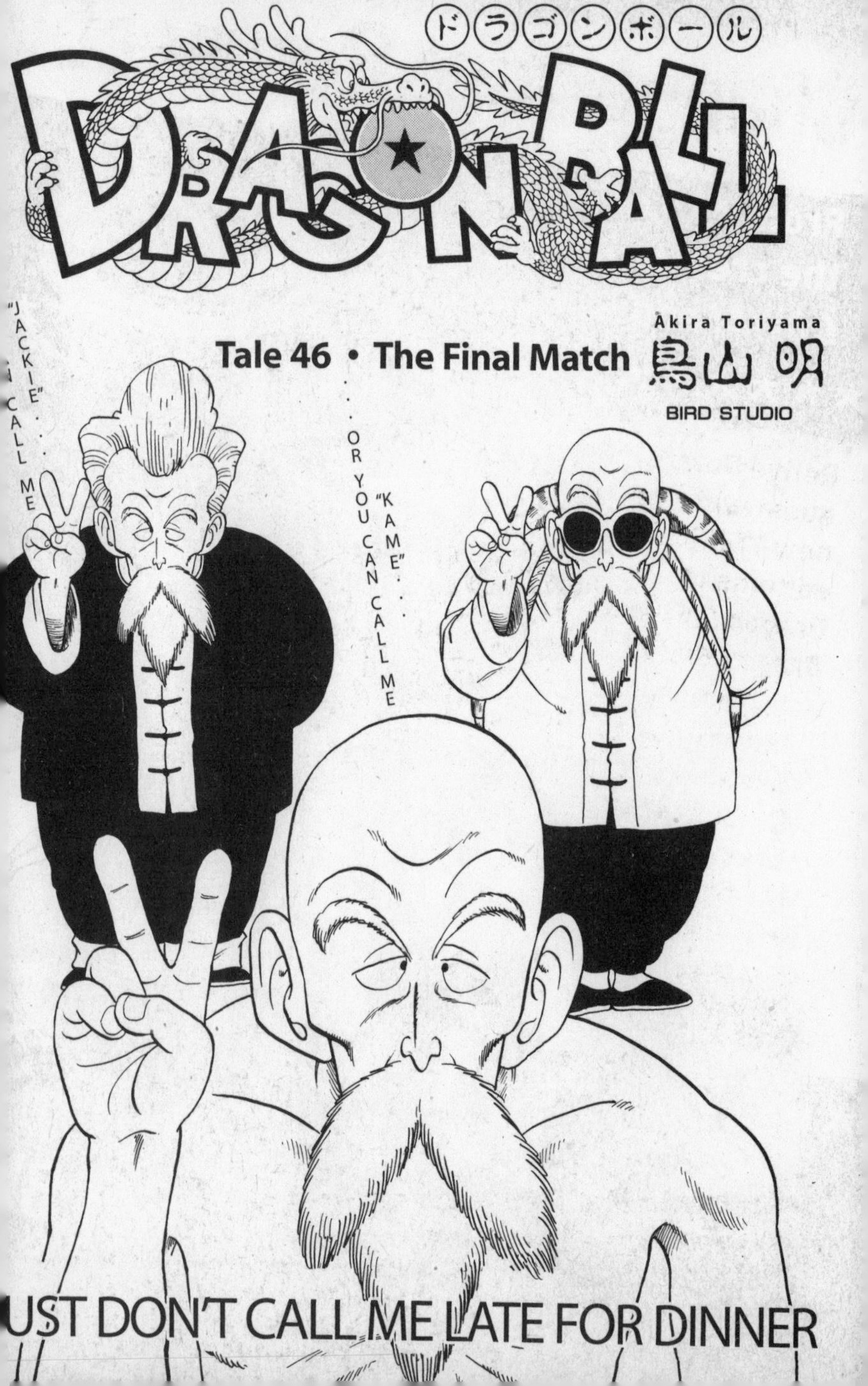
ドラゴンボール
DRAGON BALL
Tale 46 • The Final Match
Akira Toriyama
鳥山明
BIRD STUDIO
N CALL ME “JACKIE”. . .
. . . OR YOU CAN CALL ME “KAME”. . .
UST DON'T CALL ME LATE FOR DINNER

You're Reading in the Wrong Direction!!

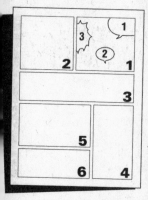

Whoops! Guess what? You're starting at the wrong end of the comic!

...It's true! In keeping with the original Japanese format, Akira Toriyama's world-famous **Dragon Ball** series is meant to be read from right to left, starting in the upper-right corner.

Unlike English, which is read from left to right, Japanese is read from right to left, meaning that action, sound-effects, and word-balloon order are completely reversed...something which can make readers unfamiliar with Japanese feel pretty backwards themselves. For this reason, manga or Japanese comics published in the U.S. in English have traditionally been published "flopped"—that is, printed in exact reverse order, as though seen from the other side of a mirror.

By flopping pages, U.S. publishers can avoid confusing readers, but the compromise is not without its downside. For one thing, a character in a flopped manga series who once wore in the original Japanese version a T-shirt emblazoned with "M A Y" (as in "the merry month of") now wears one which reads "Y A M"! Additionally, many manga creators in Japan are themselves unhappy with the process, as some feel the mirror-imaging of their art reveals otherwise unnotice-able flaws or skews in perspective.

In recognition of the importance and popularity of **Dragon Ball**, we are proud to bring it to you in the original unflopped format.

For now, though, turn to the other side of the book and let the adventure begin...!

—Editor